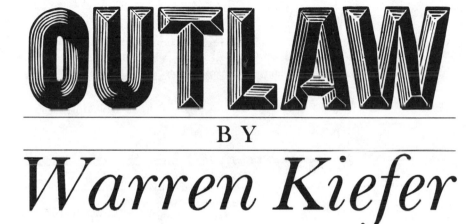

OUTLAW

BY

Warren Kiefer

Donald I. Fine Inc.
New York

Library of Congress Cataloging-in-Publication Data
Kiefer, Warren, 1929–
Outlaw : a novel / by Warren Kiefer.
p.   cm.
ISBN: 1-55611-148-7
I. Title.
PS3561.I34098   1989
813'.54—dc20   89-45343
                                        CIP
Manufactured in the United States of America
10 9 8 7 6 5 4 3 2 1

DESIGNED BY IRVING PERKINS ASSOCIATES

For Andrew and Johnny

Many of the people in this story actually existed, and where possible I have tried to be faithful to the basic facts of their lives, and to present their roles as I believe they would have played them. But I lay no claim to biographical accuracy in a work of fiction.

The research was carried out primarily from original-source material, which included hundreds of personal letters, documents and newspapers, as well as diaries, government files, military records, memoirs, training manuals, magazines and trial transcripts. Although I have tried to present the wars, scandals and other alarums with as much verisimilitude as possible, the main intent was to get the atmosphere right for the reader's entertainment.

—W.K.

PART
1

Eagle Nest

Just because I've outlived practically everybody don't mean I'm in a hurry to die. I've looked at death close up too many times and never liked what I saw, beginning with when I was real little, when my folks was trying to scratch a living out of a miserable patch of New Mexico dirt near Ruidoso. It was the last time the Apache rose up, and they massacred several families where we was, and burned the houses. They missed me because I hid out in the root cellar.

When I went back, the house was ashes, the horses was gone and my mother and father was lying in the corral all twisted and bloody. I must of stayed there several days because I remember the blow flies and the maggots on my daddy's face, but I had water from the well and carrots and raw potatoes when I got hungry. My mama had beautiful hair, I remember that. She had real pretty hair.

Some soldiers found me and I kicked and screamed because I thought they was the Indians come back. They took me to their camp and fed me and they was all right. I had no relations, so the army sent me up to Santa Fe, where a Mexican family named Montoya brought me to live at Eagle Nest. They treated me like I was their own kin, but they was so poor, I had to start work early. I speak Mexican as good as English, but I never wrote it much.

People ask me what the secret of a long life is and I tell them there is no secret. I read about Russians live to be a hundred and fifty, but it's probably Communist propaganda. Doctors have give me up for dead more than one time, but they're gone and I'm still here. My grandson Pete, who's a doctor, says I lived so long because I never grew up. If he's right, I hope I never do.

Tom Isbell used to say dying was just going home, but I ain't homesick even if I am stepping on ninety. Last year I went to his funeral in Santa Fe. That's the farthest I been since I come back to Eagle Nest. Tom was the last one but me from our old outfit, pureblood Pawnee, and he lived a month past a hundred with all his marbles. He drew a pension from the Indian Affairs people like he did from the Veterans people, but he was eighty years old before the government let him vote. Nobody has to put up with more of the white man's stupidity than Indians.

When I think about all my grandchildren and great-grandchildren I feel as old as Shank's mare. But when I get talking to my grandson Pete, I'm young again. So, in a way, I'm as vain as one of them women has her face lifted when I rattle on about what happened years ago, trying to recapture the man I was then. I know you shouldn't have favorites among kids, but I do. Since he was little, Pete always liked to hear me yarn about the early days and soldiering and all that, so what I'm telling now is mainly for him, and his kids, and anybody else is interested.

What my life was before I entered the army, I blush to tell. Mainly it was stealing. What Pete finds funny is that I started out a cattle thief, got lucky, and ended up a rancher. Like the army. The first time I went in as a private and come out a sergeant in less than six months, which was a little longer than the war with Spain lasted. The second time I went in a captain and come home a colonel. These things was accidents like the banking business. Me in a banker's chair was like a pig in a saddle, and I slid out just as quick. My wife said I could of been governor, but I liked it better when Luna was sworn into that job. Luna never could understand my objections to politics any more than he understood my stealing when he was sheriff of Santa Fe County.

After Cuba, I had no better friend than him, but we started out enemies. As long as he lived, we never had a conversation without it was an argument. Each of us always thought the other was trying to put something over on him.

I think on him now the way he looked when he was sheriff. Not real tall like me, but normal height, lean and flashy as a quarter horse, quick as a slipknot and tough. He had eyes that narrowed to slits when he was suspicious, which was most of the time, and he smiled about once a year. Don't misunderstand me. He was not a bad-tempered or mean-spirited man. He was generous to a fault if he liked you, but an unforgiving son of a bitch if he didn't.

At age fourteen I hired out as a cowhand, doing a man's job for a boy's wages and eating my weight in chili and beans. But I had most of my height, and sitting tall in the saddle put me about as close to heaven as I'll ever get. Old Man Holman, a neighbor of ours, took me on and worked my ass off, mainly because his two sons, Red and Ernie, wasn't worth a hoot. They was both older and Red was dumb as a chicken, and lazy too. Ernie was the evil one, weasel-face like his mother, a liar and a thief, but smart enough to stay on the old man's right side.

About three months after I start with the Holmans Ernie takes me in their barn and shows me a saddle he says he found and wants me to sell for him over in Taos. But I know a man don't find no saddles in the middle of nowhere, and I already seen this one once when Old Man Holman sent it to my foster dad to have the surcingle fixed. So I tell Ernie no thanks because it's stole from his old man.

"You calling me a thief, Garland?" he says to me.

"No," I say, "but you can sell it yourself, if you've a mind." Instead, he gets Red to do it. The old man finds out and whips Red near to death because Ernie don't own up to his part. That's eighteen and ninety-four when Red runs away to work for a pair of cattle thieves named Sam and Arnold Brown. A month later Ernie gets me fired, but the Brown brothers take me on too.

They was not your ordinary, run-of-the-mill rustlers. They had cow-stealing down to a fine art, and they taught me a lot. They even operated out of a ramshackle office in Santa Fe, next to the railroad building, doing some legitimate business to cover up.

Sam Brown was a heavyset, bearded fellow with brown teeth and mean eyes who'd just as soon kill a man as look at him. But he was a coward and a bully who only moved with a gang behind him. Arnold was the businessman, lean and bald as a bank clerk. He always dressed in suits and could talk his way past the devil.

You could say it was through them I met Luna. They always had four or five hands like me, only most was more experienced. One was a fellow named Moore, who'd been in jail over in Colorado. He was the biggest man I ever knew, six-six or -seven, and weighed three hundred pounds. He had trouble finding horses could carry him, and particular trouble finding them free. Mountain, as they called him, never bought anything in his life if he could steal it, except maybe a whiskey now and then.

It was him showed me how to throw a knife. We worked together a long time, and soldiered too. He was real smart about some things and dumb as grass about others. He never learned his letters, and I taught him to sign *M. Moore* for his army pay. It happens to strong men who get most of what they want by brute force and don't have to overwork their brain. I seen him knock a steer cold with his fist, but he was sweet-tempered and gentle most of the time. He never wore boots until he went in the army, but used Indian moccasins instead, and always carried an extra pair in his blanket roll. I never seen my Indian friend Tom Isbell wear moccasins in his whole life, which shows things like that ain't in the blood but is just a question of habit.

The Brown brothers' pay was high for running cattle, but low, considering they was stole. We never cut into herds on the range because there was no point in making enemies of all the cattle growers in New Mexico when you could have them for friends. We usually waited until they sold the cows to a meatpacker, then stole them from shipping pens or out of railroad cars on the siding. In that way, the Brown brothers knew their business.

We carried lead seals to lock the cars again so it was hard to tell anything was missing. If we was lucky, the buyer didn't catch on until the train got to Kansas. The risk was the railroad agents, and some of them was meaner than Sam Brown and just as smart as Arnold. The law in the Territory didn't count it much of a crime to shoot a man stealing a cow or a horse, and more than one poor devil died of lead poisoning trying to make a dishonest dollar. We had nerve in those days and a lot of luck, but as we got more successful, the railroad hired more police. That's what Luna did before he became sheriff, and he was the best.

The worst railway agent was a big fellow named Alfred S. Sorenson, a scowling Swede with platinum hair, a potbelly and legs like a stork. He come from back East in Minnesota, and had a reputation so bad it got here before he did. He had killed a dozen men, they said, a couple with his gun, but the others by beating them to death with a pick handle he always carried at work.

In the fall of ninety-six, the Brown brothers wanted to take advantage of the activity around Springer, where lots of herds was coming in from ranches east of the mountains. There was a few real cattle barons then with herds over fifteen thousand, but we mostly stole cows formerly owned by the little growers because they liked doing business with Arnold. The way it worked was this: after a rancher sold his cattle for cash, they'd be put into pens next to the siding or into the cars themselves. Then at night we'd start siphoning off to empty pens, while Arnold sold the ones we stole back to the original owner, who was in complicity with him. The rancher was happy to pay eight dollars for a cow with his brand which he already sold for thirty dollars because he could sell the same cow again for another thirty dollars the next day. They was as guilty as the Brown brothers, but they had a clear conscience because meatpackers never paid fair value.

Luna didn't look at it that way. He said a crook is a crook no matter what lies he tells himself. Anybody wonders how we got away with it for so long has to know the grand confusion of a few thousand steers and a hundred cussing cowboys at a railhead.

At Springer Arnold spent his time doing the business and collecting the money, while the rest of us snuck the cattle in and out. There was Sam Brown, me and Mountain, Red Holman, and Jake and Cody Williams. Cody was younger than me, and a good hand in spite of his being underweight and kind of sickly. Arnold Brown only hired him because Jake brought him along, but he was worth two of Jake, who was a loudmouth and lazy. I never liked working with him or Red because they was a danger, but Cody was fine, just green. It was Jake and Red Holman damn near got me killed one night.

We was cutting out thirty head from one pen to another and Jake's nipping at a bottle. Red's wandered off, it's dark as sin and I got to separate the steers we want by the brand, which I can't hardly see and have to trace with my fingers each time to be sure. I'm in the middle of the pen doing this and Jake's leaning against the gate, gargling booze, when some noise spooks the critters. Fresh off the range like that, they could be skittish cooped up together.

We'd only got about half of what we was after and the rest are still packed in so tight I can easy get gored if I don't slip out until they quiet down. My best chance is the gate, but I'm squashed between a hundred tons of moving beef and it takes time. If I try

to get over the horns, I'll get it sure, and if I fall, they'll pick me
up with a ink blotter in the morning. I can't call out, and when I
finally make it to the gate, it's closed and Jake's took off. Somebody's coming and I can't find the latch so I chance getting a horn
up my ass and climb the wire. I'm on the top with my legs swung
over when something clips my boot heels so hard my feet nearly
meet my knees. I fall in a heap of pain outside the pen and there's
this giant grinning over me with a pick handle. I don't have to see
his face to know it's Alfred S. Sorenson.

He'd of killed me, no doubt about it, because he already had that
pick handle raised to give me another whack. The stories I heard
about him was he liked to start on a man's legs and finish up with
the head after everything else was broke and the man was still
conscious. That way they buried a pulp instead of a body.

It was Luna saved my life when he caught Alfred S. Sorenson's
arm and held it back. He looked down at me, standing with his legs
apart and his other hand on the butt of a big Navy Colt loose in
a holster. "Don't get up," he says, "and if you have a gun throw
it on the ground." I didn't have no gun and it's a waste of breath
telling me not to get up. After that wallop I don't think I'll ever
walk again.

"Stand back," Alfred S. Sorenson says to Luna, "while I educate
the son of a bitch."

But Luna don't move, just signals him there's something else off
there in the dark. Sorenson goes loping away on his great bird legs,
expecting to catch Red Holman and Jake Williams. I never been
so terrified of anybody in my life, before or since. That man wasn't
normal. He liked killing and he liked to watch suffering, especially
if he was the cause.

Luna nudges me with his boot. "What's your name?"

"Garland," I say.

"Garland what?"

"Lee Garland."

"What are you doing here?"

"Working." I give him the name of the rancher whose brand is
on the steers we been putting into the next pen.

He looks at the little blackboard hanging on the wire where the
auctioneer marks the name of the buyer or seller. There's nothing
written on it and Luna knows I'm lying. He says to me, "Where you
from?"

"Eagle Nest."

He puts his boot heel on my chest so I'm looking down my nose at the pointy toe, and says in Spanish, "You're the orphan kid Hernan Montoya raised, aren't you?"

"Yes, sir."

"Is this how you pay him back?" he says, still in Spanish.

"No, sir."

"Hernan would starve before he'd steal. He took you in when nobody wanted you and you bring him shame." He bites the end off a cigar and spits it out, still looking down at me, his fingers drumming on the butt of his gun. I don't know if he's going to shoot me or what, but I prefer his lecturing to Alfred S. Sorenson's pick handle.

Arnold Brown appears then with the rancher. He asks Luna what the trouble is and Luna looks them over careful. "This kid work for you?" he says, and the rancher nods. Luna looks at the steers we cut out and says, "These yours?" and the man nods again. Luna turns to Arnold Brown and says, "What are you doing out of bed at this hour?"

Arnold Brown says, "Why don't you and I sort this out, Luna? We don't want trouble."

"You could have fooled me," Luna says.

"He was just looking after my cattle," the rancher says.

"Who says they're yours?"

"They got my mark," the rancher says.

"I don't doubt it," Luna says. "When the sun's up we'll check the brands and recount what you sold yesterday."

Well, the jig is up if they do that. The rancher's nervous now because he don't want to go to jail and he's looking at Arnold Brown to see what to do. Slick as grease, Arnold says, "Why don't we count them again right now and if there's been any mistake, I'll fix it."

Luna ponders this, and says, "I know what you're up to, but this time I'll let you correct the tally so no one is short. Then get out of here. If you or anybody working for you is within a mile of this railroad yard after sunup, you'll wish you never heard of Alfred S. Sorenson or me." I get up with my heels hurting so bad I can barely stand, and he takes me aside. "Son, you're in bad company here, but you're young so I'm letting you go. But if I ever see you with this bunch again, you'll get no more favors from me. Hernan

Montoya didn't raise you to be a cattle thief."

That night Alfred S. Sorenson never did catch up with Red Holman or Jake Williams, but I learned how he found out which pens we was working. Red had blabbed to his brother Ernie, and Ernie collected ten bucks reward from Sorenson for the information. That's the kind of bastard Ernie was, who'd sell out his own brother for a ten-dollar gold piece.

By the time I'm eighteen years old, I have four hundred dollars saved up. I own a Colt Army revolver bought off an old drunk gunfighter in Alamogordo, and a half interest with Mountain Moore in a string of mustangs. Not bad for a kid, I tell myself.

I'm in season all the time too, and know a bed is good for a lot besides sleeping. A young widow near Taos wants to go into business with me at the altar but there's no chance of that. Like they say, if you got all the milk you want, why buy the cow? My beard's coming in good by then, but I just let the mustaches grow. The trouble is, everything depends on my life of crime, and I'm building a reputation worth about twenty years in the new penitentiary.

The Atchison, Topeka and Santa Fe Railroad was a real power in the Territory then, and they was always willing to lay out money for information about me or Mountain or Red Holman or Jake and Cody Williams. They was warrants out for us in two or three counties and you couldn't trust people not to turn you in. This narrowed our social and business activity considerable.

A year after I made Luna's acquaintance in Springer, he quit the railroad and was elected sheriff of Santa Fe County, which was one of the places we was wanted but couldn't stay away from. A man could have a dandy time in Santa Fe then. There was bars and cat houses and card parlors enough for everybody because it's a Catholic town. Any place run by Catholics is generally more tolerant of people's vices than the Protestants. They're mostly killjoys who spend a lot of time praying and worrying, if you ask me. I was raised Catholic by the Montoyas and I believe it's the best religion if you're in the market for one. It don't hardly take up any time, and you can't ask more from a church than that.

Luna celebrated his first day as sheriff by shooting a man dead in front of the Exchange Hotel, which later was called the La Fonda. The dumb bunny had robbed a jewelry shop, and pulled a gun when Luna told him to put up his hands. The bullet went clear through his chest and bloodied the hat of a man sitting on a bench in the plaza. That kind of thing is good advertising for a new sheriff because it keeps the criminal elements in their place.

Anyway, I decide to steer clear of Santa Fe after that, at least for a while. They couldn't prove anything on me, and I'm only wanted for questioning, but mostly they was questions I preferred not to answer. I knew Luna was looking to give my arm a twist because I was still hanging around with Mountain and the Williamses, and working from time to time for the Brown brothers. Luna never liked it when people ignored his advice, but that didn't stop him from giving it out free all his life.

He was an old man when he died, and the vice-president of the United States come all the way to Santa Fe for the funeral. That's when Ike was president, and after the funeral the vice-president come up to me and said he understood I soldiered in Cuba with Governor Luna and Teddy Roosevelt. I guess one of the government men looked it up in a book and told him. I never could stand a patronizing politician and that's how this fellow Nixon struck me. I'm a Republican and always was, and he had my vote until he started talking, saying how much he admired what we did in Cuba back then. He says now this fellow Castro's in charge, we might have to go do it again.

I say, "Do what?"

He says, "Why, you know, Colonel Garland. Get the Commies out. Kick a little ass for democracy."

"You think that's what we done?" I ask him.

"You freed Cuba," he says, "and it's up to us to keep her free."

"I know what we did in Cuba," I tell him.

"You should be proud of it," he says, like he's talking to a kid who just got a star on his report card.

I say, "Killing people is nothing to be proud of."

"I didn't mean that," he says, backing off, sorry he brought up the subject. I know he's thinking I'm a senile old coot don't understand nothing, and he's looking shifty at the government men around him and the reporters who write it all down.

"We was dumb and clumsy," I tell them, "and lucky to come home alive. We had no business there then and we got no business there now."

"Nice talking to you, Colonel," he says, like he ain't heard a word I said. And he smiles at a photographer who takes our picture together. In nineteen and sixty I voted against that fellow for president, the second time I failed the Republican party. The first was when I voted the Bull Moose ticket for Colonel Roosevelt and he lost in nineteen and twelve.

In the late fall of ninety-six we have a good run, and Cody Williams and me decide to chance a Saturday night in Santa Fe. When you're young and got money jingling in your jeans, temptation cancels out risk every time. I figure on visiting the girls over at Mrs. Sanchez's, but Cody wants to play poker with Red Holman and some others at Gordo Martinez's bar. What nobody figures is Luna hearing we're in town and arresting Cody and Red.

The girl I'm with sees Luna come into the whorehouse, asking for me. I go out the second-story window in my BVDs without looking back. She throws my boots and britches after me, and when I count my money later, I see she took her five dollars before she tossed me the pants.

The case against Red Holman ain't strong enough to hold him, and Luna lets Cody go too after a couple of days, because the ones he really wants is the Brown brothers and Cody's brother Jake. After that scare Cody goes over to a place Jake had in Wagon Mound, which is in Mora County, out of Luna's reach.

Winters was as lean for a cattle thief as they was for the cows, unless you went to Mexico and tried your luck. But I heard such bad stories about that place I wasn't interested in doing any business there. The law was no problem, but the competition was. If they caught you, they turned you into a girl.

So Mountain and me decide to take a vacation. I knew an abandoned cabin above Eagle Nest and we go there in late November with the idea of staying until March. It's real pretty country, high and wooded and quiet. We stock the place with canned food and take along our string of horses and enough dry feed to last. We keep busy running trap lines and figure to make some money on fox pelts. The jackrabbits ain't worth nothing, but we skin them anyway because you could sell them for a quarter each. We hunted some too. There was wild turkeys then, and mule deer, which was easy to shoot against the snow so we always had fresh meat.

What I forgot was how much snow there is. Sometimes it comes down for days and we have to keep digging out the horses so they won't freeze to death. When it's too miserable to go out, Mountain shows me knife-throwing, which he is an expert at. He earned a lot of free whiskey that way, betting he could hit George Washington on a dollar bill from ten paces. He won every time and always collected the dollar too, when he took back his knife.

On good days I practice shooting with my Colt. I heard stories about gunfighters since I was a kid, but that time is past. There's still a few experts around like Luna or Pat Garrett down in Las Cruces who killed Billy the Kid, but the other ones I met was as hollow as dead oaks and just as full of air. Mountain carves my initials, *L.O.G.*, on my gun butt, and you have to admire the work.

Shooting is an expensive education even reusing the cartridges and saving the lead. I didn't have the itch to kill anybody, but I figured if I was good at placing my shots, I could slow a man down. A talent like that could make the difference if I ever come up against somebody like Alfred S. Sorenson again.

The noise of that Colt made the whole valley ring, and we was never able to hunt for a spell after I'd been practicing. One day I hit five out of six pinecones from fifty feet and figure I've reached perfection. Mountain's lingering in the cabin, watching me from the window. When I come inside again, he says, "That's good, but they was standing still."

"Moving, I'd still get a couple," I say, cocky as hell.

"While the others get you," he says.

"Can you do better?"

"Not with a gun."

"There you are. You only got one knife, so you'd be just as dead as me."

"Who you planning to kill, Lee?"

"Nobody. If I'm good and people find out, they'll stay clear."

"It don't always work that way. Up in Pueblo I seen militia gun down some of the best shots in Colorado. We was outnumbered."

"Is it true you killed a guard when you busted out of prison?"

"Naw. I just kept running."

"What happens if they catch you?"

"I'd hang. Don't matter I didn't kill anybody, I was there."

"Well, I ain't going to kill nobody," I say.

"I'm glad to hear that, Lee, because it's a bad business. Just make sure you're not around when somebody else does it."

I didn't think nothing of what Mountain said then, but it was like a prophecy that would haunt me for a long time to come.

That day Mountain's got a brutal hangover so he ain't up to

helping me with the trap line. I go out alone and find nothing except a couple of skinny jackrabbits until I get to the last trap. A lobo's caught in it, his lips curled back over his fangs when he sees me, and blood all over the snow where he's trying to chew off his mangled front paw and escape.

I could of shot him dead but why waste the cartridge? There's some piñon trees there and I start to cut one to club him with when he severs that foot and leaves the trap. Maimed as he is, there's still plenty of fight in him, and he does what I least expect, he jumps. Now the lobo is a kind of timber wolf, and no coward like a coyote, even though they're both from the dog family. There's no meaner, more dangerous animal at close range, and they got teeth like honed razors. Lobos can tear a four-hundred-pound bear to pieces without working up a sweat. This one's maybe ninety pounds, and headed for my throat.

I draw the Colt, fire and miss as he hits my chest. He bounces off my coat, taking a mouthful of sheepskin and part of my arm, and knocks me on my back in the snow, where I drop the gun. I don't even have the Bowie knife I been using to cut the tree with because that's in the snow too. He comes snarling at me again and gets hold of my foot, his teeth slicing through the boot like it's a silk slipper, but I kick him away with my other foot and stand up before he can get back at me.

Blood's all over the snow, his and mine, and when he charges again, I move behind a tree, so he misses me. Running on three legs, his balance is off or he'd of finished me fast, but he ain't likely to quit. I get the knife at last and figure I have a chance until I see two more of them coming. If they'd had half the pluck of the first one, I'd of been dinner, but they didn't. The one we caught in the trap is trying to get even with me for crippling him. The others whine and growl but they're willing to let him finish me off because he snaps at them every time they come close.

Their jaws is built for tearing, not chewing, and I heard men say they won't attack, but I'm living proof it ain't true. The next time he comes, I cut him on the chest but I can't stick him. He lets out a bloodcurdling howl, more mad than hurt, and comes hurtling back at me. It's like a signal to the others, who charge in behind him.

I wouldn't of got out of that alive if it wasn't for Mountain, who heard my single shot and dragged himself out of the cabin to see what's going on. He throws his knife and gets one of them in midair. Then he jumps on the hurt one from the trap, wrassling it from behind, and snaps its neck like a match. I'm still groveling in the snow for the Colt, expecting the third one to attack, when there's a shot and it drops in its tracks.

We're trying to figure where the bullet comes from when this fellow comes out of the trees toward us.

We ain't seen a living soul up here in weeks except some Indians running trap lines, but this ain't no Indian. It's a tall white man with a rifle in his hands and a badge on his mackinaw.

Blood is still pouring out of my arm where that varmint got me, and my ankle's on fire from the second bite. If a tree hadn't been there to lean on, I'd of fell down where I was.

The stranger looks at the wolves first to make sure they're dead, and then at me and Mountain. "It appears you boys had a little trouble," he says.

"Just lobos," Mountain says. He pulls his knife out of one he killed and wipes it on his britches but he don't put it away.

The man takes a long look at me but he don't put up his rifle or turn his back on Mountain. "You're going to die unless you do something for that arm," he says.

"Not much I can do," I say, trying to sound tough, but my voice comes out weak and scratchy.

"Tie a belt on him," he says to Mountain, "or he'll bleed to death where he stands."

"Who might you be?" Mountain asks him.

"We'll get to that," the stranger says, "after you give your partner a hand." He has a low voice, hardly more than a whisper, but there's no mistaken he just give an order. By that time, I'm feeling the pain and I don't care if he arrests us or not. Mountain puts the knife away and ties a thong from one of his moccasins around my arm. Then he lugs me down to the cabin and sets me on my blankets while the stranger brings my Colt.

He could see we ain't in a resisting mood, and after he satisfies himself nobody else is around, he kind of relaxes. Mountain gets me some whiskey and washes the torn place on my arm. I pass the bottle to the stranger and after he takes a pull, he says, "Well, now, my name is Ben Butler and I am the United States Marshall. I'm looking for a couple of boys, and if you tell me who you are, I'll tell you if you're the ones I'm looking for."

"I guess we are," I say, "but I'm in no shape to travel."

Ben Butler laughs at this and you can see he's a good-natured sort for a lawman, not like Luna.

"How'd you find us?" Mountain says. "Nobody knew we was here."

"People talk," Ben Butler says, "but the descriptions I have don't bear much resemblance to you two. You don't look like brothers."

"We ain't," Mountain says.

"Cousins?" Ben Butler says. "Or is it just a coincidence you have the same name?"

"Mine's Moore," Mountain says, "and he's Lee Garland."

Butler squints at both of us before he reaches inside his coat and takes out a paper. "The boys I want are Jake and Cody Williams. If neither one of them is you, maybe you know where I'll find them."

"No idea," Mountain says.

"You know them?" Butler says.

"Cody's only a kid," I say. "What do you want him for?"

"He and his brother Jake broke into a mail car," Butler says.

"Cody ain't a robber," I say.

"What about you?" Butler asks me.

"You got a warrant for me too?"

"You thought I did. Why?"

"I must of been delirious," I say.

"How are you feeling now?"

"Like Little Red Riding Hood."

He takes Mountain off in the corner and they start whispering. I look outside and see it's snowing again, then I must of faded, because the next thing I know this Ben Butler's standing over me with a spoon heated red hot from the fire, and I say, "What are you doing with that?"

"Going to cauterize the hole in your arm a little, so the bleeding don't start again."

"Oh, no you ain't."

But three hundred pounds of Mountain Moore drops on me, and Ben Butler's got that spoon to the wound before I can stop him. When I come to there's a godawful stench in the place from my burned flesh. I got the hole and the scars to this day and lucky it was my left arm. Ben Butler jokes, "That sure smells good, Mr. Moore. What are you cooking?"

The snow kept up and it was four days before Ben Butler could get out. He helped Mountain bind my foot and we got to be friends, considering what we was and what he was. He owns land in the valley below Eagle Nest, not five miles from my foster father's place. It's mostly timber, but with some good pasture too, and he's going to start working it in the spring. Like me, he believes it's the most beautiful country on God's earth.

We skinned them wolves and we give him the pelt of the one he killed. Winter wolf skins was worth something, and the Indians would trade turquoise and silver for the claws.

I tried to talk him out of going after Cody, and he said the government paid him fifty-five dollars a month to do his duty. But if he couldn't find him in this blizzard, it wasn't his fault. Ben Butler had a family and was reading law for the bar exam. He'd fought in the Indian Wars and was a captain in the Territorial Militia, which didn't pay him any money but brought prestige. He was ambitious, Ben Butler, and about thirty-five years old.

When he left he said, "Don't you boys break any federal laws now and spoil a beautiful friendship." He was that kind of man, God help him, and he deserved better than he got.

Wanted for Murder

Luna had a sense of humor as long as the joke was on somebody else. He couldn't take any kidding, and like most men with Spanish blood, he could be downright dangerous if he thought somebody insulted him. But he was a good sheriff, if there is such a thing, and a good governor.

I remember when he was campaigning for his second term as sheriff, the Democrat who run against him said he took bribes. Luna went to this fellow's office and called him out.

"I got the proof," the Democrat says. His name was Truman Glascock and he was a lawyer, which Luna wasn't. "Signed affidavits by people seen you take money from one Olga Sanchez, who runs a house of ill repute on Mission Street."

"You're a coward and a liar," Luna tells him. "Mrs. Sanchez runs a house of very good repute." Then he calls Glascock "crystaldick" and *"maricon,"* which means queer in Mexican, and uses some more words which brings Glascock running with two friends.

Luna laid them out like cordwood in front of a good-size crowd, and settled the election. New Mexico was like that in those days. Nobody'd vote for a pantywaist.

But Glascock files suit anyway and takes Luna to court, swearing he took bribes. I learn how politics works when Glascock calls Old Lady Sanchez as a witness.

"You give Sheriff Luna that money?" he says, bellowing like a trussed bull.

She says she give Luna money lots of times.

"For special services like seeing you don't get arrested?"

She says no, and Truman Glascock is real pleased with the way things are going. He beams a smile around the courtroom and asks what Luna's hoping he'll ask. "Well then, what was this money for?"

Old Lady Sanchez speaks up loud and clear. "Contributions to the Republican Party, all legal and aboveboard." The judge, who is Republican, says that shows public spirit, and thanks her for her testimony before he throws the case out of court.

In February me and Mountain ride over by Wagon Mound, where we learn Ben Butler never did arrest Jake and Cody Williams. Jake says he didn't have the guts, and that makes me laugh. Ben Butler could take a nitwit like Jake apart in a minute and not even work up a sweat.

Jake had broke into the mail car all right, but Alfred S. Sorenson showed up before he had a chance to steal anything and Jake ran off. So there was no felony case, only breaking and entering, which was why Butler give it up. Cody tells me he thinks the same thing happened over in Springer, because Red Holman was supposed to go with them and never showed up, while Alfred S. Sorenson was there waiting.

"And you think Red told Ernie?"

"He's dumb enough."

"Does Jake know?"

Cody shakes his head and checks to make sure Jake's not listening. "If he did, he'd kill Red Holman."

We hang around Jake's place for a couple of days, which is a real pigsty. No two brothers could be less alike. Cody was always clean and took care of his clothes and saddle gear. He was pale and skinny as a plucked bird, and didn't have good wind, but he was always game, and had the best sense of humor. He'd laugh so hard he'd get a coughing fit and you'd think his lungs was coming up. He spit pink, and when I told him that wasn't good, he ought to see a doctor, he said, "Hell, Lee, what do they know?"

Jake mostly stayed drunk and smelled like a goat if you got close. He was years older than Cody and already losir

going to fat around the middle. He bragged on himself all the time
and said he was thinking about including us in his new gang. He
claimed he knew ways we could get a lot richer than working for
the Brown brothers, but I didn't believe him.

Mountain is agreeable to going on our own, but only if we leave
Red Holman out and not with Jake as leader. I'm undecided because the money with Sam and Arnold Brown is good, and because
they're organized. We argue about it and I say let's vote. Comes
out three to one in favor of going on our own. But when we vote
again to see who's in charge, democracy don't work. I vote for
Mountain and he votes for me, and Cody and Jake both vote for
Jake. I say it don't seem right for a man to vote for himself.

"Then I vote for Cody," says Jake, "which makes it a tie."

Mountain says, "Lee ought to be trail boss."

"But I know where to start," Jake says.

"Where?" says Mountain.

"Santa Fe."

"Are you crazy?" I say.

"Last place Luna'd look," Jake says, like he had it all thought
out. "We go in at night, work and get out."

I say, "Him or Alfred S. Sorenson would hear the ruckus and
have us cold."

"We don't move no cows," Cody tells us, grinning. "Jake's got
a better idea."

"Contract paper," Jake says, real proud of himself. He had a
pasty, pinched kind of face and a scraggly beard. In spite of the flab
over his belt, he had the look of a man never got enough to eat.

"What's contract paper?" Mountain wants to know.

"You tell him, Lee," Jake says, trying to show me up and let them
know how smart he is.

I take my time. "Contract paper is what a rancher signs to sell
cows and get money up front. It's like a check anybody can cash.
Arnold Brown holds a lot of it." Mountain don't understand, and
Jake's sorry he asked. So I say, "The rancher agrees to sell cheap,
say five dollars a head below the market price, at a certain date and
certain place. He signs a paper and gets some money right away,
cha   rest when he brings in the herd. Meanwhile the paper may
        "W   ds a dozen times."
        "Watch

                    that, Lee?" Cody says, impressed.
                    wn."

"Who does he sell it to?" Mountain asks me.

"Cattle agents, meatpackers, banks," Jake says, trying to make himself important again. "Good as cash."

"And just as hard to get your hands on," I tell them, "unless you know how to blow a safe and got the dynamite to do it."

"Not so," Jake says.

"Where is it?" I say.

"Am I boss?" Jake says.

"Sure," Cody says. "It's your idea, Jake."

Mountain looks at me.

"Lee?" Jake says.

"I don't believe you," I tell him, "but if it's as easy to get as you say, then okay. You're boss."

"Easy as pie," Jake says. "It's in Arnold Brown's office."

"In a safe," I say.

"In a tin box in his desk," Jake says. "Thousands worth."

"And you seen Arnold with it?" I say, doubting him.

"That's when I got the idea."

"I don't relish going up against the Brown brothers," I tell them. "Sam would kill you for a dollar, and Arnold would find a way to make another buck off the corpse."

Cody says, "Lee's right, Jake. Arnold's awful smart."

"So smart he keeps that paper in a box you could open with a jackknife," Jake says.

We chew it over for a few hours and can't find much wrong if Jake is telling the truth, and he probably is. Only it don't feel right. If Arnold Brown leaves contract paper laying around like that, there has to be something we don't know. Jake says we can sell it down in Albuquerque easy, or in Texas. In the end I give in and go along.

Jake wants to leave that same night, but I tell him no, we take another day and plan it careful. Stealing from Arnold Brown ain't much of a crime, or even any big risk as long as he don't know who done it. But with Jake's bragging, him or Sam'll find out, and when they do, we'll be better off in jail than having them two after us. It is a dismal thought, but I don't dwell on it. Instead I think about the contract paper and what I can buy with all that money.

Me and Mountain pass the morning fixing our gear for the long ride while Cody brings up the extra horses we plan to leave in Lamy. The idea is we break into Arnold Brown's desk on Saturday night late, steal the contract paper and cut right out. We should make it to Lamy before dawn. I favor Texas as a safe place to sell it because we ain't known and it puts space between us and the Brown brothers.

When Jake finally wakes up around noon we talk over who is going to do what. Mountain will wait in Lamy with our trail gear and the fresh horses, while Cody comes with me and Jake.

Jake says only one of us is needed to break open the desk and he'll be the one. But I don't trust him alone for one second. I'm the only one besides Jake with a Colt so I'll go along too while Cody stands lookout with the horses.

After dark that Saturday we ride by Arnold's office. Sam Brown's outside, and he sees us, but we don't stop. Jake needs to spark his courage and I say we don't want nobody drunk tonight and we got to stay away from any bar where Luna might show up. Cody wants to visit a woman him and Jake know, and says I can come too for a dip in her honey pot, but I'm thinking she's got to be a hag if she lets Jake in her bloomers. I'd sooner spend my five dollars at Mrs. Sanchez's, where I can go in the back and nobody will ever know I'm there.

I leave my Colt with Cody because I can't take it into Mrs. Sanchez's and we agree to meet at midnight a block from Arnold Brown's office. That gives Jake too much time for drinking, but Cody promises to keep him sober.

I pick my way careful across town, staying away from the streets with the electric lights. I go around to the alley behind the whorehouse, where an old Indian looks after my horse. I ain't been there since the night I jumped in my underwear, and I ain't even certain the girl I had last time is still there, but I hope so because she sure knows how to sharpen a man's pencil.

Her name don't come to mind anymore, but the rest of her does. She was about sixteen with a birthmark like a plum on her neck she tried to cover with powder. Her face was plain, but she had pale white skin and stringy blond hair, which made her a change from the Mexican girls. The other whores said her daddy was a Baptist missionary on the Jemez Pueblo who chucked her out for sucking off Indians. But them women was awful liars and I doubt a preacher would do that to his own daughter.

I liked to spend time with her. She was on the skinny side compared to other women then, but she had rosy little tits and a fanny as round and pretty as two honeydews. Nothing I did with the widow woman in Taos was up to what that little girl showed me. She had the best-educated fingers in Mrs. Sanchez's place, and a tongue could raise the cock on a corpse. She'd pump you with spirit, and whimper and squeal and bite your shoulder when your gun went off. She was a body took pleasure in her work.

When I got there, she was busy, so I sat in the kitchen and stuffed myself. I got a good appetite, always have had. But ordinary food never satisfies me like good Mexican cooking. It's in the upbringing, I guess. My grandson Pete is like me, so maybe it's in the blood too, some place. When he was little I used to take him to lunch in Santa Fe with Luna, who was retired. We'd yarn about the old days and put away all the chili steak, tacos and *sopapillas* his wife could dish up. I miss those times and those people. I'd do my whole life over if I had the chance. I daydream about turning the clock back, which is what I'm doing now in a way. Luna used to say nobody dies in New Mexico, they just dry up and blow away.

Old Lady Sanchez's cook knew the way to a man's heart, but it wasn't my heart I was thinking about. When time's running short, the girl puts her face in the kitchen, gobbles a tortilla, fondles my crotch and leads me up the back stairs to her room. I get a half hour for five dollars and she tells me she don't want me jumping out her window like last time.

She asks where I been and I tell her trapping in the mountains, but she don't believe it when she sees my arm. The wound is healed but still red and ugly, and I'm kind of proud.

I tell her a wolf bit me and she says she's heard everything, but not that one.

"I swear," I say, offended.

"Look, cowboy," she tells me, "I don't go with nobody brings me grief. Who cut you?"

"Nobody cut me," I say.

"Then you was shot," she says, "which is worse."

I'm standing there in my birthday suit with a hard-on like tall timber and she's backing away, cool as spring water, making up her mind if she's going to go to work or have me chucked out. The hard-on decided her because all of a sudden she giggles and puts her little monkey hand around it and leads me over by the bed.

"I mean it," she says, with a voice that don't convince me. "Where you really been all this time?"

"In the mountains."

"Umm," she says. "With who?"

"A friend of mine," I say.

"Umm. She as good as me?"

"She's a he," I say.

"That's a surprise," she says.

"You ain't funny," I tell her.

"As big as you?"

Mistaking her meaning, I say, "Bigger by a foot."

"Ohhh," she squeals, holding my root on her fingers and currying it with her tongue like a cat lapping milk. "Bring him around!"

There ain't nothing more helpless than a man with a hard-on, which is why a woman always has the advantage. Another thing about women is how calm and collected they can be when a man's concentrating on the bullseye, like they're really thinking what they can charge you for the pleasure, or are just waiting for you to get it over with. I don't mean just whores, I mean the species. It probably comes from their natural limitations. A man's got choices, but all nature give a woman besides a inquisitive brain is two tits and a pussy.

That girl and me are doing so good after my half hour is up, I dig out another five dollars and say, "Let's keep going."

"You sure?" she says. We both look down and she laughs. "Look at little Jesus, will you? He's rising again like the good book says."

We bounce around that bed right side up and upside down until I can't do it no more. Three times in a hour is a lot even at the age I was then, considering I was still convalescing. I'm trying to get my breath after the last skirmish, and she's pulling on her stockings, when the door flies open and there's Cody, puffing and sweating, his eyes big as silver dollars. The maid is behind him, tugging on his shirt, screaming he can't come in.

Well, he's already in, and I tell her close the door, he's a friend of mine. I'm getting my britches because I see something's gone wrong and I figure it's probably Jake got drunk.

"Lee, Jake's been shot!" he says, and he's near crying.

The girl turns on me like a cougar and says, "I told you I don't want trouble. Goddamn, I should of knowed you'd be trouble!"

I say, "Hold your horses, there ain't no trouble," as calm as I can while working into my boots. "Who shot him?" I say to Cody, who's over by the window, looking at the alley and shaking like a palsied dog.

The girl starts yelling at us to get out and I tell her to shut up. But she's more scared of Mrs. Sanchez than of me, so I grab my hat and shirt and shove Cody ahead down the back stairs. "Did anybody follow you here?" I ask him.

"I don't think so," he says, gasping for air. "Lee, we got to help Jake."

"Where is he?"

"In the street by the railroad office."

Mrs. Sanchez is with the cook when we pass through the kitchen. She gives me a big smile and asks in Mexican if I'm having a good time. "Real nice, thank you, ma'am," I tell her, glad she didn't hear the girl carrying on upstairs.

In the alley, where there's nobody but the old Indian who looks after the horses, I ask Cody exactly what happened.

"Jake got drunk and went by Arnold's office and when he sees nobody's there he says he'll go ahead by himself." Cody's hacking and coughing while he tells me this. "I told him not to, Lee. I said to wait for you."

"Okay," I say. "I still don't know what happened."

"I stayed with the horses and Jake's in there a long time. Then the lights go on and there's two shots. Jake comes running out and behind him comes Sam Brown yelling Jake killed his brother."

"Did Jake get the contract paper?"

"He didn't get nothing."

The old Indian brings our horses, and Cody wants to go help Jake, but I ain't moving until I hear the rest. If it's as cheerful as what I been told so far, the less we see of Sam Brown, the better. I give the Indian a dime for his trouble, and ask Cody if Jake killed Arnold Brown.

"I don't know, Lee, honest. There wasn't time to find out. But he wounded Sam. Jake's horse was spooked and he couldn't find the stirrup in the dark to mount up. Sam Brown was yelling to stop Jake and this Sorenson comes running out of the railroad office with a baseball bat in one hand and his gun in the other and shoots Jake. He pegged a shot at me too, but he missed. We got to help Jake."

"Nothing we can do for Jake. If he couldn't ride this far, he can't make it the rest of the way." I get on my horse and tell Cody we're leaving Santa Fe.

"He's my brother, Lee!"

"Well, he ain't mine. If you think I'm going up against Sam Brown and Alfred S. Sorenson, you're crazier than Jake. Where's my gun?"

"Jake took it."

I'm so damn mad about that I put spurs to my horse and don't even look back to see if Cody's following. I don't cool down until I'm out of town and hear him come up behind me. For an hour we go between a walk and a canter without a word. Every now and then I hear Cody let go a sob which starts another coughing fit, and that only makes me mad again. Jake don't deserve a brother like Cody. What he deserves is what he got, an ass full of lead from Alfred S. Sorenson. I should of never trusted Jake, and now I'm out a Colt forty-four and on the run.

Nobody come after us and we ride into Lamy around three in the morning. When Mountain hears about Jake he looks at me like I'm the dumbest cluck ever born. "It was certain he'd do something foolish if you let him go off alone, Lee. Why did you?"

"It's my fault," Cody says.

Mountain says, "What do we do now?"

We was at a farm belonged to Tom Corbett, a friend of Cody and Jake's, and I know we can't stay there long. Cody's best bet is to head for Texas, but he's worried about Jake. This Tom Corbett says he's got to go to Santa Fe anyway about a deed, and he'll see if Jake's in jail or what. We hunker down for some sleep after he leaves, with Mountain staying awake in case somebody comes this far looking for Cody.

Late that morning, I'm at the pump having a wash when I hear my name called. I wipe the soap out of my eyes and I'm looking up at Ben Butler sitting on a big chestnut gelding. At first I figure he's after Cody, but he's smiling like he's glad to see me, so it seems he don't know yet what went on in Santa Fe.

He says I look a sight better than the last time so he guesses the wolf didn't give me rabies. He asks about Mountain and I say he's around somewheres. "You boys looking for work?" Ben Butler says.

"Could be, Marshall," I say. "We got to eat."

"You're staying out of mischief, I trust."

"Sure thing," I say.

"Well, I was just admitted to the bar," he says, "but I don't want you looking for trouble just so you can have me as your lawyer."

I get into the spirit of the joke and tell him not to worry.

"If you're serious about work, I can use a couple of good hands on my place," he says. "I'll be back from Santa Fe in a week so you have time to think about it."

"I'll tell Mountain."

"I don't pay as well as the Brown brothers," he says, "but there's a better future."

"I get your meaning, Marshall, and I appreciate your confidence," I say, hoping Cody don't come out while we're talking. No sense in Ben Butler's making that connection and spoiling his good opinion of me.

This Tom Corbett gets back after dark because he hung around Gordo Martinez's bar to hear the news. It's all bad.

"How's Jake?" Cody says, right after Corbett climbs down from his horse and starts taking off the saddle.

Corbett looks from me to Mountain, but not at Cody.

"They put him in jail?" Cody asks him.

"No," Corbett says.

"Did anybody get him a doctor?" Cody wants to know.

"Weren't no need," Corbett says. "Jake's dead, son."

For a minute I'm not sure Cody's listening because he don't react, don't say nothing. This Tom Corbett just stands there with the saddle in his arms. Then he slings it up on a post and says over his shoulder, "Sam Brown's got a bullet in his hip but he'll live. He claims Jake shot Arnold in the head and killed him."

"Jake wouldn't kill nobody," Cody says. He looks at me and he's crying. "Jake's always been a good brother to me, Lee. I know he drinks a lot and you don't like him, but he always looked after me."

Mountain puts his arm around the kid and leads him over by the barn. Funny how a man as big and hard as he was could be so gentle when the time called for it. I knew Jake Williams for the lying, bragging drunk he was, and if there was any good in him, he always kept it hid. Poor Cody didn't know it yet, but he was well shut of Jake.

"What else you find out?" I ask Tom Corbett soon as Cody's out of earshot.

"Luna locked up Alfred S. Sorenson."

"I don't believe it!"

"Luna says as long as he's sheriff, not even Alfred S. Sorenson has the right to shoot anybody in his county. He says he has nothing personal against him, but the law is the law. Luna let him out soon as the railroad paid his bail. There'll be a hearing because he killed Jake, but nothing will happen to him."

"They know about Cody?" I ask him.

"I was getting to that," Corbett says. "Luna told Sam Brown in front of everybody if he went gunning for Cody or anybody else, he'd lock him up too." Corbett laughs. "Sam Brown says, 'What kind of justice is that?' and Luna says, 'The law is what I'm paid to enforce, not justice.' It's his favorite saying."

"He'll be after Cody then," I tell Corbett, "and he didn't have nothing to do with it."

"So he says, but they got a murder warrant out on him."

"All he did was hold Jake's horse."

"Maybe," Tom Corbett says, "but Jake ain't around to testify. They got a warrant out on you, too."

"Me! What for?"

"Murder."

"I wasn't anywheres near the place!"

"Sam Brown seen you ride by the office with Jake and Cody before Arnold was killed, and Alfred S. Sorenson found your gun there."

"I was at Old Lady Sanchez's in bed with a girl!"

Tom Corbett shrugs like it don't matter to him where I was.

"I can prove it," I tell him.

"If I was you," he says, "I wouldn't want to have to."

I Make an Honest Dollar

We leave Tom Corbett's place that night but we don't get far, just the other side of Glorieta Pass below Thompson Peak. We have seven horses with us besides the ones we're riding, and enough food to carry us awhile. Mountain and me each have a hundred dollars we made off the skins, plus my four hundred dollars. Cody offers to give me a little old revolver in place of my Colt but I tell him to keep it. I got my Winchester and a double-barrel Remington shotgun, and Cody brings along a Spencer rifle must be a hundred years old. It weighed a ton and had an octagon barrel you could put your thumb inside. Fifty-eight caliber I think it was, took a slug like a cannonball, and a big paper cartridge with a fulminate cap. All it was good for was to knock down trees, but we let him bring it because he was feeling bad about Jake.

The place we camp has good water for the horses, and the grass is green and fresh. It's almost spring but there's still patches of snow, and the nights get freezing cold that high up. We make a fire and nip a little whiskey to take the chill off. Cody wants to talk about what a fine brother Jake was, and we let him, even agreeing with him so he'll feel better. The whiskey gets to him real fast, between the cold and altitude, but instead of going to sleep he starts crying again.

I curl up, but I can't sleep with all the sniffling. Cody keeps asking about the afterlife and expecting me to bring him up to

29

date. I mumble what I know, hoping he'll doze off and let me be, but that don't happen.

"You think Jake's in heaven, Lee?" he says.

If I had a grain of sense, I'd of said sure, and then I might of got some peace, but the idea of Jake Williams in a white robe playing a harp is more than I can swallow, so I say, "It ain't likely, Cody, if he shot Arnold Brown."

"I don't believe he'd do that," Cody keeps saying, "unless it was an accident. Then God would forgive him, wouldn't he?"

"I guess he might."

"But suppose God wasn't looking when Arnold got shot?"

That's the most reasonable thing I hear Cody say since he got started, but I don't say so.

"Lee?"

"What?"

"You believe in hell?"

"Nobody believes in that stuff anymore."

"You believe in heaven?"

"That's different," I say, figuring it's what he wants to hear.

"How can you believe in one without the other? I mean if Jake can't get into heaven, then he has to go to hell, don't he?"

I'm thinking Jake went to hell long before Alfred S. Sorenson give him his ticket, but I shut up. I'm wide awake and sitting up again, so I light a cigar. Mountain's quiet, tossing wood on the fire now and then. I try to recall what the Catholics say about limbo. But that only confuses Cody because he's trying to invent an excuse to get Jake into heaven, and he don't want him stopping off on the way.

Mountain saves things. "You know what the Indians believe, don't you?" he says to Cody, and I see right away the boy's interested.

Mountain spent time once with Ute hunters around Shiprock, and learned about the Indian religion. He tells Cody the Indians believe that when a man is born he takes over a spirit. The spirit is around before the man comes along and will still be there after he's dead.

Once the liquor loosens his tongue, Mountain makes up what he don't know for sure, as a kindness to Cody. "There's good spirits and bad ones, fast ones and slow ones. There's wind spirits and mud spirits, mouse spirits and bear spirits."

"Jake could of used a bear spirit," Cody says, "because he had a lot of courage and strength."

I'm thinking all Jake had any use for was a alcohol spirit, but it ain't the time for a joke so I don't tell it.

"Now these spirits hang around after a man dies," Mountain says, "for a long, long time."

"Like a haunt?" Cody says, looking out into the dark.

"That depends," Mountain says. "An Indian knows he don't have no say how he's born, but he likes to have a say about how he dies. He owes his spirit a good death, like hunting or fighting, doing what he's meant to do in this world."

"Jake died like that," Cody says. "Don't you think Lee?"

"He sure died doing what he liked to do," I say. "No doubt about that."

If Mountain had been yarning about spirits in Gordo Martinez's bar, he'd of been laughed all the way to Utah, but whoppers always sound more believable around a campfire. Mountain tells Cody that if a Indian is lucky to have a good spirit, and he lives right with it, and shows it a good death, the spirit keeps floating around after the man's gone.

Cody looks into the dark and says, "I got a feeling Jake's spirit is out there now, listening to us talk about him. I just know it, Lee. Listen!" All Cody's feeling is the booze, but me and Mountain look into the dark too, like fools, as if we half expect Jake to conjure himself up at the edge of the woods. I had no use for him alive, but I like him a damn sight less as a haunt.

I say, "Well, he ain't out there, so let's all get some sleep."

"Maybe he ain't," Mountain says, "but something is." He hardly gets the words out when there's a godawful clatter in the dark and the horses spook. I freeze where I'm sitting because all this spirit talk has got to me. Cody's got a kind of idiot smile on his face like he's expecting Jake to join the party. Mountain's the only one with any sense. He grabs Cody's big rifle and lifts it into his lap, ready. We all been looking into the fire so long we can't see a thing in the dark.

"Jake!" Cody calls. "You out there, Jake!"

"Shut up," Mountain says between his teeth, backing away from the fire with the old Spencer. Cody could hardly lift that rifle to his shoulder, and the few times I seen him fire it, he got knocked on his ass. In Mountain's hands, it looks like a toy.

Again there's a noise from the woods, and I forget all about spirits and haunts when I think we been sitting around like a convention of pinheads long enough for Luna and a hundred deputies to sneak up on us. I dive away from the fire and grab my Winchester, ready to die shooting rather than go down to Santa Fe and let them hang me for something I didn't do. I had more liquor than I needed, too.

Cody's on his feet now, staggering away from the fire like he's expecting Jake to come out of the trees and give him a hug. I back off into the shadows and cock the rifle. Then I see it. If it ain't a haunt, I don't know what it is, but it's the biggest, blackest, scariest thing I ever laid eyes on, and it's coming toward Cody and the fire. I raise the Winchester, but before I can pull the trigger, there's an explosion shakes the woods. This thing pitches out of the dark and falls headlong about a foot from where Cody's standing. Then Cody drops in a heap and don't move.

Mountain calls out, "Lee!"

"Here." I got the Winchester pointed at the thing and I come out slow.

Mountain gets there first and pokes it with the toe of his moccasin. "It's dead," he says, and I see the head then. It's the biggest goddamn grizzly in creation, twice the size of Mountain. "Some haunt," he says.

Cody's okay, just passed out drunk. We bed down finally and get a little sleep before a thunder storm hits us around dawn and soaks everybody to the skin. The lightning cracks and crashes around the peak like Fourth of July and the horses are terrified. I'm glad to see the sun come up so we can dry out and get the blood circulating again.

We skin the bear, shake Cody awake and hit the trail, headed east. We have no place definite in mind except Texas and maybe the Indian Territory. When I tell Mountain Ben Butler offered us work, he says, "If all lawmen was as decent as him, we wouldn't be on the run."

"You could of stayed," I tell him. "Luna ain't after you."

"I'd never do that," he says. "Every time I leave you alone, you get into trouble. If you ain't feeding yourself to a wolf, you're provoking a sheriff." He laughs, deep and rich and satisfying. "No, without me you'd never make it to hell or any place else."

After the pass, it's downhill to Texas, which makes it easier on the horses but is still a long ride. Cody don't say two words because he's grieving with a hangover big as that bear, and there ain't no more talk of spirits. We push hard and on the second night we camp near Anton Chico, staying clear of towns and ranches along the way. I figure we can make Tucumcari in two more days and Texas on the next.

North of Santa Rosa we leave the Pecos River Valley and head parallel to the Southern Pacific Railroad tracks. One of the horses goes lame so we only get as far as Newkirk, which is just a water tank with the name painted on it, and some empty cattle pens by the tracks. Otherwise there's nothing but tumbleweed blowing around in the alkali dust, and not a tree for fifty miles.

We're sitting under the shade of the water tank that afternoon, finishing up some grease cakes, when two fellows ride up. One claims they're cowboys on their way to one of the big ranches on the Canadian River, but I don't believe him. Their horses are all run out and they don't look like they know a cow's tit from a bull's balls, but every man's entitled to his story.

The talky one's dressed in a city suit and derby hat, ain't shaved in a week and keeps picking at scabby sores on his neck. The other one's about Cody's age, roly-poly, with straw-color hair and pimply skin, and wearing clothes way too small for him. They don't have no food, so Mountain fries up the rest of the grease cakes. It's clear the younger one's a half-wit because he sits off to one side, smiling at nothing, drooling over the food until his partner throws him a couple of grease cakes the way you would to a dog.

I'm glad they'll be heading in a different direction from us in the morning because something about them gives me the willies even though the talky one's breaking his neck to get in good with us. He says he's worked all kinds of jobs, the most recent over in the town of Vaughn, clerking in a feed store. I figure he probably stole some money or something and had to leave the store in a hurry. That's the kind of impression he makes.

Mountain beds down next to our gear so they won't be tempted to help themselves during the night, and Cody's on the other side of the fire from me. I must of slept maybe an hour when I hear a snuffling and grunting that wakes me. I lay there listening and don't know what it is. Cody and Mountain are dead to the world and the fire's nearly out.

I look into the dark until my eyes get accustomed, and I see what's making the noise. The half-wit's on his hands and knees, snorting and puffing with his pants down, and his ass white against the night sky. The older one's got his britches pulled down too, and he's locked into him like a dog from behind, pumping and pushing for all he's worth. That's the only time I ever seen two men doing it. I'd like to give them a hard kick and send them flying, but I don't do nothing. The half-wit ain't my responsibility and anyway he don't seem to mind what's happening to him. It takes all kinds I guess. I won't be seeing either of them again after morning, so I roll over and go back to sleep.

Just before sunup I hear Mountain cursing and yelling at us to turn out. There's no sign of the strangers, and two of our best horses is missing, while the winded ones they rode in on been left behind. Cody wants to ride after them, but I say no. We don't know how long they been gone or in what direction. Mountain swears he'll shoot them if we ever see them again, but I don't think we will, them or the horses.

It's a warm, dusty day. We're all in a bad humor because we been robbed and we still got our other lame horse, which slows us down. Long about noon some riders appear in the distance next to the railroad tracks. There's at least ten men, near as I can make out, and our first thought is to run. Between them and us is another water tank the railroad uses for the steam locomotives and that's what they seem to be heading for. Cody wants to cut north away from them, but I say no. If we seen them, they seen us by now, and we'd only look suspicious.

"I don't like it," Cody says.

"I don't like it neither," I say, "but we can't run now. We're damn near to Texas."

As we get closer I see these fellows got rifles, and I'm glad we didn't try to run for it. I don't see a badge anywhere. We meet up at the water tank and they are holding their guns across their saddle bows, watching us real careful. Then I see the half-wit sitting on one of our stolen horses, his hands tied behind him, grinning like they told him something funny.

I say, "Morning, gentlemen. Looks like you caught a horse thief. I'm much obliged."

A paunchy, hard-looking man with a beard rides a little ahead of the others and says to me, "Obliged for what?"

"That's my horse he's sitting on."

"And where'd you get them other two animals?" The bearded fellow points with his rifle at the sorry nags the thieves left us.

I say, "From the dummy and his partner when they stole ours."

He says, "Those horses belong to me."

"Fair enough," I say. "You give me mine and take yours back. But I sure would like to find the other one they stole too."

"What did it look like?"

"A gray gelding with a freckle face. Big horse with the eagle brand on him, same as all our stock."

The bearded man talks to the others, who keep looking at us. One of them calls out, "Where you from?"

"Mora County," I say, telling the truth.

"What you doing around here?"

"On our way to Texas."

"What's your name?" the bearded fellow says.

I try to brazen it through in case there's been a telegram about us from Santa Fe. "You boys taking a census, or what? Last time I heard that many questions was in school."

"There's a reason," the bearded fellow says.

"No doubt," I say. "You ain't riding around with all that hardware for nothing."

They talk among themselves some more before the bearded fellow says, "Mister, I'm inclined to believe you."

"No reason not to," I say.

He sends one of his men to check the brands on our other horses and the fellow says, "They're the same brand as the first two."

That seems to satisfy the fellow with the beard, and the tension goes out of the conversation. He puts his own rifle in a saddle scabbard and some of the others do likewise. There's twelve of them altogether, just like a jury, and I know what verdict they come to deliver at the water tank.

"Your gray gelding is dead," he says. "You'll find him about two miles back along the tracks."

"I'm sorry to hear that," I say.

"He broke a leg," he says, "so we shot him. This son of a bitch and his partner raped and killed a little boy in Santa Rosa day before yesterday."

They're anxious to get on with what they come to do. One of them shakes out a rope under the water tank. It ain't long enough to go over the high truss holds up the tank, so they tie it to another rope, then throw it over and make a noose.

Cody pokes me and says, "Lee, they're going to hang him!"

"Looks that way," I agree. The dummy's still grinning at every-body like this is a real joke, but he don't know it's on him.

Cody says, "Talk to them, Lee."

"And say what?"

"I don't know. Something. We can't let them do it."

"If we make a move to help him," I say, "they'll shoot us. And if that don't work, they'll hang us with him. So settle down."

One of them gets the noose over the half-wit's head and pulls it tight around his neck. The kid looks surprised, but he ain't scared. Too dumb to be, I guess. Then they tie the other end of the rope on one of the pilings.

Somebody lays a quirt across the horse's rump and the animal jumps, but he don't run. So another fires his rifle, and they start yelling, "Yaa, yaa, yaa!" and the horse takes off, leaving the poor dummy bouncing with his boots six inches off the ground. The drop don't break his neck, so he just hangs there, choking and twitching, his eyes popping out like now he wants to call off the game because it ain't fun anymore.

Mountain catches our horse while Cody fidgets, watching the half-wit squirming on the rope, his face all red and his tongue sticking out. The others sit in their saddles, calm as church. Then somebody lets out a yell because the rope is stretching under so much weight, and the half-wit's standing on his tiptoes, trying to get air.

The bearded fellow gets off his horse and shakes out another rope, slipping the noose around the dummy's ankles and pulling them off the ground again. Then he comes over to me and says, "I'll take my horses back now, if you don't mind."

"Help yourself," I tell him.

Cody can't take his eyes off the dummy, and he says, "Mister, can't you shoot him and put him out of his misery?"

"What for?" the bearded fellow says.

"Jesus," Cody says. "You did that much for our horse."

The fellow says, "If you saw the fine little boy they killed, you'd want this to last all day."

We ride on east when it's over, and after a couple of miles find our dead horse. About fifty feet from the carcass, sitting down leaning against a big rock, is the dummy's partner. We ride over to have a look, and what we see close up don't come as no surprise.

His britches are down around his feet and he's sitting in a pool of dried blood from where his parts been cut off. His crotch is alive with blow flies and his eyes are open but he ain't seeing anything. Somebody put his derby on his head and stuck his dick between his teeth for a comical touch.

We give Cody time to throw up before we move on. Mountain asks me if I ever seen anything like that before and I say no. He says he has, over in Monument Valley. "Some Utes caught a trader raped an Indian girl. He was alive when they done it."

"So was that one," I say. "The dummy got off easy."

"We don't even know they was guilty," Cody says.

"Twelve men don't go riding around armed to the teeth for the hell of it," I tell him. "They knew who they was after and what for."

"I don't know," Cody says, something still bothering him. "How could they rape a boy anyway? A boy don't have nothing to rape."

"They probably cornholed him," Mountain says.

"What's that?" Cody says.

"Jesus," Mountain says, "where'd you grow up, with a bunch of nuns? Didn't you ever learn about the birds and bees?"

"Sure, but I never heard they cornholed nobody."

That makes me think of what the older one was doing to the dummy during the night, but there ain't no point in bringing that up. We seen enough perversion for one day, so why talk about it?

Mountain's glad the posse didn't think we was mixed up with them and I'm glad they didn't know about our trouble in Santa Fe.

That puts Cody's mind back on our real problem again. "Lee, you sure we'll find work in Texas?"

"I don't know what we'll find in Texas, but if we don't like it we go on to the Indian Territory."

"What can we do there?"

"Work for a rich Indian."

"Come on, Lee, be serious."

"Anybody hires us saves hiring nine other hands."

"How do you figure that?" Cody never knows when I'm joshing.

"Mountain got the strength of three men, right?"

"Right," Mountain agrees.

"And I got the brains of three more, right?"

Cody smiles and says, "You sure do, Lee."

"That makes six. And you're three times as good as the next man so that makes nine."

"Hey, Lee, that's wonderful the way you think them things up. But you left something out."

"What's that?"

"We got Jake's spirit to guide us, too, so that makes ten."

We pass Tucumcari and the next night we cross into the state of Texas. Around Glenrio we hear they're hiring in a place called Dawn. Cody likes the name so we go there. It ain't more than a spit-puddle of a town in Deaf Smith County, but there's cattle moving through and everybody needs hands. We sell Cody's rifle for forty dollars and the bearskin for a hundred and probably could of got two. Nobody ever seen one that big and cowboys from all the outfits come to admire it. Mountain and Cody get work right away, but I wait. Nobody heard of us and there ain't no wanted posters or nothing. Communication between the Territory of New Mexico and Dawn, Texas, didn't amount to much.

I watch for several days until I see a chance to make some money without stealing anything or rustling steers out of the chutes into railroad cars. Lots of these little ranchers come in with two or three hundred head don't want to wait around for the auctions so they sell out for less to buyers with cash.

I sell off our horses, except the ones Cody and Mountain need to work, and with everything together, I have over a thousand dollars capital. The first day I buy forty steers and can't give them away. The second morning I sell them for more than I paid and have two hundred dollars profit in my britches before breakfast. If this is what business is like, we been damn fools working the wrong side of the law with the Brown brothers when we can make so much legal.

After two weeks, I tell Mountain and Cody to quit and scout the herds coming into Dawn. Every time they find a seller at a cheap price, I rent some holding pens for a couple of days and then dump the steers at a profit. Well, Dawn, Texas is good to us. In eight weeks I turn our capital into six thousand dollars and never do nothing against the law. Cody likes being in business so much, he forgets all about Jake.

We would of stayed there all summer, but I spot a railroad circular offering fifty dollars for information about Lee Oliver Garland. It's an old notice, but I know it's time we moved on.

We go to Dalhart, where there's another handbill advertising Cody and me wanted for murder, so we trot out of there fast to the Indian Territory. Even earning a honest dollar, you got to keep your eyes open. We got as far as Arkansas that year and even seen the Gulf of Mexico at Galveston, but we never stopped nowhere too long. It's like that when you're on the run.

My grandson Pete always wondered how we stayed ahead of the law in those days, and I tell him it was mainly good luck and bad telephone connections.

I Get Rich

Beginning New Year's of ninety-eight, we have ourselves a time over in Mexico, taking the train down to Chihuahua, where we check into the Victoria Grande Hotel and go on a cowboy buying spree. The saddle I order is all ticked out with carved flowers and silver-studded stirrups. I never owned anything prettier.

The whores in Chihuahua are passable pretty so Cody falls in love with one claims to be an American dancer down on her luck. Her name is Rose-of-Sharon Moriarty, but she don't speak much English. Didn't dance much either, as I recall. Damn if he don't move her out of the whorehouse and into the Victoria Grande with him. Try that on our side of the river and you'd get chucked out of any respectable hotel, but in Mexico nobody cared.

The Victoria Grande burned down years ago with heavy loss of life, but at the time I'm telling about it's one of the fanciest hotels a man could imagine. Ballrooms, barrooms, carved staircases and crystal chandeliers, turkey carpets, fringed settees and gilded mirrors. Chihuahua was rich since Spanish times, a big silver mining center where the money just poured out of the ground, so they spared no expense on that hotel. Yet it cost less to stay there than some fleabags I remember in Galveston or Amarillo.

Mountain never been in a fine hotel before, and it's a day or so before I can convince him to sleep in his bed. I'm turning down

the lamp in my own room when I hear a godawful holler and he
busts into my room backward, his knife out, panting like a cornered
bull. I expect to see ten bandits and I grab my gun, but there ain't
nobody there.

"What the hell, Mountain?"

He's trembling by the door in his BVDs, the knife still up. "I ain't
going back in there, Lee."

"What is it?"

"I don't know."

"What happened?"

"Don't know."

I push by him and step through the door into his room. There's
nothing there. "You have a bad dream?"

"I weren't asleep."

"Then what was it?"

"That bed's witched, Lee. It fires up when you get into it."
Here's a man who ain't afraid of nothing on this earth and I believe
he's lost his mind, but he ain't going to settle down until I get to
the bottom of it. I turn up the gas lamp and I go all over the bed
and show him there's nothing wrong, like you do with a scared kid.
But he ain't convinced. "It only does it in the dark," he says.

So I turn down the lamp and get into the bed myself while he
stands in the door, watching. Then I see what he's talking about.
The air's so dry there, the sheets give off a shower of blue sparks
from the friction electricity when you slide between them.

I try to explain, but he don't understand and nothing's going to
get him back in that bed. The rest of the time we're there he sleeps
on the floor with the lights on.

Mountain says if this Rose-of-Sharon's a dancer, he's a polar
bear, but he don't say it to Cody because already Cody's real
sensitive about the girl. He's skinnier than ever, and coughing
more than usual but he's happy, spending money like there ain't
no tomorrow, buying her ten-dollar dresses and five-dollar hats.
When Mountain reminds him his capital's not going to last if he
keeps it up, he says he ain't worried, he'll just make more.

Cody loved to play poker, but he was a terrible player. If he had
good cards, his face lit up like sunshine and he'd bet so heavy
everybody else would drop out. And if he held poor ones, he'd get
stubborn and stay in until he lost.

In one of the lounges at the Victoria Grande there was a poker game nearly every night. I'd sit in sometimes for a couple hours and win or lose a few dollars. The players was Mexican and American, some big ranchers who thought nothing of dropping a hundred dollars in one hand, and some cautious fellows like a gringo from Boston named Charlie Bruce who was division superintendent of the Chihuahua railroad.

Charlie's a lively little bachelor who loves a good time, but at the poker table he's all business. He has a mind can keep track of every card in the deck, which made him hard to beat. The regular players seldom pushed him on a hand because they knew he rarely bluffed. Poor Cody was easy meat for Charlie Bruce.

One day I'm having a beer in the hotel bar when Charlie comes in and sits down beside me. "You heard the news?" he says.

"Mexico's joined the Union," I say. It was our little joke.

"Wouldn't that spoil a good thing?" Charlie says. His railroad is owned by Americans and they make twice as much money off it as they do off the ones back home, so that's what he means. "It's bad news just came in on the telegraph. The Spanish sunk one of our battleships."

"I didn't know we was at war," I say.

"That's just it," he says. "We're not. Not yet anyway. The *Maine* was blown up in Havana harbor yesterday."

The truth is I don't know where Havana is. Ask me Dalhart or Tucumcari and I could tell you, but Havana was just a cigar to me then.

Charlie says, "Washington lodged a complaint with the Spanish government. If we don't get satisfaction, there'll be war."

"In Spain?" I say, dumber than a duck.

"In Cuba, most likely," Charlie says. He pronounced it "Cuber," that funny way folks from Boston talk. He tells me the Cubans been fighting for their independence against the Spanish and want our help.

"I guess we ought to give it then," I say.

"On the other hand," Charlie says, "why should Americans die for Cuba? That doesn't seem right."

"From what you say, some of us already have, whether they wanted to or not. Was they all asleep on that boat or what?"

"Apparently," he says. "Why would the Spaniards want to provoke us like that? It seems odd. Only the Cubans stand to benefit."

"Maybe it was them that did it," I say.

"A war's always good for business."

"Whose?"

"Yours and mine," he says. "The railroads will work overtime and my directors will be happy. Beef prices will skyrocket and you should make a killing."

"How do you figure that?" I say.

"The army will need meat, lots of it. What is a Texas steer worth today?"

"Around twenty dollars," I tell him.

"If there's a war, that price will shoot to a hundred. You should buy all the livestock you can get your hands on right now."

"I know something better," I say. "A Mexican steer sells for ten dollars. And if you can steal one, it's free."

"But how do you ship them in? It's against the law, isn't it, to bring them over the border?"

"It ain't easy," I say, "but there are ways."

"You rascal," he says, punching me in the arm. "I should have known. You're bound to get rich." He sips his beer and shakes his head. "I wish I could do it."

"Why don't you?"

"I don't know the first thing about the cattle business," he says, "except how to ship them."

"That's the first thing," I tell him. "It's a long drive to the border, and you got a railroad." Right then Cody joins us so we drop the subject to talk about the battleship *Maine*. Cody says the president ought to declare war on the Spanish.

"But they have the largest navy in the world," Charlie says.

"Ours is better," Cody says.

"How do you know?" I ask him.

"It's American, ain't it? So it's got to be." You could never argue logical with Cody or teach him something he didn't want to learn. He was stubborn as glue about some things, but as good-hearted and loyal a friend as a man could want. He was a terrible judge of character though, and kind of innocent too, always expecting the best in people. He wasn't stupid, but he sure could be dumb sometimes, like with his no-good brother Jake and now this Rose-of-Sharon Moriarty. If ever I seen a man pussy-whipped back and front, it was him with her.

She sashays into the bar and corners him while we're talking, dressed to the nines as usual and fragrant as a Persian flower patch. She hangs on Cody's arm, waiting for him to take her shopping. She's a looker all right, nobody can deny that, and now that he's got her all gussied up, she's looking less like a whore.

He ain't eager to take her to the shops again, but he don't have it in him to say no to that woman. He's down to his last hundred dollars, and I'm thinking we should leave town soon to keep him from going broke. But like I say, there's some things you can't argue with Cody, and one of them is her. He was already talking about taking her back to Texas.

In the bar, he says to Charlie Bruce, "How about a little poker tonight?" and I know the situation's critical.

"Bring plenty of money," Charlie says.

"I won't need it," Cody says, smiling at the girl, "because I'm going to take you like Grant took Richmond."

When they're gone, Charlie says, "I've been thinking about what you said, Lee. I get a special rate on railroad rolling stock, and shipping cattle to Juárez would only add half a dollar a head to the cost. We could go partners."

"The trick is getting them across the border," I say. "There's Texas Rangers and an army post at El Paso."

"You said there are ways."

"Sure, but I never tried them."

"Think about it," Charlie says. "I could put up five thousand dollars capital."

"So could I," I tell him, warming to the idea.

"That would buy a lot of cows," Charlie says. "At current prices we double our investment. And if the market goes the way I expect, we'll easily get rich."

"I'll think about it," I say.

"If you're worried about breaking the law, I understand. You would be the one taking the major risk at the border."

I laugh at that because he don't know my history, but I tell him, "The smart way is to start small, with fifty or a hundred head, and find the best route across. If it works, then we go for the big numbers. If it don't, all we're out is a few hundred dollars."

"Count me in," Charlie says. "Are you playing tonight, Lee?"

"I got no appetite for slaughter."

"Cody's a big boy."

"No, he ain't. He's a baby. But he's got to learn the hard lessons like everybody else."

"Don't expect me to teach him free," Charlie says.

"I didn't mean that. He'll lose his ass because you play better, and he ain't got much of an ass to lose."

I can't watch Cody's last stand, so I go with Mountain to see some cockfights. I don't know a fighting rooster from a hen, but Mountain has a knack for picking winners. "Always bet the one with the crazy eyes," he says, "even if he ain't as big as the other one."

"They all got crazy eyes," I say, "just like the owners. I'll bet what you bet." We watch about six fights, win heavy on two, and get splattered with chicken blood, before going on to the whore-house where Cody found his ladylove. I wrassle awhile with a good-natured Indian girl, and around three in the morning we head back to the Victoria Grande. Mountain's pretty drunk by that time and the liquor gives him a philosophic turn of mind, even if he don't make a lot of sense.

"Ambition," he says, "is a curse in a woman."

"What give you that idea?" I ask him.

He don't answer right away, because when he's drunk, he likes to think words over before he lets them out of the cage. "They all want to live in the hotel now, like Rose-of-Sharon. Ambition," he says again, "is a curse in a woman."

"It ain't the only one," I tell him. "Just being a woman is kind of a curse."

But the booze has disconnected him, and when he catches me by the arm I almost feel the bones give way. "Lee, don't say that. What about my dear mama, Lee?"

Before he crushes me to pulp, I say, "Your mama must of been the finest, noblest woman in the world to have a son like you." His grip relaxes and I feel my blood circulate again. It's the first I ever hear Mountain mention his mother. She must of been some kind of elephant to have him, but I don't want to die young so I shut up.

"She was, Lee. She was. And it's to my everlasting shame I turned out bad."

"You ain't bad," I say. "Wild maybe, but you ain't bad."

"It's kind of you to say that, Lee, but I know better," he says. "I went bad the day they buried her."

Curiosity gets the better of me so I ask him what he did.

"I hit the preacher, knocked him into my mama's grave."

"What did he say to make you do a thing like that."

"He said, 'Ambition is a curse in a woman.' "

"What was he talking about?"

"Mama took in boarders after Daddy died. One was teller at the bank who earned a salary, Lee, so she married him and had a baby and it died and she died. The preacher said she overreached herself and the Lord was getting even. He got the law on me."

"How old were you?" I ask him.

"About fourteen, but I had my growth."

God help the preacher, I'm thinking. "You was right in what you did. Anybody that stupid deserved to get knocked into a grave."

"I never been back," Mountain says.

"You got kin there?"

He shakes his head and says, "You and Cody are all I got."

"And Rose-of-Sharon Moriarty," I say, trying to bring a little levity into this conversation.

"She ain't really coming with us to Texas, is she?" he asks me in a panic.

"She'll only stick with Cody until his stake's gone, and that'll be tonight. Then we'll clear out and go back to work."

I get Mountain into the hotel okay, but I have to help him up the stairs. Before turning in I look in on the poker game and don't believe what I see. Cody's grinning like a toby jug with money heaped in front of him and the big loser is a rancher who wants to keep playing. But there's a time call on the next hand, so Charlie Bruce stands up and says, "Sorry, gentlemen, but we agreed to quit at this hour. There will always be another night." Cody's ahead eighteen hundred dollars and cocky as ever. It shows you can't ever be too sure of anything in this world, even losers.

I went into business with Charlie Bruce, each putting up a thousand dollars. There was a lot of hoof-and-mouth in Mexico then, and you had to be careful where you bought your stock. But I found two hundred prime, healthy steers at a small ranch not far out of Chihuahua for seven dollars a head. Mountain comes in with us for ten percent to help get the cattle into Texas. Cody ain't interested just yet because his eighteen hundred dollars gives him a new lease on Rose-of-Sharon's affections, so we leave him out.

We had irons made up with our old eagle brand to mark the steers, and Charlie printed American bills of sale that could have fooled the Supreme Court. We hurry up the branding because it takes a couple weeks to heal over, and there ain't nothing excites a cattle buyer's suspicions more than a fresh mark.

Before we ship the cows, I take the train up to Juárez with Mountain, buy horses and spend another week riding the Rio Grande until we find a place to take a herd across, about forty miles from El Paso with nothing on either side but sagebrush, rocks and rattlesnakes.

The river's wide there but only about two feet deep and not moving very fast. We ride back up on the American side and hang around El Paso a couple of days to get an idea of prices. Charlie's right about the market. Already it's moving fast. I see some real scrawny animals bought up by the army for thirty-three fifty a head.

Back in Chihuahua I hire some Mexican vaqueros to help out, against Mountain's better judgment, and we start out on our cattle drive. The leader is a fellow called Doroteo Arango. He's young like me, a baby-face villain with sleepy eyes and a loud bray of a laugh, who turns out to be one of the best horsemen I ever seen. Mountain says he's a born troublemaker and a danger, but he's a good organizer, and the other Mexicans do whatever he tells them.

After the train trip to Juárez we cover the forty miles to the river crossing easy. There ain't much for the cows to graze on, but we have plenty of water by sticking close to the Rio Grande, and we ain't trespassing other people's land. On the fourth day when I go to pay off the Mexicans at the river, this Arango kid collects all their money and none of them says a word because they're scared to death of him. I figure it's their problem, not mine, and Mountain and me go on alone.

About two miles from the town of El Paso, when I'm already counting the profit me and Charlie will make on this little herd, a fellow rides up in a wagon and introduces himself as a government sanitary inspector. He's wearing a white duster, and carries a pair of binoculars and a sawed-off shotgun. He's a mean-looking drink of water with hard, ugly eyes under pig-bristle eyebrows. "Where you boys from?" he says.

"New Mexico Territory," I say.

"Them steers for market?"

"That's the idea," I say.

"Then I guess you got a sanitary certificate," he says.

"Why would we need that?" I say.

"You can't sell them without it," he says.

I figure something's up with him but I decide to play it dumb a little longer. Until I lay eyes on this fellow I never heard of a sanitary certificate.

"It's the law," he says, looking us up and down, like he knows where the cows come from.

"If that's the case, I guess we ought to have one," I say. "Maybe you can tell us where we get it."

"From me," he says, which comes as no surprise.

"And how much does it cost?"

"Ten dollars a head," he says, which nearly knocks me out of the saddle.

"The government set the price?" I ask him.

"I do," he says, bold as brass.

"We can't afford that," I say.

"Then you better leave them animals right where they are."

"Who says?"

"I do," he says, tough as tacks.

Mountain says, "There's no feed or water. They'll die."

"Then take them back to Mexico where they come from," he says.

"So that's how it is," I say.

He pats the binoculars on the wagon seat. "We ain't asleep over here, you know. I been watching you. If you want to sell those critters in El Paso, you can't. The army won't buy them without my certificate. If I want, I can even get you arrested."

"We don't have that kind of money," I tell him.

"I see you don't," he says, smiling like he's got us where he wants us. "I'll be happy to issue a provisional certificate at no charge. It's a courtesy I provide reliable ranchers. You sell your cattle with that and get your regular certificate on payment of the sanitary fee."

"How do I know it's worth it?" I say.

"Simple. Try to move those animals without that paper and they'll be confiscated."

"And how do I know you're what you say you are?"

"Costs you nothing to find out. I'll write you a provisional certificate right now."

I talk it over with Mountain while this son of a bitch waits, and we decide to play along. "Okay," I tell him, "you got us by the short hair. I'll take one of your temporary certificates."

"Anybody can see you're a smart businessman," he says, "so I'm going to give you some free advice. If you think you can collect from the army without me, you got another think coming. The commissary department accepts delivery against provisional certificates but they only *pay* against a permanent certificate, signed by me. That clear?"

After he gives us this paper and turns his wagon around, me and Mountain drive the steers to the cattle pens on the edge of town with no more incidents, but we're both pretty downcast. Mountain says out loud what I'm thinking. "Lee, you reckon the army knows what that bushwhacker's doing? Couldn't we report him?"

"We ain't in no position to report anything and that fellow knows it. We'll still see a profit," I say, "but it ain't the business we thought it was. You know what this paper says is the official sanitary charge?"

"What?"

"Ten cents a head."

The next day, easy as pie, we sell a hundred and ninety steers to the United States Army for thirty-eight dollars each. I calculate me and Charlie are still making over twelve hundred dollars apiece, even with this crooked inspector. I ask around at the hotel by the stockyards and what I hear confirms everything me and Mountain suspect. This fellow, whose name is Brewer, is in with an army major called Dunn does the buying. Everybody knows it but nobody can do anything about it.

When I go to the fort it's plain to see this Brewer is just a lacky and the major's the real boss. "Well," the major says, real friendly, "you did some nice business there, didn't you?"

"Not as nice as I planned," I say, figuring these crooks are taking about nineteen hundred dollars of our money. But they're even greedier than I reckon, because Brewer says the price went up five dollars a head since we talked. It still leaves me and Charlie with a profit, but I tell the major it ain't worth the trouble.

"I'm authorized to purchase fourteen hundred head a month,"
the major says, "and I expect that quota to be increased." He's one
of these fellows always gets too close when he's talking to you, and
his breath's like a sewer.

Him and this Brewer can't make money on cows off the Texas
or New Mexico range because the owners got nothing to hide.
They'll get rich only with smugglers like us. So I say, "Fifteen
dollars a head is guaranteed to kill the goose because it ain't worth
the risk and the bother. But if we put it on a flat percentage of the
sale price, then we know where we are and so do you."

"What do you think, Mr. Brewer?" the major says. This officer
is not as slick as he likes to believe. His face is weak-looking with
tobacco-stained mustaches and watery eyes, and I figure he don't
want to lose us as customers.

"Depends on the percentage," Brewer says.

"I can deliver all you can take," I say, full of beans, "if it's
reasonable."

"You tell me," Brewer says.

"Ten percent," I say.

"Not less than thirty," Brewer says.

I get up to leave.

The major is pacing the floor, stroking his mustaches like he's
deep in thought. "Gentlemen," he says, raising his hand for me to
wait, "let's not lose our perspective. My duty is to insure the army
supply of quality beef at a price the government can afford. Mr.
Brewer has been of great assistance in facilitating our purchases in
spite of serious shortages, and we are in his debt."

I'm thinking if he ain't the biggest crook I ever run into, he's sure
the biggest liar. He goes on like that for a while, as if he don't have
no personal interest in how much I pay Brewer, just wants to be
fair. "How long can you guaranty deliveries?" he asks me.

"Long as you want."

"How would twenty-five percent sound to you?"

I shake my head. "Fifteen maybe, but even that's steep."

The major sighs, like he's running out of patience with a body
too dumb to understand while Brewer's sitting there like a statue,
with only his eyes moving. "What do you think, Mr. Brewer?" this
Major Dunn says. "Would twenty percent cover your costs, considering the volume?"

"It might," Brewer says.

"Is that within your possibilities, Mr. Uhh . . . ?"

"I'll have to talk it over with my partners."

"Fine, fine," the major says. "I'm sure they'll see it's a reasonable charge for Mr. Brewer's services. I'm happy to have been useful in settling this matter."

He's smiling and ready to shake hands when I say, "How do I know the percentage won't change when I get back with the cows?"

"Mr. Brewer's agreed," the major says, his face darkening over like I insulted somebody.

"He agreed before," I say, "then the price went up when I walked in here."

"You have my solemn word as an officer and a gentleman it won't happen again."

Charlie Bruce took the news like a sport and said we had to expect that kind of thing in business. The percentage was high, but so was our profit. He had somebody start sending him the daily El Paso prices on the railroad telegraph and by the time I put a thousand head together, steers were fetching close to sixty dollars.

Rose-of-Sharon Moriarty has run through most of Cody's poker winnings by then so he hires on too. I think he was beginning to see how ridiculous she made him look, but he would never admit it. The nearest he come is when I asked him what he'd do without her. He said, "The same as always, Lee. No woman's ever going to tie me down."

I take on this baby-face Arango fellow again and he brings along a dozen Mexicans who all look like they'd cut your liver out for a nickel. He's the youngest and the only innocent-looking one in the bunch, yet they're just as scared of him as ever. The wages we're paying are extra high as incentive for them not to steal from us. They work hard and Doroteo Arango collects all the money for them after we cross the cattle. Only now, one of the new ones wants his wages for himself.

"Paciencia," Arango says to him with a smile.

"Pay me," the fellow insists. Arango looks like he's going to hand the money over, but instead he flicks out a spring-blade knife and stabs him in the belly so fast I don't believe what I see. The man sinks to his knees, clutching the bloody hole in his gut while this chubby bandit just shrugs, wipes the blade on his pants and rides off. The others pick the fellow up and frog-march him behind a bluff to their horses, and that's the last we see of them.

On that first big shipment, with all our costs, including sixteen dollars a head to them grafters Brewer and the major, we clear twenty-five thousand dollars each. Charlie says there wasn't a business like this since the California gold rush.

Things Go Wrong

The next delivery of a thousand head goes like silk. Brewer is waiting for us when we cross the Rio Grande and the only other expense is two thousand dollars to some Texas rangers for looking the other way. Brewer and the major take their twenty percent and I'm on the train back to Chihuahua with Mountain and Cody, my profit safe in the vault of the El Paso National Bank.

We had other problems after that. Charlie's railroad put up the freight rates, and the Mexican ranches where we bought the steers got wind of what we was doing and raised their prices too. But we was still way out ahead because the beef market reached a hundred dollars in March just like Charlie said it would.

By then I had over a hundred thousand dollars in the bank, just short of my twentieth birthday. If anybody'd told me I'd make all that money in so little time I'd of said he was crazy. But we did, and we would of gone on doing it, except for some bad luck.

We was buying heavy at places like Rancho Nuevo and Aldama, and it was only a matter of time before the word got out we was selling contraband cattle to the American army at ten times the Mexican price.

Mexico in those days was full of bandits and cattle thieves who would kill you for the hell of it. In Chihuahua people told terrible stories about these raiders and what they did to anybody got in their way. Using the railroad to Juárez eliminated some of the risk, but it wasn't unheard of on Charlie's line for desperados to stop a train and take what they wanted, murdering anybody they didn't cotton to.

On the fifth shipment, I go to Juárez with Charlie and he says, "Lee, we're getting rich, but we both know this can't last."

"What you got in mind?"

"I see it this way," Charlie says. "War's going to break out any day and make us our first million."

I start laughing. "You sure got big ideas for a little man."

Real serious, he says, "We must increase our shipments."

"How? We're working twenty hours a day now and what we buy is going down in quality and up in price."

"Does this major have authority to buy more cattle each month?"

"Ask him. He's a terrible liar, but he ain't lied about that."

Charlie says, "There are big ranches that will sell us two or three thousand steers at a time now that we have the cash."

"We need a cattle company for that," I say. "Bookkeepers, clerks. But all we got is Mountain, Cody and Arango's Mexicans."

Charlie's thinking on a much bigger scale than me, but he's older, more experienced, and went to Harvard College. That evening in the hotel I introduce him to the major and Brewer.

You can see this Major Dunn is real impressed with Charlie, and gives quite a performance as the officer and gentleman. He says he has orders from Washington to buy up to twenty-five hundred head a month now, and the herds around West Texas are already depleted. He invites us to dinner but I turn him down. Charlie's seen me drink with some of the meanest, hardest men in Mexico, and he can't understand why I'd snub this army officer.

"He really wants to ingratiate himself with us, Lee."

"I don't mind doing business with a humbug like him, but socializing is something else. I got my standards."

We're sitting in the bar at the Palace Hotel, which was gaslit with colored-glass windows like a church, showing Bacchus and a lot of plump, naked women jumping on grapes. "Are you saying he's a hypocrite?"

"I'm saying he's a crook."

"He's only trying to make his fortune like us."

"Then he ought to get out of the army first."

Charlie's a dapper, fastidious fellow about most things, but he had a tolerance for grifters like the major I couldn't share. I guess it's the result of a college education where they teach you to be practical about people you don't like. "I respect your judgment, Lee, you know that, or we wouldn't be partners. But you're going to have to get used to dealing with worse than Major Dunn, and socializing with them too if you're going to get ahead in this world."

"I'll deal with them, you socialize with them," I say.

Charlie puts his hand out and shakes. "I'm resigning from the railroad as soon as we get back to Chihuahua," he announces.

"Suits me fine. What have you got in mind?"

"A bank," Charlie says."

"Count me out," I say. "Robbing banks ain't my style."

"I want to *form* a bank, Lee, not rob one."

"How do we do that?"

"New Mexico or Arizona is the place to set up because they will soon be coming into the Union. Lee, it's how we'll start the new century."

Charlie's never been on a cattle drive before and he comes along this time to see how it's done. We have eighteen hundred and seven steers worth a hundred dollars each, so we are pretty cocky. It's a warm March day and I don't want to push the herd so I tell Mountain we'll stop for the night before we reach the place we usually water the stock. When I inform Doroteo Arango of this, he just shrugs, but I see some of his Mexicans don't seem too eager. That's funny because driving cattle is hot, dirty work, and most hands are glad of a rest. I don't say nothing, just keep my eyes open and listen to Charlie tell me what we're going to do when a war's over that ain't even started yet.

"I've never been to New Mexico," Charlie says.

"Prettiest place on earth," I tell him.

He says, "The law requires capital of one hundred thousand dollars and at least three stockholders of sound moral character. Then we find a good central location like Albuquerque, hire some tellers and open the doors for business."

"Doing what?"

"Loaning other people's money out at interest. We'll go after government deposits and big local accounts like the mining companies and the Santa Fe Railroad. Do you have any connections there, Lee?"

"I know a few people," I tell him.

"That should be helpful," Charlie says. "There's no substitute for the personal touch in the banking business."

"Who'd be the third stockholder?" I ask, to get him off the subject of who I know at the Santa Fe Railroad.

"I was thinking of my sister," Charlie says. "She and I each with twenty-five percent, and you holding the other fifty. She's the only family I have."

"She married?"

"She's a student at Abbot Academy in Massachusetts. I'm her legal guardian since our father passed on."

After I call a halt for the night, I tell Cody and Mountain to keep one eye on the cattle, one on the Mexicans, and both hands on their guns because Arango's unhappy we ain't stopping at the usual place.

Cody says, "You know how trailhands are, Lee. They like to do things the same way every time."

"Maybe, but keep your eyes open tonight. Ride out aways every so often to make sure the herd don't wander off with them."

Charlie is happy as a kid playing cowboy and insists on taking his turn on watch with the rest of us, a Winchester balanced on his saddle horn. Nothing happens that night, and when the sun comes up like any other day, we push on along the river to the next watering place. I figure the whole thing was just my imagination, but again, about half way through the day, I see Arango and his gang bunched together and talking among themselves, something they don't usually do on the trail. By sundown, I decide on a change in plans, and I call Charlie, Cody and Mountain together to tell them.

"Arango's planning something," I say, "and I don't know what. But we got too much money tied up here to take a chance."

"I never did trust that son of a bitch," Mountain says.

"Until now him and his men worked okay, but first thing in the morning, I'll pay him off and we take the herd across alone."

Mountain says, "It's no good here, Lee. There's quicksand and we'll have to swim the critters."

"It's better than getting robbed," I say. "Tonight nobody sleeps. Each of you takes a point on the herd, while I circle between you to check. I'll spread the Mexicans out farther."

"Only four of them got guns," Cody says.

"That's four too many," I say. "So stay awake."

Arango knows I'm on to him as soon as I assign pickets way out from the herd that night, but there ain't much he can do about it without tipping his hand. Cody keeps awake, hacking and coughing, and Mountain sits his horse so silent you'd think he's asleep. But I know he's like a lizard waiting for flies, and his ears can hear the grass grow. I'm not worried about Charlie either because of the pleasure he takes in our great adventure, as he calls it.

For the first few hours everything's quiet. You'd hear a coyote once in a while, otherwise nothing but the cattle shuffling against each other as they settle down. I time my rides to pass each man every hour or so. About two hours before sunup I'm having a smoke with Mountain, thinking we'll soon get a move on when I hear a commotion about three hundred yards away where Charlie is. I tell Mountain I'm going to see what's going on. Cattle spook easy at night, so I don't call out, just mosey on over.

I'm nearly there, close enough to see his horse against the sky, when it hits me. I hear it first, like a rattlesnake sizzling past my ears. The next thing I know I'm jarred out of the saddle and flying through the air with my arms pinned to my sides.

I know what's happened before I hit the ground, but it don't help. A lariat's got me trussed like a Christmas turkey, and I land harder than a dog's dick, seeing stars with the wind knocked out of me. My Winchester goes clattering over the shale, and I'm struggling against the rope when this fellow jumps me. I feel the knife as it rips through my shirt and skitters over my ribs like a cheese grater. The son of a bitch is trying to stick me and if I wasn't wriggling so hard to get loose of the rope, he'd of done it.

We go rolling over and over until he's tangled in the rope too, but he's got the knife and my arms are free only below the elbow. I can't get a purchase to knee him in the balls, but when I feel his hand graze my face, I sink my teeth in and bite bone.

That makes him kick free for a second, long enough for me to get at my Colt. I can't draw but I can point it in the holster by raising one leg. It's a wonder I didn't blow my knee off in the dark, but the bullet only burned my britches before it passed through his chest and took half his shoulder with it.

I don't have time to congratulate myself because I hear gunfire from the other side of the herd where Cody is. I'm thinking they're killing us all and the steers will spook and I'm the dumbest fool ever lived because I knew they'd pull something like this if I didn't get rid of them sooner.

I ride in the direction of the shooting and find Cody on the ground. He ain't hurt, just mad as hell because his horse been shot. We both loose a couple rounds at the bastards we see riding off, but we don't hit nothing. I let out a holler at Mountain and he hollers back he's okay. The cows are making a racket by now, but once the shooting's over they settle down. I holler to Charlie and he don't answer so I ride to where he is.

He's unconscious and bleeding from two sucking stab wounds in his chest. Mountain tries to plug the holes and bind Charlie up with strips of blanket like a newborn baby. Charlie Bruce is a little man, and light, but he seems even littler when Mountain's working on him.

If them Mexicans had any brains, they might of got away with the herd. But they hang back because they don't have rifles and I'm glad. Mexicans don't lack grit. But they're all a little crazy, like the fighting roosters they raise. Even the smart ones like Arango don't have that extra grain of sense makes an American. That's why Mexico's the kind of confused, backward place it is.

There's no way to get Charlie to a doctor without killing him, but he's going to die anyway, so we might as well try. He's already a sickly gray color, and he don't come to when we tie him on his horse and take him across the river. I leave him under the shade of a rock and put some blankets under his head and a canteen of water within reach.

Cody and Mountain are alone on the other side with Arango and his Mexicans skulking along a rise like a pack of coyotes, just out of rifle range. I figure they'll try to rush us again when we're driving the stock across the river. I also reckon Charlie will be dead in a couple hours, and with him will go my best chance of ever becoming respectable because he had our future mapped out good, and faith in us and the country.

Before Cody starts the herd moving, me and Mountain peg a few shots at the Mexicans so they'll keep their distance. Besides the one I killed during the night, there's two more dead from Cody's rifle that we leave for the buzzards.

The crossing is a nightmare because of the bad place I picked and shorthanded like we are. Me and Mountain have to work the herd alone while Cody stays on the rise behind us to drive off the

Mexicans. As I expect, when we get half the animals across, Arango and his men rush us at a full gallop, yelling and shooting off their revolvers. They don't hit nothing, and Cody gets two more of them before they turn tail. But the cattle panic and so do some of the horses, and quite a few steers drown thrashing in three feet of water. We lose thirty more to the current and the quicksand, and have to leave at least fifty stragglers behind because Cody can't round them up alone. When we finally get all we can over, Arango shows himself on the Mexican side, his chubby killer's face all smiles. "Hey, Gringo!" he yells at me. "We ain't finished!"

Cody shoots with the Winchester but misses, and Arango just laughs. His horse rears and dances when Cody pegs a second shot at him, but the bullet only chips rock near the Mexican's head. The lucky son of a bitch is still laughing as he rides off after the others, and Cody's cursing a streak because he really wanted to kill that greaser.

I ride to where I left Charlie, wondering how we're going to bury him in that rocky soil without a spade.

I'm still thinking of myself mainly, knowing that without him, I don't have a notion where I'm going. No bank, no future, no dreams of being respectable. He almost had me convinced I could make something of myself and my conscience bothers me because I feel responsible for what happened to him. When I get to where I left him, he ain't there.

I shout for Mountain and scramble out of the saddle. It's all sandstone rocks with some sagebrush caught between the boulders and that's about it. Snake country, with maybe a blade of dry grass every hundred yards. There's a very faint sound and I stop. It's hardly more than a sigh, but I go running in the direction of it, and find Charlie propped up behind another rock in the shade, barely conscious.

I kneel down and make him take some water. "Jesus, you give me a turn," I say. I should of realized that the shady ledge I left him on turned to a frying pan as soon as the sun got high. It's hard to believe he dragged himself so far, but Charlie Bruce is tougher than I give him credit. I know if I don't do another damn thing in my life, I'm going to get him to a doctor, and somehow we do. I can't explain it to anybody, but by saving Charlie right then, I was also trying to save myself.

At Fort Bliss Brewer says he heard we had some trouble on the crossing but all I tell him is my Mexicans quit on me and we had to come over shorthanded. "You lost a lot of stock," he says, worried about his percentage. "You should be more careful who you hire."

We leave Charlie at a doctor's who takes one look at him and tells me he's going to die because his lung is punctured.

"You can help him," I say, giving him a hundred dollars.

"Not if he infects."

"See that he don't."

What to do with his share is another problem so I deposit his money in both our names, over fifty thousand dollars this time at two percent interest, which either one of us can draw out. Then I send a letter to his sister and tell her he's real sick, but don't say why. I tell her where his money is, and if anything happens, to contact me at the Victoria Grande Hotel in Chihuahua and I will see she gets it.

Mountain and Cody want to know what we're going to do now, and I need time to think. We can't have a lot of greedy Mexicans making war on us every time we move our cows. Cody says hire Americans and he's right. El Paso's full of good hands, but most of them can't shoot, and next time I want them Mexicans outgunned before we start.

But I won't hire no drunks or jailbirds, and I ain't about to take on anybody thinks they can do the job better than us, which narrows the choice considerable. Brewer recommends two friends I wouldn't touch with a pole, but Cody and Mountain turn up some good fellows they meet around the stockyards. After three days of looking, we're still shorthanded, and the major's getting impatient. The truth is, without Charlie, I'm over my head.

Time's running out and we'll be lucky to get back with another herd in less than thirty days, so I elect to hire the local boys even if they ain't sure shots. While Mountain buys some horses I go looking for guns and ammunition.

That's when I come on the funniest law I ever heard of. In this gun store where they have everything from big repeating rifles to little ladies' derringers, I tell the man I want twelve Winchester thirty-thirtys and four Colt revolvers. He says he'll be happy to sell the rifles but it's against Texas law to sell me the Colts.

I say, "Then what do you display them here for?"

"I can lease them to you," he says, "for ninety-nine years."

I tell him that's the dumbest law anybody ever invented and I been everywhere.

"This ain't everywhere, mister," he says, his nose out of joint. "This is the sovereign state of Texas where we're proud of what we got, including our laws."

I don't want to get into a pissing contest with him over Texas, so I say, "Okay, I'll lease them."

"A pleasure to do business with you," he says, changing his tune, and gets out a pile of forms I have to sign.

"I want holsters too," I tell him.

"I'll sell them to you," he says, "but it's against the law to wear a handgun in Texas, just so you know. Where you planning to take these Colts, if I may ask?"

"Mexico," I tell him.

"Work over there?"

"That's right."

"Just don't buckle them on till you cross the river."

The bill comes to over a thousand dollars and the clerk blinks when I pay cash. He offers to deliver everything to the hotel and gives me a receipt with my pistol leases.

When I get back Cody wants to celebrate, I ain't in much of a mood because of Charlie. But Cody's such a kid, he keeps insisting. There's a circus in El Paso and he's dying to go.

I give in because I don't relish sitting around the Palace Hotel alone, so we change into clean shirts, eat a good dinner and take a horsecar to the fairgrounds. The place is lit with colored electric lights and they got a steam calliope makes more noise than a railroad locomotive. We're early for the performance so we pay our admission to the freak show and go in.

You don't hear much about freaks anymore, so maybe they don't show up good on television or there ain't enough of them born these days. Some say modern folks don't want to look at freaks, but I doubt that. Freaks are a tonic when you're down, believe me. There ain't nothing like a good freak to cheer a man up.

This is a fine show and it gets my mind off my troubles. There's a sword swallower, a twenty-foot-long snake, a fat lady and another one with a beard Cody says has to be a man dressed up like a woman. The giant, who is eight feet tall, makes Mountain look puny, and we laugh because he has a midget lady in his lap they say is his wife. I don't believe it. His cock has to be big as her leg, so the question in everybody's mind is how can they get together? Otherwise all you're looking at is a ordinary giant with a midget instead of a sex puzzle only Einstein can figure out.

There's Siamese twin girls who play the trombone and the violin, a crocodile man who's also a fire eater, but he don't impress me much. I seen beggars in Mexico with skin worse than his. The seal boy puts on a good show. He has hands growing out of his shoulders like flippers, and feet where his legs should of been, and he waddles around making funny faces, balancing a ball on his nose and barking like a seal until they throw him a rubber fish he catches in his mouth. He couldn't of been more than twelve, but with freaks it's hard to tell.

The geek is just a ordinary pinhead painted up with most of his hair shaved off who I believe never set foot in Borneo. It's his feeding time and when he bites the head off a live chicken, a woman screams and faints. But Cody says she's part of the show because he seen her taking tickets when we come in.

There's a two-headed baby in a jar and a mummy supposed to be four thousand years old. But the caterpillar man's the best. He's alive, like the seal boy, and about three foot long with a worm's body dressed in a green silky striped sweater. He's got no hands or feet or hips or anything and he squirms around just like a real caterpillar. His head is an ordinary man's only he's bald. His mustaches curl around the corners of his mouth and he's got a friendly sort of smile. They give him a cigar to puff, and he winks to make us laugh. Later on in Cuba I seen similar sights. Only they wasn't born that way, the war done it.

We come out of the freak show feeling pretty good and stand around eating Cracker Jacks. I'm telling Cody and Mountain about the Texas law says you can't wear a gun when Cody says, "What about them fellows, Lee?"

Two men with their backs to us are standing a few feet away, both sporting big Colts on their hips. Between them I see the man from the gun store, and he's pointing at us. I ain't much of a runner and there isn't time anyway. When the two dudes with the guns turn around, their badges flash in the electric light. You can't hear what they say because the music is starting for the show, but one of them motions to me. I play dumb and he comes walking over, touches a finger to the brim of his Stetson real polite and says, "Mr. Garland?"

"That's right." I get a sinking feeling about this, but there's nothing I can do. Maybe it's just about the leases I signed.

"Lee Oliver Garland?"

I nod. Behind him his partner's standing loose, with his hand resting on his gun butt.

"One of you boys named Cody Williams?" he says, looking from Cody to Mountain and back again.

"That's me," Cody says.

"You're both under arrest," he says.

"What for?" Mountain wants to know.

"What's your name?" the lawman says.

"Moore."

"You're under arrest too."

The El Paso lockup ain't the Palace Hotel. It's bug heaven and they put us in with the derelicts they collect on the streets every night. I give a guard twenty dollars to get us a separate cell, and Mountain, as usual, is philosophical about it. "Inside or out," he says, "you get what you pay for."

The whole fix is my fault for leasing them Colts. I could of bought all the rifles in Texas and nobody give a damn. But as soon as I went after handguns, they had my name, big as life on the leases. The man in the gun store took them to the police department after he delivered the guns, and the police discover I'm wanted in New Mexico for murder along with Cody. At the hotel, they find Cody on the register too, and can't believe their good luck. They telegraph to learn who Mountain Moore is, and find he's wanted by the state of Colorado for killing a prison guard in a breakout. It was a hotel bellhop told the cops we went to the circus.

It's a big day for Texas law enforcement, one of the constables tells me. He's a friendly fellow named Ransom, and in the five years he's been a policeman, nobody ever caught three murderers at once. I ask what happens now, and this Ransom says we just sit around El Paso until the authorities from Colorado and New Mexico come to get us.

"What about bail?" I ask him.

"Murder ain't a bailable offense. And besides, you boys would just skip over into Mexico if we let you out."

This Ransom is decent enough, and likes money as much as the next man, so I say, "How'd you like to make a thousand dollars?"

"Who wouldn't?" he says, knowing what I'm talking about. "But I can't do it. I'd lose my job."

"Suppose there's no way they can blame you?"

"That's different," he says, all ears.

The jail security is pretty informal. Mostly what they got is drunks and Mexican illegals and small-time thieves, so no great pains are taken to keep a close eye on everybody. I'm thinking we can bust out through a window that night, if this Ransom can smuggle me in a hacksaw, but he has a better idea.

He says they have to take us to the courthouse for a hearing in a day or two, and he can arrange for the door of the Black Maria to be left unlocked. If we jump out at the right place, we stand a good chance. I give him money for horses to leave in front of the barber shop six blocks from the jail, and I give him half the thousand, the rest to come when everything's set. He never seen so much money in his life, and he looks at it a full minute before it goes into his pocket.

"There'll be a constable in the wagon with you," he says. "He'll be armed and he'll try to stop you."

"We take his gun," I say.

"That'll be hard, because you'll have irons on."

"Then we'll need a hacksaw blade to cut through them."

"You won't have time. I'll try to be the one puts the shackles on you," Ransom says, "and if I don't lock them, you can slip them off easy. But I want your solemn promise you won't hurt that officer."

"We ain't murderers. We never hurt a fly."

"You don't act like villains," he says, "or I wouldn't help out. But you must of done something to be in so much trouble."

"It's all a terrible misunderstanding," I tell him, "and I'd still like a hacksaw, just in case."

The night before the hearing none of us sleeps much. We agree Mountain will take on the policeman inside the wagon while me and Cody distract his attention. If Ransom leaves the door unlocked and we get to the horses, we're only a ten minute ride from Mexico and freedom. The plan is chancy, and everything depends on a lawman we don't even know, but it's the only shot we got. I don't care if we can't come back. At least Luna won't hang us.

Ransom passes by our cell when he comes on duty the next morning, and says everything's set. The hearing's at ten and the horses are waiting. I give him the other five hundred dollars and he's real grateful because he's married and a policeman's salary in El Paso is forty dollars a month. "Don't hurt nobody now," he says under his breath, "and don't ever let on who helped you." He slips me a hacksaw blade I put in my boot.

We're too keyed up to eat anything so we just smoke and stand around, waiting for ten o'clock to come. About eight thirty there's a commotion out front, and Ransom comes with another police-man to take us out of the cell. I hang back and catch his eye, but he just shrugs his shoulders like he don't know any more than I do. I ask the other officer where they're taking us and he says the captain wants to see us.

I'm thinking they can't be on to our escape plan because Ransom wouldn't risk telling anybody, so it must be something else. The jail's in a brand-new brick building takes up half a city block, and we walk the length of it before we get to the captain's office. He's a tough-looking, big-bellied fellow in a blue uniform, with walrus mustaches and a red-veined face. Sitting across from him is an elderly, hard-eyed, overweight lawman in a dark suit. And next to this fellow is the answer to the mystery, the sheriff of Santa Fe County, looking very smart with a new derby hat. Luna watches me like a cat looks at dinner, and I know our plan to get away just went up in smoke.

He don't say a word, just thanks the captain for his courtesy and his services to the citizens of New Mexico. The old lawman with Luna is Rufus Barry, who was a famous scout in the Indian Wars and sheriff of Prescott, Arizona, before going to work at the Colorado State Prison.

After the formalities, the captain tells Ransom and the other policeman to put the irons on us so we can travel. The other one starts on Mountain while Ransom tells me to hold out my arms. When he slips them on, he gives me a look, and I know we still got a chance because he don't lock them. He does the same with Cody, but I ain't sure Cody realizes it. The other policeman can't get the irons on Mountain, even with Barry's help, because his wrists are too big. So Luna, who could always be relied on for a keen imagina-tion, says maybe leg irons will fit his wrists, and they do.

Luna and this Barry take us to the railroad station in the police wagon, but there ain't no chance of getting away, even with the door wide open. Mountain can't free his hands, and I ain't about to pit my running skill against Luna's shooting.

We got a half hour wait for the train to Albuquerque, and Luna says, "It's been a long hard chase boys, but it's over. So I'm only going to say this once. You behave until Santa Fe, and we will show you every consideration. Try to get away and we'll shoot you dead. There's a dining car on the train and the county allows me to spend a dollar on each of you for a meal. Mr. Barry is allowed a dollar and a half because the state of Colorado is richer." That's Luna's idea of a joke, but nobody laughs. "Sit back," he says finally, "and enjoy the ride."

Even with the irons loose, I ain't optimistic. When Luna gives me a cigar and lights it, I feel as helpless as the caterpillar man.

V I

Cody Comes Through

The worst part of that train trip was trying to pretend the irons was on tight when they wasn't. Cody and me fidgeted all the way for fear they'd fall off and Luna'd discover we was free. We don't even dare take a piss and that's a hardship. We ride along all morning and I seldom seen a man in better humor than Luna. He offers to play cards but we say no. He asks us how we been living since we left Santa Fe, and I say, "Getting by in Mexico."

"That's not what I heard," he says. "What I heard is you killed three people over there, and the Mexican *federales* are after you."

"That's crazy," I say. "Why would we do that?"

"You tell me," Luna says.

"They was bandits," Cody says, "trying to kill us. And anyway we got five, not three."

Luna nods like he knows the whole story and don't believe a word of it. "Remember a long time ago, Lee, I gave you some advice? You were still a kid."

"I remember," I tell him.

"If you'd taken it, you wouldn't be chained like an animal now. You might have made something of yourself, had money in the bank."

"I did take it," I say.

"Rustling? Killing people? You call that taking my advice?"

"I ain't rustled cattle in years," I say, "and I never killed Arnold Brown. Neither did Cody."

"A jury will decide that," Luna says. "The county's got your gun and Sam Brown is a witness."

"Some witness," I say. "I was on the other side of town."

As usual, Luna's mind is closed to anything except what he already believes, and there's no way I'm going to convince him we're innocent. "What about you?" he says to Cody. "Were you on the other side of town too?"

"I was waiting for my brother," Cody says, "but I didn't know he killed anybody."

"Why did you run off then?"

"Alfred S. Sorenson was after me."

"He's another witness," Luna says, "and he saw you helping Jake into the saddle."

"So what?" Cody says. "Who wouldn't help his own brother?"

"That makes you an accessory," Luna says, "which is the same as if you pulled the trigger."

"You can't hang him for that," I say.

"We don't hang people in the Territory anymore," Luna says with one of his unfunny smiles.

"I'm glad to hear that," I say.

"We put them in our new electric chair," he says.

"What's that?" Cody asks him.

"It's a big wooden throne over at the penitentiary that cooks a man to a crisp, fries his brains like scrambled eggs."

"Does he feel anything?" Cody wants to know.

"Hard to say," Luna tells him, enjoying the conversation. "Nobody ever came back to tell us. But the way they jump around when the switch is thrown, makes me think they feel it plenty. It's not very dignified. They shave all your hair off so you get the shock better. Then they stick wires on your arms and legs, and strap you in tight and put the electric helmet on your head."

"Ain't hanging simpler?" Cody says, pale as paint.

"Hanging's old-fashioned," Luna tells him, warming to his subject, "and people have to keep up with modern advances. No state or territory worth its salt can afford to be without an electric chair today. What would a visitor from out of town say if he finds out you don't have one? You'd be a laughingstock."

"I think I'd rather be hanged," Cody says.

"That's not the idea," Luna tells him. "The idea is punishment, and if you ask me the electric chair punishes better. Why, the stink of all that burnt flesh is almost enough to put a man under. I've seen prison guards pass out from too much of it."

"Does it take long?" Cody asks him, getting paler and paler.

"Most times they don't have the required voltage, so they have to keep frying a man and frying him until he's well done. It takes a strong stomach to watch them writhing and twisting like live meat on a hot griddle."

I'm fed up with Luna's talk about the electric chair so I ask him what's going on with Spain because we ain't seen a newspaper in a couple of days.

"It looks like war," he says. "The Congress declared Cuba independent yesterday."

"I didn't know they had a congress," I say.

"They don't. Our Congress declared it for them," he says.

"How can we do that?"

"We can do whatever we want," he says.

"Suppose the Spaniards don't like it. They own Cuba don't they?" says Cody.

"We're not giving them a choice," Luna says.

Rufus Barry, who hardly opened his mouth on the whole trip, says, "They'll fight."

"Against who, us?" Cody says, amazed.

I'm thinking what rotten luck I been having, losing Charlie and the business when we should be making a million. Looking out the train window as southern New Mexico passes at sixty miles an hour, I know I don't have the courage to jump even if I get the chance.

"We'll beat them in a hurry," Cody says. "Won't we, Lee?"

"Don't be so sure," Luna says.

We all look at him as if he's crazy.

"We have maybe eighteen thousand soldiers in the entire army and one third are negroes," he says. "The Spanish have a hundred and fifty thousand soldiers in Cuba alone."

Mountain says, "But one of us black or white is worth ten of them anytime."

Luna says, "One of you might be, Moore, but I don't know about Garland and Williams here. They look kind of peaked and done in to me. Anyway, you boys don't have to worry because you won't be meeting any more Spaniards after me."

"Since when was you Spanish?" I say.

"Since fifteen and forty," he says, "when the first Luna came over from Spain."

"I thought you was Mexican," Mountain says.

"That's because you're ignorant," Luna says. "I'm pure Spanish extraction, but I was born American the same as you."

"Otherwise you'd be fighting us, right Sheriff?" Cody says.

"I am fighting you, son, in case you didn't notice."

I say, "You got your satisfaction, thanks to them Texans."

He don't like to have that rubbed in and his face clouds over for a minute. "I'd have caught you sooner or later," he says, "and you're lucky I didn't because you wouldn't be riding home in this fine train. You'd be lying out on some trail with a bullet in your gizzard."

"You'd of shot us?" Cody says.

"I shoot any lawbreaker who resists arrest or tries to get away," he says.

"But we didn't," Cody says. "We come when the man said, and we wasn't armed. The law in Texas don't allow it."

"Garland would have resisted," Luna says. "He'd never give up without a fight."

"Why say a thing like that?" I ask him. I'm flattered, but a reputation like that is no help to a man in my position.

"It's true, isn't it?"

"I ain't no gunfighter," I say.

"That so? I heard you were. Ben Butler tells me you're right handy with a six-shooter."

"Just fooling around," I say.

"That why you bought those revolvers in El Paso?"

"I leased them. They don't legally belong to me."

"However you got them, they were yours. To do what? Pot crows in a hen yard?"

"We was going to work in Mexico," I say.

"What work? Stealing cows? Murdering cattle agents?"

Luna'd made up his mind I was beyond redemption, lost to a life of crime and violence only him and the forces of law and order could stop. I didn't find out until years later the reason he was so down on me was he liked me. He said it galled him to see somebody with my spunk and brains turn bad, and if he'd been my old man he'd of straightened me out with a horsewhip before I ever got out of short pants. He never stopped telling me how to run my life, and I don't know which was more of a burden, having him for an enemy or having him for a friend.

I'm still looking out the train window while he raves on, working himself into a temper, saying he can read me like a book, telling Cody all I been thinking of since El Paso is making a break for it. "Try it," he says to me, drumming his fingers on the butt of his gun. "Just try it."

The train is slowing down as it comes into Socorro. Old Rufus Barry looks at his watch and asks the conductor how long we're going to be there. He says we'll be stopped half an hour to hook on some ore cars. Mountain's hungry, and the conductor tells him we can eat in the dining car in five minutes.

"I can't eat with these on," he says, holding up the irons.

"If you're hungry enough you'll find a way," Barry says.

"We all go together," Luna says, "single file, with me and Mr. Barry in the rear."

"I ain't hungry," I say.

"Then you can sit and watch," Luna says.

The other passengers stare at our procession into the dining car, and the waiters stand back to let us pass. Luna's in his glory, tipping his derby to the ladies, neat as a banker in his boiled collar and studs. We sit down in the far end of the car, Mountain and Barry at one table for two, and Cody and me with Luna at a table for four.

When the train comes to a stop I look out at the edge of town where the cattle pens are. Tethered to a hitching rail ten feet from the tracks are half a dozen horses, the riders all having a bite nearby.

When I look up, Luna's watching me like he's been reading my mind. Meanwhile Cody's looking at the horses, and Mountain sees them too. This may be our only chance, but I don't think about it long. Even if Cody and me can throw off the irons, we can't do much for Mountain without us all getting shot. There's no way to turn a table over on Barry and Luna because the furniture in a dining car's screwed down.

Mountain's thinking about them horses, too, so I shake my head to let him know the idea won't work, and Luna nods agreement across the table. What I don't reckon on is Cody. I'm so used to telling him what to do, it never crosses my mind he'll act on his own without my advice.

He picks up a menu and says, "Why, they have chicken soup, Lee. You got to have some of that as long as the county's paying."

"I said I ain't hungry," I tell him.

"Order it anyway," he says, "and I'll eat yours."

Everybody orders the chicken soup and when it comes it's so boiling hot you have to hold it in the spoon and blow for a minute before it's safe to sip. I got the aisle chair next to Cody, which is a mistake of Luna's and I sit there doing nothing while they're all blowing on their soup. When it happens, it catches me by surprise as much as Luna.

Cody yells, "Mountain!" the same second he throws his whole plate of soup into Luna's face. When Barry looks up, Mountain does the same, and for a minute both lawmen are drowning in boiling hot chicken soup. Luna is fast, I got to give him that. Blinded as he is, he goes for his gun, and has it out before I dive across the table at him, knocking the Colt to the floor. For an old fellow, Barry was slick, and managed to draw too, but Mountain brought his irons down so hard, he broke the poor man's wrist. The panic and confusion among the passengers having lunch helps us, and the waiters can't get out of our way fast enough. Cody picks up Luna's Colt and I grab Barry's. Mountain bulls his way out of the car, past the people waiting to eat, saying, "Excuse us, excuse us, please, folks," and we're right behind.

We ran for them horses with Mountain in the lead. But we have to help him mount because of the irons, and that takes a minute. We could hear the people in the dining car screaming for help then, but nobody come after us. Cody damn near blinded poor Luna permanent, and we was sorry about that. He had a bandage on one eye for weeks and was lucky he didn't lose the sight in it. But as Luna admitted years later, it was the humiliation that hurt most.

We flew out of that town like the devil was after us and didn't stop until the horses near give out. Cody's coughing up a storm and we have no place to go, so we head west toward the mountains and spend the night in the shadow of South Baldy. That ain't far from Magdalena, which was a small mining camp that called itself a town. I cut Mountain's irons off with the hacksaw and we thank our stars for Officer Ransom, Cody's spunk and chicken soup. If they'd left it to me to make the break, I wouldn't of done it, and I tell Cody that. The odds was just too high against us.

"When I looked out and seen them horses," Mountain says, "I

had a hunch they was put there by the Almighty for a purpose."

"I wasn't going to die in no electricity chair," Cody says, "so what did I have to lose?" I told Luna years later if he hadn't scared the kid half to death with that story, he probably would of got us to Santa Fe without a hitch.

We move deeper into the mountains just in case people are coming after us, and when I figure we're safe, we sit down to ponder our future. Cody and Mountain are in favor of striking south for Mexico. We can make it in four or five days, and nobody will follow. But I remind them that the Mexican police may be after us too.

"You can always pay them to leave you alone," Cody says, "and it's for certain we can't hang around here."

I have time to do some thinking on the ride, and I'm not so sure anymore. I keep remembering Charlie and our plans for the bank, and I don't want to spend the rest of my life running away from crimes I didn't commit. But then I'd see Luna's face, and know after what happened on the train, he'll show us no mercy. We won't be able to piss in the Territory without being gunned down. I'm almost ready to tell Cody and Mountain we'll get a move on for Mexico, when I think of Ben Butler, a lawyer now and the one man I trust who might help us.

Mountain agrees to listen to me, but Cody's impatient because he's still thinking about the electric chair. I want to write Ben Butler and explain how we're wanted for things we didn't do.

"Why should he believe you?" Cody says. "Nobody else does."

"Because I got witnesses," I say. "Mrs. Sanchez, the cook, the girl, and you all know I wasn't nowhere near Arnold Brown that night."

"Maybe not, but I was," Cody says, "and you heard Luna. It's the same as if I pulled the trigger."

"Luna ain't a lawyer," I tell him, "and Ben Butler is."

"So what can he do?"

"That's what I want to find out. If we tell him the God's honest truth, he'll help us and we won't have to keep running."

"Why take a chance?" Mountain says.

"Because we're innocent. Somebody's got to understand that."

"I don't know," Mountain says. "I don't have a prayer in Colorado if they take me back, with or without Ben Butler. My witnesses are all dead."

"Let's see what he says," I tell them.

"We can send the letter from Mexico," Cody says.

"Suppose he wants to see us?"

"He can take the train down to Chihuahua like anybody else."

"Ben Butler can't go traipsing off for no reason."

"You give him the reason, Lee," Mountain says. "Hire him."

"First we got to tell him the facts," I say, "and see if he wants the job."

"How do we get the letter to him?" Cody says. "And how does he contact us if we ain't in the Victoria Grande?"

"I'll think of something," I tell him, not having the faintest notion how to solve that problem.

"You can wait at Eagle Nest," Mountain says. "Ben Butler knows where the cabin is, but nobody else does. Tell him to meet you there if he wants to be our lawyer."

"Where you going to be?" I ask him.

"Mexico," he says.

"Remember what you told me once? Every time you leave me alone, I get into a jam."

"I was only kidding, Lee. If I turn myself in, they'll hang me, you know that."

"Nobody's talking about turning himself in," I say. "But we stick together, that agreed? If we get a letter to Ben Butler and go up to the cabin to wait for his answer, we all do it. And if we go back to Mexico, we all do that too."

Cody says, "You ain't got paper or an envelope."

"I'll find some, damn it. And you'll see. Ben Butler will come through."

I ride into Magdalena alone the next day, and a poorer place I never seen. What they mined there was silver ore mostly, but prices are down because the government makes paper money now, and most of the miners are laid off. You get used to seeing hungry faces over in Mexico, but this was the first time I ever seen them in my own country. It's funny how you tend to think poor people all have dark skin. But here are some of the poorest, and most of them are blond-haired like me. The kids are especially pitiful, with big eyes and stomachs, and little pinched faces.

The one store in town don't have hardly anything but whiskey, dried beans and some barrels of flour. There's a hotel, an Elks Club, three bars, a post office and a church, all boarded up and falling apart. Even the railroad office is closed and peeling paint because they only ship a little ore once a month. The storekeeper says if I'm looking for work, this is the wrong place to come.

I write Ben Butler that I'm innocent and say even though Cody tried to help his brother get on his horse, he was ignorant of any murder done by Jake. I say Mountain will take his chances with us too, if Ben Butler will represent him, because he never killed nobody in Colorado or any place else. I tell him we only cut loose of Luna because we was desperate and couldn't prove much from inside a jail, and we are truly sorry if we caused him or Mr. Barry any inconvenience.

That letter took me a whole day, and I read it out loud to Cody and Mountain. I said we had earned money by the sweat of our brow to pay Ben Butler if he'd defend us, but we'd understand if he didn't want to. I don't mention the Mexicans we killed or our cattle smuggling, just stick to the point. I say we want to be law-abiding but Luna won't give us the chance. And I ask him to send his answer one way or the other to the cabin, where we'll be in a week. We aren't going to give ourselves up but we'd sure appreciate his legal advice. I ask him please not to inform Luna and the Colorado authorities, but then I cross that out. If I trust the man enough to tell him where we're going to be, I have to trust him not to send the law after us.

The old storekeeper in Magdalena says he'll mail the letter from Socorro for me because he has to go down there anyway for supplies. I say I'll give him five dollars for doing that, and five dollars more when he comes back with the post office receipt.

"Be a lot cheaper to take it down yourself." He's eyeing me funny.

"Maybe, maybe not," I say, staring right back.

"The law after you?"

"What do you care?"

"I don't," he says. "I hope you write lots of letters because I ain't made ten dollars for doing nothing since I can remember."

"I'll be gone soon as you bring my receipt," I say.

"The law never comes here," he says. "Safest place in the Territory for a man to lie low. The few families that are left can't hang on much longer."

"Why do you stay?"

"Ain't it obvious?" he says. "The night life, the pretty girls. Why, a man could travel the wide world over and not find so much action."

He catches me looking at him and laughs. "It used to be like that, mister, believe it or not. When the government bought silver this town was a lively place. Easy come, easy go. Now it's gone and most of the people are gone with it. I'm too old to start again, so I hang around because I got nothing better to do."

The next day he goes off with his mule team to Socorro, carrying my letter, and I wonder if the crazy old coot will mail it or call the sheriff. He don't come back for two days and we're about to cut out for Mexico before the law shows up, when Mountain spies him coming along the road. I ride down and he hands me the receipt. I try to give him the other five dollars and he won't take it.

"We agreed," I tell him. "It's your money."

"No, sir, I got my money's worth listening," he says, and now I know he's crazy.

"Listening to who?"

"You're the talk of the town, son. They seen you leap from a moving train, shoot up a whole posse of Colorado marshalls and bend your handcuffs off and throw them away. I allow you don't look that strong, but appearances can be deceiving. Ten women fainted and three men, they say, and the law's looking for you from Mexico to Canada. They ain't had so much to talk about since Billy the Kid come through here."

"Hold on a minute, old man. That's a made-up story."

"What do you mean?" he says, and I see he's been pulling on a jug next to him and he's pretty drunk.

"I mean it ain't true."

"You saying I'm a liar?"

"Not you. Them. None of that ever happened."

"You're Lee Garland, ain't you?"

"I am."

"Well, you're famous. If you was to ride into that town today, they'd all crawl under their wives' mattresses. Only the laundry knows how scared they was. You get it?"

"I get it, but it didn't happen that way."

"What do you care?" the old man says. "They're so scared nobody's going to come looking for you."

"Did you let them know I was here?"

He squints at me and rubs his jaw, pondering. "I could tell you a tall tale you'd believe or the truth, which ain't believable."

"It better be the truth."

He offers me a pull from the jug, but I wave it away. Already I got my eye on the road behind him.

"They was going on about you, everybody telling his version about what he seen, and one fellow says to me that you must of headed up my way, and I say yes you did because you're an old friend of mine. I got the whole crowd looking at me then and I tell them you rode into town here and we got drunk together while you told me all about the shoot-up. What do you think they said to that?"

"You tell me."

"Didn't believe a word of it, don't you see? If I'd said I hadn't laid eyes on you, they might come looking, but when I tell them a story they can't match, they go back to their drinking because I got a reputation as a terrible liar."

"I'm leaving anyway, so it don't matter," I say.

"You going to Cuba too?" the old man says.

"Why would I do a thing like that?"

"There's a war. Everybody's going to fight the Spanish."

That puts to thinking again of Charlie Bruce and if he's alive or dead. A man can't plan anything in this world and expect it to work out. Charlie was an educated man and now he's probably six feet under and I can't even find out. Killed by some greaser hoping to make a hundred dollars off our cows. I hope it was the son of a bitch I shot, but that don't bring Charlie back.

I didn't think of the war then as a war. I thought of it the way Charlie Bruce did, as an opportunity that wouldn't come again. Then I stopped feeling sorry for myself and the money I was losing and I was glad that Mexican didn't get me too.

I Get Religion

We strike out for the cabin the next day after buying two mules and six horses from the storekeeper, and leaving the ones we stole for him to return to their rightful owners. He was tickled out of his mind to do it, he said, because he'd drink free for a week on the story.

Cody's jumpy as ever on the trail and we can't shut him up about Luna. He works himself into a coughing spell every little while and we have to hold up until it stops. He never heard of such an inhuman way to put a man down in his life, and I have to agree. He says he'd rather be shot or hanged a hundred times than electrified to death. He hopes we're making the right choice trusting Ben Butler. I say I hope so too and he tells me he'd still feel a lot safer taking his chances with the Mexicans.

Finally Mountain gets fed up and says, "I don't want to hear no more about it, Cody. We decided, and that's the end of it. If it don't work, we go to Mexico."

"If it don't work," Cody says, "we go to the hereafter."

"You don't hear Lee grousing," Mountain says.

"Course not," Cody says, "it was his idea."

"You don't hear me grousing neither," Mountain says.

"That's because you ain't scared of nothing," Cody says, "and I am. I'm scared of the electricity chair."

"Well, stop carrying on about it. You're the kind dies in bed when you're a hundred. Lee and me's the ones to fret. Luna wants him so bad he can taste it, and the state of Colorado's been after me since I was a pup."

"You really think so?" Cody says.

"Think what?" Mountain says.

"That I'll die in bed when I'm a hundred?"

"You got that kind of worrisome character."

"What about Lee?"

"He won't live to be thirty. Me neither."

"You're already past thirty," Cody says.

"No, I ain't."

"How old are you?"

"Twenty-eight or twenty-nine," Mountain says.

"Ain't you sure?"

"Not exactly."

"Everybody knows how old he is, so why don't you?"

"I was born in a leap year," Mountain says.

"What's that got to do with it?"

"When they skip a year like it ain't there," Mountain says, "you don't know where you are."

"Well the year's got to be there for you to skip," Cody says, "so it still makes you the same age."

"No, it don't," Mountain says.

"Figure it out," Cody says. "When was you born?"

"I don't know," Mountain says.

"Then how do you know it was a leap year?"

"I know what year it was," Mountain says, getting testy. "I just don't know what day."

"Do you know the month?" Cody asks him.

"I reckon April," Mountain says.

"Why, that's now," Cody says. "Today could be your birthday."

"It's possible," Mountain says.

"You hear that, Lee?"

"I hear it."

"What day's today?" Cody asks me.

"Tuesday or Wednesday," I say. "Maybe Thursday."

"Somebody ought to keep track," Cody says.

"It's a good job for you," Mountain tells him. "Keep your mind off other things."

"I got to be sure which day it is before I can start keeping track."

"Start with Tuesday," I tell him.

"But if you ain't sure, we could be off by two days, Lee."

"I'm sure," I say.

"Tuesday the what?" Cody says.

"Can't you figure anything by yourself?" I tell him, running out of patience. Jesus, that boy could be a trial when he put his mind to it.

"Some outfit I'm hooked up with," he says in a huff. "One don't know how old he is and the other don't know the day of the week."

"Tuesday the first of April," I say, to shut him up.

"Are you sure?" Cody says.

"I wouldn't say it if I didn't know," I tell him.

"Back there you had some doubts," he says.

"I did the calculations," I say. For a while he's quiet as we ride along. It's the first chance I get to study my thoughts without them jawing away about one dumb thing or another. Mountain ain't a talker unless Cody starts it, but once they get going, they can chase a subject harder than a jackrabbit. I don't care how old Mountain is or what day it is. All I care about is what Ben Butler's going to say when he gets our letter. I'm thinking maybe this whole ride is an exercise in futility and when we get where we're going, the woods around that cabin will be staked out with lawmen for miles. I tell myself Ben Butler's an honest man and he wouldn't betray a soul, but then I ask what would he be betraying if he just passed my letter to Luna? Nothing, that's what.

He could have had us in jail a dozen times if he'd wanted, and I'm right in trusting him. But suppose the letter don't even get to him but Luna finds out. What would Luna do? He'd keep his mouth shut, find out where the cabin was and be there with blood in his eye.

I put these thoughts out of my mind because they ain't pleasant. If we get caught this time it's my fault again and no one else to blame. I look over at Mountain and he smiles back and I feel as bad as a body can because him and Cody are betting their lives on my judgment. I don't say a word because I have to work it all out first, but I know we won't go to Mexico or the cabin. We'll wait some place else where Ben Butler can reach us with his answer.

The trail we are following is an old one from Indian times, and it winds along the western edge of the Rio Grande valley. That day, as far as the eye can see is a carpet of pink desert flowers brought out by a spring shower. Verbena I believe they're called. It's a sight you only see once a year, but it's such a beauty you love the country for it just because it can happen.

Some folks never understand that kind of thing when you tell them. Like the government people who been swarming all over this place since the Second War. They don't know a cornflower from a cuspidor or give a damn about about this state or its future. All they want to do is set off bombs and rockets. What do they care if there's still trout in the brook or deer on the mountain? Some idiot who's never been west of Delaware writes a report and the government's ready to blow half of New Mexico off the map. Well, not while I'm alive.

We pass some Apache north of Ladrones Peak, poor as mice, walking along barefoot. They keep the river in sight to the east, where people live, but they don't go near the ranches or towns because some folks will shoot an Apache same as a coyote. They don't work, not even rug making or anything, and it's a wonder they stayed alive after the last Indian War. But they did, wandering around the desert, living off snakes and lizards like the lost tribe of Israel.

It's hard to believe these was the people gave the white man the hardest run for his money. They never surrendered, never signed no treaty and never stayed put on no reservation. The poor devils kept their pride, but they sure didn't keep much else.

There's three men in raggedy vests, two women and six or seven naked kids, as skinny and starved looking as the dogs they have with them. I'd heard they was fantastic riders, but I guess it was a long time since they could afford a horse.

The men don't look at us, just stare off across the valley like we ain't even there, but the women hold out their hands to beg and the kids stare like kids the world over.

One of the women is kind of pretty and I see Cody looking her over. "Ever do it with a Indian squaw?" he says under his breath to me.

I shake my head and Mountain says, "You wouldn't like it."

"I'll bet I would."

"Try it then," Mountain says, grinning, "and she'll salt your pecker good."

"What do you mean?"

"Find out."

"Come on, Mountain! What do you mean?"

Mountain winks at me before he tells Cody, "When they don't want it, they pack sand up their snatch. Cuts a man up bad."

Cody says, "I don't believe you," but he puts a hand to his crotch as if it hurts him already, and looks at that poor Indian girl like she's got the hoof and mouth.

I tell Cody to give them the food we're carrying.

"That's real generous, Lee. But then what do we eat?"

"We'll reach Belen by sundown, and we'll buy what we need."

"Ain't that risky?"

"Not the way I plan it."

He starts unslinging the packs and emptying them until I tell him to give them the haversacks too.

Cody squints up at Mountain and says, "Did he get too much sun today or what?"

"Do it," Mountain says, so Cody tosses about two weeks of rations, corn dodgers, sacks of flour and bacon to the women. There must of been ten dollars worth of food there.

Cody says, real sarcastic, "Give them the mules too?"

The truth is, I was thinking of it, but I tell him no, because the first white man they meet will take the mules back and hang the men for stealing. The women go through the packs, chattering while the men stand around looking bored. Nobody thanks us, but you got no right to expect gratitude from an Indian.

That day my mind is far away, and I ain't concentrating on the trail, when I notice Cody's disappeared. This ain't unusual because the way is twisty, and one of us sometimes goes on ahead just to break the monotony. But before we catch up we hear two shots, and Cody lets out a bloodcurdling yell. I don't know if it's them Indians or what, but Mountain and me ride like hell with our guns out, expecting the worst. First we don't see nothing but Cody's horse. Then we spot him lying farther down the trail. Mountain gets to him at a gallop, dropping light as a cat by his side, saying, "What happened, Cody? Where'd they get you?" My mind's going a million miles a minute as I search the hills for some movement. Goddamn that storekeeper if he got the law after us! But everything's quiet except for Cody's whimpering.

I get to him and kneel down. "It's okay, you'll be okay," I tell him.

"Lee?"

His eyes is closed tight and he can't see me. I say, "I'm here, Cody, I'm here." I'm thinking, first Charlie, now him and it's all my fault.

"Mountain, you there too?"

"I'm with you, pardner" Mountain says, cradling Cody's head in his arms.

Cody's breathing hard but I don't see no blood. "Settle down and let's see where they shot you."

"I'm all washed up," Cody says. "I'm a sinner and the day of reckoning has come. There won't be no electricity chair for me and I won't live to be a hundred. I won't even live to see twenty eight or twenty-nine. What day is this, Mountain?"

"Cody!"

Mountain's so soft-hearted he don't cotton to it yet, and he says, "The first of April, Cody."

"You sure it's the first?" he says, squinting up at us.

"Show me where you're hit," I say. "Right now!"

He rolls away from Mountain and springs to his feet light as a monkey. "April fool! April fool!"

I never seen Mountain so mad. Lucky Cody scrambled over them rocks out of that big man's reach. When he got to the top of one, Mountain yelled, "I'll get you, you little son of a bitch!" and pegged three shots in his direction. We made him walk the next mile before we give him back his horse, but that night we allowed it was a pretty good joke on us after all, and Cody was real pleased.

Before we turn in, Mountain says, "You got something on your mind, Lee. When it ripens, let me know."

"We ain't going to the cabin."

"I figured that."

"Why didn't you say so?"

"I was waiting for you to."

"Everybody's always expecting me to take the lead. Who do you think I am, General Custer?"

"I hope not," Mountain says.

"Well, I ain't any kind of general," I tell him. "I can't solve everybody's problems all the time."

"I didn't mean to push you," he says, "but I got no head for planning anything past breakfast, and you know Cody's a fire-cracker can go off in any direction. Without you, we'd of been jailed or broke or dead long ago."

I feel belly-high to a toad when he talks that way. But it's a good lesson. If you want people to believe in you, they got to have a reason. You let them down once, they may forgive it. But they don't have the same confidence afterward.

All my life I wanted people to trust in me and not find out I was a fake, so I had to pretend I was stronger and smarter and kinder and more honest than the next man, or they'd catch on. People ain't stupid, so you got to show a face they can depend on, your wife, your friends, your kids, everybody. And you got to show it when it counts. I valued Mountain's good opinion, so I said, "I'll tell you when I got it thought out. Just give me time."

But Cody can't hold his curiosity back, and he keeps insisting, "What are we going to do?" until I tell him, "What Luna and the whole world least expects. Take the train to Santa Fe."

"Somebody will recognize us," Cody protests.

"When we get to Belen, we're going to sell the animals, put our guns in valises, get cleaned up and buy new clothes." Belen ain't much, just a rail junction where the spur from Fort Sumner joins the main line between El Paso and Albuquerque.

"Then what?" Cody says, looking at me like I lost my mind.

"We go find Ben Butler."

"Where's Luna all this time? Teaching Bible class?"

"Looking for a big bearded fellow named Moore who wears a buckskin shirt and a Bowie knife, instead of a respectable gentleman with no beard, a watch chain and a derby hat."

"That's wonderful, Lee! Disguises!" Cody says, as thrilled as a kid at Halloween.

"Not disguises," I tell him, "just a slight change in appearance."

"What about me?" Cody says, eager to hear.

"Luna's looking for tough Cody Williams in blue jeans and a ten-gallon hat," I tell him, "with long hair, scraggly whiskers and a revolver on his hip. He ain't going to recognize a clean-cut young fellow in a new suit on his way to join the army and fight the Spaniards."

"It'll work," Mountain says, "but he'll spot you, Lee."

"Wait and see," I tell them.

We divide up and act like we don't know each other when we arrive at the local barbershop. We all get shaves and short haircuts but Mountain keeps some side whiskers and his mustache. Cody gets himself a striped, mustard-color suit at the dry-goods store and Mountain finds a blue serge that fits him a little tight. But with a moleskin vest and a dollar Ingersoll watch, he could be the Prince of Wales.

I find everything I need, including a passable black suit with just the right amount of shine in the seat and some highbutton shoes.

Cody hires a cheap room for us at a widow lady's where she also serves meals, and we agree to meet there for supper after we scrub the trail dirt off.

It takes me a while to get clean, and the bath water looks like cold coffee when I climb out, but it helps my appearance considerable. I lay out the suit and new drawers and a frayed shirt that come with the suit, and a celluloid collar and cuffs. I darken my eyebrows and touch up the sideburns with shoe polish, and like what I see. The collar is hard to get right, but after a few misses with the stud, I have it looking passable. The spectacles do the trick. Not even my own mother would know me with them on if I had a mother, I can't see too good and have to look over the tops, but they was worth every penny of the three dollars they cost because of what they do for my personality.

When I get to the widow lady's, I see Cody and Mountain standing by the front gate talking, and they are something to behold. Mountain looks like president of a railroad in his getup, and Cody could of passed for any woman's favorite son. I walk up to them and say in a high voice, "Excuse me, gentlemen, but is this the Widow Hann's house?"

It's dark already and I got a hat on, but in the light coming from the windows we can see each other pretty clear. Cody glances up and says, "Yes, sir, Parson, it sure is," before he turns back to Mountain.

"God bless you, son," I tell him. "Now this is a stickup so give me your watch and your money."

They both stare at me stunned before Mountain catches on and says, "That's real good, Lee. How'd you do it?"

Cody busts a gut laughing when he sees how he's been taken in, and I'm glad I introduced myself on the street instead of at the widow's supper table, because the language he's using would get us all chucked out. We're a fine team all right. If Max Luna'd walked by he'd of said, "Evening, gents," and never known the truth.

I got the names we used off my suit label. Cody was Mr. Hart,

Mountain was Mr. Shaffner and I baptize myself the Reverend Marx. The Widow Hahn was pleased to make my acquaintance and says she'll have the food for us in half a shake. She's about thirty, with a nice full bosom and creamy skin, not bad looking in spite of her age. You could tell she was a Christian believer because of the way her big brown eyes lit up at the sight of me. There was eight or nine regulars at her table and she said it would be a treat for them if I would say the blessing.

I nearly give up before I start, but as luck would have it there's a big Bible on the parlor table and it seemed a natural thing for me to read at it a little before we sit down. Being a preacher, you have to make the blessing longer than an ordinary person's, so I cribbed as much as I could out of that book and tried to keep it straight until I got to the table.

I thought Cody might go off in a coughing fit when I began, but he bit his lip and bowed his head.

"Let us come before the Lord in thanksgiving," I say, "and forgive them our trespasses. Remember thine afflictions and it shall come to pass as the leopard lieth down with the spots and the serpent with the sore vexed multitude. What thou taketh up, thou shalt put down, and covet not thy neighbor, nor thy neighbor's neighbor. Wherefore suffer the vittles to come unto me, as the lambs and the catamites to the righteous. Whoa until him who beholds, and blessed be they that say unto you. For greater love hath no man. And whoever shall kill the fatted calf shall rejoice in the name of the Lord. Amen."

"Amen," the widow says, pressing my knee under the table. "It does a body good in these times to hear a man who really knows his Bible. And so young too. I do hope you'll be with us a while, Reverend?"

"I'd like to stay on, ma'am," I say, "but the Lord's work takes me elsewhere."

"Where's that?" says one fellow with yellow-looking, suspicious eyes who seen me cribbing from the Bible.

"Like the Good Book says," I tell him, "go forth and ye shall prosper, even unto the Pharisees. Ezekiel Twenty-one, verse three."

"My, oh, my," the widow sighs in admiration, passing the gravy and pressing my leg again.

"I know what the Good Book says," Yellow Eyes tells me, "but I ain't sure you do."

"Are you a minister of the gospel?" I ask him, trying not to be insulted.

"Mr. Newton is a railway agent," the widow says.

"Is that so?" I marvel, thinking it's just my luck to have a policeman at the table, especially one who keeps looking at me and Mountain as if he's wondering where he's seen us before. The best defense is attack, so I say, "I'm surprised you got time to eat while them train desperados are on the loose terrorizing the Territory."

"What desperados are those?" this Newton says in a huff.

"Why the ones shot up Socorro the other day." Mountain looks up from his plate when I say that, and Cody has a coughing fit.

"That's the Santa Fe sheriff's job," Yellow Eyes says. "It's got nothing to do with me. He's the one let them get away."

"I can understand you not wanting to meet up with them," I say. "They're bad and would just as soon shoot you as look at you."

"I ain't afraid of them."

"Well, I am. One makes Deacon Shaffner here look like a midget"—I point to Mountain—"and all three are from your regular hardened criminal class."

"How do you know so much about them?" Newton says, suspicious.

"We was on the train they shot up."

"Oh, mercy!" the widow gasps. "I hear women fainted."

"Men too," I say. "There was a lot of blood. It was no place for the fainthearted." I look at Yellow Eyes when I say that, and he focuses on his plate.

"You get a good look at them?" he asks me.

"Close as I am to you."

"Oh, Reverend," the widow says, looking into my eyes like I'm the answer to her prayers, "how you must have feared for your life."

Before I can answer, another heckler at the end of the table says, "What denomination you say you was?"

Mountain answers, "He's hardshell, ain't you, Reverend?"

"Hard as they come," I say, smiling at them and peering over the eyeglasses, trying to see my food.

"Where'd you go to seminary?" says this suspicious fellow.

Cody comes to my rescue, before I can invent a new lie. He says, bright as sunshine, "The Reverend Marx got the call, didn't you, Reverend?"

"That's about it," I say, not knowing what call.

Cody says, inspired, "He's coming to Cuba with us to fight the Spanish. What about you fellows? You signed up for the army yet?"

Cody's a genius sometimes, because that question kills the conversation and puts paid to any more inquisitiveness about my preacher's credentials. All them slackers dig into their food and never say another word, not even Yellow Eyes. They're too fat and comfortable with their salaries, so they ain't going to get caught up in no patriotic notions about Cuba. The widow gives me extra helpings of everything. "But Reverend, a man of the cloth don't have to go to war."

"My place is with the soldiers, ma'am, God bless them, brave boys such as this who are going off to die." I pat Cody's shoulder and look down the table at these other suckers, but nobody raises his eyes.

There's tomato soup and corn bread and roast lamb with gravy and potato cakes and buttered carrots with peas and berry tarts and squash pie with cream to finish off. All in all, it's a pleasurable meal, and I especially enjoy the widow's charms after the others turn in. She's greatly in need of a little spiritual comfort, poor darling, and I'm happy to give it to her. She tells me she never done it with a preacher before and she hopes I'll turn up around these parts more often.

VIII

I Volunteer

Nobody ever told me why the Atchison, Topeka and Santa Fe Railroad don't pass through Santa Fe, but I guess the men that built it had a reason. The line runs up from Albuquerque through Raton to Trinidad, Colorado. You get off in Lamy and take a shunt over to Santa Fe, where the tracks end. It's a tiresome ride, but easier than a horse, and you get there in a day.

In Albuquerque, there is a godawful commotion. Kids are waving flags and women crying, and groups of men congratulating each other on joining the army. I pity the Spaniards. They don't stand a chance against all this enthusiasm. There's a few old geezers from the Civil War wearing their uniform jackets and some real pretty girls with red, white and blue sashes over their frocks, pinning little flags on the lapels of the boys signing up. One old biddy asks me to say a prayer for her nephew and I promise to add it later to my regular prayers for the rest of the army.

We go into the Harvey House there at the station for lunch, to look at the girls waiting on table. Waitresses was a new thing then and they was all pretty. We eat fresh oysters cost two bits a dozen and have a couple of beers before catching our connection. Somebody says President McKinley's asking for a hundred and twenty-five thousand volunteers, and I reckon he's got a good start in Albuquerque. On the station platform is a bandstand set up like Fourth of July where the local bigwigs are making powerful

89

speeches. Mostly they tell how we'll kick the Spaniards out of Cuba in a week, but some admit it may take a little longer.

The coaches are full of boys going to Santa Fe to join up. Most of them drunk or getting there, and it pains me to see some fine bourbon whiskey offered I can't touch in this preacher getup. Cody thinks it's a panic. He slaps me on the knee and says, "You don't mind if we wet our whistle, do you, Reverend?" But that Cody always was a cutup.

By the time we reach Lamy and everybody disembarks for the shunt to Santa Fe, I'm about the only sober soul in the car, but going to war is fine with me if it keeps everybody's mind off us. In Lamy a dozen soldiers from the Tenth Cavalry get on the train in their heavy blue uniforms. They sit down in a group behind me and mind their own business. A week or two back, nobody'd drink with them because they was niggers, but today some fellows come over and give them a bottle of whiskey and three cheers for the army, which everybody joins in. But the soldiers are careful and sort of afraid to get into the spirit of things.

I have knowed all kinds and all colors as far away as France. I seen niggers fight in Cuba made me proud to be in the same army, and I seen Indian boys die of the fever out at Montauk without ever a complaint. I have worked with smart men and dummies, and served with brave men and cowards. A man's skin may advertise what his daddy was, but it don't tell you what *he* is. I got no time for people think otherwise, so I guess I'm prejudice.

A colored man's got as much right to be what he wants as me, but nobody admits that. If he's lazy like me, they call him no-account and say what do you expect? If he's smart and hardworking and educated, they say he don't know his place.

In this soldier group the chief honcho is a sergeant almost as big as Mountain, a good-looking black man quiet as a ghost who don't touch the whiskey. His sleeve's got more stripes than a barber pole and there's a medal on his chest. It's clear he's like a father to these boys, patient and good with them, laughing at their jokes, but keeping them in hand.

A drunk with a purple birthmark on his chin asks the sergeant where he got his medal and he says in the Apache War in eighty-five. Somebody else asks him how many Indians he killed and he says he didn't get the medal for killing Indians. "Then what'd you get it for?" the drunk says.

"Swimming," he says.

"You being smart with me?" the drunk says.

"No, sir, that's what they give it for."

"How'd that happen?" the drunk insists, still suspicious he's being ragged, but too dumb to shut up.

"We was chasing Geronimo across the Rio Grande," the sergeant says. "One of my boys got shot off his horse in the water. Another trooper went to help, but neither could swim, so I got them out."

"And they give you a medal for that? I don't believe you."

"That don't make it a lie," the sergeant says, and looks out the window.

"Hey, I'm talking to you!" the drunk says.

"I hear you," the sergeant says, looking at him like he ain't there. I'm thinking if this dumb lush ain't careful he'll wind up with more than a birthmark on his jaw. Nigger soldiers are as proud as anybody, and maybe a little extra touchy because they get small thanks for what they do.

But the drunk backs off when he sees he'll come out on the short end. "It can't be much of a medal then," he grumbles. Looking around for support, he sees me and staggers over. "What we'd like to know is how you darkies'll stand up to the Spaniards?" he says, leaning on me and waving his bottle at the soldiers.

The sergeant looks away and the soldiers don't say nothing because they're shy and embarrassed.

The drunk says to me, "We'll show them the kind of stuff we're made of, right, Reverend?"

"What kind of stuff is that?" I say, pretending I don't know what he's talking about. He thinks he's got me on his side because we're the same color, and I resent that. Nobody speaks for me.

"Why, how we'll lick them Spanish in the first fight and not need no nigger help to do it."

"I don't know about that," I say. "I'll be glad of all the help I can get, especially from real soldiers like these."

"Look again, Reverend," this dumb bunny says. "They ain't real soldiers, they're just dressed-up coons."

The atmosphere around our end of the car is sober all of a sudden. These soldiers are young and strapping, with just enough liquor to make them do something foolish. The sergeant pushes one trooper back down, but even he may not be able to stop a fight breaking out now. So I stand up and put my arm on the drunk's shoulder, whispering in his ear, "Brother, I think you're going too far."

But he says, "That's because you don't know niggers." He intends to say more but I step hard on his toes, and when he looks down I drive my fist into his middle so hard I feel his backbone. He drops the bottle and I have to turn him away fast before he pukes on all of us and goes down the aisle gasping and choking. Later I see him pointing me out to his friends.

"It ain't over yet," I say to the sergeant.

"Yes, sir, it is," he says. "We're pulling into Santa Fe."

In the confusion after the train stops I make sure to get off the other end of the car. Cody and Mountain and the whole detachment of soldiers come behind me. Cody says, "Where to now, Lee?"

There's a band at the Santa Fe station starting up so it's hard to talk over the noise. There's also some lodge delegations milling around with patriotic banners. The drunk and his friends join one group and when Mountain catches up I say, "Let's go find Ben Butler."

The sergeant says, "Reverend, can we give you an escort?"

I tell him it's a kind offer but no, I'll be fine. "The Lord works in mysterious ways."

He's poker-faced but his eyes are smiling. "When he works through you, he sure does."

Cody and Mountain hear this, and after the sergeant snaps a salute and goes off with his men, Cody says, "What was that all about?"

"Just a little struggle with the devil," I say, "but God come out on top."

"You like this preacher business, don't you?" Cody says.

"I ain't had so much fun since Mexico," I tell him, "and I never got so much respect."

There's a delegation from the Loyal Woodsmen of the World standing on the platform, and who's with them but Alfred S. Sorenson, head and shoulders above the crowd. As if that ain't enough, I look harder and see Luna leaning against a iron post, his thumbs hooked in his vest, smoking a cigar and looking in our direction. But he's got a bandage over one eye and don't see too good. I take off at a fast walk with the other two behind. A few blocks from the station we find a horse cab to the old courthouse, where I'm hoping to see Ben Butler, but he ain't there. A fellow tells me if I want him, he's at the Exchange Hotel.

We cut across the plaza to where the hotel is, and there must be five thousand people trampling around and brass bands and more banners and flags than we saw in Albuquerque. We never would of got inside the hotel if Mountain hadn't pushed through the crowd first.

When I see Ben Butler finally, I get a shock. He's in army uniform, sitting at a table with two other officers and a pile of papers. Behind them on the wall is a big banner says, "Troop F, First U.S. Volunteer Cavalry". The Territorial flag and the American flag are on each side of the table and there's a line of men waiting to see Butler and the others. The cigar smoke's thick as ground fog and the floor's slippery with tobacco juice from this mob of yelling, shoving, blaspheming cowboys trying to get into the line. The stink is powerful too, a mix of sweat, farts and tobacco, which will always be the smell of the army to me.

I ask a fellow what's going on, and he thinks I'm crazy until he sees my collar. "Sorry, Reverend," he says, "but you must be in the wrong place. We're here to join up with Captain Butler." He points to the sign behind the table before he's shoved ahead by somebody else. A sergeant's writing down each man's particulars while two corporals try to keep order in the line, but they're not having much success. We see that each time Butler and the other officers interview a man, if they like him, they send him to a shorter line with the sheet of paper the sergeant gives him. I ask another fellow what that line's for and he says it's the surgeon's examination in the next room. If you get by that you're sworn into the volunteer cavalry to fight the Spanish.

Cody's right behind me, listening to this, and he says, "Lee, let's go before somebody recognizes us. Ben Butler can't help us now."

"Hold your horses," I tell him. "We come this far and we ain't going to leave until we talk to the man."

Mountain says, "How we going to do that? We can't get closer unless we get in the line."

We're already in the line because of the way the corporals have it organized, and I see it's moving a little quicker. There's a lot of boys turned down because they're too old or too young or too fat or got a limp. Butler shakes each man's hand and thanks him anyway before he turns to the next one. In twenty minutes, Mountain's at the head of the line, but he steps aside to let me go first. The sergeant asks my name and he don't bat an eye when I tell him, "Lee Garland."

"Age?"

"Twenty."

"Military experience?"

"None."

"You ride?"

"Yes, sir."

"Shoot?"

"Yes."

"Height?"

"Six-two."

"Weight?"

"A hundred eighty."

"Ever been arrested?"

"Arrested?"

He looks up from the paper for the first time and sees the collar. "I guess not," he says, writing on the paper. "You're the first preacher we've had. You wear those eyeglasses all the time?"

"Just for reading," I say.

"Step over there, please," the sergeant says. He passes the paper over to one of the officers, who gives it to Ben Butler as I step up to the table. He looks at the paper and then at me, but he don't seem to recognize either the name or the face.

There's moments when a man's whole life can take a turn for better or worse, and most of the time we never know when they happen. But I knew this is one, and how Ben Butler reacts will settle forever if we're going to be free men or fugitives. I don't know what I expect exactly, but I can't erase the memory of the man's decency the time he spent up here at Eagle Nest when I was mauled by that lobo.

Knowing Charlie Bruce too, has a lot to do with my taking such a long chance. I have a small fortune in the bank, thanks to the business I done with him, and I want the other things that go with it. Ben Butler is about the only person in the world I trust to understand my point of view and maybe believe in my innocence.

He frowns at that paper and says to the others, "Excuse me,

gentlemen, but this application is a little unusual. I'd like to talk privately with the, uh, reverend."

He beckons me to follow him, and the crowd makes way as we go into the room where they're giving the medical examinations. He sits down near an old upright piano in the corner away from the doctor and the men stripped to their long johns. "I got your letter," he says, "and I already sent you an answer. You boys must be crazy. If I recognized Moore when he first came in, so will anybody. And they'll look right behind him for you and Williams."

"So you won't help us," I say, believing I made the worst mistake of my life.

"I can't help you," he says, "because I'm leaving. That's what I explained in my letter. I assume you haven't come to Santa Fe to give yourself up."

"I can't do that, but I didn't kill anybody."

"If you did, you sure had me fooled," he says, "because only an innocent man or a lunatic would ride in here like this."

"Then you believe me."

"Mrs. Sanchez confirmed you were at her place when Arnold Brown was killed. But Cody Williams is a different story. He was seen trying to help his brother get away from the scene of the murder."

"He didn't know Jake killed Arnold," I say.

"He's still in serious trouble. I might convince a jury he's telling the truth, but I won't be here to do it. Then there's Moore."

"He ain't a murderer either, Ben," I say.

"I didn't say he was. I talked with Rufus Barry about him and it may surprise you to know even Barry thinks Mountain Moore got a raw deal. But when he escaped from the Colorado State Prison, a guard was killed, and somebody's got to pay for that."

I say, "Mountain shouldn't have been there in the first place."

"Barry agrees."

"Then why was he going to take him back?"

"He's sworn to uphold the law, Lee, just like Luna," Ben Butler says. "I couldn't do anything for Moore even if I stayed behind."

"Now what?"

"Any good lawyer can probably get your indictment withdrawn and you'd never go to trial. I wouldn't advise Williams or Moore to hang around Santa Fe, however. Even if Cody's acquitted, Sam

Brown would probably go after him. And Colorado's still looking for a scapegoat, so Moore doesn't have much of a future."

"Thanks, Ben. I appreciate the trouble you took," I say.

"What will you do?"

"Go to Mexico."

"I thought you wanted to stop running and be respectable. That's what you said in your letter."

"How respectable would I be if I pulled out on my partners? We been friends too long."

He holds up the enlistment paper the sergeant give him. "What about this?"

"Me, in the army? I just did that to see you."

"Think about it, Lee. You could stop running."

"I don't have to think about it. You got all the volunteers you need without me. They're breaking down the doors out there."

"I could use you," Ben Butler says.

"I'd make a terrible soldier," I tell him, "but thanks anyway." I'm about to shake his hand and get a move on when there's a commotion at the door and in come Cody and Mountain like the devil's behind them.

"Lee!" Cody says. "He's here!"

I know who he means without asking. "Did he see you?"

"He knows you're in here," Cody says. He's carrying the carpet-bag with our Colts, and he gets one out, tossing the bag to me as he backs against the piano.

Before I can grab my gunbelt, Ben Butler snatches the bag and turns on Cody like a fury. "Give it here, Williams!"

Cody freezes with the gun in his hand, watching the door, his back to Ben Butler. "There's got to be another way out."

In two steps Ben Butler's on him, and with a powerful chop the gun's back in the bag while Cody's rubbing his wrist in astonishment. "Where the hell do you think you are?" Ben Butler says. "You want to make a bad situation impossible?"

"Lee?" Cody's looking at me like a trapped animal. "Don't let him take me."

"You'll do as I tell you," Butler says.

"Jesus, Ben, you can't ask him to give himself up," I say.

"You came to me for help, didn't you?" Butler says.

"I'm not going to no electricity chair," Cody tells him.

Butler says to Mountain, "Where's Luna?"

"With them other officers in the next room."

"I'll talk to him," Butler says. "All of you wait here, and strip down to your BVDs."

"Do what?" I say.

"Take your clothes off like those other men, and go over there and get in line. Now!"

He heads for the door with the bag in his hand, but it's too late because Luna's there already with a deputy and a corporal behind him. Luna nods hello to Ben Butler, but he ain't looking at him. He's squinting around the room through his one good eye.

"Morning, Sheriff," Ben Butler says. "Come to sign up?"

"I'm here to make an arrest, Captain Butler," Luna says.

"One of my men?" Butler says.

"No, but I believe you know him. That slickshit Lee Garland who nearly blinded me in Socorro. I'm told he's here."

Butler takes his arm and says, "Why don't we talk about this outside, Sheriff?"

"Because that would give him time to get away, Ben, and I'm not going to let that happen." His good eye is roaming the room like a searchlight and finally rests on me. "I do believe I found what I came for," he says in a voice like a judge pronouncing sentence. His hand resting on his gun butt, he starts toward me like he's praying I'll give him the chance to send me to Kingdom Come.

The deputy's right behind him, aping his moves, and Luna says, "Put the irons on him so tight they don't come off this time."

Ben Butler steps between us and says, "Hold on, Max. Before you make a mistake, we better have a talk."

"It's no mistake."

"There's a question of jurisdiction here," Ben Butler says.

"No, there isn't. I'm still sheriff of Santa Fe County. Get the irons on him, goddamnit!"

"Corporal," Ben Butler says, "call the provost guard," and the corporal goes running out.

"I don't need any help with this sidewinder," Luna says.

The deputy's coming toward me with the handcuffs and I'm backing away, but Butler lays a hand on Luna's arm and says, "I wasn't offering help, Max."

That stops Luna for a second. "Then maybe I misunderstood," he says, and his tone ain't so friendly.

"I was offering legal advice," Butler says.

"I don't need that either," Luna says.

"For your information, this is a temporary military installation," Butler says, smooth as butter sauce.

"Since when?" Luna says.

"Since we began enrolling men for the army. Your authority doesn't extend to these premises."

"Last time I looked, this was a hotel, not a fort," Luna says. "Now stand aside, Ben, and let me do my duty."

"Sorry, Max," Ben Butler says, "but I must do mine as well."

Luna looks at him as if he's seeing him for the first time. "I do believe you're serious," he says.

Four colored soldiers come clattering in with carbines, led by the sergeant from the train, who salutes Ben Butler.

"I am serious," Butler says. "Now, shall we go outside and talk this over?"

Luna looks around at the line of soldiers with their carbines at port arms, and tilts his derby back to scratch at his eye bandage. "You're interfering with an officer of the law in the performance of his duty," he says to Ben Butler, "and damned if I know why."

"You're wrong, Sheriff," Ben Butler says. "I just don't want to see you mistakenly interfere with an officer of the First U.S. Volunteer Cavalry in the performance of his duty. This man is here voluntarily."

"He's not in the army yet," Luna says.

"He's taking a physical examination, as you can see," Ben Butler says, "and the army is responsible for him."

Just then, when it looks like our side is winning, Cody steps out of the crowd with Mountain, and Luna nearly has apoplexy. He grabs Ben Butler by the shoulder and spins him around. "Jesus Christ, you didn't tell me they're all here!"

"Voluntarily," Ben Butler cautions, calm as a spring breeze.

But Luna's breathing hard now, and he's dangerous, no matter how many soldiers are standing by. "I thought you were my friend," he says between his teeth. "You call this justice?"

"I don't know," Ben Butler says, "but it *is* the law."

"When they leave here, they're mine," Luna says. "If I have to put a hundred men around this building, I'll get them."

"Not if they leave as soldiers," Ben Butler tells him.

"You know what they are! Why are you doing this to me?"

"They came here unarmed and of their own free will," Ben

Butler says, "to offer their services to their country."

"Since when are you taking thieves and murderers?" Luna says, madder than a snake.

"I'm enlisting physically fit men who can ride and shoot," Ben Butler says, "of sound moral character."

"There you are," Luna says. "You said it yourself. That goddamn Garland's got no moral character, sound or any other kind. Neither have those other two scoundrels. I've been chasing them since I put on this badge and I aim to get them!"

"Maybe," Ben Butler says, real soft, "but not now, and not here." Luna's glaring at the soldiers because he knows he's lost this round to Butler, but when that one eye lights on me I get the shivers. "Now, would you mind stepping outside," Butler tells him, "so the regimental surgeon can get on with his job?"

Luna turns on his heel, but he stops at the door and says in a voice quivering with anger, "If the Spaniards don't get you, Garland, I will. You can bet on it. You're finished trifling with the law in Santa Fe County, all of you!" The vein at his temple is throbbing, and he means what he says.

Ben Butler tells the guard to stand at ease, but to keep everybody else out for a few minutes. I say, "Thanks, Ben. We appreciate your sticking your neck out like that."

I'm putting my clothes back on and he says, "Where do you think you're going?"

"Out of here, if there's another way. You heard him."

"And you heard what I told him," Ben Butler says.

"But we ain't here to enlist in the army," I say.

"No?" he says. "Do you want to make me look like a liar?"

"You can't do this to us," Cody says.

"Do what?" Ben Butler says.

"Make us go in the army," Mountain tells him.

"Of course I can't. This is a volunteer regiment."

"Well, then?" I say. "We ain't volunteers."

"That's too bad," Ben Butler says. "Because you've taken up a lot of my time and I'm a busy man."

"Just give us our guns and we'll get out of your hair," I say.

"So you can shoot your way out? How far do you think you'd get? Luna with only one eye will drop the three of you before you reach the street. He'll be a hero and you'll be dead."

"We don't have no choice," I tell him.

"Sure you do," he says, smiling at the three of us. "If we find a uniform to fit Moore, you can come to Cuba with me."

And that is how we come to offer our services to the flag, and join Troop F of the First U.S. Volunteer Cavalry, later known as the Rough Riders.

Luna Gets Even

The physical examination takes about five minutes. There's the eye test and the jump test, where the doctor asks if we can see and breathe while we're jumping up and down. Then he looks us over and asks if we ever suffer from dropsy or glanders or the syphilis or dizzy spells and we all say no. Then he studies our mouths like we was horses, and sticks a finger between our balls and says, "Cough." He finds something he don't like in Mountain's shoulder and asks him what it is.

"A lump," Mountain says.

"I know that," the doctor says. "What caused it."

"Knife blade broke off," Mountain says. "It's still there."

"Ever bother you?"

"Only when it happened," Mountain tells him.

This doctor sees the scarred-up holes in my arm, and he whistles. "Ain't you the lucky one," he says. "You shoot the dog that bit you?"

"It was a wolf," I say, "and Ben Butler shot it."

"Is that so?" the doctor says. By now he's listening to Cody's chest through a stethoscope and he don't like what he hears. "You ever had lung trouble?" he asks Cody.

"No, sir."

"You cough a lot?"

"Now and then."

"Get tired easy?"

"Who don't?"

This doctor turns Cody around a couple of times and listens all over his skinny ribs. "How old are you?" he says.

"Eighteen."

"Ever spit blood?"

Cody shrugs.

"Sorry, son," he says. "The army's going to have to win this war without you."

"What do you mean?" Cody says.

"You ain't fit enough," the doctor tells him. "You could never keep up."

"I'm as fit as they are," Cody says, pointing at us.

The doctor just shakes his head and starts writing on Cody's paper. "Next man," he says.

I get Ben Butler and he takes the doctor aside to talk to him in a low voice. Finally I hear the doctor say, "All right, I'll pass him, but don't blame me when he collapses. And don't send him to me on sick call."

"I'll take that responsibility," Ben Butler says, so the doctor signs Cody fit for service, shaking his head the whole time.

We get dressed and go wait in another line to sign our enlistment papers. I leave the preacher's collar off this time and Mountain says it's too bad because it gave me a touch of distinction. Cody's grousing about how the doctor can't tell a healthy man from a cat, but I figure the doctor's probably right and Ben Butler made the mistake. There was lots of times on the trail when me and Mountain hung back to make it easier on Cody. What he lacked in strength he made up in grit. There never was a kid tried harder than him to keep up, so maybe he'll be all right. Anyway, whatever happens now has to be better than Luna, so I tell them both they better concentrate on making the army a success.

The other men in line is mostly cowhands, but some are different. The fellow in front of me is dressed in a purple velvet shirt and when he turns around I get a shock because he's full-blooded Indian. I don't know then it's the beginning of a lifelong friendship, but I might of guessed. He sticks out his hand and says, "I'm Tom Isbell and I've heard about you, Mr. Garland."

I say, "Is that so? What is it you heard?"

"You kill wolves with your bare hands." Tom's kind of short, like a lot of Indians, but built like a bull. Handsome, with a round, honest face, and eyes like two arrow points. They say Indians is solemn and never crack a smile, but that ain't true. Nobody liked to laugh more than Tom Isbell and it come from his boot heels when he let it out. He was the only one of us, except for Ben Butler and a handful more, who had military experience. He was ten years older than me and had served five years from age sixteen, being the youngest scout in the army during the Indian Wars.

I tell him I don't know where he could of heard such a tall tale about the wolf, but I can guess.

"Captain Butler's real glad to have you boys with us," he says. "You think we'll get to Cuba?"

"We better," Cody tells him. "I didn't join no army to sit around New Mexico."

Tom says, "They already got a train laid on for us to San Antonio, Texas."

"What's down there?" I ask him.

"Big army post where we train with the regiment."

"Train?" Cody wants to know.

"Cavalry drill," Tom Isbell says, and Cody starts complaining about that until I tell him to shut up.

Tom Isbell says once a man gets used to a McClellan saddle the rest is easy. Ben Butler wants to make him a sergeant but he ain't sure. Mountain asks him why not. "You got to give orders," Tom says, "and some men don't always like that coming from an Indian."

"Take the job," Mountain says. "I'll keep the men in line."

Well, Tom Isbell laughs and says he'll think about it.

Henry Haefner, a cowboy rode with me before I got mixed up with the Brown brothers, comes over to say hello. Henry's a pleasant sandy-haired fellow, a top hand and one of the best ropers I ever seen. He plays the banjo, too, and has a fine singing voice. "Lee," he says, "I told the boys you'd turn up. We never believed a word about that business with Arnold Brown."

"Thanks, Henry," I say. "I'm glad we'll have music where we're headed."

"I don't know if they'll let me bring my banjo," he says.

"If they don't, I ain't going," I tell him. There's another fellow on line with us as little and scrawny as a starved turkey, and I don't

know how the doctor ever passed him. His name is Levi Hennings
and he's got a dog looks as hungry as he does, and just as miserable. The men in the room all kick the dog out of the way, and he
complains, but they just laugh. When he introduces himself, he
says they don't want him to bring his dog along as mascot. I can
see why, but I don't say so.

Cody's already kneeling down, scratching the dog's ears. It's a
kind of spotted hound but mixed with other things. "What do you
call him?" Cody says.

"Heinz," Levi tells him.

"What kind of dog is he?" I say.

"I named him after the pickle," Levi says. "You know, fifty-seven
varieties?"

"Varieties of what?" Mountain says.

"Of dog," Levi tells him. "That animal contains the finest collection of pedigrees in the Territory."

"He don't look too healthy," Cody says.

"He's supposed to be thin," Levi says. "He's a hunting dog."

"What does he hunt?" Mountain asks him.

"Cats mostly," Levi says, "but give him a chance at a bear or a
mountain lion or a Spaniard and you'll see what he's made of."

"You a hunter?" Mountain asks him.

"I'm a jockey," Levi says. "Four-time winner of the governor's
cup. Surprised you never heard of me."

"I don't pay much attention to horse racing," Mountain says.

"Ain't no money in it for a jockey," Levi says. "That's why I do
some barbering and work as a bank teller. No money in that either,
except other people's, but I'm quick with figures. What's your
line?"

Cody looks at me before saying, "We was in the cattle business."

"You cut hair?" Tom Isbell asks Levi.

"Sure do."

"Why don't you cut mine, so they don't take me for an Indian,"
Tom Isbell says, and all the men around him laugh at that.

"Well, what do you think?' Levi says.

"About what?" Cody asks him.

"Ain't he a spectacular dog?"

You can see love on the man's face as clear as glass when he looks at that hound. Somehow it makes the hound look better, and we all agree he's a spectacular dog.

"Well, there you are," Levi says to the room at large. "He'll be our mascot."

Cody, who is always more sensitive about things like that than the rest of us, says, "Don't you think army life will be hard on him?"

This Levi says, "He don't eat hardly a thing, and he's too small to get in the way."

"I can see that," Cody says.

Another fellow barges into the discussion then, and at first I think he's just there to see what's going on because he's dressed for a wedding or a funeral in a Prince Albert coat and wing collar. "Did I hear someone say this creature is our mascot?" he says, looking down at the hound like he just did something and it smelled.

"And who might you be?" says Levi Hennings, his Adam's apple bobbing, ready to do battle.

"Are you the owner of this . . . animal?" the other fellow says.

"I am," Levi says.

"You can't be serious," the stranger says. "A mascot should be a symbol of our spirit and dedication, an eagle or a falcon at least."

"Arizona's got a mountain lion," Levi says.

"Then you see why I have to protest if you insist on bringing this poor, misbegotten mongrel along as mascot."

"I seen you somewhere," Levi says.

"Of course you have. I'm Mason Mitchell." He gives us the benefit of a right and left profile as well as a big smile to make his point. I don't know who Mason Mitchell is and neither does Mountain or Cody. But this Levi nearly faints when he hears the name, and you can see he's having a struggle between hero worship and love for his dog.

Tom Isbell knows who he is too, and so do some of the other men because they been to the moving pictures. In five minutes, everybody's forgot the dog and this Mason Mitchell's the center of attention. I can't get over how they're all falling over him, because he don't look like much to me. He's a good-looking fellow, but as a celebrity he don't measure up to the seal boy or the caterpillar man. When I say so, Tom Isbell pulls me aside and says, "He's only the greatest trick rider and the deadliest shot in the world."

"Him?" I say. "He talks like he wears lace underpants."

"No, sir," Tom Isbell says. "I seen him in the moving pictures." Coming from somebody with Isbell's reputation, I have to believe it's the truth. "I was there when Captain Butler talked to him," Tom says. "Why, I seen Annie Oakley and Buffalo Bill, but nobody can shoot like Mason Mitchell, and no Indian can touch him for riding."

Levi Hennings says, "He goes under a horse's belly at a full gallop and comes up on the other side. And he never goes aboard from the stirrup. He leapfrogs over the horse's rump to get into the saddle. I reckon Mason Mitchell's the eighth wonder of the world when he gets going. Imagine the sergeant asking him if he could ride and shoot? I guess not!" Hennings sprays you if you get too close because he's got four front teeth missing, lost in a fall as a jockey. He leans in on us and says, "Do you really think he don't like my dog?"

And Cody says, "Your dog does take getting used to, Levi. It's the kind of dog has to grow on a man."

"You're right," Levi says. "Absolutely correct."

Cody calls, "Heinz! Come here, Heinz!" But the dog don't pay no attention.

Levi says, "Here Spotty, Spotty, Spotty!" and the dog comes over and lays down at his feet.

"I thought you said his name was Heinz," Cody says.

"It is," Levi tells him, "but he don't answer to it."

A hand grabs me by the shoulder and spins me around, and for a second I figure it's Luna, but it ain't. This fellow is familiar but he was in police uniform the last time I seen him.

"Hello, Ransom," I say. "You're a long ways from El Paso."

"And you're a sight I never expected to see again, Garland. What the hell are you boys doing here?"

I ask him the same.

"Took a leave of absence from the police to get into the war," he says, laughing. "Things slowed down after you left."

"I guess you can afford it," I say, and right away he's looking around him.

"Hey, I came through for you" he says in a whisper.

"I don't know what you're talking about," I tell him,

"That must of been some shoot-out. You never told nobody who helped you?"

"I still don't know what you're talking about," I say.

"I appreciate that, Garland," he says. "I knew you was a straight shooter, but I never imagined you joining up to fight, or your friends either."

I say, "A man's got to stand up for what's right, Ransom."

"That's the truth," he says, like we're all patriots together.

At the swearing in Ben Butler makes a little speech. He says the Spanish don't understand what it's like to be free, only doing what some king tells them, like all them foreigners in Europe. Well, around here we believe every man's got a right to breathe his own air and live on his own land. That's why we're going to help the Cubans.

I didn't know it then, but he was as innocent as the rest of us about things like that. I found out since that the world is full of people don't give a damn about living free, including the Cubans. Most of them are downright comfortable with one kind of boss or another or they wouldn't put up with him. And I don't excuse the United States neither. We got socialism now and income tax and welfare and atom bombs, but damn little freedom of the kind I enjoyed when I was young. Every place you go in New Mexico today, you bump into a goddamned government fence put there by some Democrat.

Ben Butler is a fine speaker, clear and honest, and the men give him a big cheer when he finishes. Then he says, real soft and easy, "We are embarking on an unknown voyage with uncertain results. It will be hard and brutal and dangerous. Some of you will not return. Others will be sacrificing employment and business opportunities that will not come again. Think hard, gentlemen, before you take the oath. If any man wants to be excused, he should step down now. But if you stay, let me hear no complaints. No matter what comes you must bear up. Every man who swears the oath will be expected to keep it."

Nobody moves. It's like church and nobody even looks at each other. If this war is good enough for a man like Ben Butler, it's okay with the rest of us.

Remembering back on it I have to admit it was a special moment. He was right about some things. Too many boys left widows and orphans, and quite a few come back maimed or crippled. But it ain't every day a young man gets a chance to go on a adventure he believes in, and that's how we felt, even if it did turn out to be a waste of life and time.

The bar's open after that and there's high spirits as well as all the other kind. Nobody could pay for a drink, and I hear later Old Lady Sanchez picked up the bill. The only ones leave early is Ransom and two other Texans who want to stop off home and are going to catch up with us in El Paso.

I take him aside before he goes and say, "My friend and partner Charlie Bruce is in El Paso," and I give him the doctor's address. "He may be dead by now, but if he's alive, tell him I put his money safe in the bank. If he can meet the train when we come through El Paso, I'll explain everything to him. If he can't, tell him to send me a note or telegraph me in San Antonio and I'll see he gets his money."

Ransom writes it down and says he'll do me that favor.

"You can do me another one, while you're at it," I tell him. "Remember those Colts and rifles you took? Can you get them back?"

"I can try," Ransom says, "but it might cost a few dollars."

I give him two hundred to grease the wheels with his police friends and tell him to see Charlie gets the guns. If he's recovered, he may be able to do some business on his own while I'm playing around in the army. I even think about getting off the train in El Paso and joining him again, but I'd be no use as a partner with the law on my tail. Besides, I got an obligation to Ben Butler now, even if he did fox us into enlisting. Charlie and me may have missed making our first million in the Mexican cattle business, but if he's alive there may still be another fortune waiting somewhere when my patriotic duty is done.

On the train to El Paso, we hear some news gives Cody a coughing spell and makes me and Mountain almost desert the army. That's when Ben Butler comes into our car and announces that his great friend and former colleague in law enforcement, Maximiliano Luna, has taken a leave of absence from the office of sheriff of Santa Fe County and accepted a commission as first lieutenant in our troop. Everybody but us cheers and when Ben Butler leaves the car, he puts a hand on my shoulder for a second and says, "We're all in this together now, Lee, and I'm sure you boys will give the lieutenant your wholehearted support."

I know I shouldn't take a thing like that personal, but I can't help it. I was convinced the son of a bitch joined up because he couldn't leave me in peace, even in a war.

X

Indian Rules

We're a motley crowd on that train, looking more like a lodge picnic or a convention of ribbon clerks than a cavalry troop. Only a few of the officers have uniforms, while the rest of us are in levis or town clothes. Ben Butler ruled out drinking, and that don't mean there wasn't none, but mostly we just played cards and joked around to pass the time. A bunch of ignorant young men going off to fight a war is as dumb and determined as a lynch mob, but not near as dangerous because they feel really caught up in great enterprise. Nobody can understand it who ain't done it when he's young. It's like every man's been waiting for this day since he was born.

Maybe under the talk, some of us are scared, but I don't believe it. We were confident. And brave because it's easy to show courage sitting in a railroad car. We were American and unbeatable. Hell, nobody ever had beat us, and that was the proof.

Anybody with half a grain of sense knows war ain't nothing but boredom, pain, discomfort and noise. But those who come back know it's where a man learns secrets about himself he might like to forget and maybe never tells. I've heard people say that's because life is cheap, but I believe it's the other way around. Every man's life becomes precious when he don't know how long he's going to hold on to it.

On the train, our second lieutenant, Dave Leahy, who was a

lawyer and had been to college in Albuquerque, says our going to fight in Cuba don't have nothing to do with the Spaniards blowing up our battleship. The real reason, Dave says, is a young country like ours has to let off steam, and Cuba's as good a place as any to do it. We ain't had ourselves a good war since the Civil, and a country can't grow without fighting. That starts an argument because it takes some of the shine off our patriotism. But I'm inclined to think he's right.

Then the first sergeant comes into the car and says, "Listen up! Isbell, Thomas J. You are this date appointed sergeant."

Tom starts to say he didn't work it out yet with Captain Butler, but the men shout him down, and that made me feel good. You got to understand what an Indian was in those days. Nothing. And here's forty white men shouting if this Indian ain't their sergeant, they'll quit. Well, Tom accepted and went into the lavatory from embarrassment.

Then I get a shock when they make me acting corporal. "Captain Butler's orders," the first sergeant says.

"I don't have any experience," I say. "There's been a mistake.

"Take it up with Lieutenant Luna."

"He's on the train?"

"He recommended you."

I say, "What's the difference between corporal and acting?"

The first sergeant, whose name is Horace Stone, says, "Just like it sounds, Garland. Try to *act* like a corporal."

"I wouldn't know where to start."

"Start here," Sherman says, and hands me a whole handful of meal vouchers to feed the men until we get to San Antonio. He makes me sign a receipt and says, "Just see nobody goes hungry on the trip."

I spend the rest of the morning wondering what Luna's got up his sleeve besides trying to guaranty my personal downfall in the army. After we leave Albuquerque, I enjoy my first exercise of command by marching everybody into the dining car for lunch. Cody says, "Hey, Lee! Order the chicken soup," and whoops with laughter.

We're supposed to lay over about four hours in El Paso, which gives me time to see about Charlie Bruce and stop by the bank. The trouble is, we ain't allowed off the train. Lieutenant Leahy has put a guard on each car to see nobody leaves, and Mountain gets the job where we are. I tell him, "If anything happens and I don't make it before you leave, put my gear on the platform and I'll catch the next train for San Antonio."

It's a hot day and I'm late and in a sweat by the time I reach the doctor's house at three. He's operating a fistula on a kid's eye and the screaming is terrible. When the kid leaves with its mother, I go in. The doctor's in a long white apron spattered with blood like a butcher, and washing his instruments in carbolic water. He thinks I'm a patient until I ask about Charlie.

"I can't be responsible for your friend," he says, irritated. "I told him he was in no condition to travel."

I'm so relieved to know Charlie's still alive, I say, "Nobody holds you responsible, Doctor. I'd just like to know where he is."

"Everybody wants to know where he is," the doctor says. "There was a police officer looking for him a little while ago."

"That was a friend of mine."

"Mr. Bruce left this morning with a woman."

"Where'd he go?"

"Boston I believe. I told him the trip could kill him."

"Didn't he leave an address?"

The doctor shrugs and starts drying his instruments on a towel. "They were taking a train this afternoon."

"What time?"

"If it's the Fort Worth express, it leaves about now."

I ask him what I owe for Charlie's care and he says everything's paid. I rush out of there and can't find a goddamn cab anywheres. So I hotfoot it back toward the station, hoping Charlie will be on that train and hoping it will be late. I finally flag down a bakery wagon going in the right direction and get to the station in time to see the train pulling out.

A porter tells me he helped a sick man and a woman aboard a Pullman, and the description fits Charlie. I send a telegram to him on the train and then pass by the bank to make a small withdrawal, as my cash is running low. This takes twice as much time as I got, so when I get to the platform where our train was, it ain't there, and I think I got the worst luck in the world. Now I'll be in trouble with the army and late for the war. But a porter says no, the army train is still in the freight yards, just moved to another track.

When I finally find it, it's moving. I never run so hard in my life, but I make it just as the train's picking up speed. I got a stitch in my side, but I grab ahold of the rail on the observation car and drag myself up. I sit there a full five minutes before I get my wind back. Then I wander through the coaches until I find Mountain. He jumps when he sees me and Cody says, "Oh, shit!"

I say, "At least you could act like you're glad I made it."

Cody says, looking at Mountain. "Tell him."

"You tell him," Mountain says.

"Tell me what?"

Cody says, "We shoved all your gear off on the platform."

The army vouchers was in my valise and I have to pay for everybody's food all the way to San Antonio. Being an acting corporal is an expensive responsibility when you got efficient friends like mine.

Grinning like he just won at cards, Ransom gives me a sack weighs fifty pounds. In it are the four Colts and twenty boxes of cartridges. I thank him for the trouble, and give him one of the Colts. I keep one for myself and give the others to Mountain and Cody.

We pull into San Antonio at dawn two days later and tumble out half asleep. After we learn how to stand at attention and dress ranks and do right and left face, we get our uniforms. Just cheap brown canvas, stiff as cardboard, but at least we look alike. They give us boots and leggings and pants, and something the army calls a blouse which is a cross between a shirt and a jacket without the comfort of one or the fit of the other. There's a strip of tinfoil sewed into the back to protect your spine from the sun that we tear out because all it does is burn and itch.

We get felt hats go all out of shape with the first rain, and suspenders and long johns and canteens and blankets and mess tins, and they show us how to work up a horse-collar pack. We get our cartridge belts and Krag-Jorgenson carbines, which use smokeless powder and which we only fire twice before we get to Cuba. For a regiment of cavalry, we're a sorry-looking bunch because we have everything but horses.

There's rumors about when we're leaving. We hear Cuba's off and Spain's on, then Puerto Rico, then Cuba again. We learn to do everything by bugle call and almost never see an officer. The food is bad, mostly beans and pork. Mountain and Cody ask me where's the good Mexican beef we sold the major down in El Paso. Wherever he sent it, it never caught up with us the whole time we was in the army.

We have the Articles of War read to us. Mainly they say the army can shoot you or jail you if you fall asleep in the face of the enemy or talk back to an officer. Sassing an officer seems to be about the worst, judging from the amount of space they give it. They can dock your pay too, which makes us laugh. A trooper made thirteen dollars a month, and a dollar thirty extra on the battlefield.

Other volunteers are coming in by then from Arizona and Colorado and the Indian Territory. And a lot of swells from New York and Washington with tailor-made uniforms and fancy boots. One of them even has his own valet that Ben Butler sends packing the first day.

A certain amount of friction is bound to come between cowboys like us and these Eastern dudes, and one day I'm at the center.

I'm still an acting corporal when the first sergeant tells me to get together a cleaning detail outside the cook tent. I scout up five or six fellows, one of them being Cody, and a couple new arrivals bunking together from the East. One is a tall, balding fellow called C.E. Knoblauch who turns right out when I ask him, but the other one's reading a newspaper and ignores me. I tell him again to pitch in with the others. When he still pays me no attention, I get mad and say, "I don't know whether you're deaf or ornery, but I give you an order."

He looks up then, like I'm some kind of bug, and says, "Who are you to give me orders?"

Cody says, "He's Corporal Garland, that's who. Now get off your ass and help out."

"If you're a corporal," this fellow says, "where are your stripes?"

I'm thinking this son of a bitch is a challenge to my authority but if I punch him out, I'll be in more trouble than he is. If I call the first sergeant I'll get results, but old Horace Stone ain't going to like it much.

"What's your name?" I say.

"G. Ronald Fortescue," he says in a bored voice, and goes back to his paper. All the others have stopped what they're doing, waiting to see how this is going to end.

I say, "Well, Mr. G. Fortescue, I been ordered to clean this place up and that includes all paper and refuse laying around." I grab the newspaper away from him.

It couldn't of been better if I'd hit him. He jumps to his feet spitting mad and says, "That's my New York *Times!*"

"No, it ain't," I say, "it's paper cluttering up the camp." And I tear it in strips. "Now, you want to cooperate like everybody else or you want to go on the report?"

He puts his nose about an inch from mine and says, "You ignorant, cheeky lout! I could knock you unconscious."

The others are trying not to laugh now, which only makes him madder. C.E. Knoblauch comes over and says, "Calm down, Ronny. He really is a corporal."

This quiets Fortescue a little, but he's still breathing hard and looking at me in an unfriendly way. This C.E. Knoblauch leads him away and talks to him for a minute, and convinces him he better join the cleanup detail. He don't say a word and I figure that's the end of it until we get the place looking right half an hour later. He comes over to me and says, "Garland, I don't take back what I said. You are an ignorant lout, and a bully. And I loathe bullies."

"I'm also a corporal," I tell him.

"I'm speaking man to man," he says, with a real sneer, "if you are a man, that is."

Again, there's six pairs of ears listening to this so I can't just back down. "It's easy to prove." I say. "But if I take it out and show it to you, you might faint."

"Very amusing," he says. "It may interest you to know I was an intercollegiate welterweight boxing champion."

"It don't interest me at all, Fortecute," I tell him. I know his name as well as he does by now, but I want to get his goat. "Any reason it should?"

"I'm challenging you to a fight," he says.

He's a good-looking fellow with wavy black hair and a ruddy complexion, a little shorter than me, but built solid, heavier and better muscled. I can see he ain't talking up a drainpipe and I don't know the first thing about boxing.

"A fight or a boxing match?" I say.

"All the same," he says.

"Not to me it ain't. You want a fight, I'll give you one. You want to box, find somebody else."

"A fight then," he says.

"Bare knuckle?"

"Precisely."

"Anything goes?"

"You're really revolting, Garland, but I'll go along. Above the belt, anything goes, except help from a friend or the use of a weapon."

"You got it," I say.

"Now?" he says.

"Why not?"

Cody steps in and says, "Hold on, Lee. A fight will draw a crowd and the boys will want to bet the winner."

C.E. Knoblauch says, "I'll put fifty dollars on Ronny," but nobody takes him up. It's easy to see who the favorite's going to be. We agree to fight behind the cook tent at six o'clock.

When I get back to my tent, Mountain says, "You're crazy, Lee. I heard about him. He may be a millionaire but he's a expert. Knoblauch says he even boxed with Mysterious Billy Smith and Kid McCoy."

"Who's Mysterious Billy Smith?" I ask him.

"Only the world welterweight champion," he says.

"So you don't think I can beat him?" I say.

"He's going to kill you," Mountain says.

"We'll see," I say, not radiating confidence, but with a couple ideas on how I can get the edge.

"You definitely can't kick him in the balls," Cody says, reading my mind.

"I don't know anything about boxing."

"Well, you got two hours to learn," Mountain says.

"Anything goes," I say. "He agreed to that."

"He'd agree to anything," Cody says, "because he knows he's going to whip you."

In half an hour the news is all over the camp, and Levi Hennings says they're offering ten-to-one odds against me.

Trying to be witty, Mountain says, "That ain't so bad, Lee. They must think you got a chance."

Levi says, "Fortescue wants to know who's going to referee."

"What does he need a referee for?"

"That's the way things are done, he says."

"It don't matter to me," I tell Levi.

There's about a hundred troopers behind the cook tent when we get there, and fistfuls of dollar bills changing hands. Tom Isbell says, "I bet five on you, Lee," and I thank him. Mountain greases my face and torso good with lard because he says that way Fortescue's going to do less damage, but it's clear there ain't many think I got a chance. The odds are twenty-to-one by six o'clock when Fortescue shows up.

He looks impressive, I got to admit. Stripped to the waist, he's all muscle, not lean and stringy like me. When Mountain sees my face he tries to cheer me up. "You got the height and reach on him, Lee."

"So what?" I say.

By general agreement, Mason Mitchell is the referee, and he announces, "This fight will be one round as long as it lasts, Indian rules, which means, so I am informed, that the loser is the first man who wants to quit or gets knocked down and can't get up. No punching or kicking below the belt. Otherwise, anything goes. Is that correct?" He looks at Fortescue, who only shrugs, and at me. Cody draws a fifteen-foot circle in the dirt, and me and Fortescue go to the center of it. "Shake hands," Mitchell says, and we shake. Then he steps back and says, "All right, the fight is on."

I never knew what hit me when Fortescue threw his first punch. He lays me out on my back, and when I get to my knees, the first thing I see is Mountain with one hand over his eyes, shaking his head. Fortescue's standing there waiting, with his fists cocked, ready to level me again the minute I'm up. This ain't the way I planned it, and I see I got to improvise quick because he's got a punch like a pile driver, and he's fast. The men are all cheering and hooting, and Levi's dog is barking when I make it to my feet.

He hits me again, but I see it coming this time and duck, so all he gets is my shoulder. I plant two punches in his middle when he's close, but they don't hurt him because he's got a gut like a washboard. When I back off, he dances toward me, bobbing and dodging and flicking his fists like hammers.

I say, "Anytime you want to give up, Miss Nancy, I'll let you off."

"Damn you, stand and fight!" he says. He's getting mad because I ain't cooperating. All he's hitting now is my arms because I'm still backing off and the men are booing me for not standing up to him.

Well, I may be ignorant, but I'm not stupid, and I ain't about to get in the way of those fists again. I seen stars with that first punch and I'm willing to believe he's a champion boxer. But he's using about ten times as much energy chasing me as I am fending him off, and I got to wait my chance. He puts a couple more stingers into the side of my head while I'm waiting, then I see my opening. His right is his main battering ram, and the next time he throws it, I grab his arm with both hands and pull as hard as I can. He can't recover his balance in time and goes sprawling behind me. The men let out a howl and some of them is even laughing and cheering for me.

When he gets to his knees, I belt him a good one on the side of his head and the Easterners yell, "Not fair!" but Cody yells right back, "Indian rules, boys! This ain't a prize fight!"

Fortescue puts his guard up to protect his head from my fists, but this time I knee him in the jaw. He goes down in a hurry, and now he's groggy. While he's struggling to get up again, I jump on his back and knock him flat with his face in the dirt. I get a handful of hair and bang his head against the ground half a dozen times before I climb off. Then I stand next to him with my fists up like he did at the beginning and say, "Okay, you want to box? Now I'll box with you."

He's a game one, this Fortescue, I give him that. Anybody else would of give up. When he shows his face again he's cut in three or four places, mainly over his left eye, and it looks like I broke his nose the way it's bent and bleeding.

I ask him if he wants to quit but he shakes his head. The fellows all cheer him and I leave him alone while he takes the prizefighter's crouch again and throws two or three feeble punches. He's wobbly and he don't see too good, but he won't quit.

I say, "Fortescue, this ain't giving me any more pleasure than it gives you, so why not say uncle?" But his only answer is a couple more little taps I don't even feel. I turn to Mitchell and say, "If he'll quit and say I'm the winner I'll leave him alone."

While I'm looking at Mitchell, this Fortescue lands me one on the head that all but puts my lights out. I don't know where he found the strength, but it knocks me down, and when I get up, my legs feel like the Spearmint kid.

At first I just stagger out of his reach while he wastes more strength throwing punches that don't land. When my head finally clears I see by staying on his blind left side it's harder for him to tag me with his right. Each time I get a chance I pound him on the cut eye until I expect to see it fall out.

"Come on, quit!" I say. "You're finished." But he just shakes his head and keeps boxing back every time I hit him. I'm getting tired of this when he catches me a double shot in the jaw that jars my bones all the way to my knees and nearly puts me down again. One or two more like that and he's got me, so I back off once more to study my options while the crowd yells. Then I see it and wonder why I hadn't thought of it earlier, except my brain was working a little sluggish. I tempt him by coming closer, and when he throws his right at me again, I duck under it and butt him in the gut with my head hard as I can. We both go down in the dirt but I'm on top driving my fist into his bloody face again and again and he can't even see to protect himself no more.

When I roll off him, he gets up like a poleaxed bull and he don't even see me or the crowd anymore for the blood. I put my hand on his shoulder and he lashes out with that right one more time. It's a lucky punch and sends me reeling, but he can't see me to follow up.

Lucky for me, that was all he had. One more and I'd of been counting canaries. Well, the men went wild then, shouting and cheering for one or the other of us. When my head clears I can see he's hurt bad now. His face looks like he's been worked over with a currycomb, and he's totally blind from the bleeding, even though he keeps trying to wipe the blood away with one arm.

Still I have to hit him six or seven more times before his guard drops, and every blow makes more blood fly. I cut my knuckles up doing it, and his face is a pulp. It gets so bad finally I just stop and yell at him, "Goddamn it, Fortescue, give up!" But he won't quit and he's too tough to fall down, even though he can't see me anymore and can't hardly lift his arms.

Mitchell says, "Come on, old boy, it's time to quit," but Fortescue just shakes his head.

So I say, "Okay, I quit."

Cody yells, "You can't do that, Lee! You're winning."

"Not if I quit. I ain't going to kill a man to save his pride."

There's a lot of hooting about this, but I made up my mind. I'm sorry Cody and Tom Isbell and some of the other boys are losing money on me, but I ain't built to beat up on a man can't fight back.

Mountain gets a bucket and helps me wash the blood off while

C.E. Knoblauch and some of the other Easterners lead Fortescue back to his tent. I figure they ought to take him to the regimental surgeon but that's their business. The bets is paid off and there's a few long faces among my friends, but none of them criticizes what I done, even if it did cost them money.

About an hour later C.E. Knoblauch comes over, and he's got a big wad of bills and a list of all the troopers bet on me. He says G. Ronald Fortescue sent him because he ain't in any shape to come himself yet, but he wants every man to collect because I won the fight.

I say, "What about all the fellows won on him?"

C.E. Knoblauch says, "Ronny doesn't want anyone out of pocket because of the misunderstanding he caused. Those that collected will keep their winnings."

"So everybody wins?" Mountain says.

"That's right," Knoblauch says, "and I am here to pay off."

"Tell Fortescue that's real generous," I say. "Did you take him to a doctor?"

"He won't go. He's a very stubborn chap."

"Don't tell me," I say.

"He also sends his apologies, Corporal, and says he would like a return match some day, but not under the Indian rules."

"I'll bet he would," I say, "but tell him no thanks."

That should of been the end of it but after C.E. Knoblauch leaves, Ransom shows up and says Lieutenant Luna wants me on the double. Ransom has been made headquarters clerk and keeps the rest of us informed on what's going on higher up.

I ain't had two words with Luna since I enlisted, and only seen him at a distance drilling some of the men, but I know this has to be about the fight.

"What else?" Ransom says. "Fighting's against army regulations. I heard him tell Lieutenant Leahy he was going to have your ass for breakfast."

"What about Fortescue?"

"Him and Mitchell too. But mainly it's you he's raving about. He told Leahy you near blinded him when you and him had that shoot-out in Socorro. Is that true, Lee?"

"Of course it ain't. There wasn't no shoot-out and we only splashed some soup on him getting off the train in such a hurry."

This tickles Ransom and he says, "You sure are a card, Lee. If

I didn't know you better, I'd swear you was telling the truth."

That's one of my troubles all my life. When I did stick to the straight and narrow, nobody believed me because facts ain't necessarily the truth. My grandson Pete says facts are easy to distort but the truth is always there like a rock at the center. He says in medicine, doctors argue over facts all the time trying to get at the truth. Luna always knew the truth about anything, and he was usually the first one to get at it, like a dog digging a bone. But he had a talent for arranging facts to suit himself, especially if they was other people's. Ransom says Luna wants to court-martial me now.

I might of known.

XI

Choirboys

How Fortescue got himself stitched up and cleaned up I don't know, but he made it to the headquarters tent with the help of Mitchell and some friends. Mitchell's there on Luna's orders, because he was referee. Ransom tells us to wait because Luna's with the first sergeant, so I say to Fortescue, "How do you feel?"

His boots are shined and his uniform's neat, but he ain't easy to recognize with sticking plaster holding his face together. His eyes are puffed and blue, and the left one's nearly closed. He looked better covered with blood.

"Did the men get all their money?" he asks me. Mitchell has to translate this because Fortescue's lips are so swollen his words are hard to understand.

"They was real pleased," I say.

Mitchell explains, "It hurts him to talk, but he's sorry."

"So am I," I say, looking at what I done.

And this Fortescue lays a hand on my arm and pats it. "My fault, not yours," he says. "What do you think the lieutenant will do?"

"If we're lucky, crucifixion or maybe we get boiled in oil."

He asks me please, not to make him laugh.

I ain't trying to be funny. I tell him that Luna's the toughest, meanest, nastiest, orneriest, most bigoted son of a bitch I ever met on this earth, and if there's a way he can dump on me, he'll find it. I'm about to go on with my description when Mitchell jumps to his feet, yelling, "Attention!" I help Fortescue up before I see Luna in the flesh, starched and ironed as always, his mustache trimmed, fresh as new paint and looking the very picture of the model officer.

"Come in, gentlemen," he says. "You, too, Garland."

We line up inside the tent as the first sergeant gives us a look like poison and walks out.

"At ease," Luna tells us.

He paces for a minute without saying anything, deep in thought, or pretending to be. He's got a new riding crop and every so often he taps it on the table. He's got the Articles of War opened out in front of him.

"Trooper Fortescue," he says, "I am told you are a member of the New York Stock Exchange, that you play polo and sing in a passable tenor. Is that correct?"

Fortescue mumbles, "Yes, sir."

"It is your passable tenor that interests me," says Luna.

Well, I know he's the craftiest bastard in the army, and I think I got him pegged good, but this time Luna's got me flummoxed.

"Trooper Mitchell," he says, "Before being in moving pictures you were one of the stars of Christie's Minstrel Show, and are a trained baritone."

"Sir . . ." Mitchell says, starting to protest.

"I haven't finished," Luna tells him, still tapping that god-damned riding crop.

He looks me up and down, like he don't know whether to swat me with the quirt or stick it in my eye. In the end he just points it at my chin and he ain't smiling. "Corporal Garland," he says to the others, "also has a musical background," which comes as news to me. "I have heard the corporal sing a lot of different tunes since I first made his acquaintance."

"Excuse me, sir," Mitchell says, "but I think you've got the wrong men."

"For your sake, you better hope not," Luna says. "Brawling on an army post is a court-martial offense." He flicks a page or two of the Articles of War. "So is unlawful assembly to commit mayhem. So is assault on a noncommissioned officer by a private soldier and vice versa. So is unauthorized assembly for immoral purposes, which includes gambling. The penalties range from sixty days loss of pay and reduction in rank, to twenty years at hard labor. Do I make myself clear?"

"Yes, sir," Mitchell sighs.

"Now then," Luna tells us, "about the music. Colonel Wood is partial to bands, but Colonel Roosevelt especially likes choral singing. He spoke with the chaplain, and the chaplain asked me. And I'm telling you, to organize a choir."

Knowing Luna, I would of been less surprised by forty years in solitary. "How do we do that?" I ask him.

He looks from one to the other of us and says, "If you peckerwoods can round up a hundred men to watch you fight, you can round them up to sing. I have the names of everyone who was behind the cook tent this afternoon. Pass the word to those who don't want to spend their idle hours singing that I can invent other activities a lot more strenuous."

Years later when I asked Luna how that choir idea ever struck him, he just laughed. "I was madder than a snake," he says, "and I swore I'd put you boys digging a ditch all the way to Cuba. But the chaplain caught me off guard. He knew about Mitchell and Fortescue having good voices and said a choir would be more use to the regiment's morale than a lot of holes in the ground."

"He was right," I said.

"My problem was you," Luna told me. "Every time I had you by the short hair, you got off."

"Not all the way," I reminded him. "I wound up digging your goddamn ditch anyway."

"Oh, that," he says. "After the riot, the least I could do was give you some something to do with your hands."

The riot, as he called it, never would have happened without the choir.

We was up every day before dawn, and after a terrible breakfast we drilled until noon. After a lousy lunch, we drilled again until five, when we quit for a rotten supper. Then there was guard duty and cleanup details and latrine police. Everybody's complaining because we got no horses yet and we're doing everything on foot. For a cavalry regiment, our morale was poor.

The idle hours Luna mentioned was few, and for a while the choir filled them. I can't carry a tune in a shovel, so I was the organizer. Mason Mitchell knew all the hymns and popular songs, and once Fortescue's jaw healed, he turned out to be the best tenor I ever heard. Henry Haefner, who was more famous for throwing a rope, joined us too, with his high, sweet voice almost like a girl's. Mountain had a fine deep bass when he sung, and learned the words even if he couldn't read. He was the most enthusiastic choir-boy in the outfit.

Luna often wandered by to listen to Mitchell drill us on the harmony parts of a song. I'd be sort of following along, trying not to make too much noise, when I'd hear him hiss behind me, "Sing out, Garland, if you know what's good for you!"

The funny part is we were pretty good. A hundred men singing "Amazing Grace" in harmony or "Tenting Tonight" or "Old Black Joe" could bring tears to your eyes, and when we cut loose with "Onward Christian Soldiers" it'd give you goose bumps.

The word gets around San Antonio about our singing, and one day we're invited to sing a concert in the Riverside Park. We ain't been allowed out of the camp since we got there, so everybody's looking forward to going into town. We look pretty good with our hats at a rakish angle and blue polka-dot bandannas around our necks. We ain't much as soldiers yet, and we ain't been on a horse since we come into the army, but we was hot stuff as singers.

Before the concert, Mountain, me and Cody head for one of the local pleasure parlors where they say the girls ain't too hard on the eyes, but most of the choir's already there and it looks like a ten-hour wait. Levi Hennings catches up with us all excited because he just passed a nickelodeon theatre where they're showing a moving picture of Mitchell's. Everybody wants to go, even Mitchell, although he pretends it ain't one of his better efforts.

Some of us, including me, never seen a moving picture before. Out front is a big poster of Mitchell and his lady star Leonora Love. She's beautiful and he's some fancy cowboy with a big handlebar mustache and a Stetson about a foot tall. The place is packed but we all find seats down front next to the piano player.

The story's about some bank robbers who escape with Leonora Love as hostage. Mitchell's the sheriff and he goes riding after them. Everything Tom Isbell and the others said about him is true except it's hard to get used to him wearing lipstick and rouge, and funny as hell seeing all that white smoke when the shooting starts. But I never seen a better rider. And can he shoot! We shout, "Get him, Mitch!" when he takes off after the bad guys, and people in the theatre are shushing us. When one of the robbers tries to bushwhack old Mitchell, Levi yells, "Look out, Mitch, he's got a gun!" But Mitchell sees him in time and shoots him off a rock so he falls about forty feet. Some other guy tells us to pipe down, but we're caught up in the story and pretty excited. About then, the picture bursts into flame and the real Mitchell curses.

We never do get to see the end because the owner threatens to call the military police if we don't leave. He says we're a public nuisance and he won't have cursing in his nickelodeon.

Cody says, "You wouldn't even have a nickelodeon if it weren't for Mason Mitchell here."

The owner says, "Sure, and I suppose you're Leonora Love."

"Forget it," Mitchell says. "Let's go, boys."

We're in such good spirits after seeing our friend on the silver screen nobody can make us mad. So we go wet our whistles at the beer garden where we're going to give our concert. They got German waiters in white aprons and you could get a pitcher of suds for a nickel, with free sauerkraut and corned beef, which was wonderful after the army swill we been used to.

By twilight we all got a nice buzz on because the other customers keep treating us to more pitchers. We go through a river of beer in a couple hours.

It's dark when the rest of the choir shows up and the band arrives. By now the place is crowded and there's no more free tables for the people standing around. In our group only C.E. Knoblauch and Haefner are sober because neither of them touches alcohol. Fortescue and some of the others been drinking too, so everybody's in fine singing voice.

The band, in their fine scarlet coats and white duck pants, looks more like soldiers than we do. They play awhile before the bandmaster announces us on the program. As we start to get up some tough-looking Texans move in to our tables. Ransom tells these fellows we're coming right back as soon as we finish singing, but they say if we leave the tables, we leave them for good. So Cody says, "You don't understand. We been invited to sing."

One fellow nearly as big as Mountain says, "Nobody's stopping you, soldier."

"But we want to keep our tables," Cody says.

"That ain't possible," this big fellow says. We're all surprised because until now the civilians have been real friendly, but mostly older men who was buying us beer and telling us to kick hell out of the Spaniards. These fellows are different, mule skinners and gandy dancers our own age mostly. This is their town, and they're jealous.

Fortescue's behind Cody and naturally he's got to make a speech. I learned to like him after our first disagreement, and our friendship lasted a lifetime. But he always was a funny gink for all his good points, and he could irritate a saint with the prissy, affected way he talked. This was misleading, because sometimes he sounded like a pansy, and people didn't realize how dangerous he was.

The bandmaster's calling for us, and Mitchell says, "Come on, boys, we'll sort out the tables when we finish."

"This will only take a moment," Fortescue says, but the big Texan makes a bad mistake then. He picks up Fortescue's hat and shoves it at him.

Fortescue ain't about to leave now because he's been insulted and he's had enough to drink so the insult's got a sting. "If you insist on remaining here uninvited, we will find it necessary to chuck you out."

The Texan don't answer, just gives Fortescue a shove that knocks over a pitcher of beer. Mitchell says, "Oh, no! Here we go."

Fortescue wipes the foam off his sleeve and sets the pitcher upright. Then he says, calm as ice, "You deserve a thrashing for that." Fortescue was elegant even when he brawled.

I remember seeing Luna and some other officers arrive about then, but most of my attention is on Fortescue. He yells, "Indian rules, boys!" and lays the Texan out with a right to the head. He kicks the next one square in the balls and the free-for all is on, with the whole choir and half of Texas choosing up sides. There's beer pitchers broke over heads and tables upturned. The band plays and women scream. For a while it's hard to see who's winning.

I jump on a table and fire my Colt in the air, thinking I can stop things by shocking everybody. But it has the opposite effect from what I intend because Cody and Ransom do it too. Nothing slows the fight down until the local police and soldiers from the provost guard arrive. They arrest a few, but most of us get away. The concert never does happen and the place is sort of a shambles when things quiet down.

We all get back to the camp nursing our cuts and bruises, but

laughing the whole time. Except me. I know Luna seen the fracas
and it's only a matter of time before we hear from him. He's going
to take it personal. There ain't no point in trying to explain because he'll say it's our fault. But I'm wrong. He don't spread the
blame around. He puts it all on me.

Colonel Roosevelt wants us disciplined and Luna's the officer in
charge. Ransom also overheard Ben Butler tell Luna not to be too
hard on us because no real damage was done except to some beer
pitchers and a couple of reputations.

"Mainly mine," Luna says, "because I went along with that damn
fool choir idea."

When Butler asks him how the fight started, he says, "How do
you think? Your boy Garland jumping on tables like a dog with
fleas, and shooting off his pistol."

Ben Butler ain't too proud of us himself at that moment, but he's
trying to be fair. "I'm sure the boys were provoked," he says, "but
that still doesn't excuse them."

Ransom says Luna just goes on muttering about how he'll fix us,
his mind closed as usual.

He puts us digging a ditch, and the work is hot, hard and dusty.
He would of had us there in the sun, chipping away at Texas dirt
for the whole war, but the army fooled him. Two days after the
concert that never was, Lieutenant Leahy comes running over to
the headquarters tent yelling, "Get a move on! Sergeant, turn out
the men!"

"What is it? What happened?"

"The horses! They're here!"

There's some fine-looking animals all right, but not a single one
is broke to a saddle. Our work is cut out for us and Luna forgets
the ditch digging in a minute. Life around Camp Wood is a perpet-
ual rodeo with dust and sweat and yelling as we climb on and got
throwed and climb on again, until the horses get the idea.

We work in teams of two, and I pair off with Henry Haefner.
Henry throws the rope and reels the bronco in until he can tuck
the critter's muzzle under his armpit and bite down on an ear while
I climb aboard. The tenderfeet laugh at this but it's the only way
to quiet a mustang. Some hands say it's because the horse is blind
against your shirt, and with teeth clamped on his ear he's confused
for a while. But the Easterners claim it's cowboy armpits that stun
the poor beast.

A dozen men land in the hospital with broken bones and split heads before Ben Butler intervenes. He says he can't afford the casualties so he's going to show us a easier way. He gets close enough to caress the horse's neck and slip on a halter. Then he whispers sweet nothings while he eases on a saddle without cinching it up, walking the horse around. Only after he's been making love to that animal for fifteen or twenty minutes will he get on. He gets throwed too, but not often. Usually they just buck a couple of times and settle right down. The man who got one of Ben Butler's horses got a soft-mouth mount he could do anything with.

Except for Mason Mitchell. It's near dark and there's a lot of expectation when he draws his horse because we think we'll see some real fancy tricks even though the animal's just fresh broke. But Mitchell fools us and starts clowning.

First he puts the bridle on upside down and gets the martingale twisted in the saddle cinch. Everybody's howling with laughter because we know any second he's going to vault on that mustang and show us things we never seen before. But he keeps it up until we got tears running down our faces from laughing. He's the greatest actor in the world, walking around that horse like it's a giraffe. Ben Butler finally gets impatient and says, "Come on, Mitchell! The war's waiting!"

But Mitchell ain't finished. We're sitting on the corral fence, busting a gut, when he says, "Will someone please help me?" and that about paralyzes the whole troop with laughter again because the very idea of Mason Mitchell needing help with a horse is the absolute limit. Mountain plays along by going over to give him a leg up. But Mitchell even turns that into a joke by putting his right boot in Mountain's hand instead of his left so when he heaves, Mitchell winds up backward in the saddle and goes flopping off into the twilight with us about to die.

We agree it's the funniest clown act we ever seen in or out of a circus, but after supper he still ain't back. When he does show just before taps he looks like he's been dusting the prairie with his face.

He says, "I thought you were my friends, and you all sat there laughing like fools."

"But you're the greatest rider in the world," Tom Isbell says. "Everybody knows that."

"I've never been on a horse in my life."

"But we seen you!" Levi says.

"You saw a moving picture," he says, and then he tells us how it's all hokeyed up so it looks real, but it's done with other riders or fake horses.

"You have to be able to ride in the cavalry," Cody tells him. "Didn't they tell you that when you joined?"

"I always assumed when the time came you boys would show me what to do," he says.

Well, it's the biggest disillusion for all of us but we are his friends, so every man agrees we'll keep his secret.

"Mitch?" Cody says.

"Yes?"

"What did they ask you when you joined?"

"Nothing," Mitchell says. "Why?"

I say, "What he means, Mitch, is can you shoot or do we have to teach you that too?"

"I can shoot I guess," Mitchell says, "but I never tried it with real bullets so I'm not sure if I'll hit anything."

We take turns working with Mitchell until he can sit a horse proper and make it go where he wants. Mountain even gives him camphorated pork fat to rub on his chafed legs and rear end, and Mitchell limps around for a while smelling like rancid bacon and mothballs.

We forget all about why we are in San Antonio, forget about the war and the Spaniards. It happens when men are doing what they like. The food's as bad as ever and the sun just as hot, but the griping stops. It's a grand vacation from everything when all we have to worry about is teaching a horse his manners.

Then we hear we're going to have a regimental parade and there never was such a scrubbing and currying and washing and polishing as occupies us for two days. We're a sight, with every Rough Rider at his best, hundreds of horses gleaming, troop pennants snapping in the breeze and the colors rippling at the head of the regiment. The officers watch us pass in review and you can feel the pride in everybody. Three weeks before, we was a bunch of range hands and polo players, swells and cowboys. Men like Fortescue, who's a millionaire, and Mountain, who can hardly write his name. Cody, who shouldn't of been there because of his lungs, and Mitchell, who just learned to ride. Levi with his goddamned dog running along behind the troop, Tom Isbell, a full-blooded Indian sergeant, and me, Lee Garland, who never wanted to be in no army anyway, having the time of my life. It's our first formation as a mounted cavalry regiment, and although we don't know it then, it's our last.

The "Parade of the Innocents" Fortescue called it, and he was right. Looking at us then, a stranger would not have agreed. We're lean and tanned and ready for action. We counted among us men who was as hard-bitten, slit-eyed and tough as any on the Western frontier. Cowboys, miners, gamblers, hunters, gold prospectors, Indian-fighters, mule skinners and the like. But all of them was innocent when it come to the war we was going off to fight.

Quite a few didn't come back or come back with scars that never healed or died of fever after they got home. We even had a deserter or two. Colonel Roosevelt and some others got famous out of the war and served their country in other ways.

The men liked Roosevelt, which was funny in a way, because he wasn't such a likable man. He's arrogant and opinionated and don't care whose toes he steps on. He's critical of everything we do and as tough on the officers as he is on the men. He has a way, like a lot of Easterners, of looking down his nose, which some people say is snobbish but in his case is mainly because he can't see without his eyeglasses.

There ain't nothing he won't do for the men. He has more energy than ten of us, and he's criticized by some because he's always out front taking the bows. But he was out front dodging the bullets too, and why he wasn't killed God only knows.

He went to bat for us in Washington to get the new Krag carbines we carry, when all the other volunteer units still had old Springfields from the Civil War. It's him gets us cotton uniforms when the rest of the army goes to Cuba dressed in blue wool. He tried to find us better food and medicine there too, but didn't have much luck, which ain't his fault.

After the war, and after he become president, and even after he left the White House, he didn't change except maybe to grow more sure of himself with so much responsibility. I didn't know it in the army, but he was a genius. All his life he wrote books and letters and articles and God only knows where he found the time because besides politics he was a family man with a houseful of kids.

He wrote me a letter after the First War. I still got it here somewhere. It says, "No principle of justice, no ideal of right and

no belief in a cause can replace a son or make up for his lost life."
It was how I felt then and still do. One of his own boys was killed
in that war.

Once I met a man who'd known him since they was kids. He said
he wouldn't give a Confederate dollar for T.R.'s chances as a boy.
He was skinny and had the asthma, couldn't see a goddamned
thing and stuttered when grown-ups spoke to him. But he lifted
weights and went working on a ranch and run a mile every day and
learned to box. He was a man knew how to overcome his liabilities
and he was afraid of nothing.

Years after the war, at a Rough Rider reunion over in Las Vegas,
I ask him about that. I say, "I seen you do some damn fool things
under fire at Las Guásimas and Kettle Hill," and he laughs. "Tell
the truth, Colonel," I say, "was you ever scared?"

And he says, "I'll tell you, Lee, because you were there. I was
scared to death of losing my specs and making a fool of myself."

I been around almost ninety years and we was only in Cuba fifty
days, but every minute of it's etched in my head with acid. I don't
know why that should be except I never got closer to my own life
than there. It's when I really smelled it and felt it and knew there
wasn't any other reason for anything in the world than just Lee
Garland being alive. I learned then that no hereafter could ever
measure up to the here and now, for all the complaining we do.

I believe that was something the men sensed about Roosevelt
too. He was in love with life and always give it everything he had.
He wasn't a man you could get close to like Ben Butler, and he
probably wasn't half as good a military mind as Colonel Wood or
Luna. I've heard criticism and backbiting from people not good
enough to black his boots, jealous politicians and armchair generals mostly, people who like the taste of sour grapes. They called
him a crank, conservationist, opportunist, jingoist, what-have-you,
before his career was over. And he was all of them things. But he
was a great American too, a man who understood our possibilities
as well as our past. He was reckless and stubborn, a show-off and
a dreamer. But he knew what most politicians never learn or tend
to forget, that if a man loves his land and what it gives him, he dies
in its debt.

A day or two after the big parade we're jacking our gear to leave
for Tampa, Florida, when Levi shows up in a state. "You fellows
seen Heinz?"

Mountain burps and says, "What I had for breakfast might of been him, Levi, but I can't be sure."

And C.E. Knoblauch tips one of the buzzacot ovens we're loading in Levi's direction and says, "Take a look, Levi. There may be enough left here to identify."

"Stop kidding," Levi says. "I can't find him anywhere and I been all over camp."

He's so sad the men feel sorry for him and we mount a search as soon as we jack the last kettle into the last wagon. Usually when the dog ain't with Levi he's hanging around the cook tent, but nobody's seen him all day. Then Ransom says he spotted him outside the fence, humping a fox terrier around nine o'clock. We tell Levi we'll cover for him while he goes looking, and we all get back to work.

Fortescue and I are among the lucky ones who get passes that afternoon, and he wants to close out his local bank account. The manager kisses his ass and says he'll transfer Fortescue's sixty thousand dollar balance immediately back to the Chase Bank in New York. "Jesus," I say, "how much money have you got?"

"I'm not sure," he says, "because I have trouble keeping up with the market out here. But the last time I looked, my net worth was around ten million."

"Your old man give you all that?"

"By no means," he says. "I inherited two million dollars from an uncle but the rest has come from my own profitable investments."

"You got to show me how it's done when the war's over."

"Do you have any capital, Lee?"

I'm thinking of his ten million when I say, "Only about a hundred fifty thousand."

He stops dead in his tracks and looks me in the eye. "Really?" he says, "or are you pulling my leg?"

"Really," I tell him.

"Forgive me for saying this, but you don't give the impression of a man with that kind of money in the bank."

"I don't try to," I say. By now we're out of the bank, waiting at the trolley stop. San Antonio's got the new electric ones, not the old horsecars like in El Paso, and one of them comes along at a hell of a clip and screeches to a stop for us. We climb on but the motorman won't take our nickels because we're soldiers.

"I had no idea," Fortescue says to himself, amazed, like my having money suddenly gives me a whole new dimension in his eyes. "But you can't leave all that capital in a bank. It's criminal."

"I can't carry it around," I tell him.

"It should be in the stock market," he says.

"How do I do that?"

"Any brokerage can invest it for you. Railroads, manufacturing, government bonds, whatever you want."

This is the first time I heard anybody talk sense about money since Charlie Bruce. Most people don't understand it at all. They think it's something you have to work for and earn, while any thief or banker knows that ain't the case at all.

"What looks good to you now?"

"I favor petroleum stocks, or anything to do with the war," he says with a smile. "Wars are always profitable. You could say I joined the Rough Riders to protect my investments. What about you, Lee?"

"You could say the army was the lesser of two evils."

"What was the other evil? A pregnant girl?"

"Jail," I tell him, and he busts out laughing. "I think it's time for a drink, don't you?"

"One thing is certain," Fortescue says. "We can't go back to that beer garden again."

We head for the Alamo Hotel, which ain't as picturesque as the Exchange in Santa Fe or as luxurious as the Victoria Palace in Chihuahua, but it's one of San Antonio's best, a far piece from Camp Wood or the beer garden. We ease into big leather sofas, light up two Havanas from the cigar counter, and order us some whiskey and ice.

Fortescue raises his glass and says, serious for a minute, "Here's to us, Lee. May we both come back in one piece."

I drink to that. We're on our second whiskey, talking about the investment market when I see a woman in the outer lobby. She's got her back to me but the view I get is inviting. She don't turn around and after a minute or two I'm dying to see the other side and not paying much attention to Fortescue's explanation of the petroleum market. I excuse myself to visit the men's room just so I can get a look.

She's standing like she's waiting for someone and she's good-looking all right, with a birdwing hat and pale blue dress, and a upswept hairdo sets off her face just right. I know that face. I walk up to her and say, "Hello, Rose-of-Sharon. Remember me?"

"I beg your pardon," she says, in a accent as thick as enchilada sauce.

"Lee Garland from Chihuahua," I say.

"*Dios mio!*" She throws her arms around me like we was long lost cousins and wants to know what I'm doing playing soldier and how's Cody and Mountain and Charlie Bruce. Women ain't allowed in the Alamo bar, but just then Fortescue comes out and sees us in each other's arms. I introduce him, and Rose-of-Sharon's girl friend shows up so we all go for a drink to another place and then to a vaudeville show.

Rose-of-Sharon's still working the same trade but at a higher level. She was cruising the Alamo for customers when I showed up, she tells me, but there's nobody they'd rather spend some time with than me and my friend. They got a place we can all go to which ain't a whorehouse, but it's expensive. I say how much and she says how long?

"Until ten or eleven?"

"Fifty dollar," she says, always the business woman.

"I thought we was old friends," I say.

"That's why so cheap," she tells me.

"You know how much a soldier makes?" I ask her.

"Come on, Lee," she says. "You got money. You go make war, get killed, no more fooky-fooky. What you want, fancy tomb?"

She always was one to put a man's world in perspective. "Okay," I say, "but I pay for both of us and you tell your friend not to say anything about the two of you charging."

"So he think it's free?"

"That's the idea."

"She won't like that."

"It's his birthday. I want to give him a present."

"Oh! You're crazy man, Lee, but I love you," she says, and agrees to keep quiet about them being whores.

Fortescue's having fun with the other one and Rose-of-Sharon arranges everything. Her girl friend at least speaks English, and I can see she's charmed by Fortescue's manners as well as his physique. The place they take us is real respectable looking, like a private home with a nice big parlor, and where each girl has her own room.

I disappear with Rose-of-Sharon after a while and she gives me a workout. I seen then what got Cody so interested. She's all curves and silky skin under her corsets, and she likes to give a man a good time. She knows so many ways to stick it in and take it out and play with it and diddle it and lick it and ride it without making you come, that when a body finally does get there it's like a Vesuvius eruption.

Maybe it's because I been so long without a woman, but I don't think so. Rose-of-Sharon Moriarty was a first-class whore, and they're few and far between, like the top of any profession. She could be a pain in the ass, and a vain, greedy little minx, but when she worked, she give you your money's worth, even at fifty dollars a throw.

It's after ten o'clock when we take the trolley back to camp. Fortescue's happy as a horned toad and says we couldn't have spent our time better. "By the way," he says, "many happy returns."

"What?"

"Happy Birthday. You should have told me earlier."

"It ain't my birthday," I say.

"But the girl told me it was," he says.

I'm beginning to get a glimmer of something here and I say, "What else did she tell you?"

He hesitates like the gentleman he is, and says, "Well, that's all, Lee, why?"

"She didn't suggest you pay my bill for me as a birthday present?"

He laughs, a little embarrassed. "As a matter of fact she did. Until that moment I wasn't sure they were . . . professional ladies."

"And you paid it."

"Well, yes."

I tell him about my conversation with Rose-of-Sharon Moriarty and the hundred dollars I give her and we sit there in the trolley car, laughing like fools at how we got taken.

It's a half-mile hike from the end of the trolley line to our tents and we're picking our way along in the dark when I hear a whimpering and see something off the road. I walk over to investigate and find Heinz cowering in the shrubbery. He's been in a fight and part of one ear's chewed off. He can't walk but on three legs so I pick him up and carry him

The sentry on duty is Henry Haefner so he don't even look up when we come in. It's long after taps and the men are sound asleep, but we take the dog to Levi's tent, figuring he'll be happy to see him. Ransom's his bunkmate and he rolls out to tell us Levi never come back since morning. He's still out looking for the dog, and now the provost guard from Fort Sam Houston are out looking for him.

Ransom tends to the dog but the next morning at reveille, there's still no sign of Levi Hennings. We start jacking baggage into freight cars, and by five o'clock when we board the train, Levi still ain't showed. Nobody in the provost marshal's office knows where he is, and Tom Isbell says our headquarters will have to put him down as absent without leave if he ain't on the train when we pull out.

"What do we do if Levi don't show?" Cody asks me. "We can't leave old Heinz."

"Then put him out of his misery," Mitchell tells him.

"I'll take him," Mountain says. "I'll carry him in my shirt."

The train pulls out at two o'clock in the morning and it takes us five miserable days to reach Tampa, Florida. Anybody'd think the railroads is working for the Spanish the way they treat us. There's no ice to cool the cars and no food for the men. Sixty horses and fifteen mules die from lack of water, and Colonel Roosevelt says he'll see the railroad president in hell before he'll let the army pay the bill. When the train finally gets to Florida, Levi Hennings is posted as a deserter.

XII

I Fall in Love

Tampa's the best training in the world for the war in Cuba. I mean, learning how to sleep in the heat and eat in the rain, with centipedes and scorpions for company, and our first bouts of fever. But what excites us most is the new Colt machine guns Fortescue's millionaire friends, Lieutenant Kane and Sergeant Tiffany, buy the regiment with their own money. Nobody'd fired the guns yet, but they could shoot five hundred smokeless-powder rounds a minute and was supposed to be ten times as reliable as the old Gatlings. We also have a field gun that fires a twenty-pound charge of dynamite, a new kind of shell that's propelled by compressed air and the newspapers say will blast the Spaniards out of Cuba. Everybody stands around admiring it when it arrives.

We set our dog tents where they tell us in a hollow next to a mangrove swamp behind the Tampa Bay Hotel. It rains every day for a couple hours and the water drains into our camp instead of out of it. The mosquitoes are ferocious and the flies around the horses and mules drive us all crazy. Malaria starts up and some cases of typhus. The only one who don't have to shit eighteen times a day is Mountain because he mixes his own remedy from kerosene, mint and Fuller's earth. It stops him up pretty good, but nobody else can swallow it. He's also addicted to pipsissewa tea, an old Ute Indian remedy, and he carries a supply of the leaves with him. It's bitter as gall but it works.

Cody's the hardest hit, but he won't turn in sick. He loses five pounds a week and says he has to push his asshole back in place every time he stands. But he hangs on somehow, and don't complain. He could never keep up in the best of times and I tell him just between us, "Damn it, turn yourself in and the surgeon will discharge you. You got no business being here anyway. Luna's not chasing you now."

"I can't do it," he says, paler and more peaked than ever.

"You mean you don't want to. I can loan you enough money until you get on your feet and you won't have to go to Cuba."

"I can't, Lee."

"Why, for Christ's sake?"

His eyes start to water and he says, "I just goddamn can't!"

"We're not going to carry you, Cody," I warn him. "Every man's got to pull his load."

"You sound just like a corporal, you know that?"

"Do yourself a favor, Cody,"

"I'll do my share," he says.

"And if you can't," I tell him, irritated, "you figure me or Mountain will always be there to help. Right?"

He grins like a little kid and says, "I know that, Lee. Ever since Jake died I knowed I could count on you both."

"Well, goddamn it, there ain't no guaranty of that in a war! What do you think Jake would do if he was in your shoes?"

"He'd of run off from the army long ago," Cody says, and I know he's growing up a little, even if he is still a damn fool kid.

Mountain nurses Levi's dog until his bites heal, but that poor hound wasn't the same without his master. He moped around, ate poorly and got scrawnier than ever, a poor excuse for a mascot. But we wasn't much to look at as a regiment either, so it evened out.

There was always poker games or Mexican monte, but the popular new game we learn from the colored cavalry is craps. It's fast, easy and portable. A poncho throwed down anywhere serves as the table and somebody always has dice in his pocket. It's also very democratic with black men and white men, rich men and poor men all able to get in the game. It's amazing to see the sums wagered in a crap game between troopers only make thirteen dollars a month. More than once I seen three or four hundred dollars riding on one roll of the dice. We all try our luck, and as usual the rich get richer and the poor go broke.

Whiskey is scarce and women even scarcer around the camp at

first. But where there's soldiers sooner or later you're going to find both aplenty. At night if we ain't too tired, we walk the four miles to Last Chance Street, as the soldiers call it, which is nothing more than some tents and shacks on a sandpit near Ybor City. It wasn't no city, just poor niggers and Cuban refugees huddled in a tropical slum. Every tent is a bar or a whorehouse, and in between are stands where fat mammies sell fried chicken and pork ribs cooked over charcoal, the only decent food most of the men get in Tampa. A chicken wing costs a nickel, whiskey is two bits and the whores charge a dollar.

Those of us can afford it wander over to the Tampa Bay Hotel instead, and sit drinking soda pop or whiskey. The hotel has a huge red brick rotunda in the Moorish style, five hundred rooms, a million dollars worth of furniture, a casino and an indoor swimming pool. Fortescue says it's an insult to the eyes. But the view from the veranda is like a postcard, with oleanders and coconut palms and swamp oaks covered with gray moss like Christmas decorations. Women come to the Tampa Bay Hotel too. Not whores but relatives and officers' wives. When a man spends his time night and day with a hundred other horny-handed, cussing, sweaty bodies just like himself, it's a pleasure just to see a woman sometimes. They move different, smell different and sound different, and it's the difference a man misses as much as the honeypot.

One day when I'm enjoying the view over an iced sarsparilla with Mitchell and Fortescue before getting down to serious drinking, I see a woman makes me hold my breath. She can't be more than seventeen, with auburn hair swept up under a straw boater, and eyes green as emeralds. In them days with ankle-length skirts and tight corsets you couldn't always tell how good a woman's body was until you got her undressed. But with some women you just knew that what was underneath had to be as slick as what was showing, and this girl is that kind.

We all watch her come out of the rotunda and look around the veranda for a chair. Her style of beauty is the haughty, heartbreaking kind that you'd risk your neck for a smile. Each of us is about to offer her our chair when a busybody waiter says, "Right over here, miss," and points her to a wicker rocker a good safe distance from where we're sitting. She orders a root beer and starts fanning herself with one of them little fold-up fans women carried in their purses. Our conversation is stopped dead until Fortescue says, "Whoever loved that loved not at first sight?"

"Shakespeare," Mitchell explains. *"As You Like It."*

"As you like what?" I say, dumber than a duck.

"The title of a play. Lee, we're going to have to educate you in the finer things of life."

"Like what?"

"Theatre, opera, ballet," Fortescue says. "It's the only way you'll ever interest a girl of her quality."

"Who says I want to interest her?"

Mitchell says. "Is she or is she not the most beautiful creature you ever laid eyes on?"

"She is," I say, telling the truth.

"Then how can you say you don't want her?" Fortescue says. "Everyone wants a woman like that, but the race goes only to the swift. And to be swift, you need polish."

This is only a harmless game we're playing, and cheaper than losing at craps. She can't hear us, but I feel she knows we're talking about her because every now and then she glances our way.

"Women of her class don't even kiss before marriage," Fortescue warns me.

I laugh at that. "Jesus, you're full of shit."

Mitchell says, "We start by cleaning up his speech."

"I don't use bad language in front of women."

"That isn't what he means," Fortescue says.

They don't get to start the lesson because at that moment Luna strides on the porch, saying, "Garland, get over to headquarters on the double! The colonel's looking for you."

"Colonel Roosevelt?" I say.

"Corporal, how many colonels do you know?"

I'm about to risk asking what Roosevelt wants me for when this girl rises from her chair. "Excuse me," she says.

Luna turns around, very polite, and clicks his heels with a small bow. You'd think he was in the Spanish army instead of ours when a woman's around. "Yes, miss?" he says, all *caballero*.

She gives him a sweet smile but she's speaking to me. "Are you Mr. Garland?" she says. Her voice is as soft and pretty as her face.

"Yes, ma'am," I say.

"Mr. Lee Garland?"

"That's right."

She starts to tremble and her eyes get misty in spite of her smile.

"You are the Mr. Lee Garland associated with Mr. Charles Bruce?"

"Charlie was my partner," I say, and then the dawn begins to come. But before I can say anything else she drops her fan and throws her arms around me.

"Oh, Mr. Garland," she says. "At last I've found you! Oh, God bless you, Mr. Garland!" And she starts to cry in my arms while I look over the top of her head at Fortescue and Mitchell, who stand with their mouths open like two dummies watching a sideshow.

Luna's the first one to get his bearings. "Are you Miss Bruce?" he says.

"Yes," she says. "I'm Caroline Bruce."

"My compliments, miss. I am Lieutenant Luna. I'll tell Colonel Roosevelt you have Corporal Garland in hand so we can call off the search." Then he turns to me and I never seen him so polite. "Corporal," he says, like we was old pals from Sunday school, "why not escort Miss Bruce to one of the lounges, where you'll have some privacy?"

"Thank you, sir," I say, and give him a snappy salute.

I steer Caroline Bruce toward the rotunda while she says, "Please forgive me, Mr. Garland." She's daubing at her eyes with a little silk handkerchief, but she's smiling. "I'm afraid I've embarrassed you in front of your friends."

"Nothing to forgive," I say. "I'm glad you found me."

Fortescue and Mitchell are still staring after us so she stops to apologize. "Mr. Garland is my brother's dearest friend," she tells them. "Charles would not be alive today if not for him."

I'm still in a bit of a whirl myself when I finally sit down with her alone in one corner of the lounge. It is cooler under the big ceiling fans. "How is Charlie?" I say.

"Quite well, Mr. Garland, after a very tiring journey."

"He's here?" I ask her. We're sitting side by side on a divan. She's wearing a linen dress the color of frosted mint and a couple locks of her hair is loose under the straw boater. Up close I can see her skin is as beautiful as the rest of her, and she has slender, graceful hands. I wish I was back on the veranda with her arms around me again, but talking with her is fun too.

"Charles is resting, but in a while I'll take you up to see him." I tell her how happy I am they made the connection, and she says,

"We were so afraid you would not be here."

The telegram I sent from El Paso didn't catch up with them until they got to New York. Charlie wired me in San Antonio but that message was lost somewhere in the army. When he heard the regiment had moved here, he decided to come in person.

"We tried to find you, Mr. Garland, but no one knew where you'd gone," she says.

"I had some business over in New Mexico," I say.

"Oh, Charles told me about your bank. He said you were modest and unassuming, Mr. Garland, and I see for myself he is quite right. I believe he was mistaken, however, to call you rough and cynical."

"Well, I don't know," I say.

"A cynical man would not have saved my brother's life and his money. Could it be a pretense on your part to conceal a loyal and generous heart?" she says, smiling.

I'm not about to disabuse her of this notion even though I am embarrassed. I don't know it yet, but I'm in love with her already. It never happened to me before, and never would again the same way.

"He'll be so pleased to see you," she says.

Charlie Bruce is on the balcony of his room, dozing in a deck chair with a quilt tossed over his feet. He always was a little, skinny fellow, but now he looks smaller than ever. Lying there with his eyes closed, he could pass for a corpse. He's lost a lot of weight and is pale as skimmed milk. His cheekbones stick out and his eyes is sunk, and most of his hair has turned gray. He looks like the middle-aged ghost of the young man I remembered.

"Charles?" she says softly. "Look who's here!"

Only when he wakes up and sees me does the old Charlie Bruce show through. He don't say nothing, just gets up and shakes my hand. He's so skinny you could play a tune on his ribs, but he says he already gained back ten pounds because of Caroline's good nursing. She says, "There's whiskey, if you would like a drink, Mr. Garland."

"I would," I say, "and it's about time you called me Lee."

"Lee," she says, and squeezes my hand.

Charlie tells me it was a near thing in El Paso, because one lung got infected and the doctor cut him open twice to get the pus out. I recall that doctor with his bloody apron and the screaming kid and I guess Charlie's lucky to be alive.

He shows me the scars from the surgery and the knife wounds and they still look ugly.

"What did you tell her?" I ask when Caroline's out of the room.

"The truth. She is only eighteen, but she understands a lot about life, as you will see. Now tell me about yourself. Why did you disappear so suddenly? I heard you were in some sort of trouble, but I wasn't well enough to go find out."

I give him a kind of edited version, leaving out the parts about jail and Luna, and me and Cody being wanted for murder. There's always time to tell the rest.

"Why the army? Was it a spur of the moment decision?"

"You could say that."

"Lee, I can't start the bank without your capital."

"As soon as I get out, we'll do it."

"There's no reason to wait until then," he says. "I can get things going alone."

"You don't look like you're ready to go back to work yet."

"It's the best medicine for a chap like me, Lee. And I'm stronger every day thanks to Caroline."

"Whatever you say, Charlie."

"Who knows how long this war will last? A year or two?"

"I doubt that."

"It's a shame to lose the time until you return."

"If I return," I say.

Caroline comes back in time to hear this last exchange and stands by the door with a pale, disturbed expression on her pretty face, like I already got killed and she's just arrived for the funeral. Charlie sees this and says, "You'll come back all right."

"I believe that too," I tell him, "or I wouldn't go."

"Please don't even think otherwise," Caroline says.

Trying to make a little joke, I say, "If them Mexicans couldn't put paid to Charlie's half of the partnership, I reckon no Cubans will cash in mine."

That lightens the mood a little except for a trace of fear that lingers in Caroline's beautiful eyes.

"Just don't talk about it anymore," she says, yet in the short time I know her in Tampa, she's the one keeps bringing it up. I know why and I'm flattered. She's attracted to me, and like a little kid trying to keep the boogey man away, she believes if she harps enough on the possibility of my getting killed, it won't happen.

A morbid fascination with death was almost a fashion then. In the popular plays artists, poets and immoral women was doomed by consumption, while pretty wives mainly died in childbirth. Sweet little kids perished from pneumonia or diptheria, but husbands got slaughtered in train crashes or carriage accidents. Bachelors usually had to drown at sea or find a Indian war to get killed in. The trouble is, real life wasn't much different.

Charlie says to me that afternoon, "Lee, you'll have to trust me completely."

I say, "If we can't trust one another we got no business starting up a bank together. Just tell me what I have to do."

That evening I eat supper with him and Caroline at the hotel but Charlie leaves early because he needs his rest. Caroline walks me out to the veranda afterward, where we sit talking for hours, mainly about what we'd like to do. "You're the most exciting man I've ever met," she says, "and I know I should not say it. Do you believe in love at first sight, Lee?"

"Well . . ."

"I've embarrassed you, haven't I? Forgive me. Charles is always saying I'm too open and forward."

"In fact I was discussing that very topic this afternoon with some friends of mine." What I want to say is I believe in any kind of love if it's with her, but I'm kind of tongue-tied. When I'm about to shake her hand and say good night, she gets up on her tiptoes and kisses me in front of all the people sitting around.

This may sound dumb but I never been kissed before, except by my mother and I don't remember that. By the time I get my wits together to say something or kiss her back, she's gone. It don't seem like anything very important today, but in eighteen and ninety-eight, it took some courage for a respectable young lady to kiss a man in public unless he was her brother or her daddy.

I'm standing there like a poleaxed pig when I hear Fortescue say, "Nightcap, Lee?" Him and Mitchell are still on the veranda drinking, and some other Easterners from our troop are with them. I sit down because I need a drink.

"As Ronny and I were telling Corporal Garland earlier today," Mitchell says to the group, "a man needs polish to catch a girl like that. Maybe he'll tell us where we can get some."

My time with Caroline is short, but sweeter than anything I ever knew before. By the third day when Charlie goes off to rest and I'm alone with her, we've told each other our whole lives. When we're alone we hold hands and touch and can't take our eyes off each other. I tell her finally, "It is love at first sight, Caroline," and she answers demurely, "It would seem so, darling Lee, and what do we do about it?"

We take long, lazy walks along the beach in the late afternoons after I get off duty, sip drinks on the hotel veranda and have supper every night. Some of the time I'm listening to Charlie talk business, but mostly now I'm ignoring him and yarning with Caroline. He notices this and don't seem too happy about it, but Caroline tells me in private not to worry, he's always been jealous of any man she looks at. When I give him my power-of-attorney on the sixth day, Charlie says, "Hurry up and end the war, Lee," but his eyes are telling me, "Hurry up and go to war, and leave my sister alone."

The next afternoon when I go to collect her for our walk, he's waiting for me on the hotel veranda and says she ain't ready yet. "Sit down, Lee." His tone tells me this is going to be serious.

I sit, but I don't give him any encouragement to say what's on his mind.

"Caroline is all the family I have and she's very young," he says finally. "She's a very affectionate and emotional girl, and totally inexperienced with men. Don't misunderstand me, but it's not in her best interest to be seen alone with you so much."

"I thought we trusted each other," I tell him.

"Lee, I know you would never betray our friendship by taking advantage of an innocent child."

"Caroline's no child."

"I'm asking you man to man to see this from an objective point of view. A marriageable young girl's reputation is all she has until she finds a husband, so if Caroline is indiscreet and allows her natural affection to focus on someone she has no intention of marrying—"

"How do you know what her intentions are?"

"Certainly you're not serious," he says in alarm. "You've known each other less than a week."

"I am serious, Charlie, but you can relax. Caroline and I ain't planning to get married just yet."

"You mean you've asked her?"

"No, but I intend to. Meanwhile, we're enjoying each other's company while we can, trying to crowd in a few days before I leave."

"You're compromising her, Lee, and people are talking."

"Who's talking?" says Caroline, who arrives then and comes directly to my side.

"Some of the officers' wives," he says, "who are from our set at home."

"Oh, Charles, don't be such a ninnie," Caroline says. "They're jealous because I've caught such a handsome, gallant beau."

"Caught?" Charlie says.

"You heard me, brother darling," Caroline answers him pertly. "Lee, have I caught you or not?"

"Roped and thrown," I answer, and Caroline wrinkles up her nose and hunches her shoulders in a giggle of delight.

The expression on Charlie's face at all this is just plain horror. "Caroline!" he says. "You have no shame!"

"Don't worry, Charles. You have enough for us both."

If she'd said to me then, "Desert the army and run off with me," I'd of done it and not looked back, but she was too honorable even to think such a thing. Instead she pecks Charlie on the cheek to make him feel better and tells him we're going for our walk.

"You're both behaving like children," he says. "Lee, I expect you to be a gentleman and take my advice, even if Caroline lacks common sense. I am responsible for her, after all."

"Not any longer, dear brother," she says gaily. "According to the law in Massachusetts, at eighteen I'm free to make my own decisions."

The more pressure Charlie puts on Caroline, the more determined she is to spend all the time she can with me, and the harder he presses me with his old-maid attitudes, the less attention I pay him. What Caroline says is true. Charlie's jealous of any attention she gives to me. Two days in a row, he announces that they're leaving Tampa, and both times she says, "I am not leaving until Lee sails."

I don't want to be the cause of trouble between brother and sister, and I tell Caroline so. We're splashing barefoot along the edge of the bay just before twilight one evening with a big orange sun sinking into the sea. She's got her skirts tucked up and locks of hair falling loose, and we're holding hands, pretending to look for seashells. She stops and puts her hands on her hips and says, "See here, Lee Garland, do you love me or don't you?"

"You know I do."

"And I love you, so that's that. I'm deeply fond of my brother, but I'm tired of his objecting to everything I do. For the past four years he had me locked away in a notorious girls' prison, and—"

"Come on, Caroline. I hear the Abbot Academy's a fine school." She had a vivid imagination and liked to overstate things sometimes.

"That didn't make it any the less a prison," she says, sticking her chin out stubbornly. "It was run on the principle that all girls are innately wanton, and must be constantly protected against themselves."

"Maybe they're right," I say, trying to kid her a little.

The reflection of the setting sun paints her cheeks all gold and rosy as she looks up at me. "Do you think I'm wanton?" she says, narrowing her eyes and moistening her lips with her tongue in a way that makes the skin on my neck prickle.

"A little," I tell her.

"How wanton?"

"I don't know."

She goes up on her tiptoes and kisses me, putting her arms around my neck and pressing her whole front against mine. It's a long, wonderful kiss that gives me an erection fit to bust my britches. I'm trying not to let her feel it because I don't want to shock her and spoil everything, but she don't let up on the pressure so I finally give in because she's writhing and gyrating against me. Then suddenly she breaks away with that lovely laugh she has, as if she's just played a joke on me, and runs up the beach, calling back, "Catch me if you can!"

I stand there for a bit, waiting for my crotch to soften up, then I go after her. She's gone into a piney grove above the high-water mark and when I get there, I don't see her anywhere. I walk among the trees where it's nearly dark, looking for her in the shadows, knowing she's going to jump out on me when I least expect it. She does, too, catching me around the waist from behind and crying, "Bang! If I were a Spaniard you'd be dead, Lee Garland!"

I grab her and lift her off her feet and she kisses me again and we flop down on a carpet of pine needles, rolling around like two kids. But it's more than that, because our lips stay together and before I know it my hands are all over her and she's pressing harder. Then I'm stroking her silky drawers under her dress and she's as soft and sweet and velvety as a colt's nose.

"Love me, Lee," she says, and I do. Women wore a lot of complicated clothes in them days, with hooks and stays and underpinnings too numerous and complicated to describe. Only they knew all the secrets of how to get in and out of them, so a man had to fumble around or wait while they undressed themselves. But there we are finally, naked as Adam and Eve, making love in this pine grove. All that was missing was the snake, which in that country is a miracle because there sure was enough of them around.

Caroline's a virgin, which is a new experience for both of us, but my loving her don't seem to hurt. She whimpers and cries out once or twice but then she wants me as much as I do her. Her body's more beautiful than I could have guessed, with breasts as firm and tasty as peaches, and thighs so silky soft I wanted to lose myself between them. Nothing in my life ever made me feel better than Caroline's legs and arms wrapped around me and her little moist kisses in my ear. "Hold me! Hold me, please!" she cries as we both come together like an electric shock. When it's over, and we're laying in each other's arms Caroline says, "Lee, I'm sorry. That really was wicked."

"We love each other," I say, "so it can't be wicked."

"I don't mean because of what we did," she sighs. "But because of what I've been keeping from you."

"What's that?"

"Our love was all foretold to me by a necromancer."

"A what?"

"A fortune-teller."

"You mean you knew what was going to happen?"

She nods and starts to weep, so I hold her tight and say there's nothing to cry about. She says, "But there's more, my darling. I was told I'd meet my true love on this trip, that it was in the stars, and, and . . ." She's sobbing and I'm fit to be tied.

"Well, you met him and he loves you, Caroline," I say, "so it can't be that bad."

"But it is," she cries, "because she said I will lose you as soon as I find you."

"Not if I can help it."

"But you can't, my dearest. It's in the stars."

I don't know why women believe in claptrap like that, but there's lots of them who do, and Caroline, bright as she was, is no exception. She's really upset and nothing I say can change her conviction. She reasons that because half the prophecy's already been proved by meeting me and falling in love and consummating it so fast without a long courtship or getting married, the other half about losing me is sure to follow. And that means, although we don't say it, that I'll probably get killed in Cuba. It fits in with all that morbid romantic stuff women fill their heads with.

After a while we get dressed and walk back to the hotel, where I tell her I'll join her and Charlie for dinner in an hour. She's smiling again by then, as cool as if nothing ever happened, even though what we did would change both our lives forever.

At dinner Caroline's more beautiful than ever but she don't say much while Charlie drones on about capital reserves and treasury deposits and how much profit our bank can make. Then all of a sudden Caroline bursts into tears and leaves the table without touching her dessert. I start to go after her, but Charlie says, "No, leave it, Lee. It's just her time of the month."

I don't tell him I know better. Instead, I say, "She's convinced I ain't coming back."

"Then why upset her more? You see how distraught the poor girl is already."

Like an idiot, I listen to him and don't go after her.

She sends me a present the next morning with a note. The present's a red flannel bellyband to wear under my shirt, which people in those days believed kept off tropical fevers and such. It ain't much good for that as things turn out, but Caroline made it herself.

I remember the note because I read it over enough times. "Dearest Lee, I feel I have known you forever. If I was too bold and wicked, forgive me, but I could only follow my heart. It is love at first sight just like in the fairy tales and you are right about my foolish belief in prophecies. Come back soon, darling Lee, to one who prays that God may bless you and keep you always. Your faithful, loving, Caroline Bruce."

I'm drilling my section, thinking on her words and touching the bellyband hot around my middle, when Ransom comes cantering up. I never realized how a woman could enter a man's life and put everything else in the shadow like Caroline did. I'm a sleepwalker giving orders because every time I close my eyes I see her face.

"Lee, did you hear what I said?"

"What?" I look around to see Ransom shouting at me to pass the word we're leaving for Cuba.

PART
2

XIII

Invasion

That night we spend packing, and the next morning we're sweltering in the heat, watching the transports at anchor in the bay, when
Ben Butler calls us to attention. The good news is we'll board the
S.S. *Yucatan* within the hour. "But," he says, "only baggage mules
and artillery horses will accompany us. Our own mounts will stay
behind."

We're stunned. He's just told us we've been converted to infantry by the stroke of an army pen. Fifth Corps headquarters says our
horses will follow on another boat, but nobody really believes it.

We bob around for a week on that floating furnace before we
leave because the navy says the Spanish fleet's waiting out in the
Gulf of Mexico. If they don't kill us, the food will. And the bunks
are made for Singer's Midgets, so close one on top of the other,
that a man has to get out and in again if he wants to roll over.
"Always take the top one," Mitchell says, "because what goes
down may come up, and you don't want to be under it when it
does."

Just before we sail a steam launch chugs alongside with two
regular army provost guards and a prisoner in chains. It's the
hottest day yet and nobody pays attention until Heinz starts barking to beat the band because it's Levi, looking the worse for wear
after hopping freights from Texas to the Tampa docks. After they

155

get the irons off him, Luna says, "You're restricted to quarters, Hennings, until we get to the bottom of this." Levi's got Heinz in his arms by now, scratching what's left of the chewed ear. He gives Luna his best gap-toothed grin and says, "Why, I wouldn't miss this war for anything, Lieutenant!"

I read once we was the biggest military expedition that ever left the United States up to then. Sixteen thousand officers and men, with eighty-nine newspaper reporters, an observation balloon and some other cargo we discover by accident the first night out.

The bunks down below are too suffocating for all but the hardiest troopers, but there's always a breeze on deck and every man tries to find a spot to curl up where he won't get shouted at or stepped on. On the top deck, where it's forbidden to go, Cody found room for a dozen men to stretch out in comfort. We have to sneak up at night but it's easy. I organize everybody while he leads the way. There's Mountain, Mitchell, C.E. Knoblauch, Fortescue, Ransom, Levi, Tom Isbell, Marcus Russell from New York, Henry Haefner and "Bronco" George Brown, another New Mexico cowboy.

We're at our most vulnerable in the passage, with me and Cody at the front and Mountain bringing up the rear, when Ham Fish, a sergeant friend of Fortescue's from New York, bumps into us.

"You ain't going to report us, are you?" Cody says.

Ham says, "Wait right here, all of you."

"What are you going to do?" I ask him.

"Get Ted Miller and join you," he says.

"For Christ's sake hurry up," Cody tells him. "If Luna catches us, he'll chain us to them bunks."

Cody's hideaway is splendid, with more breeze than any place else on that old scow, and there's room for everybody if we move a few crates. They're longer than ordinary ones, and mostly empty, but it don't dawn on anybody what they are until Cody drops one like it bit him. That's when I see they're tapered.

Bronco George Brown gives it a hard kick and says, "No place to put our horses because they're sending our coffins?"

Mitchell's reaction is more philosophical. "It does give one pause to contemplate eternity," he says.

"Not my eternity, by God!" Mountain swears, and he heaves it over the side to fall fifty feet and splash into the sea. Then everybody pitches in without another word. We just chucked the fourth one over when we hear a shout from the deck below. Officers are down there smoking and they seen the coffins sail by.

"Who's up there?" one of them calls out.

Fortescue's the fastest one on his feet and yells something like, "This is First Officer Smith! Please stand back from the rail down there! We're splicing keelhauls on the starboard larboard!" Then he shouts at us like we was sailors, "All right, men! Make her fast!"

Miller and Ham Fish get into the act, saying things like, "Aye, aye, sir! Belay the binnacle pin! Batten the belly hatch!" until Fortescue has to threaten them with his fists to cut it out.

He yells, "That'll do, men!" and calls down to the officers, "Carry on, gentlemen. Sorry to have disturbed you."

We're snickering into our shirts and he snarls, "Shut up, damn it! They may still come and have a look."

But nobody does, and we sleep on them coffins every night of the trip, staying cool and talking quiet

"You think the Spaniards will put up a hard fight?" Cody asks one night.

Levi says, "The president got that all calculated."

Ted Miller says, "My father told me the last thing in the world Mr. McKinley wanted was this war."

"How does your father know that?" Levi asks him.

"They're friends," Miller says.

Bronco George Brown says, "If your old man knows the president, Miller, how come you ain't an officer?"

Ted Miller is smug. "Being an ordinary trooper in the Rough Riders carries more prestige, George. I thought you knew that."

"Hear, hear!" Fortescue says.

And Ham Fish says, "Let's drink to that!"

"Drink what?" Mountain says, and damn if Fish don't come up with whiskey from one of the coffins that he'd squirreled away for our private use. How he got it on board he never said, but like all of us, he was learning to be resourceful. It was scotch, which nobody from the West ever tried, but it wasn't bad if you like the taste of creosote.

Knoblauch don't drink and there's plenty to go around. Fish pours it into our tin cups, and we drink toasts.

Mitchell says, counting heads, "To us, the thirteen immortals!"

"Maybe we ought to go find another immortal," Cody says. "Thirteen's kind of an unlucky number."

"There's Heinz here," Levi says, holding up the dog. "That makes us fourteen."

"To Heinz, the fourteenth immortal!" Knoblauch says. "May his fleas grow and prosper!"

Fortescue says, "We few, we happy few, we band of brothers. For he that sheds his blood with me shall be my brother. Be he ever so vile, this day shall gentle his condition. Did I get it right, Mitch?"

"More or less," Mitchell says, and we keep on toasting until we are all in pretty wobbly condition. Henry Haefner wants to sing quartets with Fortescue, Mountain and Mitchell, but I talk them out of it. The hardest job now is trying to stay quiet and not give away our hiding place to the whole ship.

I ain't superstitious, but in all the years since, I often wondered about us up there with them coffins. We chucked four of them overboard and within two weeks four of the "immortals" was dead. Fortescue always said it was only a coincidence, but I'd of felt better about it if the numbers didn't match up.

The fifth day at sea when everybody is bored out of his skull and even the card games are dragging, Ben Butler streams a target about four hundred yards behind the ship, and we all take turns potting it with our new Krags. Then me and Cody and Ransom bang away at tin cans with our Colts until Luna appears. I think he's going to tell us to quit but instead he borrows Cody's revolver, spins the cylinder and tells Mountain, "Toss one can, Moore, but toss it high."

"You ever seen him shoot?" Cody whispers to me.

"No, but I seen him show off."

When he draws, it's a blur, and he turns the can into a cheese grater before it hits the water. The performance lasts about a New York second and the men all shout for Luna to do it again. But he hands Cody's gun back and tells him to save the bullets for the Spaniards.

Cody shakes his head in amazement. "I must of been crazy throwing soup on him that time. He could be in a circus."

"Don't ever tell him. He's sure to take it the wrong way."

Some days we can see Cuba on the horizon now. Purple-green mountains in the haze. Half the men are seasick so you have to watch where you step. At night searchlights crisscross the sky. God knows what they're looking for because there wasn't no airplanes around in those days.

One afternoon the convoy sails in close to the coast and every-body gets a good look. White sand and water blue as birds' eggs. Some ragged-looking Cuban troops go galloping along the beach and they wave at us. Their horses ain't much bigger than donkeys, but like Fortescue says, "At least they have horses."

We're all wondering where we're going to land and when, and there's a lot of criticism of our generals. The ones we seen around the Tampa Bay Hotel wasn't impressive. Shafter, who's the head of the invasion, weighs three hundred pounds and has to be lifted into his buckboard. He can't walk much either because he's got the gout and only has the use of one foot. I guess he could kill a Spaniard if he sat on him, but that's about the only way. He used to have a big reputation as an Indian fighter, only we ain't going to fight Indians.

Joe Wheeler, a spidery old geezer in charge of the cavalry, was a Confederate general thirty-five years ago and a politician ever since. Like Shafter, he don't exactly inspire overconfidence in the men.

Most of the time I'm daydreaming about Caroline and wishing the war would end that minute. I win three dollars from Ted Miller when I pot five flying fish in a row. I offer to let him try only he ain't handy with a six-shooter. When a curious whale surfaces near the ship, he says, "Maybe I can hit that."

Everybody sings a dumb song we learned in Tampa called "The Animal Fair":

> *I went to the animal fair*
> *The birds and beasts was there*
> *The big baboon by the light of the moon*
> *Was combing his auburn hair*
> *The monkey he got drunk*
> *And sat on the elephant's trunk*
> *The elephant sneezed and fell on his knees*
> *And what became of the monk, the monk?*
> *Oh, what became of the monk?*

One morning I wake to a dawn that's all baby pink and a sudden shock when the deck stops vibrating. It takes me a minute to realize the engines have shut down. Then I hear the anchor chains rattling in the bow and somebody says, "We're here."

"Where?"

"The Animal Fair," Fortescue says. The place is called Daiquiri, like the drink. It is June the twenty-second, eighteen and ninety-eight, and we're going to fight the Spaniards.

If ever an army deserved to get shot to pieces or drowned or captured because of sheer stupidity it was us, but again we was lucky. The surf is rough and the lifeboats bob around like corks. Several men get their hands and legs crushed as we bang against the side of the ship and everybody's shouting to look out or hurry up. The wagoners and mule skinners whip our baggage animals over the side, making them jump into the sea because swimming is the only way they'll reach the beach. But half the poor beasts drown because they get confused and head in the wrong direction.

As we're being rowed in to a pier on the beach, the navy puts on a show bombarding a hill, and you can actually see the shells going through the air, which ain't true of a bullet. I make everybody wrap the breech of his Krag in oiled flannel and plug the muzzle with a cotton patch. As dumb and disorganized as we are, the Dons are even dumber. Not a single enemy soldier's there to greet us, so our regiment gets ashore without losing a man. Some of the other outfits ain't so lucky.

The pier is crowded with colored soldiers from the Tenth Cavalry. One big fellow catches me when I nearly go into the water.

"Why, if it ain't the Reverend from Santa Fe," he says. "What's a smart man like you doing in a low-down place like this?"

"God's will, Sergeant, and I could ask you the same question."

"You didn't come all the way to preach?"

"That was only a getup," I tell him. "I was on the run from the law the last time we met."

He busts up laughing and sticks out his hand. "Carl Washington," he says, "and any time you're on the run again, remember you got a friend in the Tenth Cavalry." Somebody shouts his name and he goes running to the end of the pier, where one of his troopers has gone down in fifteen feet of surf with all his gear. I seldom seen a big man so fast and then I recall he got a medal for swimming. He's out of his shirt in seconds and off the end of the pier like an acrobat. C.E. Knoblauch, who's a swimming champion, leaps in after him to help.

But it's a long time before they find this poor soldier, and when they do, there ain't no life in him. Then Carl Washington and Knoblauch are back in the water again because some other poor devil took a header. They save a dozen more, but before we all get ashore, there's two drowned bodies on the beach, both of them from the Tenth Cavalry.

I'm sitting with Knoblauch, Cody and Fortescue under a palm tree when Carl Washington wanders over later to thank C.E. for his help. C.E. says he's sorry about the two men they couldn't get in time and Carl Washington says, "So am I, but there's others owe their lives to you."

I tell Sergeant Washington to have a seat, but he stands around awkwardly for a minute like he can't decide. Fortescue offers him a drink of scotch whiskey, but he turns it down because he's temperance. "Well, thanks again," he says finally, but he still don't go or sit down. What a damn funny country we come from where men of different color can save lives together and then can't be comfortable socializing afterward. I know Carl Washington wants to get a few things off his chest, and me, Knoblauch and Fortescue would like to know him better after what we seen him do that day. But it ain't going to happen.

"Do you mind if we attend the burial?" C.E. Knoblauch asks him.

"You'd be most welcome."

When the men from Washington's squadron lower those two unfortunates into the hot sand, their bugler plays taps and a white chaplain who looks like he don't want to be there says some words in a hurry. They fire a volley over the graves, so the first shots we hear in Cuba are a salute to our own dead.

Right after that we march about half a mile to a pretty valley of green grass on the edge of the Daiquiri River where we make camp. The grass is higher than our tents and it's home to just about every crawling thing on earth. Apart from the lizards and snakes and scorpions, there's tarantulas big as dinner plates and about a million land crabs, which Mitchell says signed an alliance with the Spanish.

We bed down in some discomfort after a dinner of hardtack and beans, when Ted Miller doing sentry mistakes a land crab for a Spaniard and blows it against a tree. It's a ugly-looking thing, a five-pound spider with two big claws and colored pink, blue and yellow like a bad bruise. Luna comes running to find out what the shooting's about.

Miller ain't had the pleasure of Luna's undivided attention yet and I feel sorry for him. He's holding up this dead crab, saying, "I'm sorry, Lieutenant. I thought it was the enemy creeping up on us."

"The enemy?" Luna says, in a tone that makes Miller feel smaller than the crab.

"Yes, sir."

"You know who the enemy is, soldier?"

"Yes, sir. The Spaniards."

"Have you ever seen a Spaniard?"

"No, sir."

"Then how do you know this is not a Spaniard?" He points at the crab and some of the men snicker.

Before he can start torturing poor Miller, another shot rings out, and the battle of the land crabs begins. It goes on all night, and after reveille, Luna lines us up before we have coffee and says, "The United States government did not spend a million dollars to send you here to destroy the wildlife on this island, nor did Cuba ask for help against the land crabs. The next moron who shoots anything that isn't a Spaniard will deal with me personally. Do I make myself clear?"

The march to Siboney that day scars everybody's memory. The trail's narrow and full of roots, with vines and branches brushing our shoulders at every step. There's oleanders and orchids and jasmine blossoms big as cauliflowers. But there's also holes to fall into or jump over, depending on how wide awake you are, and a wet heat so suffocating and heavy it turns your lungs to lead and makes your head pound.

Men from the regular army in their blue wool uniforms drop out from heatstroke. The Spaniards don't bother us but the mosquitoes do. Carrying a carbine, a hundred rounds of ammunition, canteen, poncho, shelter half, tin cup and blanket, it ain't easy to swat a mosquito, and even harder to keep your balance when you miss.

"How far to Gethsemane?" Mitchell says, but nobody laughs. The men start leaving gear along the trail to lighten their loads. It's only twelve miles to this place, but it feels like a hundred, all up hill.

Most of the canteens are empty before we're half way there, and it's a long time before we come to a creek to fill them again. I'm so thirsty I'm ready to drink it dry, but when I dunk my canteen to fill it, Mountain stops me. "Don't, Lee," he says. "Use mine. It's still half full from this morning."

"What about you?"

"I'll get by."

"Then so will I. Give it to Cody." Pride talking, when my body's crying out for a drink. "This water's okay," I tell him, looking at the creek, but he shakes his head. Mountain knows better.

We stagger into Siboney after dark and make camp. It's a grubby, depressing place with most of the buildings falling down But we finally get decent water, even if nobody can focus on his drinking cup from fatigue. We hunker down near the railroad tracks and try to get a little sleep, but as tired as we are it don't come easy. I clean my Colt and the Krag and tell the others to do likewise. The smell of gun oil is a comfort, and the steel is cool to the touch.

Six Cuban soldiers ride into our camp around dark and the leader nearly shoots Levi's dog because he's barking at them. They're a poor-looking lot, niggers, whites, and Carib Indians dressed in dirty white pants and straw hats, without shoes or shirts or saddles. They gobble our hardtack like angel cake.

Only two of them got guns while the rest carry machetes except one who's got an old bayonet stuck on a bamboo stick. They're surprised to hear some of us speak Spanish as good as they do and the leader wants to know where we come from. We ain't been told much by our own army so I decide to use this moment to get a little information. I ask him how many troops are up ahead and he says there's more than we are.

"We haven't seen any yet," I tell him.

"They're waiting for you," he says, laughing.

We march next morning before the heat's too bad, but the sweat puddles under our belts anyway, and runs into our eyes and off our noses before we cover half a mile. We start out in column of fours and wind up Indian file with men using axes and shovels to hack away at the scrub. Then without warning, the world becomes water. Rain comes down so hard it turns the trail to soup, with water so dense it chokes off your air, and the noise of the deluge too loud for any conversation. After about fifteen minutes it stops

like somebody turned off a hose, and there's only warm steam
rising from the mud and a symphony of singing frogs.

Mitchell says, "Welcome to Cuba," and Fortescue says, "That
must have been the rainy season."

We take off our clothes to dry but the mosquitoes ain't had
dinner yet so we dress again in a hurry and stand around soaked.

Ben Butler makes his rounds that night with Luna, telling the
men we may see action tomorrow because the regiment's moving
up to some hills near a place called Guásimas.

What he don't say is that where there's hills, there's valleys, and
we got to pass through one to get up to the other. Then he adds,
"Stay alert, follow orders, and shoot only when you have something to shoot at. Good luck and God bless you."

When he's finished, it's Luna's turn. Instead of the kindly, fa-
therly tone Ben Butler always uses, he just starts barking. "I want
no shirking, no talking and no horseplay on the march. If I hear
a shot fired without someone in authority giving the order, the man
responsible will deal with me. The Cubans say the enemy is well-
armed and entrenched, and I'm telling you his only interest is in
killing you. We're not out to beat him tomorrow, just find him and
dig in. Any questions?"

"I have one, Lieutenant," C.E. Knoblauch says. He's got his hat
off, and his bald head shines white in the reflection of the campfire.
He's younger than Mitchell, but he looks forty at a time like this.
"If the Spanish run when we attack, do we follow?"

"Not unless you get a specific order to pursue."

Levi says, "Where will you be, Lieutenant?"

"All over any man who doesn't follow orders. And I don't want
that hound of yours underfoot in the morning. Tie him to a tree
and leave him behind."

"He's a valuable scout dog, Lieutenant."

"He's a pain in the ass, Hennings, and I won't have him barking
at every lizard we pass on the trail and giving away our position."

"What do I do?" Levi asks us later. "You heard him."

"Ain't you learned anything in the army, Levi?" Cody says. "The
lieutenant give you an order but he didn't say what to tie him
with."

"You mean like a string instead of a rope?"

"I don't see no rope around, do you?"

"But where will I find string?"

"Thread's better," Mountain says. "I can loan you some."

We sleep soaking wet and roll out at three in the morning. Ransom says our Colt machine guns won't be available because some quartermaster lost the ammunition, and the dynamite gun, which is supposed to be our secret weapon ain't showed up either and nobody knows where it is. He says Roosevelt's throwing a conniption fit because we're going into action half-cocked and underequipped, but we are going.

Some journalists show up that day. There's Ed Marshall from the New York *Journal* and Stephen Crane from the *World,* who's a famous writer although I don't know it until Fortescue tells me. He's not much older than me, and kind of shy, unlike Marshall, who's asking everybody questions. They're going with us in the morning, which seems foolish, but that's the kind of reporters they are.

Richard Harding Davis is with them too and we all heard of him. He's an elegant dresser about six-four in a long white duster with fifty pockets. He hobnobs with the officers mainly and only talks to enlisted men if they are New York millionaires.

Fortescue can't stand him, and C.E. Knoblauch agrees. He wipes the oil off his revolver, sights it at the reporter's back and pulls the trigger as he says, "Bang!"

Cody says, "He looks like a real gentleman to me."

"Well, he's more of a lady," Fortescue says, "if you really want to know," and the other Easterners smile.

"What do you mean by that?" Cody asks them.

"Acey-duecy," C.E. Knoblauch says, but Cody still don't get it.

"He likes men," Mitchell explains.

"What's wrong with that?" Cody wants to know, and they all bust out laughing, which only increases Cody's confusion.

"Instead of women," Mitchell adds.

Cody thinks about this for a while before he tells them, "We met a couple of those once—me and Lee and Mountain. Peter asses."

The Easterners double up and Cody gets prickly. "Well, that's what they're called, damn it, because one puts his peter in the other one's ass," which makes them New Yorkers laugh harder than before.

Fortescue asks what happened to the peter asses and Cody tells him, "One they hung, and the other they cut his parts off and let him bleed to death."

"Come on, Cody," Mitchell says, not believing a word.

"Ask Lee," Cody says, offended.

"It's true," I say. "They raped and murdered a little boy."

When we set out again around six with Ben Butler in the lead, the sun is already hot, and clouds of flies and beetles join the mosquitoes to keep us company. Mitchell says he wouldn't mind the war so much if we could have it in New York City.

"What do you miss most?" Cody asks him. "The wine, the women or the song?"

"The sidewalks," he says.

Cuba Libre

We get an order to load magazines but not carry a round in our chambers because Luna don't want nobody stumbling and shooting the man in front of him by accident. We hear Roosevelt yelling at people to shut up and march quiet, which strikes everybody funny. He has a pair of lungs on him would do credit to a carnival barker.

Ed Marshall, the reporter, keeps right up with us the whole time. I ask him why, when he could stay back at headquarters and write his stories after the fighting is over.

"It's his bad conscience," Fortescue says. "He's one of the reasons we're here," and Marshall laughs. What Fortescue means is that the articles in the papers about Cuba for the last couple of years inflamed a lot of public opinion. Marshall's boss, William Hearst, is at headquarters right now telling General Shafter how to run the war.

"I wish they'd get it right," Mountain says. "So far I ain't impressed."

"How come you're with us and not the regulars?" Cody asks Marshall.

"Where else could I find the social register, half the New York stock exchange and a wild West show all in one place?"

"Just make sure you spell my name right," C.E. Knoblauch tells him, "with a *K.*"

"As in k-n-i-t-w-i-t," Mitchell says.

The chatter dies out as the heat and fatigue build. For a time the only thing we hear are cicadas in the trees and a bird every once in a while. Levi's dog trots along with his tongue hanging to the ground, too hot to bark even if he felt like it. Men start to drop out before we been on the trail two hours, and nobody's thinking of the Spanish. Water's all we got on our minds as Ben Butler calls a halt.

When we start up again, the pace slows. The undergrowth on both sides of the trail is thicker than ever, and there's a kind of yucca they call Spanish bayonet can slash right through a uniform, and the wound always infects.

About quarter to nine we see our first Spaniard, laying belly up on the trail, his empty eyes looking at the sky. He's got a bullet hole in the side of his head and his neck's been sliced halfway into his shoulder by some Cuban's machete. He's a starved-looking kid in a blue-striped cotton uniform that's more holes than cloth, and a pair of worn-out plimsolls I'd be ashamed to give a beggar.

We're coming out of the thick undergrowth now into a little valley at the bottom of a hill. There's kind of a meadow with high grass and bushes all around and a few wooded copses.

"Perfect place for an ambush," Mountain says to me.

"Flankers, fan out!" Ben Butler calls to us, and we start to spread ourselves right and left, running through the grass past the bushes and the trees. Spread out and flop. Then run and flop again. When we practiced this in Tampa everybody looked before he flopped because there was always a snake or a scorpion there ahead of you. Now that don't seem important, and we're a good deal quicker to hunker down.

The heat's coming off this meadow like a open furnace door, but I don't mind it now because we're exposed and the sooner we get across that place and onto the hill, the better.

The funny part is I don't even know we're under fire when it starts. There's no bang or crack because the shooters are too far off, and no smoke to show where they are because they use smoke-less powder. Then I see something slice the grass like a invisible buzz saw near my feet and hear a kind of *z-z-zeu* and that's it. Then another and another, like berserk bees. Levi's dog goes crazy chasing them, and there we are all standing up, making fine targets for the Spanish, but with nothing to shoot at.

Then I see Tom Isbell go down with blood pouring out of his neck. Mountain is closest to him and rushes over, but Tom just motions him to keep moving, and then Mountain is hit.

I been asked what a bullet sounds like going into a man, and I can tell you it's the most sickening sound there is. It ain't sharp and it ain't a thump. It's like when you beat a carpet to get the dust out, and once you hear it you never forget it.

Isbell gets up, but he don't run ten feet before he goes down with another bullet in him. Mountain's got a bloody hip but he don't pay it more attention than a mosquito bite. I see my first live Spaniard then, dodging between two bushes, and I kill him. Cody's out ahead of us and I don't know how he got there. He's yelling, "They're over there, Lee! In them trees!"

Damn if I can see them except for the one I shot. The grass is moving in places like a wind's blowing over it, but it ain't no wind, it's Mauser bullets ripping in at us from two sides. We're running and flopping and I'm yelling, "Keep your intervals! Don't waste your fire! Spread out!" I see a flash of white shirt which turns into another Spaniard. I shoot on the run and miss. He aims at me point blank and I feel my balls draw up into my stomach, waiting for the bullet. But it ain't my time yet, and I hear the bullet pass. His straw hat flies off with half his head on my second shot.

Cody goes down just ahead of me and my heart's in my throat. I don't want nothing to happen to that kid and I rush to see how bad he's hurt. He rolls over cursing, "Levi! Chain your goddamn dog!" Cody's okay, he just tripped over Heinz, who scoots off into the grass again, chasing Mauser bullets.

Ham Fish is ahead of us, with part of his section. I see that fatal wind bend the grass again, and him and a guy named Culver drop. Next to me I hear Marcus Russell say, "Hot work, Lee!"

Before I can answer he sags to his knees with a hole over one eye and a fountain of blood pumping out the back of his head.

At this rate there won't be nobody left by the time we get to the hill. I step over Henry Haefner's body in the grass and think he's dead because he's on his back with his eyes and mouth open. Then I see he's breathing, and when I slosh some water on his face, he gives me a weak smile. I say, "Hang on, Henry. Somebody will get you pretty soon."

I pass the place where Fish and Culver are. Fish's been hit in the side and Culver's got a chest wound. Both of them are conscious, and Fish is in pain, but Culver looks worse. He's Indian like Tom Isbell but right now he's whiter than Ham Fish. I kneel down next to them and Fish says, "The same bullet got us both, can you believe it?"

Culver's trying to get at his canteen when he passes out, and Fish says to me, "You don't happen to have a drink, do you? I can't seem to find mine."

I hand my canteen to him but he don't take it. "Go on!" I say, pushing it into his hand. He's looking at me but he still don't take it because he's dead.

The Mauser slugs are thrashing the grass like snakes wherever you step. One of them knocks off my hat, but I put it back on again and another one grazes my shoulder as I hurry to catch up with Cody, who's kneeling to reload.

Fortescue's a few feet away, and for a second I think he's dead too, because he don't move. Then he fires a round and a Spaniard spins out of a bush not thirty yards from us, hit, but running. I drop him and Fortescue looks over his shoulder, scowling.

When me and Cody reach a stand of trees near the bottom of the hill, a bullet goes clean through one where I'm crouching, dropping wood chips all over me. I never seen anything like them Mausers for muzzle velocity. One of our rounds wouldn't penetrate more than a couple inches of that wood.

"You're hit, Lee," Cody says.

"No I ain't."

"Then whose blood is it?"

I look down at myself for the first time and see he's right. One whole side of my shirt is soaked red but I don't feel nothing except a little tenderness in the shoulder where the bullet grazed me.

About then, Davis, the reporter, goes running by with a revolver, shooting at the hill. I'm thinking whatever else the boys from New York say about the man, he ain't no coward.

Mitchell catches up and so does Levi Hennings. I don't see Luna nowhere but I hear him every now and then shouting at somebody to move up or spread out. C.E. Knoblauch gets his hat shot away and his skinny bald head sticks out of the grass like a turkey gobbler's. More men drop as we get closer to the hill, and Fortescue shouts, "There's a machine gun up there!" Which explains why the men are being scythed down with the grass. Our conversation is cut short when a bullet tumbles Mountain and he don't move. His whole head's covered with blood. I figure he's dead so I leave him.

All of a sudden the bullets ain't tearing up the grass anymore and seem to be going over our heads. The Spanish machine guns was set for longer range, which is why once we passed through that valley of death, we was under their line of fire.

It never occurs to anybody we're taking a licking. We just keep going. At the bottom of the hill I see Roosevelt for the first time about two hundred yards to our right making a fine target, high on his horse, running here and there.

More Spaniards are breaking cover now. The ones that hit us from the tree line are showing themselves, trying to make it to the hill, but not many of them do.

Ed Marshall's taking notes on the battle, calling out, "Well done, boys!" He tells Knoblauch, "I'll get your name right, Cyril, don't worry!" and Cody stops shooting and turns around to Knoblauch. "Cyril?" he says to Knoblauch. "Is that what the *C* stands for?"

"That's right," Knoblauch says.

"Well, you never told me," Cody says.

"You never asked," Knoblauch says.

Cody flushes another Spaniard from the bushes and Knoblauch kills him.

"What's the *E* stand for?" Cody wants to know.

"Cody, shut up and move it!" I tell him.

"I was only asking."

On our left two more enemy soldiers make a dash for the hill, firing in our direction, and poor Ed Marshall goes down with a bullet in his spine. When a rifle explodes twice in my ear and the two Spaniards fall, I turn to see the ghost of Mountain Moore blotting out the sun, his body covered in enough blood to scare all the Spaniards out of Cuba. But he's grinning and wiping it out of his eyes with the back of his hand.

"I thought you was dead," I tell him.

"I tried it, Lee, but it didn't take."

"Get to the rear," I say. "You need a doctor."

"What about you?" he says, pointing at my bloody shirt.

"I just give you an order."

"Great place to make a reputation, ain't it?" he says, cheeky as ever.

"Mountain, you hear me?"

"Leave him be, Lee," Cody says. "He's too dumb to know if he's bad off or not."

"Don't call me dumb," Mountain says.

"Dumb, dumb, dumb," Cody says, and Mountain makes a grab for him. But Cody's too limber and dodges out of the way. "Come on, dummy!" Cody yells, and he's off and running up that hill.

We all start after him on what is later called our "gallant charge against a heavily entrenched enemy position on the fortified hills of Guásimas" by Mr. Richard Harding Davis, who watched us go.

C.E. Knoblauch actually took the lead when Cody's wind ran out before he got halfway up. It caught the Spaniards by surprise I guess, because they began to empty out of their trenches and run down the backside of the hill. Not all. Some stayed and fought and was killed by us. After five or ten minutes, the firing stopped. It was only ten o'clock in the morning. It had lasted about an hour.

The first thing we go after is water because there's nothing makes a man thirstier than fighting. "It wasn't what I expected at all," Mitchell says.

"What wasn't?" I ask him.

"The war," he says.

"What did you expect?"

He shrugs. "I thought I'd be afraid."

"Who had time?" Levi says.

"I saw Lee waving," Mitchell says, "but I never saw the battle."

I still don't know what panicked them Spaniards. They was dug in and had us outnumbered and outgunned. If the battle had lasted another ten minutes we'd of been too cut up to make it to the top of that hill and could of been slaughtered easy.

"The fortunes of war," Mitchell says.

"Dumb luck," I say.

"Dumb, for sure," Levi says. "If I'd known what I was getting into I never would have got into it. Heinz neither. Did you see him snapping at them bullets down there? How many you think he swallowed?"

Luna comes out of nowhere, yelling at us to break it up. "This is not a church social. They need help with the wounded. Garland, send a dozen men on the double!" He sees Mountain and says, "What the hell are you doing here, Moore? I ordered you to the rear."

"So did I," I tell him.

"It looks worse than it is," Mountain says.

"Then go wash yourself," Luna tells him, "because you are not an appetizing sight." He sees me then and his voice drops. "I'm sorry, Garland," he says. "I didn't realize you were hurt."

"I guess it won't kill me."

"Good," Luna says. "We're all heroes. Before those bastards counterattack up the back of this hill, Garland, I want ten men on each flank, the rest in the middle and everybody dug in."

"I don't have that many men," I say.

"You do now. You're taking over from Isbell as sergeant. Knoblauch!"

"Sir!"

"You'll replace Garland as corporal. Mitchell!"

"Sir!"

"You're in charge of Marcus Russell's section. The rest of you men get to work. It may be hours before the Hotchkiss guns catch up so I want you ready to repel the enemy now. Do I make myself clear?"

Everybody nods and grumbles. The heat and the fighting has taken the starch out of us, but what's clear is it ain't softened Luna one bit. Yet he makes Mountain sit down so he can look at his head. There's two slices in his scalp about four inches long. One on top and one over his left ear. That's where all the blood come from. He's also got a flesh wound in his side where a bullet passed clear through his thigh and didn't hit more than skin.

Luna makes me sit too, and I wince when he touches the shoulder. But he says we can report to the surgeon after the worse wounded are seen to.

He tells all of us, "You gave more than you got. And I'm proud of you. That's all."

I follow Luna a ways down the hill. "Lieutenant?"

"What is it, Garland?"

"How many did we lose?"

"Too goddamned many," he says.

"I saw Tom Isbell go down."

"He's still alive, but his war's over."

"Ham Fish is dead," I say, "and Culver."

"You're wrong," he says. "Fish and Haefner were killed but Culver will make it."

I say, "Any chance you or Captain Butler can requisition some rations? We don't have anything and the men will be hungry."

"I'm in command of the troop now," Luna says.

"Where's Ben?"

"He's dead, Sergeant. I thought you knew."

The news of Ben Butler's death hits me hard. Seventy years later I still get mad. I always had trouble separating anger from grief and it's hard to forgive a man of his quality for dying.

When the word gets around the hill, some of the toughest, meanest soldiers in the troop got tears streaking their cheeks. "Not old Ben," they say. "Not the captain."

I believe we was afraid after that. Not cowardly or scared in the usual way, but afraid of something bigger. If a man as mighty and well-loved as Ben Butler could get killed that easy, then everything we bet our lives on was precarious.

Luna was a fine officer and a good leader, but Ben Butler was more than that to all of us and we took his death personal. He was the best we had to offer, the kindest, toughest, smartest, most decent man in the Territory. But all the things he was couldn't save him, and all the love we had for him wasn't enough either.

Cody ties up my shoulder for me, and cleans Mountain's wounds because he still refuses to go to the rear. From the top of the hill that night we look across to the Spanish campfires and wonder about tomorrow. It seems funny not having Ben Butler drop by to tuck us in. He always made the rounds at taps and knew every man by his first name.

Luna's on the hill with the first ray of dawn, brisk and irritable as ever. He lost his riding quirt in the battle, and now he's got nothing to tap or point with except a stick he cut along the trail. With that he indicates where he wants the common grave dug for Ben and the others.

"The chaplain will be here soon, Sergeant. Where's Mitchell?"

Mitchell comes up behind him and wishes him a good morning.

"Ben liked a good hymn, Corporal. Could you put part of our old choir together again and sing him one?"

"Yes, sir."

"You and Fortescue and Haefner?"

"Haefner's dead, sir," I remind him. He's confused for a second when he hears this and his face looks a hundred years old, all bleary-eyed and drawn.

"Did I say Haefner? I didn't mean Haefner. See what you can do." And he walks off.

We have thirty-four wounded, not counting me and Mountain, and they are a bigger problem than the dead because some are bad hit, and as usual, the army's short of everything. Our field hospital is still floating around on a ship somewheres off the coast and there ain't enough stretchers so we have to make do with rifles and dog tents to carry the men. Bandages and antiseptic are short, and so is ether. But heat, mosquitoes and land crabs are plentiful, and become the biggest hardship for the wounded, because they got no defense.

The chaplain takes forever to come, so we don't have the funeral until the heat is fierce and the bodies are taking on a smell. He's a tall, bony man with a high-pitched voice, and what little hair he's got is combed over a bald spot that's all sunburned. He's in a hurry again, like at the funeral for Carl Washington's drowned men, and he keeps losing his place in the prayer book. The burial detail covers the bodies with grass and palm leaves, and Colonel Wood says our comrades have not died in vain.

Fine words, I hear them said again over so many other friends in the weeks that follow. If you ask me all soldiers die in vain no matter who wins.

That don't make me a pacifist. I believe men enjoy killing each other and war's just a ritual excuse they invent. My grandson Pete disagrees. He's as quarrelsome as Luna sometimes and even though he's a doctor, he loves to argue the eternal questions. He believes in what he calls the "perfectability" of man, and says there's no reason to think we're not getting better each generation. He throws medical evidence at me about how everybody's taller and smarter and healthier than they used to be, so why shouldn't they be improving their morals too? "Common sense," Pete says, "dictates our survival in a nuclear age. If we can put a man in space we can save the species from extinction."

Pete's an optimist, but I ain't seen nothing in ninety years leads me to agree with him on this. Common sense don't dictate nothing because we got other fish to fry. If we didn't like wars so much, we wouldn't have them. If we wasn't so contrary, we'd learn from our mistakes and not make the same ones over and over since the Babylonian time. Just look at us! If we don't blow ourselves up first, we'll drown in our own shit or else starve to death because there's too many souls for too few rations.

"Rock of Ages" was what the boys sang before they threw the dirt on Ben Butler. I had to go off by myself then, and I remember Cody coming after me. "You all right, Lee?" He hangs around a few minutes, kicking dirt and chewing on a piece of grass. "Remember when Jake died, what Mountain told us about the Indian spirits?"

"Cody, leave me alone."

"I thought we could talk a little."

"Some other time."

"What kind of spirit you think Ben had, Lee? Wise old owl maybe? Only he wasn't so old, was he?"

"There ain't any spirits, Cody! Grow up! A man gets shot, he's dead. Don't you smell anything? That's Ben Butler! He's buzzard meat. So's poor Russell and Haefner. Now go away and leave me be."

It's as if I slapped him and he starts to walk off.

"Sit down," I tell him. "But shut up."

Well, if there's one thing Cody can't do it's that, and I should know better than to ask the impossible. After about a minute he says, "Lee?"

"What?"

"I don't think that smell's from the grave. It's Heinz. Your boot's covered with dogshit."

Leave it to Cody. That's the trouble with grief. You mainly feel sorry for yourself because your world's interrupted when somebody you care about leaves you high and dry. And in the end it all comes down to dogshit.

An army captain rides up then on a mule and hails us. He ain't from our regiment, but dressed in blue with infantry insignia.

"Yes, sir?"

"What's your name?" He's a handsome dude and he looks familiar.

"Sergeant Garland, sir."

"I'm Captain Fall," he says. "Where's Ben Butler?"

Thinking he wants to know where we buried Ben, I answer, "There on the hill."

"Be a good fellow and tell him I'm here, will you?"

"Captain, he's dead."

He just climbs off his mule and wipes the sweat off his face with a kerchief before he says, "Ben dead? I always counted on Ben."

"Well, you can't count on him no more," I tell him. "None of us can." As I hear my voice choke, I know I'm trying to convince myself as much as him. I have to bury Ben Butler now and can't do it.

He lays a kindly hand on my shoulder and says, "Well, son, I have a Spanish prisoner. Can you take him off my hands?"

"Leave him with us, sir," I tell him, glad to get my mind off the funeral and onto something else.

"Garland, Garland," he says. "You from New Mexico?"

"Yes, sir."

"There was a man wanted for murder, name of Lee Garland. Any relation?" He laughs at this, like it's the joke of the year.

"I'm Lee Garland," I say.

He looks at me as if he don't believe it. "Not the same?"

"The same."

"Ben was trying to get your indictment quashed."

"It was him took me in the Rough Riders."

"Jesus Christ on a crutch!" he says. "Ben Butler dead!" He whistles up a soldier down on the trail who leads out this scared-looking fellow in white pants.

I only met Captain Fall for a few minutes that first time, under circumstances which was sad and miserable in the extreme. But as soon as he says who he is, I recognize the name. Albert Fall was an important personality in the Territory, a judge on the Supreme Court and a close friend of Ben Butler's. Like Ben, he was looking ahead to a big political future, even if he was a Democrat then.

He's a man you wanted to trust, but a different kind from Ben. Not modest and quiet at all, always tearing around with his ambition sticking out as obvious as elk horns. What might of been obnoxious in anybody else, was attractive in Albert Fall because you felt all he wanted to do was take you along with him, a quality that wins a young man over in a second.

Captain Fall don't stop at Ben Butler's grave. He just salutes the hill and says in an ordinary voice, "Good-bye, Ben. And may the devil reserve a special place in hell for the greaser that did you in!"

"See you, Garland," he shouts as he remounts his mule and kicks him into a trot. "Finish this goddamn war and let's go home!"

The prisoner is nervous and scared and surprised I speak Spanish. He's older than the other enemy soldiers I seen so far, well fed and his pants got a red stripe on them.

"I am Cuban," he says. "Let me go, please."

"Then why are you wearing a Spanish officer's pants?"

"I took them from a dead man to escape."

Miller and Knoblauch join me and I send Miller to tell Luna about the prisoner. Then I make him turn out his pockets, and he's got three letters on him, all in Spanish. He denies they belong to him and says they was in the pants he stole from the dead Spaniard. He's also wearing a gold signet ring that looks a bit rich for a Cuban rebel.

"Where'd you get that ring?"

"I found it."

"Lucky fit."

He's sweating pretty hard now and not just from the heat.

"You know what?" I say. "I think you're a Spanish officer and a sniper." The letter I'm reading is an order to a Lieutenant Mancebo to lead a group of sharpshooters along our line of advance. The other two letters are from the lieutenant's family.

"I am Cuban," he says, and by insisting on it, he only irritates me. He hopes I'm dumb enough to believe him and turn him loose so he can rejoin his unit. But I've heard enough Cubans talking Spanish to know they don't lisp like this fellow.

Just then our brave Cuban allies ride up, the same bunch been with us on and off since we landed, led by this mean-looking nigger laughs at everything I say. Mostly they been pillaging our supplies and staying out of the fight, so I got no use for them. But they see the prisoner and come swarming around like kids after candy. I wave them away with my Colt, but their interest don't lag. They all got Mauser rifles now, scavenged off the battlefield, and they're still carrying their machetes.

The leader grins at me, showing a great mouth full of pearly teeth. "Cuba *Libre!* We beat them good, eh, chief? How come you keep this one alive?"

"Stand back," I tell them. "He's my prisoner."

The leader busts a gut over that. "Sure. Yours, mine, everybody's."

Ted Miller comes back with the news that Luna don't have time to interrogate the prisoner and wants him sent to the rear.

"He can't go without a guard and I ain't got the heart to ask anybody to take him in this heat."

"What about them?" Miller jerks a thumb at the Cubans.

"He'd never make it alive with them clowns. No. Leave him here for now. He'll keep." I tell the leader again, "Stay away from him. He's ours."

"We watch him for you," the Cuban says, and his men all get the giggles again.

"Just stay away from him!"

I start up the hill with Miller behind me and we ain't more than halfway when a scream freezes me in my tracks. I turn and see the Cuban leader holding up the prisoner's severed hand, the one with the gold ring. I give a shout, but before I can move, the son of a bitch gives the Spaniard a couple whacks with his machete and the man is cut to pieces still tied to the tree. I'm about to blow that piece of shit out of the saddle, when Miller catches my arm.

"Don't, Lee! There'll be hell to pay."

The Cubans ride off, laughing.

Miller and I cut what's left of the Spaniard away from the tree and leave him there on the ground.

I feel worse than when the boys was singing hymns at Ben Butler's grave. It didn't do me no good to cuss out that Cuban bastard. The man was my prisoner and I let them kill him.

Nobody's going to blame me, nobody's even going to care. I tell myself that if the dead man had told the truth and admitted he was a Spanish officer, he'd still be alive. But I know it ain't true. I still would of left him tied to the tree and them Cuban cutthroats would have done the same thing. How could I let a helpless man be butchered by a bunch of bandits.

I got his letters in my pocket. One from his wife I didn't finish reading. And one from his kid saying, Papa, please hurry home. I tear them up and let them fall to the ground.

"It's not your fault," Miller says.

"How many goddamn things in this world ain't our fault, but we just let happen?"

"Come on, Lee. He's the enemy. Yesterday he was trying to kill you."

"Yesterday we both had a chance. Today he didn't."

We walk off down the trail in the direction of the beach. It's quiet except for the cicadas. "Are you superstitious, Lee?"

"No."

"Neither am I," Miller says, "but I have a feeling I won't see home again."

"I got no time for that kind of talk."

"Sorry." He's a fine fellow, this Ted Miller, always the first one to volunteer for anything, but he has it in his head he ain't going to make it through Cuba and I finally ask him why.

"I've had the idea since I put on the uniform that I'd never take it off."

"Stay in the army and become a general. Like Shafter."

"God forbid."

"Or old Joe Wheeler."

"Spare me that."

"There must be somebody you respect."

"There's Luna, and Colonel Roosevelt and you."

"I thought we was having a serious conversation."

"You don't know how the men depend on you," Miller says. He's thoughtful for a while before he tells me, "You're a talisman. Everybody wants to stay close to you because you're lucky and they know you'll bring them through."

"Well, there you are. I always had a horseshoe up my ass and if it works for them, it'll work for you."

We come quite a distance down the trail by then and we're all alone. I stop for a smoke, then turn back. As I move a hole explodes in the tree where I struck the match, and me and Miller hit the dirt. A second later I hear the crack of a rifle.

I remember the orders the Spaniard was carrying as another bullet tears the leaves a foot away. We roll into the thicket. Neither one of us has a rifle and I don't have the faintest notion where the shooter is even if I could hit him with my Colt.

We lay there five minutes without moving before I see something coming through the grass in my direction. I don't know if it's a sharpshooter or a boa constrictor, but either way he's dead. A flash of white appears and disappears and that's no snake. Then the grass parts not five feet from me, and it's Levi's dog.

"Go on, get! Get out of here, Heinz, goddamn it!" He's licking my face like he ain't seen me in a week.

Ze-e-eu! A bullet smacks the grass a few feet away. The dog tries to bite it and runs in circles looking for more.

I hear voices coming up the trail from the beach, and recognize Levi yelling for his dog. Old Heinz stiffens when he hears him, but he don't run off. That hound always did have a mind of his own.

"Levi!" I holler. "Stay down! Snipers! Move off the trail!"

Another ze-e-eu between me and the dog and I roll deeper into the undergrowth while he snaps at the grass.

"That you, Lee?" Levi and the others can't be more than forty yards behind us.

"Keep down!" I tell them.

"You seen Heinz?"

"Call him, will you? He's drawing fire."

Thwa-a-ck! against a tree right above the dog, who's growling now, the hair on his back up.

"He'll find him, Lee! Just tell him, 'Point.' "

"Point, Heinz!" I say. "Point, boy! Go on, Heinz, point!" But I might as well be talking to a deaf-mute, the way that dog ignores me. "Heinz, you dumb fleabag, point!"

Ze-e-eu! Ze-e-euu!

The dog goes crazy chasing them bullets and I'm thinking he ain't only useless, he's a peril because that shooter can see him. Then I remember the first time I ever seen him at the medical examination in Santa Fe. He wouldn't obey Levi either until he called him by another name. But I don't remember the name. I whistle at him and he don't even look. He's too busy watching for the next bullet. I ain't anxious to shout at Levi anymore because every time I open my mouth that bastard shoots and every time he shoots, he gets closer.

Then I remember. "Spotty?" I whisper, and damn if that mutt don't prick up his ears and look at me. "Point, Spotty! Point, boy! Where is he, Spotty? Go get him, Spot!" Well, you have to understand he is a miserable-looking dog, always was. He's short half an ear from his San Antonio fight, and the Cuban diet ain't done him no good either. But he stiffens right up when I use that name. His tail goes out straight and his nose quivers in the air. Then he takes off through the grass like bees are after him and a second later he appears on a little rise about fifty yards ahead of us, howling and barking at the foot of a coconut palm. A patch of white appears in the green thatch of leaves above, and I know I just got lucky.

"Lee, you there?" Levi yells, but I don't answer. I'm too busy working my way closer to that tree.

Ze-e-eeu! I get it in the foot. When I get up I'm limping but I make it to a bush before he fires again. All I see now is the top of this palm tree. He's in it someplace but I only got six rounds and a target about twenty feet in diameter.

I wait.

When I see the little patch of white again I shoot.

He don't fall so I don't know whether I hit him or not, but when I move again he don't try to get me. Heinz is still going crazy at the base of the tree and the sharpshooter don't shoot the dog either, so I figure I did some good. But then maybe that's what he wants me to think, so I lay there in the weeds until Levi comes running. I expect him to get it, but he don't.

"Lee, you all right? Where's Heinz?"

When the others catch up, Mitchell empties a magazine into the top of the tree and we see the man up there, caught in the branches a hundred feet off the ground. I guess he's dead because he ain't moving. The only thing happened to me is he shot my boot heel off.

San Juan Hill

We march in fits and starts the next couple of days, and more men come down with fever. Finally we reach a hilly glade where Luna tells us to dig in because it's exposed to enemy fire.

As soon as we finish and everybody falls exhausted into his own little piece of trench, we get orders to move out. Ransom's the bearer of this disturbing news, and Mitchell has a laughing fit he passes to the others. It's a weak, hysterical kind of mirth, the sort that only takes over when men been fighting and digging and marching half-starved and thirsty for a week. Fortescue starts a chorus from "The Animal Fair" and Ransom appeals to me, "Tell them, Lee! You're in charge."

"I can't control them. They're feverish and crazed from the heat, Ransom. I wouldn't push."

"Luna will throw everybody off this hill. Don't say I didn't warn you."

Mitchell says, "Okay, you warned us."

Miller says, "Ransom, you're as tiresome as the lieutenant."

Ransom says, "He better not hear you call him lieutenant. He's a captain now."

Fortescue says, "Ransom, old chap, are you familiar with the ancient Persians?"

"The ancient what?" Ransom says.

"Persians," Fortescue says. "Xerxes, Darius, Cyrus?"

"I don't believe I'm acquainted with them," Ransom says.

"The Persian army policed an empire that stretched thousands of miles, and they used men like you to carry messages."

"So?" Ransom's a favorite target of Fortescue's humor and he's suspicious, but the word "police" catches his interest.

"So whenever a messenger brought news the Persian's didn't like . . ." Fortescue says with a dramatic pause, "they killed him."

"So?"

"So beware, Ransom."

Ransom puts his hands on his hips and says, "So you're going to kill me? Don't make me laugh!"

"We are not the ancient Persians," Fortescue explains solemnly. "We are modern American empire builders."

"You're crazy, that's what you are," Ransom says. "Lee's right. The heat melted your brains."

"Modern American empire builders do not kill messengers," Fortescue continues. "They take their pants!"

Poor Ransom don't have a chance. Fortescue tackles him and they get his leggings and britches off, leaving him standing on the hillside in only his long johns and hat.

"Goddamn you!" Ransom yells. "How am I going to report to the colonel like this? Give me back my pants! Lee!"

"I told you they was out of control. You didn't listen."

"It ain't my fault you got to move out," Ransom pleads.

"But you brought the news," Fortescue says.

"I got orders!"

"Thank your stars we're not Persians," Mitchell says.

"Come on, fellows. Please?"

Knoblauch says, "Should we take a vote?"

"I move we get off the hill," Miller says.

"I second that," Mitchell says.

"All in favor?" says Fortescue, and we all shout, "Aye!"

"What about my pants?" Ransom hollers.

"What pants?" Cody says. "Anybody seen Ransom's pants?"

We go down into another valley in the heat. Across it and up another hill. There ain't no sign of the enemy. It rains and we slip and fall in the muck. Sometimes there's so much water, it's like standing under a barrel somebody knocked the bottom out of. When the sun comes out, so do the horseflies and seven different kinds of flying beatle. Cuban mosquitoes don't keep regular hours either so we have them for company all the time.

Nobody talks. The energy just ain't there. Mountain kills a snake as big as a fire hose and we leave it thrashing and twisting on the trail. We curse the rain but every time the sun comes out, we curse it too, and wish it would start raining again. It always does. We fill our canteens with the water running off our hat brims, like having a spigot in your head.

We reach a hill where we can see through the wavery heat to the red-tile rooftops of Santiago in the distance. But between us and the city twelve thousand Spaniards are working like ants, digging trenches, and we see them plain, their straw hats bobbing up and down.

At Guásimas we was four hundred against two thousand. How we won, nobody knows. Now there's a lot more of us. Not just the Rough Riders but our black friends from the Tenth Cavalry, as well as the Ninth Cavalry, which is another colored regiment, the First Cavalry, which is white, and more regular and volunteer outfits. The artillery's catching up and long lines of muddy mules straggle in with ammunition and rations.

Mountain cooks us rancid sowbelly and hardtack, and Fortescue says he wishes he had invested in pork futures. "Next war," he says, "I'm going to stay home and make money."

"You got more than you can spend now," Cody says.

"The key words are 'stay home,'" Fortescue explains.

The next morning I see Shafter followed by five or six staff officers, one of whom is Captain Fall. While the general's talking to Colonel Roosevelt, Fall comes over to gossip with us and bum a cup of coffee.

"Tomorrow," he says, "Shafter's taking Caney."

I ask him where it is and he draws a triangle on the ground. "This is us," he says, indicating one point of the triangle. "This is San Juan Hill, and over here is Caney." San Juan Hill is the one where the Spaniards are digging. "There'll be seven thousand of us swarming over that place tomorrow. The Dons won't know what dropped on them."

The enemy occupies some buildings and a blockhouse on the hill, a stone fort with walls three feet thick. We got a one-mile march along a narrow trail and a small river to cross just before we break out of the jungle. Then it's only four or five hundred yards up a steep grassy slope to where the Spaniards are.

Captain Fall says if four hundred Americans could drive two thousand Spaniards off the ridge at Las Guásimas, he ain't worried about what we're going to do to them tomorrow. "Before noon we'll have Santiago at our feet," he says, "and the Spanish army at our mercy."

Looking at the confusion around me I ain't so sure. The place we're camped is a quagmire with different regiments milling around. Besides that, common sense tells me we're going to be ass-deep in Mauser bullets the next day, but listening to Captain Fall you'd think the Spanish are no more nuisance than bugs at a picnic. He could sell hair to a bear, that man, and he done a lot for our morale on the eve of the battle.

When General Shafter finishes looking through his spyglass at the Spaniards, three men lift him on his buckboard and he goes off with Fall and the other staff officers trailing behind.

That afternoon we draw rations for three days. Hardtack, green coffee beans, moldy sowbelly and canned tomatoes. The tomatoes are finished as soon as we get our hands on them and the other stuff we put in our horse-collar packs. We break camp and move to what's going to be the firing line in the morning. It takes three hours because of the traffic and the mud, but on the march the observation balloon arrives tethered to a wagon full of gas machines. It's a fat yellow bag of silk, bigger than a house and lighter than a bubble, oscillating on the end of a cable. Two men climb into a basket and they reel it out over two thousand feet above us. Everybody's gawking because it's such a spectacular show.

The rain begins again but the balloon don't come down. Levi says, "Ain't that a caution, Lee? I bet they can see where the whole Spanish army is."

Fortescue says, "And the whole Spanish army knows where we are as long as it stays up there."

The moon comes up just before dark but it ain't nearly as impressive as the balloon. We hunker down for the night without our tents. Luna comes around to see how we are and says with his usual tact, "Tomorrow dead and wounded are to be left where they fall and tended to later. Keep your intervals and make every shot count."

I roll out around four A.M. and clean my guns. Breakfast is hardtack soaked in water. This is the coolest hour of the day but it don't stay that way for long. The sun comes up like a great red fireball, and five minutes later we're all pouring sweat even though we're just sitting. In my case it's a touch of fever and I feel a little giddy even in the shade. Then Captain Grimes's artillery clatters up a few yards from us, the horses plunging and struggling under the drivers' lashes to get the cannons into position.

Grimes is a prissy little fellow with glasses and a mustache that looks pasted on his lip, but they say he's the best gunner in the army. He's walking around the guns like they're his pets, patting them and stroking them, and peeking through a little brass rangefinder he carries, telling the cannoneers what adjustments to make.

Roosevelt's with us on his horse, calm and quiet for a change, eating a sandwich everybody wonders where he got. We wait and wait and start to get nervous because no order comes to advance. Ransom says Shafter's down with the gout and can't make it to the battlefield.

An aide gallops up and talks to Grimes, who raises both arms as if he's about to lead an orchestra. When he brings them down the cannons open fire. The first barrage deafens all of us and a big cloud of white smoke hangs over the guns because we don't have smokeless powder.

When the shells hit, the enemy lines come alive like somebody kicked an anthill and I'm thinking this ain't going to be so bad because there won't be many Spaniards left by the time we get over there. That's when it happens. A whistling sound and a tremendous explosion that throws dirt all over us and leaves my ears ringing. For a second I think one of our cannons blew up, but they're still there. We're all looking at each other, wondering what it is when we hear the whistle again and we duck. This time it's right over our heads and it rains shrapnel.

I hear groaning from the ground nearby and see a trooper with his leg nearly sliced off. A horse is down and thrashing around, but the officer riding him jumps out of the way. Roosevelt's been hit too, but only a small cut on his wrist, which he ties up with his bandanna.

I call out to Mitchell and C.E. Knoblauch to report their sections but Mitchell don't answer. Instead Fortescue hollers that Mitchell's been wounded.

Before I can get over to see how bad he's hurt, more shells come in from the Spanish lines. They can't miss with our goddamn smoke to sight on, and I'm hoping somebody will get us off this hill before we all get blown to smithereens. Grimes's battery is still firing, but to us now it feels as if he's doing more harm by giving away our position than damage to the Spanish.

Except for the burst that got Mitchell and the others, most of the shells go over our heads to the rear or fall short. It's ugly music in the air all the same, not a tune I'd ever care to hear again. While it's going on, funny enough, my mind's some place else. I'm not even daydreaming about Caroline or thinking of food and water. I'm concentrating hard on New Mexico, trying to conjure up these here mountains around Eagle Nest, the most beautiful place on earth. I'm remembering the clearness of the air, the ponderosa pines and the smell of a piñon fire, the rich feel and color of the grass in spring and the look of the shady pools where the trout hide. In my head I see sunlight playing on the aspen leaves, and little clutches of pink and yellow wild flowers that grow by the river. I think of birch trees in the snow and my horse's nose as he drinks from the spring, ice crystals forming on his whiskers. I don't know why I recall all that, lying on my belly in the Cuban heat, but I do, and it comes in my mind to this day whenever I think of that bombardment.

My grandson Pete says these are the defenses of the human brain, and because I got total recall they're all lodged in my head with my war memories. He says I was probably so shit-scared of them shells going off I just had to push my imagination back to some comfortable thoughts to keep my sanity. He's usually right because he studied them things as a doctor.

Caroline liked to say nature was my religion and Eagle Nest was my church, and that by keeping them in mind on the battlefield, it was my special way of praying. But she was always trying to work God into any situation she didn't understand.

I think the explanation's simpler. The noise, the heat, the fever, the bugs, the rain and the Spaniards was all telling me I was going to die and I just wanted the best part of my life in my head when it happened.

Poor Mitchell lost a lot of blood. When I tell him he'll live, he says, "Lee, old friend, I've gentled my condition." As a Red Cross man helps him to the rear, he waves us a weak salute with his good arm.

When the bugle finally sounds the attack, we move out as if the devil's behind us, tripping over the heels of the men in front, looking more like kids let out of school than soldiers charging the enemy. We don't have the cannon fire to worry about anymore, but that's when the sharpshooters start in the treetops, taking a toll.

We step around dead men and horses, and pass stragglers from other units, regulars and militia in blue uniforms who join us. There's a stream of wounded toward the rear, some of them hurt real bad, and most sort of hypnotized by the pain. One quiet fellow being carried is losing a terrible lot of blood where the head of his prick is shot away, and another one is screaming who don't seem to have a mark on him. When Luna catches him by the arm he shakes loose. "Where's your rifle?" Luna says. "Get back to your outfit and fight!" But the poor bastard falls in a heap because he's got a hole in his back as big as a baseball.

The San Juan River ain't much as rivers go, about thirty yards across and knee-deep where the ford is, but there's no cover, and bullets are churning the water like hailstones. Because of the wounded and the general confusion, our column is now down to single file. I holler at my people to spread out and run because that's the only way we're going to make it across that stream.

Red Holman, who I've known since we was kids, comes running back from the stream screaming, "It's no good, boys! It's no good! Fall back! We're beaten!" He practically collides with Cody, who calls him a goddamn scrimshanker and shoves him out of the way with his rifle butt. The rest of us move around him like he's got the plague. Nothing ever happened to him for running away because the generals didn't want to publicize a bad apple. There was a few others like him in Cuba, but they was the exception, not the rule.

Roosevelt's already cantering into the water ahead of us on his horse, yelling at everybody to get a move on, and waving a sabre to get our attention. Most of us think he's a damn fool to expose himself, but the men holler back at him, "We're coming, Colonel! Hold your horses!"

And we go.

One of his aides, Lieutenant Shipp, is shot out of the saddle right next to him. When I pass Shipp on the riverbank I see he's dead. Ahead of me, a police detective named Haywood who is a New York friend of Roosevelt's goes down on all fours, puking blood into the water. Sam Goldberg, a redhead telegraph operator from

Santa Fe gets hit in the spine and both lungs. That creek's frothing with Mauser slugs and I don't know how the rest of us escape being struck down. The big yellow balloon comes floating over the river and we all watch it like idiots. Fortescue swears we ought to shoot it down. "That's what's drawing all this fire on us!" he says.

The balloon finally collapses and we watch it drift down like a big busted beachball to settle in the jungle. I read after the war there was more than four hundred men wounded and killed in a space no bigger than a city block because of that balloon, but nobody could ever tell me if it was us or them that shot it down.

Luna nails a sharpshooter in the top of a coconut palm, dropping him on the trail in front of us like a buckshot bird. The Spaniard's dressed in a quilted green vest like a life preserver and sand is running out of the bullet holes. The quilting was supposed to be a kind of armor, but it didn't help him much.

Roosevelt passes the order to move off the road into the thicket, without slowing down the advance. That's fine, except there's barbed-wire fences, and wire cutters was only one of the things our side forgot to bring to this war.

Cowhands have crossed enough fenced land back home to have it down to a fine art. One man holds two strands of wire apart while the other fellow passes, then vice versa. But when the Eastern city boys try it, there's cuts, scratches and torn britches everywhere.

Luna's got Lieutenant Shipp's horse now, and he's every place at once. "What's holding you back!" he hollers at us. "You people want to live forever?" We stir ourselves because there ain't a lot of point in staying where we are, thirsty, tired and suffering from the heat. There's no let up in the enemy fire.

I see black faces around us, men in blue uniforms hunkered down, shooting at the hill ahead. "You from the Tenth Cavalry?" I ask one fellow and he shakes his head. Then another black man says, "Over here! What do you want with the Tenth?"

I yell back, "Are you in Sergeant Washington's troop?"

Another voice calls out from the grass, "Is that you, Reverend?"

"It's me, Sergeant. What's a smart fellow like you doing in a low-down place like this?" and his laugh ripples back to me.

I'm glad to see these fellows because they are some of the best soldiers in the regular army, but I'm thinking if they're mixed in with us, then there's even more confusion on this battlefield than

I thought. I don't know whether it's us or them, but somebody's in the wrong place.

Roosevelt's arguing with an officer in blue I never seen before, but I guess he's one of those in charge of Carl Washington and his people.

"I have no orders to advance beyond this point," the regular says. He's a handsome fellow on a skittish horse, and he's dancing all around Roosevelt during their chat.

"Then stand aside, sir, and let us through!" Roosevelt tells this officer.

"As you wish, Colonel," he says, and gallops for cover.

Roosevelt's crazy, but we ain't going to heaven where we are so we might as well try the hill. About then a fellow dressed like a department-store dummy in a seersucker jacket and white linen pants, flops down beside me. "John Black Atkins," he says in a real fancy accent. "The *Times.*"

"Lee Garland," I say. "Keep your head down."

"Are you really going to charge that hill?"

"It looks that way," I tell him.

"You can't possibly go it alone as infantry," Atkins says.

"We ain't infantry," I tell him. "We're Rough Riders."

"You're mad," Atkins says, "whatever you call yourselves."

The Spanish fire is like corn popping at us now. It's irregular, but every so often they get off a volley and the grass bends ahead as if a giant comb's being passed through it.

At that moment Roosevelt is galloping back and forth like a lunatic, while Luna's gone crazy with the rest of them, pounding into the lead, and waving his hat like he's at a cattle roundup.

Lieutenant Leahy jerks in the saddle before I hear the *chunk, chunk!* of the bullets that hit him. It's like they say, you never hear the one that gets you because it's there before the sound. He slumps forward with his head over the horse's mane, saying, "Help me, somebody, help me down." I grab his bridle and try to keep him from falling and my hand's all sticky where I'm holding him by the hip. Miller helps me get his boot out of the stirrup so I can ease him to the ground. "I'm sorry to put you out, boys," he says. "I'm real sorry."

That's when the fire is the heaviest. A corporal raises his arm to motion people forward and his hand turns into a bloody stump.

One trooper gets it through both cheeks, while another has his kneecap blown away and a West Point cadet on his summer vacation is gut-shot.

Henry Meagher, another Oklahoma cowboy, is laying on his belly next to Ted Miller when a bullet strikes his cartridge belt and a dozen rounds go off around his middle like firecrackers. His own bullets cut him up around the ass and one of them creases his heel, but otherwise he's okay. His bunkmate McGinty loses part of an ear and they can't stop laughing at their luck.

The heat is cooking us. We're pinned down, but we can't stay where we are. Mountain rolls over next to me and says, "Lee, you got to do something." It's the first time I ever seen him drink from his canteen so I know we're in trouble. That man wasn't frightened of anything other than some sparks in a Mexican bed. But he don't want to die here any more than the rest of us.

Roosevelt charges out again, swearing a blue streak and pointing toward the hill. Luna's shouting too, "Go, go, go!"

I say to Mountain, "Let's do it," and we run forward. Levi goes down right away and Cody pauses to see how bad he's hit. But Levi ain't hurt. His leg just fell asleep from squatting in the grass too long. Fortescue brings his men forward and some black troopers join us. The colonel's in a canter now and we're trying to keep up with him.

For a minute or two it's going fine and we're part way up the hill. Then Roosevelt reins in his horse because there's another goddamned barbed-wire fence across our path and we're stalled right under their rifles, the men milling around bewildered. That's when I see Carl Washington rise up out of nowhere, shouting at his people to charge that section of the fence. They fling their bodies against the wire, a dozen yelling troopers with Washington in the lead. When one of the posts snaps off under their weight, ten yards of fence go down.

Graceful as a toe dancer, Roosevelt's horse, Texas, steps over the wire and canters up the hill as we pour through after him.

It's hard for the enemy to miss. But we're giving it back now and that makes a difference. Run, kneel, shoot. I don't know how the colonel stays alive. Sometimes he's galloping between us and the Spaniards and we hold our fire for fear of hitting him. Levi Hennings tumbles into the dirt with a bullet in his leg, but Heinz don't stop.

"We're going to make it, Lee!" Miller yells. Luna's on foot now, keeping up with us. Carl Washington's a few feet behind me with Knoblauch in the lead. Then Miller goes down. When I stop and ask him where he's hit, he says, "I don't know."

"I'll be back," I tell him, and keep going.

Our people are swarming all over that hill. I don't know where they come from all of a sudden, but it's a lovely sight to see. When I reach the first trench it's empty except for dead Spaniards, and we keep going till we get to the second one.

The colonel's off his horse too, running with the men. I see two Spaniards from this second trench aim at Roosevelt and I empty a Krag magazine in their direction, dropping them both. We're on the top finally, congratulating ourselves, and thinking the battle ought to be over. But it ain't.

There's another hill right next to us so full of Spaniards, it's raining Mauser bullets again heavy as ever. Me, Mountain and some others crouch down behind the biggest iron kettle I ever seen, about eight feet in diameter and six feet deep, a thing Cubans use to boil sugar in.

The joke is that San Juan Hill is where all the shooting's coming from, and we either take it too, or get the hell off the one we're on. I look around and wonder how many more hills our luck is good for. The way men have been falling since we started out this morning we're going to be a pretty small army before we get to Santiago.

Somebody comes up with our flag then and sticks it where we can all see it. The damn fool is hit while he's doing this, and drags himself off into a trench, but we give him a cheer for his trouble.

Ransom squirms his way over to where we are and I ask him what's going on. Before he can answer shells explode overhead again and the kettle rings like a fire gong from the shrapnel. I'm thinking every time we get on a hill we get bombarded and every time we move off we're chewed up by their rifle fire. Then I hear another sound from behind, a kind of dull *drrumm-dum-dum-dum,* and nearly wet myself when somebody says, "Spanish machine guns!" But Ransom says, "No, that's our Gatlings," and he's right. They're raking the trenches on San Juan Hill. Puffs of dust stitch the dirt in front of the Spaniards and at last their fire lets up a little. After a couple minutes even the enemy artillery slacks off.

Our infantry starts up the other slope, their blue shirts against the green grass in the sun. Little pinpoints of fire pick at them from the Spanish trenches, and they look pitiful and disorganized, scrambling around, spread out, holding their rifles across their chests, slipping on the grass. There don't seem to be very many, not nearly enough for what they're trying to do.

I'm thinking there's been a terrible mistake here. Somebody gave the wrong order and these poor dumb bastards don't know it. It ain't heroic or gallant or brave, just pathetic. The only thing you can admire is the stubborn way they keep going, slipping and sliding and falling. I want to call out for them to come back, not even try it. We must of looked just as stupid stumbling up to where we are. Then I see Luna coming toward us at a run and he's in a fury. "Goddamn you for laggards!" he yells at us. "Who told you to stop? When I say go I mean go! Off your asses! Go! Go! Go!"

Cody says, "We didn't hear you, Captain."

"You hear me now, by God! Garland, get these men moving! The colonel's out there all by himself!"

It's easier at first because we're going down the back side of this slope. But the Mauser fire don't let up, and bullets pluck at my clothes like the enemy's trying to get my attention. We're at the bottom before I see Roosevelt again, on his way up the other hill already, on foot like the rest of us.

A huge explosion tears into a part of the Spanish blockhouse, and Ransom yells, "The dynamite gun, by God!" He must be right because the shell is too big to come from the Hotchkiss one-pounders or any of the other artillery we got.

A captain from Shafter's staff is shaking his head like he's got water in his ear. A bullet took out one eye and he can't see from the other one for the blood. Another man's rifle stock is split into two huge splinters and he's trying to pull one of them out of his thigh.

First there are men ahead of me and then there ain't. I'm yelling the whole time and climbing on the slippery grass and trying to make every shot count. I remember squatting for a second behind a shredded bush where a bird's singing for all he's worth. Who ever heard of a bird singing in the middle of a battle?

A Harvard kid from Fortescue's section runs ahead. He's shot in the face, but he don't go down, just drops his rifle and turns around on the slope like he ain't interested in the war anymore. His brains are all over his shirt but he staggers twenty feet before he falls dead.

Spanish faces appear and disappear, and I concentrate on hitting them. Twice I empty my Colt and reload, and the second time I only got four cartridges left. We're not more than thirty yards from the trenches when Fortescue catches a bullet in the foot and goes down cursing. But he sits there calm as Christmas, firing round after round until we get in his way and he has to stop. Cody's way behind because the second hill climb is too much for him, but Mountain's never more than five yards from me the whole time.

We're so close to the trenches now, we'll be thumb wrassling the Dons in a minute. This ain't the same bunch we beat at Guásimas. They don't run away and they ain't throwing up their hands in surrender neither. They got no chance because by now we're all over the place, but I guess somebody forgot to tell them.

One little greaser in front of me wounds two troopers before I shoot him in the head. Another one in the trench takes aim at Knoblauch and I'm so close I can't miss, but when I pull the trigger, the Colt clicks on an empty chamber.

The Spaniard turns his Mauser on me. Now *he* can't miss and for half a second I'm as close to dying as I ever been. In fact I'm already dead, looking into that man's eyes. But Mountain shoots first, so I get to tell the story instead of that Spaniard.

After another ten minutes San Juan Hill is ours, but we work all afternoon getting the wounded down to a dressing station near the river. There's damn little shade and the surgeons operate nonstop. When they run out of bandages they use torn-up underwear, Spanish uniforms and pieces of tent to wrap the worst wounds. Buzzards circling overhead mark the hospital, and more than one man is shot by sharpshooters while he's waiting his turn.

We near drown ourselves in water, we're so thirsty. Mitchell's doing better than I expect, and so is Levi. Fortescue's still cursing because he can't stand on his damaged foot. But Miller's the worst hit and I'm surprised he's still alive. The bullet went in his left shoulder and come out his right, and he's having trouble breathing. At least we move him to a little shade and Levi and Fortescue stay with him.

The enemy finally stops shooting around sundown and we find a mess of rice and beans in the captured blockhouse so we have a pretty good supper. Luna's been hit by four pieces of shrapnel during the afternoon, but nothing serious. He's as cantankerous as ever and cusses us out for the sloppy way we come up the hill, taking our own sweet time. But we know he's satisfied because he even pats me and Mountain on the back for what we done, and Luna ain't a backslapper. When we hunker down to get some sleep after dark, he goes off to check on the other wounded.

XVI

Staying Alive

After the battle for San Juan Hill there weren't any more death-defying charges or colorful skirmishes to entertain the reporters, but there was still a lot of shooting and dying to do before the enemy was ready to give up. According to what we hear, one of our generals wants us to attack while the other one want to retreat. I ain't any more fond of San Juan Hill than I am of the rest of Cuba. But we bought and paid for it, and there's no way we'd give it back without a fight.

Early on the morning after the battle we're sitting in the shade of the blockhouse wall drinking bitter, half-roasted coffee we ground with our pistol butts. I slept bad the night before, with chills and fever and nightmares about Alfred S. Sorenson chasing me. It ain't enough I got the Dons on my hands in the daytime, I got to put up with him in my dreams.

Luna says, "If we'd pushed the attack yesterday when we had the momentum we'd be drinking this in Santiago." Momentum? The man's never satisfied. "Garland, who are the best rifle shots in the regiment?"

"You mean, besides me?"

"Don't try my patience, Sergeant."

"The best is Bill Proffitt. He's even better than me." Luna's eyeing me and drumming his fingers against his tin cup. "What do you want him for, Captain?"

"A hunting party."

"To hunt what?"

"Spanish snipers."

"We could also use C.E. Knoblauch and Cody."

"We?" Luna says. "We!"

"You want the best, don't you? That includes me. Now if you want second best you got a broader choice."

Guerrilla sharpshooters have been shooting stretcher bearers and wounded men, and Colonel Roosevelt wants them cleaned out of the trees like the varmints they are. It's hot as whore's breath when we leave, and the bombardment's started. I'd rather be hunting an armed man in a tree any day than waiting for a cannon shell to drop on my head.

Bill Proffitt is a tall, leathery fellow with his neckerchief tied round his head like a pirate. Luna lets him get away with it because Proffitt says it keeps the sweat out of his eyes better than a hat, and it's the only way he can see to shoot.

I suggest bringing Levi's dog with us but Luna won't have it. We all carry extra canteens, pistols and our Krag carbines, but nothing else. We ain't on the path fifteen minutes when we hear shots ahead near the ford. A negro soldier tells us it's a sharpshooter who's been plaguing that part of the trail since yesterday afternoon. Proffitt disappears into the thicket and for ten minutes we don't hear or see nothing except the mule trains on that path, going and coming with rations and ammunition. Then there's a single shot.

Proffitt reappears and says, "One less," and we start off again. During the next hour, we see more men wounded and the sight ain't pretty. These guerrillas are using the Remington rifle, which shoots a bullet with a brass jacket that heats up and deforms in the air. When this slug wallops a man, it tears a worse hole than shrapnel.

Proffitt kills two more within an hour, working with Luna from opposite sides of the trail. When we're almost to Siboney and can see the beach, me and Knoblauch flush another one in our rear and kill him.

Siboney is a major depot now, with all kinds of stuff coming off the ships and being piled up on the beach. Luna gets us the best meal we had in days, and then we strip down and dive into the lukewarm sea. After we come out and dress again, I watch the rations and ammunition being loaded for the front.

There's two hundred unguarded mules strung in picket lines farther up the beach, and I tell Knoblauch to come with me while Cody explains to Proffitt how we used to operate with the Brown brothers back in New Mexico.

The army mule is smarter than your average mule because he's been educated by lazy men who expect him to do everything. So when he sees work threatening him, he protests, especially on a hot tropical day in the middle of a war.

The bray of an army mule is especially unnerving to an innocent horse-lover like C.E. Knoblauch, and he's looking both ways, expecting the skinners to come running. It may be the most penetrating sound there is, worse than fingernails on a blackboard and louder than Spanish shells passing through the air. It can tear its way through wooden planks, brick, rock or cement, and it shatters bottles and windowpanes better than a slingshot. As if that ain't enough, when a mule sees the bray ain't getting him anywheres, he lets off a long bloodcurdling moan mournful enough to break your heart.

"Lee, for God's sake, what do we do?" I tell Knoblauch not to let them critters go no matter what vaudeville act they put on. The mule skinners down by the beach don't even look up.

We get in line and when we get to the sergeant who's dispatching the hardtack and sowbelly, Cody hears him ask another soldier where the mules are that are supposed to take provisions to Shafter's headquarters.

"Right here, Sergeant!" Cody sings out, and this quartermaster waves us past the piles of hardtack and sowbelly, telling me, "Your pickup is with Sergeant Driscoll."

I lead our mule train to where this Driscoll is standing. "You'll have to wait until my men finish eating," he says, "unless you want to jack the load yourselves."

"We're in kind of a hurry," I say.

"It's up to you, Sergeant." He holds out an inventory and a pencil and I scrawl, "Sgt. Alfred S. Sorenson, Hdqtrs, Fifth Army." Then the four of us move like lightning to get them mules loaded and out of there. There's cases of corned beef, bags of flour, sugar and coffee, tinned peaches and pears, condensed milk, tomatoes, potatoes, onions, sides of bacon, matches and tobacco. I never seen such riches in my life as that day on the beach.

"Now what?" Knoblauch says.

"You and Cody get them mules moving. Fast!"

Bill Proffitt's about the quietest man I know in the army. I seen him play poker the whole night in Tampa and never say nothing more than, "Hit me." After Cody and Knoblauch are gone, he says, "Lee?"

"Yeah."

"What're we waiting for?"

"Luna."

"There's more sharpshooters along that trail."

"How do you know?"

"I seen one, smelt others."

"Christ, Bill, Cody and Knoblauch are perfect targets, creeping along with them mules!"

Proffitt nods.

"Come on. We'll explain to Luna later."

But that ain't necessary because he shows up. I tell him we're in a hurry because Proffitt seen some more snipers. I don't mention our supply train, but I don't have to. This dumb quartermaster sergeant comes running across the beach just then, yelling, "Sergeant Sorenson! Sergeant Sorenson!" I try to ignore him but he overtakes us, all out of breath, "You forgot your receipt!" He sees Luna and gives him a salute. "Sorry, sir, but I know how particular they are about these things at headquarters."

Luna returns the salute and takes the paper. "Sergeant Sorenson?" Luna says to me.

"He obviously got me confused with somebody else," I say. "You know the army."

"I know you," he says, smoothing the paper out to read it. "I also know Alfred S. Sorenson and there's no way he could be confused with you even if he was in Cuba, which he is not." His eyes go down the list as he reads out loud. "Sugar? Bacon? Flour? Tobacco?"

"I arranged for a few supplies."

"Fancy groceries is more like it. Do you have the remotest idea the kind of trouble this can bring?"

"Only if we're caught."

"You are caught, Garland! I just caught you! Where are these provisions now?"

"On the mules. Come on!" I take off down the trail after Proffitt, and Luna's right behind me.

"What mules?"

"Well, we couldn't carry it all by ourselves," I say. "There must be a ton of food there."

"The commanding general's rations, you arrogant, irresponsible saddlebum! You can't just steal a little hardtack and sowbelly, you have to go after Shafter's dinner!" He's wound up tight as a dollar watch now and there ain't no way to slow him down. Not even a Spanish sniper can interrupt one of his morality lectures, and anything I say is like throwing gasoline on a fire.

He goes on. "Poor Ben Butler must be turning in the ground. You can't even maintain a veneer of respectability out of respect for the man's memory. Well, once a thief, always a thief! Where'd you steal the mules?" The whole time he's raving we're hurrying to keep pace with Proffitt up ahead.

"We borrowed them off the picket line."

"Borrowed! Anyone see you?"

"Nope. Just like the Brown brothers, don't worry."

"I don't need to be reminded of the Brown brothers. What do you suppose will happen when the headquarters people show up and discover those supplies were stolen?"

"Nothing. This is the army. The only two thieves they can identify is you and me. But they'll be looking for a Sergeant Sorenson who don't exist and they don't know your name."

"Don't think for a minute you can involve me, Garland. You got into this mess by yourself."

"Driscoll gave you the manifest," I remind him. "You accepted it and didn't say anything."

"You son of a bitch!"

There's gunfire on the trail and we break into a run. The mules are standing on the path in the open and there's no sign of Knoblauch or Cody. A bullet kicks up dead leaves near Luna and we both dive into the thicket. Then there's two more shots from a Krag and Cody whoops, "Got the greaser!"

It takes us four hours to get back to San Juan Hill with the mules. I don't see a single sharpshooter the whole time except a couple dead ones, but Proffitt and the others make the road safe at last. We kill eleven snipers that day all told and C.E. Knoblauch also bags six guinea hens for the pot.

I hear no more about Shafter's groceries, not even from Luna. Mountain cooks the best meal in Cuba that night, but I can't keep it down. The fever comes on me worse than ever around sundown, and I feel like I'm drowning in a hot-water tank. I have a lovely long conversation with Caroline but it's interrupted by Alfred S. Sorenson stalking me again with his pick handle.

Any schoolboy today knows you get malaria and yellow fever from mosquito bites, and typhoid and swamp fever from lice or bad water. But back then, not even the doctors understood how you caught a fever, let alone how you cured it. There was measles laid a lot of us low, and meningitis and heatstroke. The disease and suffering was just part of having a war.

What I catch first is the malaria, which the red flannel bellyband Caroline give me don't have no effect on. As fevers go, it's one of the reliable ones. You can set your watch by the attacks. Every second afternoon you feel cold and clammy in the boiling sun and your teeth start to chatter like you're bare ass in a blizzard. If you eat, you puke. You sweat, see visions and talk out of your head. You're hot and dry as a bone before the sweats begin, then you're oozing water out of every pore. You're fine again in the morning.

The Spaniards make a few feeble attempts to come up the backside of the heights again, but they scatter as soon as the Gatlings open up. Our Colt machine guns fire on them too, using captured Spanish ammunition at five hundred rounds a minute. The only trouble is they never get to shoot a whole minute because they jam up. It's the same with the dynamite gun. Every two or three shells they have to take it apart and fix it.

One way or another the Dons keep their distance. At night we see their campfires and always know where they are. Mountain says it shows they got more sense then we do not to come looking for a fight and I guess he's right. Every day there's a rumor we're going to attack Santiago but it peters out before breakfast and we just lay there and cook in the heat or soak in the rain.

General Shafter's groceries give out after a few days, but by that time some more hardtack catches up with us. The sowbelly that comes with it nobody can eat, not even Levi's dog, so we live on the hardtack.

Our wounded are at a place where the operating table's just boards set on sawhorses and covered with white oil cloth. They call it a hospital but there's no roof and no beds, and the only shelter is from ponchos rigged over the litters. Some men don't even have clothes, and they suffer terrible blisters from the sun. Many die.

I'm visiting there when they take the bullet out of Fortescue's foot. They got chloroform, but only enough for the real bad cases like stomach and chest wounds, so they give him a razor strop to bite. He's pouring sweat before they begin and it ain't from the heat. When the surgeons go for the bullet Fortescue starts screaming. They got tools like a carpenter, and they dig and gouge and chisel around the bone in his foot like it's a piece of ham. His screaming goes on for minutes while I force my mind to focus on something else. I remember the crazy times in Chihauhua and conjure up the anatomical parts of Rose-of-Sharon Moriarty one by one. I recall walking on the Tampa beach with Caroline, and I imagine Eagle Nest in the winter. But it don't help when I'm listening to the real sound of war, a grown man howling like a gut-shot dog.

A few days later Captain Fall brings us good news. "Jesus, Garland," he says, "you look like refried beans."

"It's just the fever."

He's studying me with them shrewd eyes he has. "I've seen dead Apache with more meat on their bones than you." He looks around him and shakes his head. "The campaign's over."

"Since when?"

"Since our navy sunk the Spanish fleet in the harbor yesterday. Didn't you hear it."

"Yesterday all we heard was that Shafter asked Washington, D.C. for permission to retreat."

"You heard right," Fall says.

"Are they all crazy at headquarters or what?"

"What do you expect from a fumbling old fart who left most of our artillery in Tampa, ignored the navy's plan for the invasion and landed his army in the wrong place? Then sent everybody down the Guásimas road when he'd been told the enemy had it enfiladed, and across Bloody Ford with that goddamn balloon marking you like a gravestone!"

"Why don't McKinley replace him?" I ask Fall.

"Why would he want to do that? Shafter came, he sat and he conquered. The world believes he won a great victory." After

Captain Fall rides off, I get to thinking we can't hang around here much longer. If the Spanish don't give up soon, we'll have to attack Santiago while we still have the strength to walk there.

These days the latrines are flecked with blood and quite a few of the men have all they can do to drag themselves from their places in the trenches to where they squat. Some are letting their cartridge belts out a notch because their bellies are swollen from lack of food. Just about everybody's gums are bleeding and there ain't no shortage of runny sores and painful infections from the different kinds of insect bites.

Mountain's dropped at least fifty pounds, hunched over like an old man because the wound in his hip won't heal. Cody's so skinny a breeze would carry him off, and Knoblauch could pass for a mummy from Egypt. I don't see myself and I guess it's just as well. If I look like I feel, I could hire out to scare babies.

That's when the Vitagraph movie people show up to take our pictures. They ask where Mason Mitchell is and are disappointed when I tell them he's back at the hospital wounded.

With them is an obnoxious little staff lieutenant in his tailored blue uniform, and when he starts ordering my men out of the trenches I say, "Hold on there a minute, sir. We can't do that."

He says, "You'll take orders from me while these people are here, Sergeant. Now do as I say."

The civilian in charge of the picture people is more diplomatic and he says, "What I'd like is about a dozen of your men down at the bottom of the hill, Sergeant, if you don't mind, with their rifles and bayonets. Could you do me that favor?"

This fat lieutenant speaks up. "We're filming the charge up San Juan Hill, Sergeant," he says. The little butter tub whips out a sheaf of papers and shoves them at me. "I have permission from Colonel Roosevelt himself to call upon any soldiers in this regiment."

They put their camera about thirty feet from us up the hill and the civilian says, "Now boys, fix your bayonets, and charge at a run. Six pass on one side of the camera and six on the other. Look mad and pretend you're shooting Spaniards."

When I say I'm not sure we should be doing this, the civilian fellow says, "You're not going to let Colonel Roosevelt down, are you?"

I can see some of the men want to do it, so I say what the hell.

But I tell this fellow we didn't use bayonets and we didn't run, we walked up the hill.

He says running looks better and anyway we only have to run a few feet past the camera. What he don't tell us is that he wants to do it about ten times, and he keeps moving the camera up the hill till we're nearly at the top. I say, "This is as far as we go," and this lieutenant draws his sabre.

"Stand aside, Sergeant," he says, and puts himself in front of the men.

The cameraman starts to turn the crank and the civilian says, "That's good! That's very good! That's what we want. Right on by, sir! Keep it up!"

The men stumble past the camera just below the brow of the hill and squat down, but this dumb lieutenant keeps running with his sabre in the air until he's at the highest point. I yell at him to come down off there because of the sharpshooters, but he's too full of himself to pay any attention. Then *zee-eeu! zee-eeu!* two Mauser slugs whistle over, one of them raising the hair on his neck, I guess, by the astonished look on his chubby face.

He drops the sabre like it's hot and dives in the mud, soiling his nice new uniform. "Did you see that? They shot the sword right out of my hand!"

Luna seen it too, and the sight brings a rare smile of pleasure to his face. "Garland," he says, "the colonel says to give these folks anything they want."

"I think we got enough," the civilian fellow says, real nervous now. "You've been very helpful, gentlemen. Thank you."

Luna has a letter for C.E. Knoblauch, and we all gather round because this is the first mail anybody got since we joined the army, and it's kind of a miracle.

"Who's it from, Cyril?" Cody asks him.

Knoblauch busts out laughing because the letter's a summons for jury duty in New York. If he don't show up, there's a hundred-dollar fine.

Different kinds of lice find human beings good to eat, and in Cuba we got them all. The seam-squirrel's a greedy little gray-backed varmint likes to take all his meals where you can't scratch, the hair mite favors the hot climate inside your hat, and the common crab louse's taste runs to the tender regions near a soldier's pecker.

The only way you get rid of seam-squirrels is to burn them, but that means burning the clothes too. A bald man like C.E. Knoblauch has no trouble with hair mites but the crab lice plague us all. They hate to leave a comfortable crotch unless they're drowning, and the rare times we're able to bathe in the surf ain't enough to discourage them.

I'm aching all over after the film people leave and I feel terrible. My head's about to split and I can't eat a thing. I got a fever too, and it ain't the day for my malaria. When I lay down, I can't hardly get up again, and in the morning I can't get up at all. I remember everybody looking like they're under water, all blurry and indistinct, and the sun hurts my eyes even when they're closed. What I got is the typhoid and it makes you forget you're lousy. Otherwise it ain't a disease I'd ever care to associate myself with again.

I'm out of my head most of the time, can't eat nothing, and can't hardly move without the ache in my bones turning the simplest muscle twitch into an agony. I know I'm dying but I can't believe it takes so long. Levi nurses me and Mitchell helps him, even though he ain't in too good a shape himself. They take turns sponging me down with lukewarm river water feels like ice. The doctor forces some bismuth down me but I just spit it back, and he gives up. The rule is if a man can't keep down his medicine, they save it for someone who can.

Pete says I survived the typhoid and malaria because I'm tough, but that ain't a satisfactory explanation. Hundreds of men died from fever in Cuba, and most of them was tough. On the other hand, a man like Cody, who's frail as a girl, don't come down with nothing.

When the enemy finally quits in the middle of July, our army's a shell. Twenty-four thousand Spanish soldiers surrender to Shafter, who has about twelve thousand, a third of us in the hospital. We also get tons of stores, artillery, machine guns, wagons and the city of Santiago. The day of the surrender is the first day I'm able to swallow anything and keep it down.

"Lee," Mitchell says, "it's over."

I need a while to understand he's talking about the war. I still can't move much, but the pain is almost gone. Luna says I'm too ornery to die, but if it wasn't for my friends looking after me, I'd of been dead long ago.

Captain Fall drops by to cheer us up and says Roosevelt's working to get us out of Cuba before we all crepate. So far Washington don't seem to be paying him too much attention, but Luna says they will because Roosevelt's got too many connections.

Fall gets us moved to the old Santiago Yacht Club overlooking the harbor. The huge rooms have parquet floors and lots of light and ventilation. Each cot's got a mosquito net, and when there's a little breeze off the water we feel it. But after a few days, the place is so full of sick and wounded, you can hardly pass between the cots.

Luna's got the malaria too, but he's holding together. One visit he even smiles, but he don't realize that a smile on him is about as natural as a skirt on a dog. I ask him what's wrong.

"Nothing's wrong," he says, still grinning.

"Then why are you smiling?"

"What's the matter with my smiling?" He's frowning now.

"You know something I don't know?"

"I know a thousand things you don't know, Garland, and most of them you'll never learn!"

"It's something in particular, ain't it?" I say.

"It's nothing in particular," he says.

"Something you're keeping back."

"It's nothing I'm keeping back!" He ain't even trying to smile now. He's standing with his hands on his hips and he sounds more like his normal self.

Fortescue hears and hobbles over. "What's the trouble, Captain?"

"Goddamn it! He's the trouble! You can't even have an ordinary bedside visit without him starting an argument!"

"An argument about what?" Fortescue says.

"He won't tell me," I say.

"Jesus Christ, Garland, you're the goddamned limit! Your mind's twisted!" One of the nurses appears and tells Luna to please lower his voice because of the other patients. He mumbles about getting back to the troop, and he leaves.

"What was the matter with him?" Fortescue asks me.

"Who knows? When he come in he was smiling."

Roosevelt announces that the whole regiment's going home. Those too sick to travel will be cared for at the hospital, but those who can muster aboard ship will be taken.

The doctors say I can't stand the trip and will die, but I know if I stay where I am I'll die sooner. Sitting up on the edge of my cot makes me dizzy with weakness. But when Mountain comes for me, I tell him to get help before he busts his wound open, but he says I don't weigh much over a hundred pounds anymore, and for him that's nothing.

He scoops me up like a child and carries me five blocks to the pier, where the Rough Riders are shuffling up the gangplank of a ship called the *Miami*. The big man must of been a sight with me like a corpse in his arms, because the men stand aside to let us come on board.

When Roosevelt hears about it, he wants me taken back to the hospital because he's afraid I'll spread whatever I got to the other men. But Captain Fall talks him out of it. Luna told me later nobody thought I'd survive more than a day or two anyway, and the colonel agreed to let me die among my friends.

There's six of us to a fancy, white-painted passenger cabin with two bunks. They put me in the lower one and Mitchell in the upper, while Cody, Mountain, Fortescue and C.E. Knoblauch take turns on the deck. The cabin's ventilated and I can see a small part of the sky through a porthole.

Mitchell says, "I have enjoyed accommodations like this on other voyages gentlemen, but never so cheap."

Fortescue says, "Boys, we made it! Let's drink to that!" and he breaks out a bottle of cognac Luna give us in the hospital. Everybody takes a few drops in his mess cup except Knoblauch, who don't drink, and me, who can't, but Mitchell puts some on his finger like you would for a teething baby and wets my lips. "There you are, Lee, old friend. That counts even if you can't swallow it."

Mitchell says, "To all who fought and bled!"

Cody complains, "That leaves out me and Knoblauch."

"Mosquito bites count," Fortescue tells him, "and you both shed enough blood scratching them." Then Mountain raises his cup. "To Lee Garland, the man who pulled us through!"

They all clink their cups at me where I can see. I don't know if it's the pus in my eyes, but everything's wavery. There I am, dying in that bunk, and yet I remember the moment as a happy one. I guess because a man don't always get a chance to die in such good company.

The trip took a week, maybe two. They wash me and feed me and clean up after me like a baby. Then one day everything's still and somebody says, "We're home, Lee."

The place is on the tip of Long Island at Montauk, where there's nothing but surf and potato fields because the army decided they ain't about to turn us loose on the population until we're certified noncontagious. An old side-wheeler ferries us to the pier, where there's lines of horse-drawn ambulances waiting in the dawn. Soon I'm in a clean hospital tent set up between sand dunes with a yellow quarantine flag flying over the place. They call it Camp Wikoff.

A hospital orderly brings beef extract but there ain't enough to go around so I miss out. Later another orderly shows up with some cold oatmeal and I get a spoonful, but thank God Mountain finds me in the morning or I sure would of perished.

It's September and the Atlantic Ocean off Montauk is gunmetal blue and cold, but the days are warm and sunny, and everybody bathes in that wonderful foam. Them that can't walk, like me, get carried down to the edge by their friends.

We're issued new uniforms because the old ones are falling off us. Fortescue's mother comes out from New York in her private railroad car with a ton of food, medicine and Dr. Wallace Graham. He's a famous professor at the Columbia Medical College, a big, handsome man with a white goatee and a walking stick, and he's Roosevelt's doctor too. By the time he sees me, I'm able to walk around a little. He pokes and prods and tells Fortescue I should be in the hospital in New York City.

When Fortescue explains that the army won't let us leave yet, old Dr. Wallace Graham says, "We'll see about that." He also wants to X-ray Fortescue's foot and Mitchell's shoulder, and his X-ray machine is in the city. A week later the surgeon-general declares us noncontagious and the army turns us loose. My back-pay comes to ninety-six dollars.

The whole regiment assembles one more time and Colonel Roosevelt shakes every trooper's hand. The men present Roosevelt with a bronze statue of a bronco buster made by Fred Remington, and there's tears in his eyes when he thanks us. His voice chokes up too as he recalls some of our dead by name and how much has happened in these few months. Butler, Ham Fish, Miller, Russell, and Haefner gone. Tom Isbell still laying in a Cuban hospital with seven bullet holes in him. Levi, Culver, Mitchell, Lieutenant Leahy, Mountain, and me wounded or with the fever. To me he says, "Sergeant Garland, I'm especially happy to see you on your feet again." And to the general with him, "This is the cowboy I told you about who saved my life." Somehow I make it through the ceremony, leaning on Mountain.

Emma Fortescue would of taken the whole regiment home if it fit in her private railroad car, but she can only squeeze in about a dozen of us. Me, she puts to bed as soon as I'm aboard, and her butler brings hot milk-and-barley soup prescribed by Dr. Wallace Graham. The others lounge around smoking and drinking and ogling the fancy trimmings on the trip. By the time the train pulls into Long Island City at sundown, we're all asleep. Two men in white coats help me and Fortescue and Mitchell into a horse ambulance and we're taken to Roosevelt Hospital. Both men need the kind of operations doctors never could of done on the battlefield.

The first thing I do as soon as I'm able is write a long letter to Caroline, telling her I'm okay and I love her. I explain that there's no way I could of let her know what was going on before now, but I hope to be out of the hospital soon and get up to Boston. I kid her a little about not writing me, but I know she probably did and her letters are God knows where because nobody except Knoblauch ever got any mail the whole time we was in Cuba. I say the flannel bellyband she give me probably saved my life. It ain't true, but I figure it's something she'd like to hear. I ask after her health and say I'm recovering my strength. I sign it, "Your faithful friend and admirer, L.O. Garland."

Our room is like a railroad station before train time. I never knew two people could have so many friends as Fortescue and Mitchell. Not just the Rough Riders who are around, but half of New York it seems to me, male and female, and they all come with flowers or baskets of fruit or candy. We laugh when we think only a month before the best we could hope for was some of Mountain's hardtack soup with a little moldy sowbelly to flavor it.

One morning the nurse announces we got two colored gentlemen as visitors. Mitchell says, "We don't know any colored gentlemen." But I should of guessed who it was before Carl Washington appears, filling the doorway. He looks like a general in his brand-new blue uniform with heavy gold stripes filling both sleeves and his medals on his chest. He's carrying a little potted geranium and his broad black face lights up in a huge white smile when he sees me. "Well, Reverend," he says real slow, "I just had to find out what a smart man like you—"

"—is doing in a low-down place like this. Sergeant, how did you find out I was here?"

"First I heard you was dead but nobody knew where they buried you. Then a fellow says he thought you was taken away by some New York doctor so I tried four hospitals and at last I find you here, looking well to my intense satisfaction."

We all shake hands and I thank him for the flower.

"I'm a trifle embarrassed about that," he says, "because I bought it for your grave. But I'm glad you like it anyway."

After he leaves, I tell Fortescue and Mitchell about Luna chasing us when he was sheriff, and how I posed as a preacher. Mitchell says it explains why Luna still has it in for me, but I disagree. "He's got his own ideas about right and wrong, and he don't understand anybody ain't as perfect as he is. He excuses Mountain because he can't read or write, and Cody because he's sickly and kind of innocent. But he never could find an excuse for me except wrong-headedness, and he's got no patience with that."

I weighed a hundred ten pounds when they took me into that hospital and a hundred fifty when they let me out, still thirty pounds shy of my weight when I entered the army. But I'm alive and that's the whole point of the exercise.

The days roll by and no answer comes from Caroline. I begin to get edgy and wonder if I got the address wrong or what. I'm feeling better and I've written her four or five more letters and also one to Charlie Bruce telling him to come see me. We got a lot of unfinished business and I'm anxious to sit down and make plans.

The hardest one to write is to Ben Butler's wife, which Luna will take with him to New Mexico. He's as awkward as a pig at a picnic when he comes to say good-bye to us. At the door he barks, "Fortescue! Mitchell!"

They both say, "Sir!"

"You're welcome to ride with me anytime," he says, which is about the highest compliment a man like Luna can pay you.

"So long, Captain," Fortescue says. "Thanks for the war." As wars go, it wasn't much. A couple of battles and the surrender of a third-rate power to an army of scarecrows. There was more mistakes than glory and more misery than action. None of us asks if it was worth it. Wars never are, I guess, to men that fight them.

I've lived seventy more years since then, yet it don't seem like any time at all has gone by. Life's a card trick, if you ask me. When I was young, a summer was forever. Now if I blink, I miss a whole year. It's the mind that betrays you. I ain't soft in the head, but I ain't exactly your average senior citizen either.

XVII

My Eastern Education

Mountain says, "I don't like to leave you, Lee."

"I'll be all right," I tell him. "I got the best doctor in America and half the regiment running in here every day checking on me. There's no way I can get into trouble."

"What about us?" Cody says.

For the tenth time I tell him it's all fixed with Captain Fall and Luna. Fall is still a justice of the Territorial Supreme Court and Luna's still the sheriff of Santa Fe County. Cody and Mountain both got letters from them in case they get stopped by any lawmen on the way home, and Captain Fall promised me he'd get the warrants and indictments withdrawn as soon as he arrived in Santa Fe. There's nobody going to put them in jail now because Luna wouldn't stand for it, and Albert Fall wouldn't either.

"I don't know," Cody says. "What about Sam Brown? He'll still be after me because of Jake killing Arnold."

"That's ancient history, Cody. If the law says you're innocent, and the law right now is Luna and Fall, then that's the end of it. Sam Brown don't want to go to the penitentiary and that's just where Luna'd put him if he touched a hair on your head."

"I ain't afraid of Sam," Cody says.

"Course you ain't. You just stood up to a army of Spaniards, didn't you? That's more than Sam Brown ever did. Just behave yourself and leave the rest to Max Luna."

213

"I wish you was coming with us," he says. "I ain't never been on my own before."

"You been on your own since you joined the army. You just didn't know it. Now get out of here and stop worrying." New York ain't no place for them to linger. In such a great modern city there's too much temptation for Cody and not enough room for Mountain.

Dr. Wallace Graham sends Fortescue home as soon as he can limp around with his cast and a cane, and after Mitchell has the last stitches taken out of his shoulder, he moves to the Lambs Club, where he lived before he joined the army. I'm the one they keep till last and Dr. Wallace Graham only lets me go because Emma Fortescue insists I'll put on more weight at her house than at the hospital.

The Fortescue place on Fifth Avenue ain't a house at all. It's a five-story mountain of granite set down bang in the center of New York City. Fortescue says it ain't the biggest private home there by a long shot, but it does occupy half a city block. It's a copy of an Italian palazzo his parents stayed in on their honeymoon, only the New York architect designed it bigger.

It's raining the day Fortescue takes me there in a fancy carriage, but we don't get wet because the coachman drives right inside the front of the house under a overhang. I can walk okay, but three fellows in striped jackets come running out to help me anyway. They're part of a staff of twenty-eight servants that keep the place clean, cook the food and wait hand and foot on Fortescue, his father, Emma and anybody else happens to be around. The family's got three carriages, a fast little cabriolet fly Fortescue runs around in, and a stable full of sleek horses.

The butler lets us in through a normal-size door cut out of another door ten feet high. The front hall's about the size of the Santa Fe Courthouse with checkerboard floors in different color marble and a huge staircase nobody ever uses because there's an elevator. We go into the library, which is only a little smaller than the hall, with balconies and ladders so you can get at the million books lining the walls.

I look around and tell Fortescue I don't understand how a man in his right mind could leave all this to join the army.

He says, "Well, I did, Lee, and I'm not sorry. But I'm awfully glad to be back."

"I can see why. You're going to have to give me a minute to get the range, Ronnie. You got a map of this place so I don't get lost?"

There's drawing rooms and parlors and a Turkish smoking room with beaded curtains, and a billiard room. There's even a gymnasium on the top floor with punching bags and medicine balls and ropes and pulleys and weights and Indian clubs. A full-size boxing ring's set up in the middle of it, lit by a big skylight, and Fortescue says when I'm feeling better, he'll teach me how to fight like a gentleman.

The dining saloon sits ninety people at a table the size of a bowling alley and the ballroom is bigger than the Albuquerque depot. Paintings and bronze statues are all over the place like a museum, and a Irish maid serves me breakfast in a bed could hold six elephants. There's a bell system to call the servants and brass speaker tubes in every room you can talk through to any part of the house.

In the library is a machine I never seen before which Fortescue says is a stock ticker. He explains how it's connected to the stock exchange so on days when he don't feel like going to work, he can keep up with his money. There's also a telegraph and two telephones, which a clerk operates every day from six in the morning, getting messages from London and San Francisco and Boston. I ask Fortescue why they need all this if they got offices downtown, and he says because of the time difference with Europe or California, and for confidentiality. I see what he means when I come down at six o'clock one morning and see his father dictating coded telegraph messages to the clerk.

Mr. Fortescue's a lively old geezer who spends an hour every morning in the gymnasium doing sit-ups and throwing the medicine ball with one of the young fellows works there. Him and Fortescue don't have much to say to each other but they both compete for Emma's attention. The old man walks thirty blocks to his bank every day and thirty blocks home, unless it's raining. Fortescue was born in this house and so was two older brothers, who both died of pneumonia when they was small. He tells me the family's always been in banking or the stock market, but that him and his father have different ways of looking at life. Fortescue's made his own fortune in about five years, buying and selling stocks and properties his old man wouldn't touch, and he says part of the reason they don't talk is the old man's jealousy.

"Everything I've ever done, he's been against," Fortescue tells me, "even when things turned out well."

"He ought to be proud of you," I tell him.

"If he is, he'd never admit it. He went to Princeton, but I chose Yale. He insisted I row, and I boxed. He's an ardent yachtsman, while I prefer polo. He assumed I'd join him in the bank, but I bought a seat on the stock exchange instead. He buys municipal bonds, while I prefer petroleum stocks. And to top it off, he had just arranged a safe naval commission for me last spring when I shocked him by enlisting in the Rough Riders."

"Did you do all that because you wanted to, or was it contrariness?"

"I have to be my own man, Lee. Like you."

"I never had your choices," I say.

"Not the same ones, perhaps," Fortescue says, "but you had others. I've seen you stand up to Luna and I know he wants to run your life as much as any father."

"He wants to run everybody's life," I say. "If the war and Ben Butler hadn't come along when they did, he'd of run my life right into the jailhouse."

"Yet he recommended you for the medal."

"What medal?"

"I signed a deposition in the hospital. So did Cody and Lieutenant Leahy, and several of the others."

"Deposition for what?"

"For San Juan Hill."

"Why me?"

"Don't you remember what you did?"

"Sure. I got to the top. That ain't nothing to give me a medal for. The colonel got there first."

"He's been recommended too. The names of several men who distinguished themselves in Cuba have been forwarded to the War Department and the Congress for the Medal of Honor."

"That ain't fair," I say.

Fortescue laughs and says, "You're a hero, Lee. Wait until your little Boston love hears about that!"

"It ain't right."

"You were in the thick of it with the colonel from the first, bullying us up that hill, and you saved Roosevelt's life. It's eminently fair, Lee, and every man agrees. I thought you knew or I would have told you sooner."

Thinking back on it after all these years, I still don't believe it was right to single me out. We all took the same risk and climbed the same hill, and it was the colonel who really led us. But like they say, in love and war, nothing's fair. I blame it on Luna. He admitted there was others he wanted to recommend too, but he decided on me because it would be a thing I'd have to live up to.

Charlie Bruce finally shows up with all the plans for him and me to incorporate what he calls the Southwest Century Bank of New Mexico. Charlie's been back and forth a couple of times to Santa Fe, and down to Albuquerque to select the location, and to Washington too, getting the charter and corporation papers drawn up and making contacts. I've already had two or three long distance telephone conversations with him during the last two weeks so I know more or less what he's been up to.

What I don't know is anything about Caroline because she never wrote back and each time I ask about her on the telephone, he is mysterious and says he'll tell me everything in person. When I take him aside in Fortescue's library and ask him again why she hasn't contacted me, he's embarrassed.

"Lee, I know you were fond of Caroline but it would really be better if you forgot about her."

"Why?"

"She's young and inexperienced and romantic. I'm afraid she may have led you on without realizing it."

"What are you talking about, Charlie? Why didn't she answer my letters? Don't she want to see me? Or is it you? We're friends, so don't lie to me. If you think I ain't good enough for your sister because I didn't go to Harvard College, say so and I'll understand. Anyway, I'll try to understand."

"Good lord, no, Lee! I owe you a debt I can never repay. I had no idea you were serious about Caroline."

"Sure you did, Charlie, or you wouldn't have tried so hard to bust us up. So level with me. If we're going to be partners, I got to know where I stand."

He hooks his thumbs in his vest and shakes his head, staring at the carpet. "It's all been a terrible misunderstanding," he says, looking at me. "I have avoided telling you until now."

"Telling me what, Charlie?"

He lets out a long sigh before he answers me. "Lee, if things had worked out differently, I would not have opposed your courting Caroline on your return. You thought I was being stuffy about it in Florida, but I only hoped to protect my impulsive sister against herself."

"What are you trying to say, Charlie? I just want to see her."

"At the moment, that's out of the question."

"Why? I'll go to Boston."

"Caroline's not in Boston. Look, Lee, she may have said things before you went to Cuba that you had every right to take seriously, but she was infatuated and afraid you'd be killed. That may have been why she behaved as she did. But on our return to Boston, she met someone else who swept her off her feet."

"I don't believe it."

"I'm afraid it's true, Lee."

"Who?"

"It doesn't matter, does it?"

"It ain't over until I hear it from her."

"That's impossible. Caroline was married in August and is traveling in Europe now with her husband."

His words hit me like a Spanish bullet and for a minute I can't even draw a breath. The idea that she could have met somebody else and fallen in love and married him that fast after being in love with me don't make sense. This is not the girl I knew in Tampa. Yet Charlie does his best to convince me that I'm wrong, because he says I didn't know her at all.

"I love my sister," he tells me, "but she is capricious, and always was, so you must not take her behavior as a personal affront. Put her out of your mind, Lee, I'm telling you as a friend. You see why I could not explain all this on the telephone."

"So she didn't even get my letters."

He puts one hand on my shoulder and sighs. "I can't tell you how hard this is for me, Lee. But I was powerless to prevent her from doing what she was determined to do."

"Didn't you try to talk her out of it?"

"You saw how she was in Tampa, always doing exactly what she wished and ignoring my advice. Between us, I'm relieved that she married, as sudden as it seemed at the time. Caroline is so impetuous there's no telling what kind of trouble she would have got into on her own. Now, at least, she has a husband to guide her."

When I find out who the son of a bitch is I ain't any happier. He's a director of the railroad Charlie used to work for in Mexico and his name's Woodrow Sloan. He owns woolen mills in Massachusetts and a couple million sheep out West, and rides around on a hundred-foot yacht when he ain't counting his money. My only comfort is he's fifty years old so maybe he'll die soon and I'll get a second chance with Caroline.

Fortescue finds the whole thing as hard to believe as I do, but like Charlie, he tells me you can't look back. What he finds odd, he says, is that he never seen anybody more in love than Caroline Bruce was with me. Mitchell ain't surprised because he says beautiful women are natural bolters, which is why the institution of marriage exists. It ain't to tie a man down, but to keep a rein on a woman's flightiness.

I don't know. They're only trying to make me feel better, but that's impossible. The idea of a future without Caroline never occurred to me until Charlie Bruce slammed me in the gut with it. Emma Fortescue sees what's happened and her immediate solution is to fill the house with pretty debutantes.

Toward the end of October there's a army ceremony at the Seventh Regiment Armory where I get my medal together with Colonel Roosevelt, and Emma gives a small dinner for fifty people that night in my honor. All the Fortescue friends are invited, as well as Mitchell and Knoblauch with their young ladies. Emma asks Honora Stockton for me.

Honora is her niece just turned eighteen. She's pretty enough with dark hair and gray eyes, but kind of tomboyish, and real outspoken like Emma. Her father was a family blacksheep who embezzled money from the Fortescue bank and run off with an actress when Honora was small. The mother is an invalid, so Emma practically raised her, sponsored her as a debutante and, according to Fortescue, is trying to get her married off well because she don't have a lot of money of her own. It's easy to see she's Emma's favorite because she's smart and got a good sense of humor. But so far nobody's beat a path to her door because she's too forward, Fortescue says, and smarter than most of the men she meets.

"She's the best of the current crop," he tells me. "By far the most intelligent and the most beautiful."

I ain't planning to marry anyone now that I lost Caroline. But

Emma's right about me needing female company, and I see a lot of Honora Stockton. Sometimes she comes along with Emma, or I take her out alone. She's such good fun I almost forget she's a girl. We go riding in the park and she takes me to see my first horseless carriage race around a track at the Hippodrome.

One evening we all go to Fourteenth Street to see a moving picture of Bob Fitzsimmons and Jim Jeffries boxing, and *The Charge Up San Juan Hill,* starring "America's Heroic Rough Riders." It lasts about eight minutes and is billed as "a motion picture spectacle filmed during the fiercest fighting of the recent war by our brave cameramen at great risk and peril." Some of it's the movie they took of us running up the hill, but most of it was made some place else with actors and fake palm trees. Me and Fortescue have a laugh or two, and so does Emma when we tell her how they done it.

The next day, at Mitchell's invitation, I take Honora and Emma to Brooklyn where he's making a cowboy picture, and I get as big a kick out of it as the two women. It's called *Law of the Range* and poor Mitch spends most of the afternoon bouncing up and down on a sawhorse while a workman rolls a endless cyclorama of a desert scene behind him.

Some days I meet Honora and Emma for tea at the Fifth Avenue Hotel and tag along while they shop at Wanamaker's Department Store or Abercrombie's or Altman's. Emma takes me to Fortescue's tailor for suits and a overcoat, and chooses the material at the shirtmaker's. I even get fitted for dinner clothes and buy a silk topper because you can't go out at night in New York except in white tie and tails.

I kind of like the way I look in this monkey suit, and Emma shows me off to Fortescue, saying, "Have you ever seen a more elegant young man, Ronnie?" All the time she's teaching me things I don't know, like which fork to use for the fish and which spoon for the soup.

We go to the theatre, usually with Mitchell and some actress, and I get to see Maude Adams and de Wolf Hopper and John Drew on the stage. Afterward, there's supper at the Bellerose, lobster newburg and champagne with Mitchell's theatre friends, who kid him about making moving pictures. It's just jealousy because none of them is half as famous as he is by now.

Nora and I do a certain amount of kissing and groping around in the backs of carriages and taxicabs after these outings, but when I'm feeling her, my mind can't help imagining Caroline. The weeks go by, but the pain of losing her ain't any less. It's a dull, constant ache somewhere deep in my guts, like grief.

Knoblauch and Fortescue ride me about Honora and the other debutantes I take out. Fortescue says to watch my step because they're all looking for husbands.

"Rich husbands," I say, "which leaves me out."

"You'll get there, Lee," he says, "with a little help from your friends." He's right, too. When I was still in the hospital, he invested my money for me and by Christmas I'm already fifteen thousand dollars richer, plus what I spent on clothes and things. It beats working, I tell him, and it sure as hell beats the ninety-six dollars I made fighting in Cuba.

On nights when I leave Nora with my balls throbbing, me and Fortescue journey across town to spend a few hours at Madame Dubonnet's establishment on Twenty-first Street. It's a far cry from Old Lady Sanchez's place in Santa Fe, with fancy gilded sofas, girls pretty enough to be actresses and crystal chandeliers. Fortescue laughs when I point out it's got to be the only whorehouse in the world with a stock ticker.

The first time I go, I ain't sure what I can accomplish, but the little chestnut-haired beauty I pick makes me real comfortable. When she takes off her clothes, she's got a rose in her pussy, to make it smell nice, she says. Her arms are chubby, but her tits are sweet as apples, and she's just as juicy down below. She costs thirty-five dollars, but the money's well-spent. For a man who ain't had a hard on in two months, I do all right and get two rides for the price of one because she likes me.

In November, when the colonel gets elected governor of New York, there's a victory party at the Waldorf Hotel. I go with Fortescue and Mitchell, and find most of the local fellows from the regiment there. Colonel Roosevelt's on top of the world and he makes a pretty speech, saying we won him the election in Cuba.

Living at Fortescue's house is one of the happy memories I have from that time, and it's mainly Emma Fortescue made it so. She ain't pretty, probably never was. Too sharp-boned and tall to be delicate, and too energetic and intelligent to be a wallflower. She runs the place, as Fortescue says, with an iron hand in a velvet glove. Yet she's got a good warm nature and treats everybody the same, with none of that talking-down-the-nose manner some of these New York people have.

It's Emma and Honora who introduce me to New York. While Fortescue's at his office, they take me to the aquarium down at the Battery and to see the ice skaters in Central Park. Emma shows me Grand Central Station and Grant's tomb and the Madison Square Garden. One afternoon she even takes Honora and me to the Eden Wax Museum, where we go through the Chamber of Horrors. They have criminals being executed in India and some other gruesome exhibits remind me of some of the things I seen in Cuba.

Fortescue's disappointed about my going into the banking business because he's hoping I'll stay in New York and play the stock market with him. But New York ain't for me in the long run, as much as I like it, because it ain't New Mexico.

Charlie's lawyers draw up the partnership agreements for us, and everything goes fine until I give the notary public my date of birth. One of the lawyers overhears this and says I ain't legally of age. He's right, I guess, because I'm still shy of my twenty-first birthday. When they ask if I got a legal guardian, Charlie Bruce don't know what to say and Fortescue doubles up laughing. Finally this lawyer says it's okay if I have a guarantor sign with me, so Fortescue comes to my rescue.

A couple nights later at Emma's big New Year's farewell party I kiss Honora Stockton and wish her a happy New Year.

She says, "Lee?"

"What?"

"It's been wonderful."

"I enjoyed it too, Nora."

"Will you write me?"

"Sure."

"Promise?"

"I promise."

"And come back soon. I'll miss you." Then she gives me a little present which for a minute I think might be a red flannel bellyband, but turns out to be a French silk foulard.

"I wish you weren't going, Lee."

"So do I."

"Think of me."

"I will."

"I'll never forget you."

Maybe I'm growing cynical about women since I been in the East, but it seems to me I had this conversation before.

The Southwest Century Bank

Charlie plays poker most of the trip to New Mexico and makes himself some money. I sit in on a few hands and lose because I can't keep my mind on the cards. Being around him only makes me think of Caroline more than ever, and a terrible depression settles on me. I try to read the books Emma gave me and wind up staring out the window at nothing while half the United States passes by. We're traveling first-class Pullman and have our own drawing room, but I'm in no state to appreciate the luxury.

I spend my time drinking alone after we leave Chicago, telling myself I'm alive and got my health back, I'm richer than I got any right to be and I'm about to make a whole lot more money. I got New York connections and a bunch of fine friends. But I got no appetite for all that dining-car food, and the booze goes down like water with no effect except a hangover. I just ain't fit company for nobody.

I ask myself a thousand questions don't have no answers until at last I say, "See here, Garland, pull your socks up! Half the human race is female and you ain't off to a good start if only one of them can get you down like this!" But I ain't listening. All I see is Caroline on the veranda of the Tampa Bay Hotel, and hear her speak my name. I try to conjure up the scent of her cologne and remember the fine little beads of sweat like morning dew on her brow. I think about her eyes and shiny hair and the graceful way she moves.

To help my self-esteem I compare her to Honora Stockton, who I know is sweet on me. Nora's every bit as pretty, and smart and lively, and by now I know her a lot better than I knew Caroline. Nora's sure as hell more loyal and sincere, too, but she ain't Caroline Bruce and that's who I'm in love with.

People might say I'm as big a fool today as I was then. But for a few days in Tampa we was both in love for the first time and we knew it. It can only happen once to anybody and the honey-sweet taste of it is still there on the back of my tongue after a whole lifetime.

The day we're due in Albuquerque, I got a hangover fit to kill a buffalo. We're crossing over the continental divide near Glorieta and the glare on the snow outside hurts my eyes. I cut myself shaving and bleed all over the washbasin. Charlie's already having breakfast in the dining car when I walk in, and he says, "Are you ready to take off your hair shirt?"

"What's that supposed to mean?"

"You've been wallowing in self-pity since I told you about Caroline. It's time you got over it."

"I'll be all right," I tell him.

"I hope so because you have to make a cold-blooded business decision and I don't want your feelings clouding your judgment."

"Don't worry about that."

"Do I have your word you'll keep an open mind?"

"We're partners, Charlie, so get to the point. If you're in favor of whatever it is, I'll probably go for it too."

"We've been offered a two-hundred-thousand-dollar loan against collateral amounting to forty percent of our stock," Charlie says. "It means we can capitalize the bank at half a million instead of the three hundred thousand we now have. We would still be the controlling stockholders and managing partners. The increased capitalization would qualify us for Treasury Department discounts available to Territorial banks over a certain size. In short, it puts us into a different class."

"It makes sense. Who's the generous investor?"

"Woodrow Sloan."

"Are you crazy! The son of a bitch steals Caroline and now you want to let him take over our bank? Oh, no, Charlie. Not while I'm around to stop him!"

"Think about it a minute."

"I don't have to think about it. We ain't even open for business yet and you want a sidewinder like him in with us? He may marry your sister, Charlie, I can't stop that, but he ain't having ten cents worth of stock in our bank. No, sir!"

"I'm sorry, Lee, because we'd be eligible for federal deposits, which we aren't now. But I told him I couldn't accept unless you concurred. I'll write him today."

"You do that, Charlie, and send him and his bride Lee Garland's best wishes for their happiness."

"Lee, please."

"What the hell do you expect? I'd rather have Arango and his Mexicans in business with us. At least they stab you from the front."

"It's unfair to infer Woody Sloan is a snake in the grass. He made the offer in good faith as a gesture to family solidarity. There are no strings attached."

"He's a string and I ain't part of the family! Woody, is it? You and him must of got real chummy while he was sparking Caroline behind my back."

"It wasn't behind your back. What was she supposed to think when she heard nothing from you? It's not as if you and she were engaged, Lee, or committed in any formal way."

"She could of waited."

"She was determined."

"How hard did you try to stop her?"

"My God, Lee, it wasn't a matter of life or death."

"No? Since when?"

"You know what I mean. We're not smuggling cattle over the Mexican border anymore and you're not off potting Spaniards in some foolish little war. You must learn to live in polite society if you're going to be a successful banker."

"Remember Brewer and Major Dunn?" I say.

"How could I forget them?"

"You think they're polite society?"

"I found the major presentable enough."

"Well, you can add Woodrow Sloan to your presentable list. On one condition, Charlie. You deal with him. If you say we need his money to get this Treasury business, take it. And as soon as we make enough profit of our own we buy him out. Agreed?"

"I understand."

When we get off the train, the New Mexico air cures my hangover in a minute. In Texas all you breathe is dust, and Florida and Cuba is pure humidity. New York might be tolerable if the elevated trains weren't dumping coal dust all the time, but New Mexico's the only place I know where every breath's a pleasure.

It's cold on this January day. The sun's bright as ever and the Sandia Mountains got snow on them. I'm alive and back home where I belong. I fill my lungs again and again, standing there on the station platform until Charlie says, "Are you all right, Lee?"

"Never felt better," I say, and it's the truth.

Before we go to the hotel, Charlie shows me the place he leased for the bank on the northeast corner of Central Avenue and First Street, a block from the depot.

"It will be the first thing a man sees when he gets off the train, and the last before he leaves town." Charlie has a sign hanging out front that says:

Soon to Open on These Premises:
THE SOUTHWEST CENTURY BANK OF NEW MEXICO
Courtesy - Integrity - Security

We spend eight thousand dollars on furniture, adding machines, a telephone, locks, bars and a one-ton safe to make the place live up to this motto, with the name in goldleaf on the windows. Charlie is president and I'm vice-president, and Lieutenant Dave Leahy, who's finally out of the army and the hospital, is our legal counsel. Dave rounds up two Albuquerque businessmen for directors and we steal one teller each from the other two banks in town. But the best thing is I hire Levi Hennings as cashier.

When the Southwest Century Bank opens in March of eighteen and ninety-nine, it don't cause much of a stir. There's already the Albuquerque National Bank and another private bank, and they ain't worried about competition from a little pissant operation like us. But that's where bankers ain't as smart as they should be.

Charlie's right about getting the extra cash from Woodrow Sloan even though it galls me to admit it, because the Treasury deposits earn us enough to pay expenses. Customers start trickling in, but they're mostly small-fry.

I bring in our biggest account by accident one Saturday night when I visit Sadie Apodaca's establishment in Old Town to get my ashes hauled. Before I leave, Sadie says she wants to talk with me private. She's a fat old bag with little beady eyes and skin like a toad, but she's jolly enough if she likes you, and she pours me her best whiskey.

We speak Spanish, sitting there in her private parlor, which smells like a perfume factory. She gets right to the point, which is how much interest our bank pays. I tell her two and a quarter percent a year, and she says I been recommended by her friend, Old Lady Sanchez, in Santa Fe. "If I come to your bank will you take my deposit?"

I tell her she can open her account Monday morning.

"The other banks don't want my business," she says.

"Mrs. Apodaca, the last time I looked your money was the same color as anybody else's."

She pours me another whiskey. "Will my money be safe?"

"We got insurance on all deposits."

"Olga Sanchez tells me you're the insurance. She says nobody would rob any bank you own because they'd never get out alive. Is that true?" When I laugh she says, "I am serious. Would you shoot someone who tried to rob your bank?"

"Dead in his tracks," I tell her.

"Good. What time may I come and see you Monday?"

"We open at eight."

She's there at five minutes past the hour, and Levi brings her into the little office I use in the back, where the big safe is open behind me. She's looking very respectable, I see, not painted up or dressed colorful like you'd expect of a woman in her profession, and carrying a big carpetbag. I offer her a cup of coffee and she says, "Show me your gun."

"My gun?" For a minute I think she's joking, but she ain't.

"I want to see it."

I open the drawer of the desk and take out my gunbelt. The oiled Colt's in it's holster where it's been since I come home. I lay it on top of the desk.

"Is it true you've killed many men with that gun?"

"A few."

"When they were trying to rob you?"

"Not always."

"I'm here to make a deposit," Mrs. Apodaca says.

I put the Colt away and get out an account card and passbook for her to sign. "How much will it be?" I ask her.

"Forty-one thousand dollars," she says, and starts taking bundles of bills from her bag.

When Charlie comes in, I have to show him the cash before he'll believe it.

I don't tell him about showing Sadie Apodaca my gun because it ain't exactly part of the dignified impression we're trying to create. But I do mention that she's worried about scaring off our respectable customers if she comes in here to bank.

"What did you tell her?"

"That she's welcome anytime."

Charlie looks at me for a long while before he says, "You wouldn't drink a beer with Major Dunn, yet you tell a whorehouse madam the door to your private office is always open."

"What's wrong with that?"

"You played cards in Chihuahua with thieves and murderers, but you won't sign a simple bank letter to Woodrow Sloan."

"I got my standards, Charlie."

"And damned peculiar ones they are. When will you learn that appearances are important to a bank."

"So's a forty-one-thousand-dollar deposit."

Charlie's a businessman and wants the money, but he knows in the long run Sadie Apodaca's presence might hurt us. "How do you keep her away without offending her?" he asks me.

"When she wants to deposit money I'll pick it up, and if she wants to withdraw it, I'll take it personally."

"She'll see through that."

"Not the way I'll do it."

"Another thing. Speak to Hennings about that dog. It's always underfoot. If he insists on bringing it to work every day at least he can tie it out back."

"He'd quit if you made him do that."

"I loathe that dog," he says, "but we can't afford to lose Hennings at this time."

"Then forget it. I'll see if I can talk him into giving Heinz a bath, but I don't guarantee anything."

Charlie looks around at our little bank and heaves a great sigh. Nothing's turning out quite the way he planned. The two tellers we hired can't add a column of figures to save their lives and if it wasn't for Levi hovering behind them, they'd never be able to check out their cash and go home at night. With all Charlie's running around, very few of the real money men in town show any interest in transferring their loyalty and their cash from the competition to us. Except for Sadie Apodaca, all our other depositors so far are nickel and dime and we only make about fifteen loans in the first two months we're in business.

Then all of a sudden things get better. One of the idiot tellers comes into my office one morning and says there's a fellow at the window don't speak English wants to see me.

"What's he speak?"

"Well, Mexican," this teller says, like it's a dirty word. Three quarters of the population in the Territory speak Spanish, and half of them speak only Spanish. The trouble is most of the Anglos look down on them and don't bother to learn the language.

This fellow's tickled pink I talk the lingo. He tells me Sadie Apodaca recommended our bank, and gives me a note signed by her in Spanish that says, "This is Jesus Maria Chavez who works hard but can't write. He is rich and honest."

Mr. Chavez don't look rich. He looks like an illiterate sheepherder, which is what he is. But he opens an account by depositing a wool company check for four thousand dollars. Over the next month or so, we get so many Old Town customers we probably should have called ourselves the First Enchilada Bank. But Sadie Apodaca's still number one. I never knew there was so much money in the whore business until I become a banker.

I go see her right after she makes her second deposit and say it's dangerous riding around the streets of Albuquerque with so much cash in her purse. I wear my Colt and say, just call me and I'll pick up your money or deliver it personal.

After that she's on the telephone every Monday.

"Lee? I got twelve hundred twenty-nine dollars."

I strap on my Colt and pick up the money. Sometimes her neighbors bring their deposits to the whorehouse too. I don't mention this to Charlie because he wouldn't appreciate me using Sadie Apodaca's place as a branch office. But one day when he sees me wearing my gun and toting a money bag, he says, "The vice-president of the National Bank doesn't go around with a revolver on his hip, and neither should you. What kind of an impression will that make on customers?"

I point to our motto on the window. "Security. They see my Colt and don't worry about their money being safe."

"That isn't what security means," Charlie says. "It signifies we won't default as small banks often do."

"That may be what it means in Boston," I tell him, "but out here security still means a Colt."

Charlie screws his face into a frown and shakes his head. He looks like the perfect banker when he does this, with his thumbs hooked in the pockets of his vest. "Lee, we have to look serious if we're going to attract important clients."

"What's more serious than a gun?" I pat the revolver as I take my gunbelt off and put it back in the drawer.

I agree to be a little less conspicuous just to make him happy, and when Mountain comes down to visit I offer him the job as bank guard.

"I don't believe I'm cut out for that, Lee."

"How's Cody?"

"Still pale as a painted post, but he got himself a new girl friend over at Old Lady Sanchez's."

"Sam Brown around?"

"Him and Alfred S. Sorenson are in business with the Holman brothers. He still talks about settling Cody's hash one of these days, but mostly when he's drunk. He's full of hot air, like a lot of them."

"Don't count on it. Sam's a mean piece of work and Cody ain't that fast. What does Luna say?"

"Same as you. It sure would help if you was around, Lee. Cody don't pay much attention to what I tell him."

"Remind him that he can't afford trouble while he's got Ben's wife and kids to look after. Cody's sensitive about things like that."

I hate to see Mountain leave. Being with him again makes me realize the banking business is boring compared to everything I ever done before. Charlie Bruce is my partner, but I'm always trying to keep up appearances with him. With Mountain or Cody or Fortescue even, I don't have to act like something I ain't. It don't matter how many black suits I own, I'll never be the banker Charlie wants me to be. A good example is when I make a loan to

Bert Bishop, who was in the Rough Riders.

I barely know him because he wasn't in Ben Butler's troop, but he says he's running a cattle herd with his daddy out on the east mesa toward Tijeras Canyon, so I figure he's good for the loan. He don't want his father to know about it, because he got a girl in the family way and needs two hundred dollars to fix things with a Mexican doctor. He signs a paper to pay back twenty dollars a month with interest.

When Charlie asks what collateral Bert's got, I tell him his old man.

"Then his father should have co-signed the note."

When I explain Bert Bishop's peculiar circumstances Charlie gives me his banker's frown. "Lee, you can't loan our money for abortions. A man's got to have a better reason."

"It seems like a good enough reason to me."

"And an army friendship isn't sufficient collateral."

"It was the Rough Riders. That's different."

"All right," Charlie says, "so they're all gentlemen in the Rough Riders and they pay their debts. We'll see."

I ain't worried until Bert Bishop's first payment's due, and he don't turn up. Levi sends him a letter. He still don't show and when the second payment date comes and goes with no twenty dollars, I ride out to the Bishop place to pay him a visit.

His old man's a leathery, squint-eyed piece of work, horny-handed and stoop-shouldered from forty years of punching cattle. He's branding calves when I get there and peers up at me through the smoke. "Owe you money, does he?"

"He owes the Southwest Century Bank," I say.

"Well, he owes me, too. You'll probably find him in some bar or whorehouse, but you won't find your money, I reckon."

The next day Levi tells me our man's in a card game right around the corner in Ned Bungle's saloon, and he's winning. I pick up Bishop's note and my Colt and wander over to take a look. It's only two in the afternoon, but sure enough, Bert Bishop's got a stack of twenty-dollar gold pieces in front of him. He don't notice me when I pull up a chair behind him. He's about to bet his cards, but I put my hand down over his on the pile of dollars.

He looks around with a start to see who's playing jokes, and then gives me an uncertain smile. "Oh, it's you, Garland."

"I'm calling in your little bank loan, Bert. Here's your note. You can tear it up if you just count out two hundred dollars plus four dollars interest and late charges."

One of the other bravos asks who the hell I think I am and I tell him. When Bert don't show no sign of paying up, I take off my Stetson and indicate he should drop ten gold pieces and four silver dollars in it and we're square.

"I'll be damned if I will! This is robbery!"

"I'll count it then," and I begin, saying, "these gentlemen are witnesses."

But Bert Bishop's stupid as well as greedy and he wants to fight me over it. He don't have a gun showing, but I ain't taking no chances. I give his chair a shove and he crashes over backward. Then I draw my Colt and point it at him while I finish counting out the money. I put the note where everybody can see it, holster the gun and walk out of the saloon. Nobody comes after me.

I ain't back an hour, when Charlie comes charging in and demands to know what in God's name I been up to. "It's all over town you held a man up at gunpoint. I do everything to build a serious reputation in this community, and you tear it to pieces in five minutes playing gunfighter!"

"Calm down, partner. First, I wasn't playing, and second, I was helping establish our reputation for seriousness in certain circles."

Charlie's wringing his hands like an old woman. "I don't know what to do with you. This is not Mexico."

"Maybe I was too quick off the mark, Charlie. But Bert Bishop's a deadbeat, and when I heard he was sitting with a pile of money practically around the corner, I thought it was time to collect."

"Did you *have* to go after him with a gun? Who will borrow money from us with that kind of reputation?"

The funny thing is his question gets answered a hundred times over the next few months. Our Mexican business doubles, then triples, and we hire two Spanish-speaking tellers. The Anglo business picks up too. Shopkeepers and cattlemen start coming in, and small mine operators. It ain't a get-rich-quick scheme like our cattle smuggling, but it's a steady, profitable spiral up.

Charlie's getting postcards from Rome and Paris and other places, although we never talk about Caroline. Until one day he holds up a letter from her and says, "Lee, I'm an uncle."

It takes me a few seconds to put it together, and when I do, that old hurt hits me in the gut again. "Congratulations," I tell him.

"A fine healthy boy in London. Motherhood should settle Caroline down if anything does. What shall I send as a gift?"

I ought to be happy for her too, I suppose, but I'm not. I'm still grieving because she should be having my kids.

"This calls for a celebration," Charlie says. "Lunch at the Harvey House?"

"You go ahead," I tell him. "I'm just going to catch a beer at Bungle's saloon."

He frowns and gives a little shrug. "You're not still carrying the torch I hope."

"Course not. It was a long time ago."

"In that case I'll join you."

I know some day I got to make my peace with the fact I lost Caroline and won't ever get her back. But not yet. Right then I just wanted to feel sorry for myself alone and not with Charlie.

Bungle's wasn't elegant, but it was a serious saloon, with sawdust on the floor and a room where ladies could be served if they was escorted. The owner, Ned Bungle, had come West with Winfield Scott to fight Mexico in 'forty-six, worked as a scout and buffalo hunter, prospected for silver in New Mexico, found it, and traded his mine claim for the saloon.

When I'd walk into Bungle's for a beer, Ned would always say, "How many poor widows did you foreclose on today?" or "How many orphans you throw in the street?" It was his idea of a joke. His other idea of a joke was a string of dried-up old Indian scalps hanging behind the bar like black flywhisks. Ned claimed the owners were Apache he killed in his scout days.

When a pair of drifters tried to hold him up one night, he killed one and made the other drag his partner into the street before he shot him dead too. Ned said he killed the second one outside because he didn't want any more mess in his bar.

He gave no credit except to one old geezer called Argus Haverill, a retired miner who once belonged to the Wobblies up in Utah. This was funny because Ned Bungle thought McKinley was practically a revolutionary. Once Charlie says to Ned, "I don't understand how a man with your principles gets along with a bomb-thrower like Argus Haverill. He's in favor of blowing up every bank in the country."

"So'm I," says Ned.

Argus Haverill could be real impolite, and he was nearsighted as a fish so he made mistakes. He'd go stomping across the room to some poor bastard minding his own business and say, "Get your goddamn feet off Ned's table!" when the man's feet was flat on the floor the whole time.

If some drinker didn't pay up fast enough Ned would ignore him, but Argus would catch his arm before the last sip and say, "Ain't you forgetting something, partner?" On the other hand, if a man passed out, he'd leave him be. Argus didn't believe it was fair to eject a customer who bought enough whiskey off Ned to get that drunk.

The free lunch was still a respected institution in Albuquerque then, and nobody did more to keep it alive than Ned Bungle. His Chinee cook filled the board with roast beef and coleslaw and ham and boiled potatoes and chili every day. Beer was a nickel a glass, ten cents a mug or three for a quarter. Bar whiskey was ten cents too, but good bourbon cost fifteen.

The saloon's crowded that day but Walter Wideman makes room for me and Charlie at the bar. They are great pals, but I don't cotton to him. He asks me in a sarcastic way where my gun is, but I don't pay him no attention.

He's running on now about his new automobile which cost a thousand dollars and how he's getting ready to double his fortune in the timber business with a partner who's due in from Santa Fe any minute.

Naturally Charlie tells him he just become an uncle, so they drink to that and I listen to him tell about Caroline again. Charlie never shuts up about how rich Woodrow Sloan is, and what a wonderful brother-in-law and partner he is. Lots better than Lee Garland, I'm thinking with a bitter heart, but what the hell, I can't blame Charlie even though I'd like to. It's just I wish he wasn't always so impressed by people with money.

I seen it in New York at Fortescue's house. He was bowled over by all that luxury. Even though Charlie didn't grow up poor, he'd never been close to the kind of millions people like Fortescue and Knoblauch had. He never said so, but I know he couldn't imagine how they ever picked somebody as rough as me for a friend.

Fortescue called Charlie a social climber. "Watch out for him," he told me. "He'll walk over anybody to get ahead."

There's a small ruckus behind us caused by Argus Haverill. I hear him say, "You can't come in here! No Injuns allowed in Ned's place!" and a voice answers, "Out of my way, you color-blind old coot!"

Towering over the crowd, pushing Argus aside and coming straight out of my worst dream is Alfred S. Sorenson, his Kewpie-doll face as scarey as ever. Lots of Swedes have real whitish hair and light-colored eyes, but close up Alfred S. Sorenson is practically albino, with hairless cheeks like a baby's, and eyes set close in a face as cold and hard as sharkskin. Only somebody as blind and crazy as Argus Haverill would mistake him for a Redskin.

My personal acquaintance with him was limited to the time he went after me with his pick handle and Luna stopped him. I never forgot the expression in his eyes as he stood over me, the kind of joyful cruelty you see in kids who torture animals.

Luna always said Alfred S. Sorenson was cunning like most lunatics. What they'd call a psychopath today. He wore no smile, no frown, no nothing except the kind of evil interest a snake shows before it strikes. His size told you he wasn't normal, with his wide hips and tiny feet, hands like big rubber mittens and a too-small head. He was nearly as tall as Mountain, but as grotesque and out of proportion as a whale on stilts.

I get the fantods just seeing the son of a bitch and I'm about to move some place else to eat when Walt Wideman says to me and Charlie, "Boys, I'd like to present my partner, Alfred S. Sorenson."

I got a beer in one hand and my lunch plate in the other, but Sorenson don't make a move to shake hands. He don't say anything either, just looks down at me and nods.

"We've met," I tell Wideman.

"Of course! You used to work around Santa Fe, didn't you, Lee?" Wideman says.

"If you call it work," I answer, and Wideman smiles.

"I call it getting away with murder," Alfred S. Sorenson says in a flat, high-pitched voice like a woman's that makes him sound as ominous as he looks.

I stiffen, but Wideman and Charlie take it as a joke, and Charlie says, "Well, we're certainly putting in the hours now, Mr. Sorenson. Getting a new bank started these days is no picnic."

I'm eating but not tasting until Wideman takes Alfred S. Sorenson to see his new car. When they leave, Sorenson gives me the fisheye without saying anything more to either of us.

Charlie fills his plate and says, "Odd sort of duck. Have you known him long?"

"A few years."

"Wideman tells me he was a very effective railway agent in his time. But they let him go. Why would they do that?"

"He's crazy."

Charlie laughs. "He can't be crazy if he's in business with Walt Wideman. Everything Walt touches turns to gold."

"I mean *crazy.* The man's a killer."

"To hear you talk, they're all desperados."

I tell him about Alfred S. Sorenson's reputation, about the men he killed back in Minnesota and out here too.

"Look at your friend Luna. He probably has just as many notches in his gun and you don't call him crazy. You respect him."

"Alfred S. Sorenson don't use a gun. He beats his victims to death with a pick handle."

"I fail to see the distinction," Charlie says smugly.

"The distinction is Luna ain't a born killer but Alfred S. Sorenson enjoys it."

While Charlie's mulling this over, I start to put some numbers together I don't like. If Alfred S. Sorenson's teamed up with Sam Brown and the Holman brothers like Mountain says, how does a respectable businessman like Walt Wideman fit in?

When I lay all this out for Charlie, he just shrugs. "You're the one who's always saying most men here have colorful pasts, Lee, so why are you surprised?"

"I'm talking about the present, not the past."

"I'm sure Walt knows what he's doing," Charlie says.

At that moment, there's a racket like gunfire outside, and most of the customers rush to see what's causing it. Charlie says, "That's Walt's new motorcar," and he's right.

There's less than a dozen automobiles in Albuquerque then, and every time one appears on the streets, it draws a crowd. Mostly kids but lots of grown men as well. Most of Ned's customers are on the sidewalk, admiring the machine, a little yellow four-cylinder Duryea with brown leather seats, shaking and trembling because the engine's ticking over. Wideman's put on a smock and goggles now, standing in front of the car with a crank in his hand.

Argus Haverill's peering at the fenders up close and says, "Can I sit in it?" The Chinee cook wants to sit in the car too.

"I don't know," Wideman says.

I say, "What's the harm, Walt? Let them sit in it." Wideman gives in and says, "Wipe your boots first and don't touch anything." The Chinee climbs in the rear while Argus gets behind the wheel, grinning at the crowd and clasping his hands over his head like he just won a prizefight. Them two are a funny sight, especially the Chink in his pajamas and pigtail.

"What's this for?" Haverill says, pointing at a handle.

"That's the brake," Wideman says.

"And this?" He's squinting at the different things that stick out from the steering wheel.

"The spark."

The Chinee squeezes the hooter and everybody laughs.

"What's this do?" Haverill says.

"Don't touch that," Wideman says, but it's too late and the car leaps forward like a bee-stung bronco. Wideman goes on his ass in the dust and everybody jumps out of the way as blind Argus and the Chinee go bouncing down Second Street in the yellow Duryea. Everybody's laughing except Ned Bungle, who's shaking his fist after the car and yelling, "You get back here, goddamn it! You got people to feed!"

Wideman runs after the car, but he ain't got a prayer of catching it. Horses bolt and people scatter. A man on a bicycle gets thrown through the air. Then the Duryea disappears and only the dust lingers over the street. We're about to return to the bar when there's a shout and the car comes back. It's still veering from one side to the other, tilting up on two wheels and almost turning over, but headed our way as everybody runs and ducks. Everybody except Ned Bungle, who charges out the saloon door with his big old buffalo gun, shouting, "Stop, goddamn it, or I'll fire!"

Argus Haverill throws himself out of the way just before old Ned shoots the Duryea square between the headlamps, but a mudguard hooks Ned in the thigh and sends him ass over tea kettle like a matador in a bullring. With the Chinee screaming at the top of his lungs, the car clears twenty feet of board sidewalk and plunges through the window of Quintero's barbershop before it comes to a stop.

For a minute I think they're all dead behind the smoke and dust. The Duryea's a wreck and so is Quintero's shop front, and Wideman's cursing Ned for seven kinds of an idiot because his radiator's punctured by the bullet, and it's hissing steam.

But Ned Bungle ain't about to listen to that kind of talk. "The machine had it coming," he tells Wideman, reloading his buffalo gun and hanging it back over the bar, "and if you bring another one around I'll put it out of it's misery just as fast!"

Wideman turns on me. "It's your fault, Garland!"

"My fault?"

"You and your big mouth. I never should have let them near my automobile! Who's going to pay for my car?"

"Well, I ain't," I say.

Most everybody's laughing so hard the tears are running down their cheeks, and I forget all about Caroline and her new baby and Alfred S. Sorenson in the excitement. That's when I see him again, standing off in a corner of Bungle's saloon, his arms folded in front of him, them evil eyes staring back like he's been waiting for me all these years.

XIX

Friends and Enemies

I usher in the New Year and the twentieth century over French champagne at Sadie Apodaca's place with all my best customers invited as my guests. Charlie says a whorehouse ain't a fit place for a respectable banker to give a New Year's party, so he stays away. But the customers don't. The Southwest Century Bank enters the new century growing like a prairie weed, the envy of our competition. Prejudice helps us, too. Not just with the Mexican business but with other elements in the community as well. Take Jews.

It starts one day in the spring of nineteen hundred when Levi says there's a local businessman wants to see me about a five-thousand-dollar loan. Five-thousand-dollar loans ain't something we make every day so if this fellow is good for it, we're interested.

The man's about forty, with a black serge suit so shiny it reflects the light, a long beard and a round black hat he don't take off. He owns a small notions and dry-goods store in the wrong end of town and wants to buy a big building on Central and Fifth so he can sell to the carriage trade. My first reaction is he's a waste of time, but I hear him out anyway.

He offers as collateral a three-thousand-dollar time deposit, his old store, which is worth another thousand, and the new building the owner's asking seven thousand dollars for. He can afford to buy the building without the loan, but then he won't have cash to put in his stock.

By the time he's spelled all this out, I'm impressed. If this funny-looking fellow's telling the truth, he's exactly the kind of customer we want. He says he can furnish commercial references that show he pays all his bills in cash and on time. When he's finished talking, he sits there looking at me through watery eyes, like he's been crying. I tell him I got to clear a loan that size with my partner.

"Then the answer's no," he says in a funny accent, getting up to leave. "Why don't you say so now and save us both the trouble?"

"Why do you say that?"

"It always is no," he says.

"Other banks turn you down?"

He shrugs as if it don't matter and I say, "Look, if the figures you give me are honest, my partner will go along."

"Even I'm a Jew?" he says. His name is Simon Glasinsky and his whole family works in his store.

"If we turn you down, it won't be for that," I say. Hell, I don't even know what a Jew is then, but I figure I better check with Charlie before I put my foot in it. "Come by tomorrow."

"What for?" he says.

"I'll give you your answer."

"You mean you might change your mind?"

Charlie likes the numbers but he's nervous about approving the loan when I tell him why the other banks refused Mr. Glasinsky. Charlie says he's got nothing against Jews, but he can't think of anything good to say about them either. "They're Shylocks," he says, "and they know things about money we don't."

Levi Hennings laughs at this. "That's bullshit, Charlie, and you know it. The other banks are stupid." Charlie hated Levi calling him by his first name because he felt it showed disrespect, but he never said anything because Levi was too valuable an employee to offend.

Dave Leahy found Mr. Glasinsky's deeds in order and I finally talked Charlie around, so we grant the loan. After Mr. Glasinsky and his wife sign the mortgage papers, he looks at me with his eyes twinkling and says, "If I don't pay, what happens? You shoot me?"

Charlie don't know he's joking so he has a seizure when I say, "That's right, the Southwest Century Bank don't fool around."

What Charlie don't understand about a man like Simon Glasinsky is he had to have a good sense of humor or he never would of made it to America. He's from some place in Russia where being a Jew is worse than being a colored or Indian. Over there, Mr. Glasinsky tells me, just breathing's enough to get you killed.

He became a lifelong friend, and his grandson Sy Glass is my lawyer today. Sy don't have the patience Old Man Glasinsky had, or the wisdom. Don't get me wrong. Sy's sharp. Graduated with highest honors and went to Congress and made a pile of money lawyering. But where young Sy may know all there is to know about the law, old Simon understood the law ain't worth a damn without justice.

At the turn of the century Albuquerque was a comfortable place to live, not a bunch of office towers spread all over the goddamn mesa and smelly with truck smog like now. Central Avenue was cobbled for about fifteen blocks and so was the downtown cross streets for a couple blocks either side. The trolly line ran from Old Town all the way up to the university and they was even talking about taking off the horsecars and electrifying it. The population was close to fifteen thousand with more saloons than churches, but the center was still the Santa Fe depot on First Street.

This is the town Fortescue sees the first time he visits on his way to California. He's concentrating on the petroleum business now and running from Texas to the West Coast and down to Tampico, Mexico, financing oil wells and setting up new companies. He's still after me to come in with him and says he's making more millions than he can count, but I tell him I got my obligation to Charlie and the bank.

"Lee, how much did you make last year?" he asks me.

"About six thousand dollars," I say.

We're standing in front of the bank looking down Central Avenue toward Mr. Glasinsky's new "department" store. "I make that in an hour," he says, shaking his head like I'm the world's biggest dummy.

"You always said money ain't everything."

"I still say it. But do you enjoy what you're doing?"

"Once in a while."

"That's not good enough, Lee, for a man with your energy and imagination. I'm talking about the creation of a whole new industry based on the internal-combustion engine!"

We walk on down to Bungle's saloon, where I point out the scalps behind the bar and tell Fortescue about the time Ned shot Walt Wideman's Duryea. "Petroleum is the future," Fortescue says as Ned sets up the drinks. "The gasoline age has arrived. Did you know there are already nine thousand motorcars in the United States?"

"They better keep clear of my place," old Ned grumbles, "or they'll all get what's coming to them."

"And tomorrow?" Fortescue says. "Millions of horseless carriages with an unquenchable thirst for gasoline, which a year ago was still thrown away! Stove oil, it was called, and refineries dumped it into streams because it was explosive and didn't burn like kerosene. There's no end to the need. The oil man will be the new Midas."

"Which is what you want to be."

Fortescue smiles. "Rockefeller and some others in Ohio have organized refining and distribution very efficiently, and for obvious reasons they're in no hurry to increase the crude-oil supply. Yet it's just lying in the ground, waiting to be taken out, and most of it's here in the West." Fortescue puddles a few drops of whiskey on the bar and draws his finger through them, making dry lines across the wet. "Of course you have to know where to drill. If you drill here"—he indicates a dry spot—"you get nothing. Here"—he stabs at a wet place—"you get rich."

"How much does it cost to drill a well?" I ask him.

"A few hundred dollars in some places. Thousands in others."

"You think there's any oil in New Mexico?"

"Most of it's being found in Mexico, the Indian Territory, west Texas and California."

Fortescue's like a kid when he gets excited, and it's clear this petroleum idea has captured his imagination. He tells me about the company he's already formed to lease rights around Tampico, and says I'm a fool if I don't throw in with him.

Ned says, "You boys want another bourbon while you're making all them millions?" I nod and he brings the bottle. "If I was younger I'd come in with you," he tells Fortescue, "because you got the enthusiasm."

"There you are, Lee! A man with an eye on the future!"

"I don't know about that," Ned says, "but anything's got to be better than this goddamn business."

"Why, Ned," I say, "you run the best saloon in the Territory and make a good living at it."

"Running a bar ain't a living, it's a penance." He recites a line of his favorite poem. " 'When Saint Peter sees him coming, he'll leave the gate ajar, for he knows he's had his hell on earth, the man behind the bar.' "

"Lovely," Fortescue says with real appreciation.

"I hope you ain't a banker like your friend here."

"Ned don't like bankers," I tell Fortescue.

"Listen to him," Ned says to me.

"And go into the oil business?"

"It's outdoor work, ain't it?" Ned says. "That's what you're cut out for, like me."

"Then what are you doing behind that bar?"

"Paying for my sins," Ned says. "Ain't it obvious?"

I only been to see the Montoyas once since I come back from the war, but I send them money regular and get news about how they're doing. Never too good, in spite of the whole family working hard, because there's just too many mouths to feed. I been planning to take some days off to visit with them here at Eagle Nest, and go see Cody at the same time. Fortescue comes with me.

This is still the most beautiful spot in New Mexico, and one of the few places in the world where it's possible to believe things never change. I'm glad my grandson Pete and his family can come to breathe the air. But that's only one of the reasons I won't give it up.

The time I come up here with Fortescue, I promised Mountain I'd have a talk with Cody on the way, and I do when we get to Santa Fe. Me and Fortescue both. "Save your money," we tell him. "Stay clear of Sam Brown and Alfred S. Sorenson, and look out for Mrs. Butler's cattle."

"Don't worry," Cody says. "I can take care of myself."

"Since when?" Fortescue says, which makes Cody laugh.

"I miss you boys," he says. "I miss the life we had."

"Especially the canned beef and the bugs," Fortescue says.

"I'm serious," he tells us. "It ain't every day a man can be surrounded by his friends like in Cuba."

"You call the Dons friends?" Fortescue says.

"You know what I mean," he says, kind of sad. "They were the best days of my life."

Mountain finds an elegant mare for Fortescue and I borrow a big old chestnut gelding from Albert Fall. I load one packhorse with so many different size blue jeans, shoes, flannel shirts and long johns as presents for the Montoya kids, I look like a traveling pedlar. Fortescue shows up with a saddlebag full of all-day suckers and about a year's supply of jawbreakers.

It's a real June scorcher the morning we set out from Santa Fe, and I calculate the seventy-five mile ride will take us four days. As far as Taos, it's easy even though it's all uphill because the road's in good repair for the diligence that runs from Santa Fe.

We pass painted mesas and sandstone mountains under a turquoise sky. We see sunsets that take our breath away and ride past miles of silvery aspen and little fields of lush grass. There's brooks and springs and wild flowers. Daisies and violet-colored sage, buttercups and pink carpets of verbena.

We get drenched in a shower and wait by the side of an arroyo as a flash flood goes by that only lasts a minute. A solid wall of water ten feet high and fifty feet across that could sweep us and our horses to Kingdom Come. By the time we get to Taos, Fortescue's run out of words to describe what he's looking at, but he agrees it's the most exciting country in the world.

The ride from Taos to Eagle Nest is over a narrow trail that crosses the continental divide not far from Wheeler Peak, the highest place in the Territory, more than thirteen thousand feet. In some of the hidden places, big patches of snow still survive, and everywhere you smell the special perfume of New Mexico which comes from the piñon wood.

We catch fat trout in the streams and I shoot a wild turkey. We see bear and deer and foxes, and Fortescue says for the first time he really understands New Mexicans because he had no idea the place was such a paradise. "In the regiment," he says, "we joked about the passionate attachment you people had for this place, but could never imagine why."

Eagle Nest lays in a broad meadow at the head of Eagle Nest Lake, surrounded by some of the most spectacular peaks in North America. Who's got a right to the place anyway? Ask Sy Glass, my lawyer, and he'll tell you it was once part of the old Maxwell Land Grant before Hernan Montoya bought it, and before I bought the rest of it. But that ain't the point. Nobody can really own a place like this, not even the birds or the animals or the Indians who was here before me. We all just borrow it awhile if we're lucky, and if we look after it like I always did, it pays us back in lots of ways.

Eagle Nest belongs to the wind in the aspens, to the sun and the seasons, that's all.

In the old days there was seven or eight ranches in the valley, all but one of them small, and Hernan Montoya's place was the smallest. He had a rambling old house, a falling-down barn and some sheds and chicken coops set out on less than five hundred acres. The good thing about it is it straddles the Red River and most of it's in the big valley meadow. Hernan's only cash crop is horses. The few cows and sheep he raises mainly go to feed and clothe his family. All the grown boys are off working at other ranches, and they send money home when they can, but they leave their wives at Eagle Nest with Hernan and Mama. The house never has less than fifteen people in it, most of them women and kids.

The dogs give such an alarm you'd think a circus arrived. Mama comes out of the house, wiping flour on her apron, with a couple of the little ones tagging behind. She's a fat, dark-skinned woman with a wide happy smile who don't speak no English. When she sees me, she shoos the kids out of the way and comes running. I catch her in my arms, and she's weeping and laughing at the same time. The kids take the horses and we all go clumping up on the veranda, past the strings of chili peppers drying in the sun. Mama sends one of the boys after Hernan while I get hugged and kissed by all my foster sisters and sisters-in-law and nieces and nephews.

Mama rattles on at Fortescue, who don't understand a word, and it's all talk about food and settling down and why don't I find a wife to look after me. The whole time she and the other women are putting together the typical Montoya lunch, which is about a ton of good Mexican food with chicken and chili and *sopapillas.* As poor as Hernan Montoya was, you never went hungry at his table.

We wait for him to arrive before I break out the clothes and things for the kids. He's a short, wiry man, slit-eyed and wise. He tells me I look a damn sight better now than when I first come back from the war, and he's glad to see I'm getting my weight back.

"Not according to Mama," I tell him.

"She wants the whole world to be as fat as she is," he says. Miguel, the oldest boy still at home, takes his father's horse. As soon as the boy is out of earshot, Hernan says, "You on the run again?"

"Can't I visit without being a fugitive?"

"You don't usually. How is your business?"

"It's going fine."

"Imagine, you a banker." He laughs and shows perfect, white teeth, all his own. I don't know how old he is, maybe fifty or sixty, but like Mama, he don't have a gray hair.

"How are things here?" I ask him.

"Not good," he says. "I got the best remuda in years, and prices aren't bad. But the Holman boys want to buy me out."

"So what's the offer?" Hernan was always on friendly terms with Old Man Holman, but he's dead now, and Red and Ernie are a different story. They been pressuring their smaller neighbors like Hernan, forcing them out of business and buying their land at bargain prices.

"Twelve dollars an acre," he says.

An acre's worth at least twenty dollars in that valley and land like Hernan's along the river is worth more.

"I'm too old to go any place else," he says, "and anyway, why should I? But they're tough."

"They can't force you."

"That's what you think. They bought Baca out at six dollars an acre a couple of months ago."

"That ain't buying, that's stealing. Why did he sell?"

"He was losing too many sheep."

"To them?"

Hernan nods.

"Didn't he go to the law?"

"You know how it is up here, Lee. The biggest man around is the law, and right now that's Ernie Holman. He says his offer drops a dollar a month. I ask if that means he won't offer nothing after a year, and he says my place won't be worth nothing. They got no interest in the stock, so I suppose they're after the timber."

"I'll have a talk with Ernie."

He laughs. "That might scare them off awhile. But once you're gone they'll start to squeeze me." He indicates the children playing near the house. "I got to think of them. If the Holmans pay me five or six thousand dollars now, it's still a lot of money."

Mama's yelling at us to come and eat, and I got to save Fortescue from a tangle of little nieces and nephews climbing all over him. "Give me time to think about it," I tell Hernan.

The kids are in a permanent state of giggles with Fortescue's Spanish, and after we plow through Mama's lunch, he becomes the hero of the hour when he breaks out the all-day suckers. I spread the clothes after the table's been cleared and Mama makes a ceremony of holding up each pair of shoes or each garment for everybody to admire before she bestows it on the lucky child.

Hernan and me and Fortescue sit on the veranda afterward, letting the meal go down easy, and as soon as we get on the subject of horses, Hernan recognizes that Fortescue's an expert too. We go down the valley to see his current crop of fourteen geldings and seven mares he'll sell in the fall. Nobody's got a better reputation for turning out smart animals, because he believes intelligence is more important in a horse than it is in a cowboy.

"Take this fellow," he says, referring to the big stud he's riding. "He's tall and heavy, but he's smarter than me, and he passes on his brains to his children. I breed him with short-legged mares and get a nice mix." He indicates the grazing animals he plans to sell.

"They'd make fine polo ponies," Fortescue says.

"I don't know about polo," Hernan tells him.

"How much are you asking?" Fortescue says.

"You interested?" Hernan don't turn his head, but I see him glance over at Fortescue.

"I might be."

"Which one?"

"All of them."

"There's twenty-one horses there," Hernan says.

"I know."

"I'll have to think about it," Hernan says.

"I thought you wanted to sell them."

"They're all I got."

I have to laugh at the two of them dodging around each other. Born horse traders, Hernan and my friend.

"I'll pay what they're worth," Fortescue tells him.

"I don't know," Hernan says. "They're between two and three years old. And they're saddle broke, which adds to the value. What would they be worth where you come from?"

Fortescue smiles. "Between four and five hundred."

"I'm counting on getting more," Hernan says.

"How much more?"

"Between seven and eight hundred."

"That's a bit steep, Mr. Montoya, even for me."

"Let me think about it," Hernan says, and we go look at some sheep he's got penned in a corral for shearing. One of Hernan's little grandsons comes over to see what we're up to, and my foster father scoops him onto his shoulders for a piggyback. "This is about the size Lee was when he come with us," he tells Fortescue. "I thought he was deaf and dumb at first because he didn't talk."

Fortescue asks how they came to adopt me.

"I was down in Santa Fe selling remounts to the army. Some troopers bring in this little stray thing, shaking and starving. You couldn't tell the color of his hair he was so dirty, but he had these blue eyes, big as saucers, so they knew he belonged to one of the families wiped out by the Apache. Finally they found out his name and that he had no kin, so I put him on the saddle and brought him home."

"Biggest mistake you ever made," I tell him.

"There was times when I wondered," he admits to Fortescue. "Lee was a wild kid, you know. Running with that Brown brothers gang down in Santa Fe. Luna come up here once on account of him."

"You never told me that," I say.

"Luna says to me, 'Hernan, I can't be responsible for what happens to that boy. If you don't do something, he'll end bad.' Well, Luna was right. He turned into a banker."

Fortescue has a good chuckle over this, which is what Hernan intends. He puts his grandson down and lights his pipe. "Lee don't get home too often, but he's still Mama's favorite," he says between puffs.

That afternoon I take Fortescue on a long ride up the mountain so he gets a view of the valley. I bring my Colt and he's got a Winchester in a saddle scabbard in case we see a turkey. "I envy you this place," he says.

I tell him about the pressure from the Holmans.

"What are you going to do?"

"Hernan will die if he has to sell out. But he ain't a lawyer and I ain't a *pistolero.*"

"These Holmans can't be that powerful," Fortescue says.

"In this valley they are."

"You've got money, Lee. Connections."

"That don't count in Eagle Nest," I tell him.

"Everybody's vulnerable," Fortescue says. "We just have to find out where the Holmans can be threatened."

"We?"

"Certainly. If I'm going to buy those horses, I have an investment to protect."

We're sitting in a little meadow nestled against the cliffs at the highest point of Eagle Nest, where the house I live in now stands. I used to come to this spot as a kid because you can see for miles along the Sangre de Cristo range. The air's clear and dry, and even on a June afternoon, it ain't hot. "I thought about this place a lot in Cuba," I tell Fortescue.

"I can see why."

"Sometimes I wonder if it ain't all in my head, like they say beauty's in the eye of the beholder. The sky, the mountains, the smells, everything. More than just the peace?"

"You haven't had much peace in your life."

"I wasn't thinking of the ordinary kind. It's what comes from feeling you're part of the land yourself, yet you're carrying the whole thing around in your mind. I'd have to defend it, wouldn't I? I couldn't let anybody take it away because then I'd be losing part of myself. I'd be worse than dead. I'd be crippled."

"Mitchell feels the same about Union Square," Fortescue says. "He's not as mystical as you, but he's just as biased."

I know he's pulling my leg, but I'm still serious. "It's something else too," I tell him. "Something impossible to describe but even harder to give up." We sit without saying anything for a while until Fortescue points at the sky where a bald eagle's circling. "They nest in them rocks higher up," I say. "That's where the place gets it's name."

"Does he see us?"

"He sees everything. But what he's probably looking at right now is a jackrabbit lunch." The bird dives as I say this, straight down like a bullet, braking with his wings a split second before he crashes into the meadow a hundred feet away. He's big and when he takes off again he's carrying a four-foot timber rattler in his claws. With the extra weight, he's got to pump like hell to gain altitude, but he knows what he's doing. He climbs back into the sky with this thing thrashing in his talons, higher and higher, until he's gained maybe two or three hundred feet.

"Now what?" Fortescue says.

"Watch."

The bird drops the snake twisting through the air to crash

against a rocky outcrop. In half a second the eagle's there too, screaming and grabbing it again. We see the rattler whip and thrash, wrapping its body around the eagle so he can't fly.

"Who wins?" Fortescue says.

"Don't bet on the snake," I tell him. The bird's tearing at the rattler's head with his beak by this time, pulling it apart. After a while we mount up and let the horses pick their way back down the steep trail. When we get to the meadow we give them a good run along the river bank toward the pasture where Hernan's working the new ponies with young Miguel. I see they got company, three men on good mounts, two of whom I recognize as Red and Ernie Holman. The third man's a rough-looking geek with a battered sombrero pulled down low over his eyes, wearing a long white duster. I don't see who he is until I'm right in front of them.

"Hello Brewer," I say to the man in the dirty white coat. "How's the sanitary business?"

"What the hell are you doing here, Garland?" Brewer says, like he owns the place instead of Hernan. He ain't lost none of his charm in the two years since I last seen him in El Paso with the major.

"I live here," I say. "Didn't anybody tell you?"

He's glaring at Red and Ernie Holman like he could kill them, and for fifty cents he probably would. I never had any love for either of the Holman brothers. Red's the one was in the Rough Riders who hightailed it to the rear when he seen the enemy, and Fortescue recognizes him. When Red ain't harassing his neighbors, he runs with Sam Brown and is a great pal of Bert Bishop's, the fellow tried to stiff me on that loan.

Ernie is older and quieter, the leader of the two, with a mean, pockmarked face and squinty eyes.

Red Holman's fidgeting in the saddle under Brewer's stare. "I didn't know you was around, Lee," he says with a nervous smile.

"Well, I am," I say.

"I heard you and Bert Bishop had a little trouble."

"What trouble was that, Red?"

"You held a gun on him."

"You heard right."

"That's no way to treat an old army pal, Lee."

"Exactly what I told Bert when he tried to beat me out of two hundred dollars."

"How come you're wearing a gun now?" Ernie asks me.

"I heard there was varmints around."

"There's always varmints," Red says.

"Not the kind I'm talking about."

"Is that a threat?" Ernie says, a lot faster on the uptake than his brother.

"No, sir," I tell him, my hand resting on the Colt. "It's a solemn promise. This ranch ain't for sale and the stock is counted. If any go missing, or anybody bothers my old man, I'll know where to look."

"I hope you don't mean that personal," Red says, smiling and trying to make a joke of it.

I don't answer him. I don't take my eyes off him neither.

"I got to be getting back," Brewer says. "See you, Garland."

"What brought you up here, Brewer? Sanitary problem?"

He looks at the Holmans like he could wring their necks. "They thought there was," he says. "But them ponies look healthy enough to me."

"Nice of you to take a interest," I tell him.

When they leave, Hernan says, "You know that inspector wanted blood from my horses? Says they have to be killed if they have this disease. Then you ride up and a miracle happens. They all get better." He can't stop laughing for a minute. In Spanish he says, "They thought you were going to shoot them!"

When I translate for Fortescue he says he wasn't too sure what I was going to do himself.

"If they bother you again, wire me," I tell Hernan. "But you don't sell, understand?"

The next morning I hear the horse traders dickering on the veranda. Hernan says, "Okay, five hundred fifty dollars because you're Lee's friend," and Fortescue says, "Done."

We toast the deal over coffee while Mama's stuffing food in our saddlebags to eat on the trail. Hernan says him and Miguel will ship the horses from Santa Fe next month and I agree to arrange the details. When Fortescue asks if he can pay by check, Hernan tells him that's fine, so Fortescue writes it on the kitchen table and gives it to Hernan, who's too much of a gentleman to look at it, just folds it and slips it into his shirt pocket.

Our departure is as noisy as our arrival, with the dogs barking and the kids running so close to the horses it's a wonder they ain't stepped on. Mama's mopping her eyes with her apron, and Hernan just touches the brim of his Stetson as we ride off.

We ain't gone fifteen minutes when Miguel comes tearing after us bareback on one of the ponies, Fortescue's check in his teeth. "Lee," he says, giving me the check. "There's been a mistake. Papa says it is way too much."

Fortescue doubles back when he sees Miguel, thinking there's trouble. Miguel says, "They agreed five-fifty."

"Twenty-one times five-fifty," Fortescue says, "is eleven thousand, five hundred and fifty dollars. What's the problem?"

When I tell Fortescue what Hernan understood, he can't believe it. My old man wanted five-fifty for *all* the horses, not five-fifty each. He thought he was selling twenty-one polo ponies for twenty-six dollars apiece.

"He gave you that price," I say, "because you're a friend of mine. He was hoping to get thirty or thirty-five dollars each."

We're both laughing and poor Miguel don't know what to make of it. Fortescue says, "A deal's a deal," and tries to give him back the check.

"I know my old man. He won't take it."

"Okay. There's been a misunderstanding. We'll split the difference. That's fair."

"He won't do that either."

"You see that he does."

"Some horse traders," I say. I send Miguel to tell Hernan I'll work it out with Fortescue and send the right amount. Not to worry.

"It's easy to see why he stays poor," Fortescue says when the kid rides off.

"What ain't easy to see is how you ever got rich."

When we get to Santa Fe we hear Colonel Roosevelt's been nominated candidate for vice-president of the United States on the Republican ticket with McKinley. All of us congregate at Gordo Martinez's saloon that night for a celebration. Besides me and Fortescue there's Mountain, Cody, Luna and Horace Stone, our old first sergeant, Tom Isbell and a bunch of others. Albert Fall joins us too, and we all sign a telegram of congratulations promising Roosevelt the same support we gave him in Cuba. Not long after that, Fall quit the Democrats and turned Republican because of his great admiration for the colonel.

I'm sorry to see Fortescue go and I ain't sure I'm doing the right thing not quitting the bank and going in with him. The truth is I'm bored and Charlie's beginning to get on my nerves because he's behaving more and more like a banker, which makes him critical of practically everything I do.

In October me and him have our first major disagreement when he wants to approve a twenty-thousand dollar loan to Walt Wideman's timber company. I say no because Ernie Holman and Alfred S. Sorenson are on the company's board of directors and because the company's only capitalized for five thousand bucks to begin with.

"Are you implying that Walt Wideman isn't good for it?" Charlie says, amazed at me. "He's the richest businessman in town."

"I'm implying he's mixed up with a bunch of crooks who'd cut his throat for that kind of money. You're breaking your own rules, Charlie, if you loan twenty thousand dollars to a company never had more than six hundred on deposit here, and you know it."

"I trust Walt implicitly," he says.

"Then loan the money to him against his house and brickyard, not against so-called timber rights we don't even know are real."

"Of course they're real."

"You seen the trees?"

"I've seen Sorenson's assessments. Just because you dislike the man is no reason to doubt his ability."

"I know his ability, and it's with ax handles."

"Walt Wideman always pays his bills."

"Then make him put up personal collateral."

"I refuse to compromise my friendship with the man and all our chances of future business by insulting him."

"Then you co-sign the note."

"Are you refusing the loan if I don't?"

"Sorry, Charlie."

"All right," he says, "if that's the way it has to be," and he goes on the note for Walt Wideman. But it's the beginning of the end of Charlie's friendship with me.

I'm kind of relieved a couple weeks later when he tells me I'll be on my own for a few weeks because he's going to visit Caroline and her husband back East, his first vacation since we started the bank.

"I trust you won't embarrass us while I'm gone," he says stiffly. "Just stay in your office and leave your six-gun in the drawer."

When I see him off at the train I think about giving him a message for Caroline. But what message? That I'm still alive? I guess she knows that and couldn't care less.

I hardly ever think of her until now with Charlie going back to Boston. But all of a sudden she's in my mind again, beautiful and wonderful as ever, crowding everything else out, and losing her was like the worst thing ever happened to me. I drop into Bungle's for a drink instead of going back to the bank, and Ned says, "Hey, Lee, Levi Hennings is looking all over for you."

I think, the hell with Levi and the bank, and I have a few drinks. I ain't going back there today. But the whiskey's small comfort so eventually I wander on home. When I get there, my landlady says Mr Hennings has been by twice and to the railroad station and everywhere trying to find me because of some urgent thing at the bank.

Levi's sitting at his desk when I walk in, and if I didn't know better I'd think he'd been crying. He looks up when he sees me and I figure either Heinz got run over by a horsecar or we been held up.

"What is it?"

"Cody's dead."

"Cody!"

"Somebody killed him, Lee. Tom Isbell telephoned."

X X

Alfred S. Sorenson

I've made some sad journeys in my life, but none sadder than the ride up to Santa Fe, where poor Cody's laying dead. Knowing that Luna or Mountain or me will surely get his killer don't make me feel any better. All I see is Cody alive, barely nineteen years old, laughing and joking and throwing his money away on Rose-of-Sharon Moriarty, or running up that damn hill in Cuba ahead of Mountain and me, or pulling his April Fools trick along the trail.

Maybe he wouldn't of made it all the way to a long life because he was reckless and innocent, and the bad lungs would of got him in the end. But he sure don't deserve this. I know it ain't my fault directly, but I still feel it is. I should of looked out for him better and made sure nobody never got the chance to kill him. I should of done a lot of things I didn't do and now it's too late.

When I get off the shunt at the Santa Fe depot, Mountain and Tom Isbell are waiting. "Where is he?" I ask them.

"Over there at Morton's Funeral Parlor," Tom says.

"I want to see him."

Tom says, "It's kind of late and Morton's in bed by now."

"Then we'll get him up."

Mountain says, "Maybe you better not see him, Lee."

"Why not?"

"Morton couldn't do much with the body."

"I'll see him."

The lights go on inside and old Morton lets us in. There's three or four coffins standing upright around the room and another one with the lid closed set up on two sawhorses. Morton starts apologizing, saying he done the best he could, but there wasn't much to work with.

"Coyotes get him?" I ask Mountain.

"No."

Morton's looking from Tom Isbell to me to Mountain, his hand on the lid, explaining, until Tom tells him to shut up and I say, "Open it."

What's inside the coffin is the remains of a human being, but just barely. I seen some pretty ugly things in the war, men torn up and blown to pieces, and gut-shot and head-shot, but I never seen anything worse than poor Cody.

He's naked in the coffin because Morton says they wasn't planning to show him to nobody before he's buried and he couldn't dress a body in that condition even if he wanted. Most of Cody is black and swollen from bruises, and smashed bones are sticking out of the flesh in his legs and arms. Some ribs too jut out like spikes from one side of his chest. His left shoulder ain't even there no more, it's been battered into his chest so hard. I recognize him only by one side of his face. The rest of his head is crushed and split like a melon, the hair and brains and teeth matted together with dried blood.

I walk outside to the dark street by myself. What's clear is Cody was kept alive a long time or he wouldn't be all swollen and bruised like he is. He was beat by something like a crowbar or pick handle, and then finished off by bashing in his skull.

After they douse the lights in Morton's, Mountain and Tom Isbell come out. I ask Tom if Luna got Alfred S. Sorenson or Sam Brown locked up yet.

"There's nobody locked up, Lee," he says.

"Can't he find them?"

"Luna needs proof before he can arrest anybody."

"The proof's in that coffin, Tom. It used to be our friend Cody Williams. Does Luna doubt who killed him?"

"He's got to be sure, Lee," Mountain says. "Come on, let's get a drink and I'll tell you from the beginning."

"What do I care about the beginning? I just seen the end! That's poor Cody in there! Our Cody! And you tell me nobody's doing anything about it?"

Mountain calms me down after a bit and we go to a bar nearby, where he tells me the story.

Three days before, one of the cowhands working with him and Cody on Mrs. Butler's place finds a fence cut and a hundred fifty-five cows missing. Cody and Mountain pick up the trail and follow the thieves, but after a couple of hours, Mountain's horse goes lame and he has to turn back. Cody rides on alone, figuring to see where the herd stops to water, then he'll come back and get Mountain and the others.

But when he ain't back by the following morning, Mountain figures maybe he got throwed or his horse give out, so he goes looking for him. The trail's easy enough to follow, and five miles from where Mountain doubled back the day before, he sees Cody's horse grazing loose, but no sign of Cody or the stolen cattle. That was Friday.

"How many men was you following?" I ask him.

"Three or four, with extra horses."

"Sam Brown?"

"I don't know."

I say, "Goddamn it, a hundred fifty-five steers don't just disappear! Find the cattle and you find the killers."

"We found two strays on the road to Lamy today," Tom says, "but nobody knows how they got there."

"Sorenson or Sam Brown left them there," I say.

"We got no proof, Lee," Tom Isbell says.

"Who else has been threatening to kill Cody for two years? And who else beats people to death?" I stand up to leave. "Are you coming or do I go after them sons of bitches alone?"

But they're looking past me at Luna, who just walked in. He points me back to the chair. "Sit down, Lee."

"What are we going to do about it?" I say. "Let them walk free? You know it was them. It had to be!"

"Most likely. But nobody appointed you their executioner. Now I'll tell you how we're going to do this and you're going to listen. Tom and two other deputies are leaving at daylight to scout the route between the Butler place and where Mountain found Cody's horse. Maybe what they killed him with was just thrown into a thicket or left along the trail. A survey crew saw some men driving a herd near there on Friday. The description they gave me of one of them fits Alfred S. Sorenson."

"Is that all?" I say.

Luna looks at me through them special X-ray eyes he's got and says, "No, but it's a start. I also talked to Red Holman, who claims he knows nothing about Cody or the missing cattle, but I don't believe him. So we're going to talk again and see if the surveyors recognize Red too."

"What about Sorenson?"

"He's made himself scarce."

"And Sam Brown?"

"Unavailable. Red Holman swears he hasn't seen either of them."

"Do you believe that?"

"You know what I believe," Luna says "If that survey crew can identify Red, I'll hold him."

"He didn't kill Cody," I say. "Red's dumb and he's bad, but he wouldn't do a thing like that. Alfred S. Sorenson's the guilty one. Him and Sam Brown."

Luna agrees. "Those acquainted with Mr. Sorenson's reputation know he often carried a hickory pick handle he referred to as his 'old persuader.' " By now it's after two in the morning and Luna tells Tom Isbell, "Be ready to ride by four."

"What about me?"

"You're going to behave until I've got them behind bars. We're doing this right and we're doing it legal. Is that clear?"

"What's clear is we get them, one way or the other."

"That's not good enough, Lee. Do I have to take your gun or will you give me your word you won't do anything crazy."

I get to my feet and back off from him a little. "I'm not giving you my gun and I'm not giving you my word, Max, except to swear I'll kill them both if you don't."

He comes over and puts his hand on my shoulder, walking me out of the bar. "Let the law do it, Lee. I'm asking you in the name of our friendship, and for Cody. The last thing in the world he'd want would be to cause trouble between us."

"What the hell kind of friends are we if we let them bastards get away with it?" The tears are running down my cheeks then, the rage and grief boiling over.

"If you can't give me your word, at least give me time," Luna says, real calm. "A few days, Lee, to do it right."

I go back to Tom Isbell's place with Mountain and try to get some sleep, but it don't come easy. All I can see when I close my eyes is Cody all battered and broken in his coffin, and I got an anger so fierce I know I got to kill them two if Luna don't. I'll give him the time he asked for, I tell myself, but if they're still walking free after that they're as good as dead.

In the morning I'm still so full of grief and hatred I don't hardly hear the eulogy Albert Fall delivers at the funeral. Nobody talks much. Cody was a great favorite, and Sam Goldberg, the telegrapher who was lung-shot in Cuba and is still in a pushchair, says what's on everybody's mind. "If poor Cody had to die, why didn't it happen then? Not here like this."

I go for a long ride out of town. I ain't hungry and I ain't thirsty. It's like I got a fever again only my head is clear and I feel them murderers drawing me back like a magnet.

Two or three times I rein up with only one thing in mind, to turn around, go back and gun them sons of bitches down. Then I think of Luna and I know he's right, only it don't answer the need. Nothing does. The tears dry on my face before they even get shed and I don't know if it's the wind or the anger. Rage keeps sweeping over me like a hot breath from hell and I run that poor horse ragged. When he starts to give out, I finally turn him around and let him take me back to Santa Fe. It's sundown when I ride up to Luna's office and see a dozen lathered mounts tied out front.

Some of the men there was in the Rough Riders, special deputies who volunteered to help because they was friends of Cody's. They're tired and frustrated from a long day on the trail, and they're waiting for orders from Luna. Tom Isbell found a pick handle, only it ain't going to help at any trial because it's charred from where the murderer chucked it into a campfire. There's a lot of grumbling because they're in a lynching mood, but when Luna glares at them they shut up.

Dave Leahy's there too, giving legal advice. He thinks there might be a case against Alfred S. Sorenson even if the pick handle is half burned, because only somebody trying to hide a murder would throw a perfectly good tool in the fire.

The more I hear, the more I think there ain't going to be any electric chair for Sorenson and Brown. Luna's got Red Holman locked up because the government surveyors identified him as one of the thieves driving off the Butler steers. He swears he knows nothing about who killed Cody, but Red's more scared of Sorenson than he is of the law.

After a while, I just drift out, trying not to call attention, but Mountain comes after me. I tell him I can't stand to hear all that jabbering. "Luna and everybody else knows who killed Cody. So why are we flouncing around like a bunch of women?"

"We ain't a lynch mob, Lee. It don't work that way anymore. You heard Luna."

"I'm going to find Sorenson."

"Don't do it alone."

"Stand aside."

I'm on my horse by this time and Mountain's holding the stirrup. "If you go I'm going with you," he says.

"Suit yourself." I kick the horse into a canter and leave him standing there.

I cut across town to the Brown brothers' old office and turn up the alley behind the railroad building, planning to go in the back way. Mountain catches up and asks me what I aim to do if I find them.

"Listen to them tell me how they killed Cody."

"Lee, this is a bad idea."

There's a horse tethered in the alley and an electric light is on in the office. I drop my own reins over the hitching rail and unholster my Colt. The only sound I make comes from the cylinder as I check the cartridges for the hundredth time that day and try the door. A shade's drawn on the back window so I can't see if anyone's there. The door ain't locked, but I just kick it in and follow through with the Colt in my hand, hoping.

The goddamn place is empty, with drawers turned out and papers on the floor and Arnold Brown's old strong box open on the desk. I holster the Colt and try to think what I'm going to do next. My back is to the door and I hear a voice say, "Turn around real slow with your hands in the air."

I do as I'm told and see Brewer in his long white duster, pointing a sawed-off shotgun at my gut.

"Well, well, well" is all he says. "I thought I heard prowlers and I was right."

"You can put it down. I'm looking for Sorenson."

He lowers the shotgun real slow like he ain't sure of me, but it's still pointing at my feet. "So am I," he says, his mean, greedy eyes taking in the mess, "but it don't seem like he's here."

"What do you want with him?"

"He owes me money. Find any around?" He stirs the papers on the desk with the muzzle of the shotgun.

"I just got here," I say.

He looks at me hard from under them pig-bristle eyebrows and smiles. "I guess a big banker like you wouldn't be rifling Sam Brown's strong box now, would you?"

"That don't even deserve an answer, Brewer."

He finally relaxes and puts his gun up. "I guess not. What are you after? You think they killed your friend?"

"You tell me."

"If you're studying possibilities, Sorenson's a good one." He sees a shadow in the doorway then and whirls, raising the shotgun, but it's just Mountain. "I might of known," Brewer says with relief. "Thunder always follows lightning."

"You got any idea where they went?" I ask him.

Brewer sits himself on the edge of Sam Brown's desk, working a chaw of tobacco from one cheek to the other like a cow chewing cud. "Seeing as we're friends," he says, eyes darting from me to Mountain and back again, "maybe we can help each other. The way I see it they got a short life if you catch up with them before the law does. Am I right?"

"What do you care?"

"I don't like people owing me money when they die," he says, "and they owe me two hundred and thirty dollars."

"So?"

"You guarantee I get it and I'll help you find them."

"How you going to do that?"

"I know where to look and you don't. Is it a deal?"

"Why not?"

"I always said you was a smart businessman, Garland. I'll tell you something else. Find one and you'll find the other one."

There's only two ways out of Santa Fe in them days if you don't walk, and that's by horse or train. If Sorenson or Sam Brown made a run for it during the day, somebody would have seen them and I would have heard about it at Luna's office. So that means they're probably still somewhere in town and planning to get out tonight.

Brewer works his chaw awhile before he says anything. "I ain't mixing in no murder, Garland, understand that. But Sorenson owes me because I certified some steers for rail shipment."

Mountain says, "With Ben Butler's brand?"

"You know me. Brands ain't my worry, just sanitation. If I cared where a cow comes from, how much business would I do?"

"Where are they now?"

"Probably on their way to the Kansas City stockyards."

"Brewer, you ain't being helpful."

He moves away from the desk and pokes around Sam Brown's papers before he picks one off the top of the pile. "Maybe here," he says, handing me a Santa Fe freight schedule marked up in pencil. "If they drove them steers to Lamy, they could be loading them now."

"Just the two of them?"

"They had plenty of help," Brewer says. "The Holman brothers and a flashy hand named Bishop. I'd look in Lamy."

"Luna's got Red Holman in the lockup."

"Good place for him. Don't forget our deal, Garland, if you find the others."

The cows they stole are worth eight or nine thousand dollars if Sorenson can sell them some place else, and Brewer's probably right about them using Lamy as the shipping point. I can ride there in a little over an hour. But if he's wrong, it's a wild-goose chase and a wasted night, putting me no closer to Cody's killers. The sensible thing is to tell Luna, but I ain't been sensible since I seen Cody in his coffin. So instead of going after the law first, I start right out for Lamy, thinking Mountain will get the deputies. Except Mountain refuses.

"Cody went up against them alone," Mountain says, "and look what happened. So I'm coming with you."

We ride hard, lathering the horses, and get there just after midnight. The freight yard's on the edge of town. There's lights in the dispatcher's office, and a couple more in the yard, but mainly it's dark. An engine's getting steam up and there's freight and cattle cars standing on the track behind it. I tell Mountain to keep out of sight but make sure the locomotive don't pull out while I check the cars.

I hear the steers shuffling and smell the cowshit before I get there. It's dark as pitch and I can't make out the brands between the slats, but I'm willing to bet they're the steers was stole from Ben Butler's widow.

The next car's empty and so's the next one, and there's no sign of Sorenson or anybody else. I pass another loaded car and almost think I made a mistake before I hear voices. They're talking real low, almost in a whisper, standing in the shadows on the other side of the boxcar near the open door. It's Alfred S. Sorenson all right. No mistaking them stork legs, even in the dark, and the other one has to be Sam Brown.

I hear Brown say, "Goddamn it, Red Holman ain't my worry. You're the one took him on!"

"He was supposed to be here hours ago." The second voice is Alfred S. Sorenson's, high-pitched and squeaky.

"How the hell do I know?" Sam Brown says. "Him and Bishop didn't sign on for no killing."

"If Luna's picked him up, God help you," Sorenson says. "The law could be on their way here right now because you were too lazy to bury that body."

"Oh, yeah? Where was you when the heavy work had to be done? Afraid to get your hands dirty?" I see Sam Brown's legs start to walk off and the stork legs follow.

Then I hear Brown let out a yell and Sorenson says, "If Luna arrested him, he'll be after us next, and it's your fault!"

Sam Brown's trying to answer but his voice is choked off because Sorenson's got him by the throat. Sam's no slouch. He's tall, built strong and always got a gun around him somewhere, which he's real handy with. But he's no match for Alfred S. Sorenson. Sam Brown can hardly get air.

"Stupid, stupid!" Sorenson shakes him like a chicken before he lets him go.

When Sam finally pitches to the ground both his hands are clutching at his neck and he can't get his breath. "You ever . . . lay a hand . . . on me again," he croaks, "I'll kill you!"

Sorenson's laugh comes out a girlish giggle. "Kill who? You couldn't even finish off a skinny kid like Williams without my help!"

I'm thinking maybe the best thing could happen now is they kill each other, but when I think of what Sorenson just said about Cody I know I want that pleasure.

The truth is I intend to murder these two without giving them a chance at me. I don't care if I shoot them in the front or the back except I want them to know what's happening and who's doing it. But we're on opposite sides of a freight train in the dark and all I see is their goddamn legs between the wheels. If I walk around the train I risk letting them spot me too soon and missing them. So I back down aways to the next car and crawl underneath.

I'm duckwalking between the rails, with one hand on the rods to feel my way when there's a godawful screech of iron, sparks fly in my face, and I get knocked on my ass across a railroad tie with my head in front of the moving wheels. I see them wheels coming like meat slicers aimed at separating me from myself, but instinct's working better than my brain because I roll away just as they scrape by. The cars skid about six feet and stop, and I'm laying underneath, my heart going a hundred miles an hour.

The choof and chug of the engine covers any noise I make, and when I'm sure the goddamned boxcar ain't going to move again I roll out from under it. I'm crouched on their side of the tracks now, about twenty feet away. Okay, I tell myself, do it!

A brakeman's coming along the train on the far side, carrying a lantern. I hear a commotion around the dispatcher's shed and Mountain yells, "Hold it right there, Bishop!"

Sam Brown and Alfred S. Sorenson hear it too and come padding down toward me, heading for the rear of the train. I stand up just before they reach me and point the Colt at them.

"That's far enough," I say.

Sam Brown reaches for his gun, then changes his mind, but Alfred S. Sorenson's a lot quicker off the mark. He bends down like he's going to button his shoe which I don't expect, and before I see what he's up to, he springs and butts me in the chest so hard I go over backward. I shoot, but miss him. That seems impossible when you're two feet from a target as big as him, but it happened.

The shot brings Mountain running. "Lee! Where are you?"

Sorenson gets off a round at me, which also misses in the dark, and both him and Sam Brown run as the train starts to move. Brown trips and falls, and I sprint right on by him because I want Sorenson first. Between the darkness and the smoke curling back from the engine I can't get a clear line of sight, but when I see him hoist himself aboard the first car I shoot. At first I think I missed. But as the train gathers speed, he loses his grip and falls, nearly going under the wheels. Meanwhile Sam Brown's on the train and shooting at me. Two bullets kick up earth near my feet and one knocks the wind out of me when it ricochets off the buckle on my gunbelt.

I lose sight of Sorenson for a minute in the smoke until I pick out a pair of skinny legs moving behind a line of empty cars on the siding. Mountain's behind me so I shoot and by some freak of luck I hit what I'm aiming at. When I get to him, Sorenson's on his knees in trouble because my last bullet got him in the hip.

Mountain's there now too, holding a gun on Bert Bishop, who says, "What's the matter with you boys? You lost your minds?"

"You murdered Cody Williams!"

"I never murdered nobody," Bishop says.

I smack him with the barrel of my Colt as two railroad men show up, lighting the place with their lanterns. "It wasn't me," Bishop cries, holding his head and pointing at Sorenson. "They killed him!"

Sorenson's still trying to stand but he falls against a switchbox and cries out in pain. I point the Colt at him and say, "You killed Cody."

"I never laid eyes on him."

"You killed him, you son of a bitch! You and Sam Brown broke all his bones and then you killed him! Which arm did you start with! This one?" And I shoot him in the arm.

Bert Bishop yells, "Jesus Christ, he's crazy! Stop him!" The scared railroad brakeman jumps out of the way, but I grab his lantern to keep the light on Sorenson's face.

"Lee, that's enough!" Mountain's trying to pull me off and hold onto Bert Bishop, who's twisting like a stepped-on snake.

I'm close enough to Sorenson to see his little pink eyes on fire with hatred. "How long did you torture him before you killed him?"

"I didn't torture anybody."

"You tortured Cody and you killed him!"

"You can't prove it!" he says, clutching the wounded arm.

"Which leg did you break first!" I cock the Colt and aim at his good knee.

"Help me! For God's sake, stop him, somebody!"

Mountain's telling me to put the gun down, but it's like his voice is faint and very far away.

I can't stop if I want. I hunker down and press the hot gun barrel against Sorenson's pink skin until he flinches. "You killed him piecemeal, you bag of shit!"

"Sam Brown did it! He was getting even for Arnold."

"You broke all his bones! Then you killed him!"

"No, I swear!" he whimpers. "Get a doctor, please! I'm bleeding bad!"

"Say it so I can hear! You did it!"

"I told you it was Sam! What does it matter?"

"The next bullet's in your gut, you lying yellow bastard!"

"Help me! I can't move!"

"You never gave Cody a chance."

"Who gives a shit!" he cries suddenly. "Goddamn you, get me to a doctor!"

"Lee, give it up!"

When I step back then, the railroad men think it's over. Mountain's pulling at me but I shake him off. The bile in my throat's still hot and choking, and I ain't satisfied yet because I only see Cody crushed and murdered by a man I've feared and hated since my boyhood. I feel no pity for him bleeding against a railroad switch, mocking my weakness, so goddamn cocksure I lack the guts to shoot him. Who cares about Cody, he says? What does it matter how he died or who killed him, he wants to know? There's only one answer to that and I got it.

I fire the last shot into Sorenson's face while he's looking at me, and pull the trigger on the empty chambers until Mountain takes the gun away.

"Jesus Christ, Lee, what have you done?"

"Where's Luna?" I ask him. "I got to talk to Luna."

XXI

Murder Again

"You couldn't leave well enough alone, could you?" Luna says to me the next morning. We're sitting in his office in the Santa Fe County Jail drinking coffee. I know I'm in a mess, but I feel better than I did the last two days. Like I vomited up something bad stuck in my gut and now I'm on the road to recovery.

Maybe ten minutes after I shot Sorenson, Luna and a dozen deputies showed up in Lamy and arrested Bert Bishop. Brewer had told Luna where we'd gone. If I'd had sense enough to talk to him myself before riding off half-cocked we probably would of caught Sam Brown too, and everything would of turned out different.

Luna's dressed in a natty dark suit this morning because he's got to go into court later on. When I turned myself in the night before, I told him my side of the story and now he's telling me, "I don't suppose it occurred to you that Sorenson was the key witness against Sam Brown."

"I didn't think of that."

"You didn't think period. If I'd caught them with those cows, they'd be falling all over one another with accusations. But Sam Brown's hundreds of miles away by now and you made sure Sorenson can't testify against anybody ever again."

"I'm sorry, Max."

"Contrition's not your strong suit. You take upon yourself a function reserved to the state by law, and execute the man in front of five witnesses. Not one or two. Five!"

His gun and his derby are on a hat rack near the door, and he's got a rolled up newspaper in his hand, using it like his old riding quirt to emphasize every second word. He's already read half the paper, about the theft of the Butler cattle, Cody's brutal killing and his own investigation. Luna had a word with the editor, so my name ain't mentioned. Yet. All it says about Sorenson is that he was "shot when officers sought to arrest him."

"Mountain will swear Sorenson was trying to escape when you shot him, but that doesn't mean you're safe. Bert Bishop saw you do it and so did those railroad employees."

"Who'd believe Bert Bishop?"

"Hard to say. But the whole town will believe the brakeman and the dispatcher. Sorenson had a sister, by the way, and she's already been to Truman Glascock, the Democrat county attorney."

"I really am sorry for the trouble, Max."

"Your lack of faith in the law I understand. But your lack of confidence in me is hard to swallow. Do you think I'd have let those bastards go free? I'd have personally strapped them into the electric chair myself. But without Sorenson, I can't hold Sam Brown on a murder charge even if I find him."

This is a different Luna from the one I'm used to. He ain't angry or raising his voice. He's talking calm and making sense, and I feel a sadness in him that would break a lesser man's heart. For the first time I realize he's as tore up about Cody as I am. I ain't sorry I killed Sorenson, but I'm sorry I put Luna in a position where he's got to violate practically everything he believes in to help me. I try to explain that there wasn't no other way I could handle it, but he tells me, please, to shut up.

"What happens now?"

"That bastard Glascock will worry the thing like an old bone to get at me." Luna gives a bitter laugh. "He's waited long enough. Ever since Old Lady Sanchez made a jackass out of him in court."

"Max," I say, "whatever you have to do I understand."

He paces some more, slapping the newspaper against his leg. "I wish I knew what to do," he says. "According to some people, shooting Sorenson was no great crime, but it was a killing, and as sheriff I can't ignore it. So there's the dilemma." He glances at his pocket watch, hooks his badge on his vest and straps on his gunbelt. "I've got to see Albert Fall in chambers. Maybe between us we can invent some way to save your hide without compromising the entire system of justice in this Territory."

He calls Tom Isbell to keep me company, puts on his derby and goes out with his shoulders hunched, looking eighty years old.

Tom says, "This don't make sense to me, Lee, you in the lockup." He's got a tin of Admiral Dewey cigarettes with him and offers me one. Ready-made cigarettes was a new thing then, and very popular, but I always preferred a good cigar. "If you want to clear out," Tom tells me, "go ahead."

"You'd lose your job if I did that."

"Never. I'm a war hero, remember?" He tilts back in his chair, blowing smoke at me, his brown Indian face frowning at the world. "If I was you, I'd cut out."

"Tom, I've embarrassed him enough."

"You'll be a worse embarrassment if he has to jail you."

"What about Bert Bishop and the Holmans?"

Tom Isbell shrugs. "We can't arrest Ernie and we'll probably have to let Red and Bishop go. The government surveyors saw Holman driving some cattle but there's no way to show they was Mrs. Butler's or that he stole them. And Bert Bishop claims he was just passing through Lamy when Mountain assaulted him, and he don't know why."

"All thanks to me."

Luna's got a telephone in his office, and while me and Tom are talking, it rings. Luna wants me in Albert Fall's chambers in the courthouse right away, so we walk. The morning is hot but crystal clear as usual, the New Mexico spring turning to summer, with a bright, friendly sun glaring back at us from adobe walls and dusty streets. On the courthouse steps a reporter from the Santa Fe *Chieftain* wants to talk to me, but I got nothing to say.

Albert Fall in his judge's robes is just as impressive as he was in a uniform. He comes around his desk to shake my hand and tells me what we're going to do while Luna drums his fingers on his knee and stares at the ceiling. Fall's chamber is as dark as a cave, with only a little sunlight coming through the heavy curtains behind him. Law books cover the walls, and the furniture is all polished oak. You feel the majesty of the law in there all right, like a big, suffocating blanket. I know they're my friends, but I don't know how far they can go to help. Listening to Fall talk and seeing Luna's expression cloud over every so often, I'm beginning to think they can't go far enough.

Al Fall peers at me from across his desk, looking very judicial, and says, "Since Truman Glascock has requested your arrest on a first-degree murder charge, there will have to be a hearing."

"Tell Glascock where he can put his request," Luna says. "If I have to defend one of my deputies every time he shoots a murderer trying to escape, there's no way I can keep the peace in this county."

"I'm not a deputy," I say.

"Yes, you are," Luna says. "You just weren't listening when I swore you in yesterday."

Albert Fall says, "By trying to pass Lee off as a deputy sheriff, you may only dig yourself in deeper."

"I'm already over my head," Luna says.

"Glascock has witnesses and he wants the press at the hearing. Bert Bishop may not be any threat because of his unsavory reputation but you have some frightened, hardworking railroad men who know what they saw and have sworn to it."

"It was dark in the switchyard," Luna says. "Nobody's eyesight's that good."

"Is a hearing necessary?" I ask them.

"That's my point," Luna says. "If my other deputies and I give our statements, that should be the end of it."

"If I refuse to hold a hearing, they'll crucify me. Glascock will only take his motion to another judge, and would certainly get what he wants by pointing out that I am the same person who quashed a previous murder indictment against Lee." He raises both hands arms upward like he's about to surrender. "Therefore . . ."

"It's necessary." I answer my own question.

"Who's your lawyer?" Fall asks me.

"Dave Leahy," Luna tells him, insisting, "I believe you have a choice in the case of a deputy just doing his duty."

"Max, that may be a legitimate defense at a trial as long as your boys are willing to perjure themselves," Fall says, "but in view of my actions on Garland's behalf in the past, it's not sufficient grounds to deny a hearing now, and we'd never get away with it."

"Tell Glascock you'll hear a motion for a lesser charge, assault with intent, or negligent homicide."

"That would only incite him to greater effort. With the witnesses he has, he won't stand still for anything less than a first-degree murder indictment." Albert Fall turns to me. "I hope you under-

stand this has very little to do with you. Max Luna's the one Truman Glascock wants to destroy in court, to make him appear a
reckless incompetent, unfit for public office. Glascock is the Democrat's candidate for mayor and he knows he can't win against Max."

All my worst feelings about the law come back and I get the
fantods when I hear them talk about actually accusing me of murder. Fall says to Luna, "Make sure your deputies tell a consistent
story."

"I'll see to that," Luna says, "but Dave Leahy will have to paint
those railroad fellows like blindmen or liars."

"Dave's good, don't worry."

"And we never had this conversation, Lee," Fall tells me.

"What if it goes wrong?"

"I'll see that it doesn't," Fall says.

"I mean if Glascock gets another judge."

"Remember what I said a moment ago. It's Luna he's after, not
you." Albert Fall gets up from behind his desk frowning, his robes
trailing from his arms like black batwings, and comes around to put
a friendly hand on my shoulder. "Lee, we came through the war
together, and we'll get through this. It's serious, but maybe with
luck, in two weeks you'll look back and laugh. See you in court."

Outside Luna says, "You don't have to do it."

"What do you mean?"

"I'll hold the warrant until you're clear of the Territory. You're
free to go."

"They'd ruin you."

"I said you're free to go."

"Any mess is my own fault. I'll take my chances."

"I'd still prefer a lesser charge."

"What difference does it make?"

"As long as Glascock knows when he's beaten, none at all. Fall's
convinced an imbecile like him won't be able to prove enough to
get you arraigned. But if anything goes wrong and you have to go
to trial on a lesser charge, the worst that could happen would be
some prison time, which could always be appealed or suspended
or fixed."

"What are you saying, Max?"

"It's not important."

"Don't I have a right to know?"

"A conviction in this Territory for first-degree murder carries a mandatory death sentence," Luna says in a flat voice. "But you won't be tried or convicted, so don't worry about it."

"But if I was, Al Fall couldn't help much, could he?"

"Nobody could," Luna says, and a chill runs down my spine.

Dave Leahy ain't any more pleased about Glascock's motion than Luna, and he says Albert Fall's only trying to protect his own political career by making it impossible to criticize his handling of the case. Luna tells Dave the same thing he told Albert Fall, that Truman Glascock can never prove a murder was committed as long as the deputies testify there wasn't.

Leahy says the point is to get me off the hook, not to make things hard on Glascock or easy on Albert Fall.

I listen to Luna telling the deputies what they have to say in court, and I almost get to believing it myself because he makes them go over it so many times. The gospel according to him is we all rode out to Lamy because of a tip that the killers of Cody Williams were seen there with the Butler cattle. I come across the two malefactors first next to the freight cars and tell them to give up. Instead they draw their guns and we have a shoot-out in the dark. Sorenson is killed, but Bishop is captured and Sam Brown gets away. All Luna wants to establish is that more than one law officer fired at Sorenson.

It's a pretty good story even if it ain't exactly the truth. What it boils down to is the word of Luna's deputies against these railroad employees. Dave Leahy says he don't want me to testify.

Albert Fall gives a newspaper interview saying where there is any doubt about the performance of a law officer like Mr. Garland, it should be resolved in a public forum such as his court. The interview runs three columns without a mention of Alfred S. Sorenson.

My hearing is scheduled for Thursday, the twenty-ninth of June, nineteen hundred, with Justice Albert Fall presiding. The headline in the *Chieftain* that day says "SHERIFF ACCUSED OF MURDER," which don't exactly please Luna. I guess the printer didn't have room for the word "DEPUTY" in front of it, but Luna says, no, the editor's a Democrat out to get him. The courtroom is jammed because Leahy's brought as many war veterans, cattlemen and registered Republicans as he can find while Glascock's invited union men, store clerks and Democrats. In the end the balance is about even.

Truman Glascock tries hard to be dignified, but his bellow

bounces off the walls like a cannonade as he tells lies about Alfred S. Sorenson's career as railway agent, businessman and cattle grower. This last brings a laugh even from some of Glascock's friends because the whole county knows about Mrs. Butler's stolen cows. So he concentrates on telling instead about the decent citizen who's life was cruelly and brutally cut short by the known killer sitting in this courtroom, a man who's been charged with murder before and got away with it.

Dave Leahy's on his feet objecting because according to legal rules Glascock's not allowed to mention my previous problem with the law. Albert Fall tells people to disregard what they just heard. But half of them are wondering who else I killed besides Alfred S. Sorenson.

My respect for the law never was too high, but listening to them go through this dance diminishes it to just about nothing. Who ever heard of anybody telling somebody they got to disregard something scandalous they just listened to? Fall don't say what they heard's a lie, only that it ain't pertinent.

I feel better after Dave Leahy makes his opening speech. He's still gimpy from where he was shot on San Juan Hill, and uses a cane to support the weak leg. His voice is full of conviction, and his big, florid face is as friendly as an old hound dog's.

"This decorated soldier, wounded in gallant service to his country, this fearless young peace officer should not be here today defending his precious honor against these vicious calumnies. Deputy Sheriff Garland acknowledges he did draw his weapon and fire it in pursuit of three notorious wanted criminals, Samuel Brown, Alfred S. Sorenson and Hubert Bishop."

Glascock objects to Leahy's calling Sorenson a "notorious wanted criminal," and Albert Fall says, "I don't understand the nature of your objection, Mr. Prosecutor. Alfred S. Sorenson was wanted in this Territory for serious crimes at the time of his death." Dave Leahy says he's glad the county attorney brought up the matter of Sorenson's notoriety because he'd like to clarify it.

Glascock says, "That won't be necessary. I withdraw my objection."

"Oh, no trouble," Dave says, flashing Glascock a quick, friendly smile. "I have a telegram here from the federal marshall's office in Minneapolis, Minnesota, which says, 'Alfred Sven Sorenson, age thirty-four, height six-feet-five-inches, weight two hundred forty pounds, wanted for questioning in connection with the murders of farmhands Knud Hansen and Lars Christiansen December fif-teenth, eighteen and ninety-two in St. Cloud.' And that's not all," Leahy continues, changing papers. "A telegram from the sheriff of Mankato County, Minnesota, says he's also wanted there on suspi-cion of murdering Annie B. Rutledge, bookkeeper, and Louis T. Weyerhauser, saloon proprietor."

Truman Glascock heaves a sigh like a steam locomotive and says, without getting to his feet, "Please, Your Honor. Mr. Sorenson is not the subject of the motion before the court. Lee Garland is, for murdering him."

"Garland did not murder anybody!" Leahy yells at him.

Albert Fall tells them both to shut up, and when there's silence again, he says, "Counselor, please confine your statements to the events surrounding the night Sorenson died."

Leahy then tells how the sheriff's investigation of the Butler cattle theft and the brutal murder of Mr. Cody Williams led to Sorenson, Brown and Bishop. He winds up saying that during Captain Maximiliano Luna's absence from the county in the recent war with Spain, the criminal element got out of hand. So many of our brave boys was away in the army like Deputy Garland, the outlaws thought they could get away with murder. Well, they were wrong, Dave Leahy says, because enough good men returned to make it hot for them. He says it's absurd that a deputy sheriff of Santa Fe County should be criticized for doing his duty and ridding the Territory of a vicious killer. He says he could of asked that the motion be dismissed but I insisted on having my day in open court to vindicate my honor.

I did?

Leahy's limping around the front of the crowd now and looking into their faces one by one. Although he's addressing Judge Fall, he's really talking to them. "Here's a young man accused of a crime when there was no crime! Only a shoot-out between officers and outlaws! It was a dark night, there was no light except some kero-sene lanterns. Maybe Deputy Garland's bullet found its mark. Maybe someone else's did. Lawmen in pursuit of an armed fugitive should not be brought to account for doing their duty when they risk their lives in the dark against desperate killers—"

"Objection!"

Leahy quickly says, "Let me rephrase that last remark. A law officer like Mr. Garland should not be required to risk his life in the pursuit of a dangerous criminal only to become a victim of politics."

Fall frowns at Leahy. "Get a rein on your tongue, Counselor."

"Excuse me, Your Honor. I was only stating what I thought were facts known to everyone."

"Do get on with your presentation. And hurry it up."

"I'm finished, Your Honor. Deputy Sheriff Garland should not be in this courtroom. The grateful citizens of Santa Fe applaud him for having done his duty."

Some people clap and Albert Fall beats his gavel. Then the clerk swears in the first witness, a hungry-looking fellow in his forties named Vic Hunsel. He's wearing his bib overalls and carrying his Santa Fe Railroad cap in his hand.

Glascock asks him to tell in his own words what he saw.

"Well, Garland had his gun out and he took my lantern and shined it in Sorenson's face. He says, I mean Garland says, 'You killed my friend Cody Williams, you no good so-and-so, and I'm going to kill you!' Then Sorenson says he didn't kill nobody and Garland shoots him."

"In the head?"

"First in the leg or the arm I think it was. Then he tries to make him say he killed this Williams kid."

"How far away were you when this happened?"

"I was about six feet away when this happened."

"Then what?"

"Well, Sorenson's screaming in pain for somebody to stop this maniac, but nobody dares, and Garland shoots him dead."

"Tell us what happened after that, Mr. Hunsel."

"Garland says, 'Come on, boys. Let's go see Luna.' They made us carry the body over to a wagon and then they all ride off."

"Was it your impression that Garland was following Sherrif Luna's orders when he murdered Mr. Sorenson?"

"It sure looked that way."

Dave Leahy gets up shouting an objection, but he's a little late because of his leg, so everybody heard the answer.

Judge Fall orders the last part stricken from the record because it's only conjecture, but now the crowd's looking at Luna.

Albert Fall calls a recess for lunch and Dave Leahy's boiling mad because the crowd's got two hours to think about Hunsel's version.

When Luna hears me say to Tom Isbell that Hunsel was only telling the truth, he gets his dander up. "You trying to make a fool out of me?"

"I can't lie to Tom," I say.

"Nobody's asking you to lie. Just shut up!"

The afternoon starts off with Dave Leahy calling Hunsel back and telling him to answer yes or no to all questions.

"You are married to Alfred S. Sorenson's sister?"

Glascock jumps to his feet. "Your Honor, please. This has nothing to do with what we're talking about here."

"It has a lot to do with it," Leahy insists.

Fall says. "You may answer the question."

"Yes." Hunsel's looking real shifty and nervous now, like he's afraid of what else Leahy might ask him.

"Before coming to New Mexico where did you live?"

"In Joplin, Missouri."

"Were you ever arrested in Joplin?"

"No."

"Now, Mr. Hunsel, think carefully before you answer the next question, and remember you are under oath. Do you drink?"

"No."

"You were never a drunkard?"

"No!"

"Your Honor!" Glascock says.

Fall says, "What are you trying to prove, Mr. Leahy?"

Dave Leahy waves a paper in the air. "Twenty-one arrests for drunkenness in Joplin, Missouri, over five years."

Glascock is protesting loudly. "Your Honor, counsel is presenting allegations about the witness's personal life that have nothing to do with what we're after here!"

"The facts show the man's a lush and a liar."

"Mr. Leahy," Fall says, "please get on with your questions and confine them to the motion before this court."

Leahy turns back to Hunsel. "At the railyard, you are responsible for closing and sealing all freight and cattle cars that go out, is that correct?"

"That's one of my jobs."

"Do you ever leave any of those railroad cars open?"

"No."

"In fact you arranged to leave a number of them open the other night so Alfred S. Sorenson and his accomplices could load stolen livestock after the regular crew had gone home, didn't you?"

"No!"

"Were you paid to leave them open or did you expect to collect later on?"

"They didn't pay me nothing!"

"You just did it as a favor, then, is that it?"

"No."

"But you did leave the cars open?"

"No."

"Then who did?"

"I don't know."

"But they were open."

"I don't know."

"You mean you didn't see them open?"

"No."

"Did you see them closed?"

"No. Yes! I don't know."

"Do you wear eyeglasses, Mr. Hunsel?"

"No."

"Your eyesight is perfect?"

"It's good enough."

"But not good enough to see an open boxcar door, something that's ten feet square, five times the size of an ordinary door?"

"It was real dark."

"You swore this morning you saw a dozen things much smaller than that in the dark. How do you account for that?"

"I don't know."

"I have one more question and you may go." Leahy limps over to a place between Hunsel and the crowd where he can look from one to the other. "Answer yes or no and remember that you are under oath. Are you being paid to testify here today?"

Glascock practically screams his objection and says it is insulting to the witness. Fall agrees that unless Leahy has proof of such a payment, he must withdraw the question.

"Your Honor, I'd like some time to deal with the matter and respectfully request a recess until tomorrow."

"It's just a delaying tactic, Your Honor," Glascock protests, "I'm ready to call my next witness."

"I'll make the rulings in this court, Mr. Glascock," Fall says sharply. "I warn you, Mr. Leahy. You better have something convincing to show me in the morning."

"I'll do my best, sir."

When we get outside, Leahy's eyes are dancing. I ask him if he's got any proof about Hunsel getting paid and he says he wishes he did have, but he don't.

"Then why wait until tomorrow?" I ask him.

"Fall will bawl me out for wasting the court's time, but we accomplished our purpose by showing the witness is related to Sorenson and is an ex-drunk. So far so good."

"Where'd you get all that stuff from Minnesota and Missouri?"

"Judge Fall got it by telegraphing some old friends."

Afterward when I'm having coffee with Mountain and Tom Isbell, Mountain says, "You know, Dave Leahy asked that Hunsel fellow a lot of questions, but never once asked him if he saw you kill Sorenson."

"Dave ain't crazy," I say.

I have nightmares about Cuba that night and dream I'm caught under the big yellow balloon with my feet tangled in vines, while machine gun bullets are hissing around me in the elephant grass. I'm trying to wake up, because if I don't before the bullets reach me, the dream won't be a dream anymore and I'll be dead.

Cody's tied to a tree and Cubans are hacking at him with their machetes, and they're coming after me next if I don't find Alfred S. Sorenson and kill him.

It must of been three in the morning before I settle down, and then a dream happens that's almost worse than the nightmares. I'm at the Tampa Bay Hotel again and there's Caroline. I walk toward her across the veranda and when she sees me, she comes running. "Lee!" she cries. "Oh, Lee! You're back! Oh, my darling!" and throws her arms around my neck.

She's dressed in one of them organdy summer frocks and smells like rose petals. "But you're married," I say. "You have a child. What are you doing here?" And she says, "That was all a terrible mistake. I've been waiting for you the whole time. How could you doubt it?" I hold her in my arms and breathe her scent and feel her hair against my cheek and then I wake up, sure she's in the room with me because the dream's so real. But it's only Tom Isbell on the other bunk, and the smell ain't rose petals, it's tobacco and farts and stale whiskey.

But the sweetness of the dream lingers in my head for a long time, as if that's the truth and me being here ain't any more real than her marriage to someone else.

When Luna comes in at seven he gives me a funny look, but he don't say anything. He's as spruced up as ever, pants creased, hair brushed, mustache waxed, and smelling of bay rum from the barber shop where he just been shaved.

"You look like something the land crabs have been after," he says, and tells Tom Isbell to bring the barber to shave me too.

"Max?"

"What?"

"Nothing."

"What's on your mind?"

"Remember where we was two years ago today?"

"On the *Yucatan.*"

"Cody and me and Mountain and a bunch of others found a stack of coffins and started throwing them over the side. It was crazy but nobody wanted his coffin going with us to Cuba."

"I know."

"Tom Isbell tell you?"

"Who do you think was on the deck below when you all went up there. You made more noise than monkeys."

"Was Ben Butler with you?"

"Ben, Dave Leahy, me. We were enjoying the peace of a tropical evening when you started heaving those boxes over. Ben said to leave you be because he didn't want the coffins on board either."

"Sometimes it's like I dreamed the whole war. Cuba, the fever, everything. Ever feel that way?"

"No, but I don't have your vast imagination."

"Tell me something."

"If I can."

"Why'd you make me acting corporal on the train when only three days before you was trying to put me in jail?"

"For the same reasons I promoted you to sergeant."

"Which was?"

"Because you're a natural-born leader. Satisfied?"

"I suppose."

"Now you tell me something."

"What?"

"Where'd you get the money to start that bank?"

"You think I stole it, don't you?"

"It has crossed my mind."

When I tell him about running the Mexican cattle and the fat profits we made off the army, he busts out laughing so hard one of the deputies thinks he's having an attack of something. It's one of the few times in all the years I knew Luna I ever seen him really laugh. It's so surprising, he even puts me in a good humor, which is a small miracle on that morning. He says, "I might have known you'd be the only one in the world to screw the Mexicans *and* the U.S. government at the same time."

On the way to court, Dave Leahy asks if we both been drinking this early in the morning because Luna still lets go a chuckle every now and then for no reason, which makes me laugh. When Dave asks what's so funny, Luna says, "I'm funny. To think all these years I worried about him when he should have been taking care of me."

"Let's keep a sober countenance, boys," Leahy says. "We still need every bit of luck to get through this ordeal."

When court opens Albert Fall expresses his agreement with Glascock and his extreme displeasure with Leahy because he don't have proof Hunsel was paid for his testimony. Then the clerk calls the next witness.

The dispatcher is Cecil Burden, a pinched-looking man in his forties with the bigoted, suspicious face of a church deacon, and drooping mustaches that partly cover a purple birthmark on his jaw. He's dressed in a frayed Sunday suit and he wears a brass watch chain with a lodge emblem on his vest. I got the feeling I know him from somewhere, but I don't want to stare. He wasn't in the army, so maybe I just seen him around the railroad yards.

Glascock asks him to tell the court in his own words what he saw the night Sorenson was killed.

"A cold-blooded murder," he says. "Committed by that man there," and he points at me. "He wanted Alfred to confess he killed Cody Williams. He'd have confessed to anything with Garland pumping bullets into him." Jesus, I'm thinking, this ain't how it's supposed to go!

"Alfred?" Leahy says. "*Alfred?*"

"Alfred S. Sorenson," Burden says, a little flustered.

"Please go on," Leahy tells him in a velvet voice.

"Yes, sir. Well, after that, Garland put his gun to Al—to Sorenson's face. I didn't hear what either of them said, but he shot him and kept pulling the trigger after he ran out of bullets. Then he said he had to talk to Sheriff Luna.''

Leahy limps over in front of Burden and leans on his cane. "Mr. Burden, were you a friend of Sorenson's?''

"I knew him.''

"Were you surprised to see him that night?''

"No. His brother-in-law worked with me.''

"Did you know Sam Brown?''

"I believe they was in business together.''

"By 'they' you mean Sorenson and Brown?''

"And some others from Albuquerque.''

"Were you aware they were wanted by the law?''

"No.''

"When deputies arrived looking for them, what did you do?''

"Nothing.''

"Did you know the gang were loading stolen steers?''

"Of course not.''

"Before you went to work that night, Mr. Burden, did you meet with Sorenson and Brown or Bishop or Red Holman to discuss a fee for using the cattle cars you dispatch?''

"No!''

"I object, Your Honor!'' Glascock hollers. "The witness is an honest working man!''

Fall's looking hard at Leahy, waiting for an explanation.

"I have a witness, Your Honor, who saw Burden visit Sam Brown's office on the afternoon of the day in question.''

Burden jumps out of the chair like he's been stung and hollers, "That's a damn lie!''

On the sea of memory, an old wreck like me can sometimes pretend to be a pretty sleek yacht and get away with it. At least that's what I warn my grandson, Pete, who's always ready to listen. I wasn't no hero even if the army did give me a medal, and I wasn't no villain either, even if I did commit a murder. I don't say I was right or wrong because morality's got nothing to do with it. A man knows what he is no matter what excuses he invents for himself. Hardly anybody thought killing Sorenson was much of a crime. In some circles it even increased my reputation as a serious person.

Glascock should of known that you don't embarrass Luna. Max

Luna was not only tough and smart, he was proud and loyal. It probably come down from his Spanish ancestors who settled the Rio Grande valley before it was even part of Mexico, back in the fifteen hundreds. Pride and loyalty was what kept them alive when they didn't have much else. Loyalty to their friends, and pride in themselves as men. They'd kill for one or die for the other, and anybody who trifled with them, did so at his peril.

That's where Glascock was dumb. He knew Luna for the honest lawman he was, and thought he could use that honesty against him. He didn't reckon that a special kind of man will perjure himself and get others to do it too, before they'll abandon a friend.

Finally Leahy tells Burden in a real soft voice, "You were going to be paid for helping those outlaws! When events didn't work out as you planned, you decided to get even by falsely accusing an innocent officer! That's the truth, isn't it?"

"No!"

"Objection! Objection!"

Dave just limps back to his seat and says, "I have no further questions," waving Burden away with his hand.

That afternoon Tom Isbell goes on the stand and tells the story Luna cooked up. The next deputy tells the same story and so does the third. By the time the last one's finished Glascock's so mad he don't even ask him any questions. Then Leahy surprises everybody by calling Luna to the stand. I figure he just got him up there to give me a character reference, but Dave wants him to please tell the court how Sorenson was shot.

"When he made a run for it my officers opened fire. That's all. They told you the rest."

"Sheriff Luna, will you tell the court where you were at three o'clock in the afternoon of the day in question?"

"Watching Sam Brown's office."

"Why was that, sir?"

"I was shorthanded because my men had gone after evidence to prove who killed Cody Williams. So I took my own turn keeping an eye on Brown's office."

"Did they find that evidence, Sheriff?"

"They did."

"Objection, Your Honor! This has nothing to do with the motion before the court!"

"Mr. Leahy, what is the point of these questions?"

"Your Honor, I'm only trying to show that Sorenson had a powerful motive for running that night."

"That's not necessary. Continue, Mr. Leahy."

"Sheriff, did you see anyone go in or out of Sam Brown's office while you were watching?"

"Yes."

"What time was that?"

"Three-thirty P.M."

"Can you identify that person, sir?"

"I certainly can. It was that gentleman over there." And he points at Burden.

Burden's on his feet, his face red, screaming, "That's a lie! I don't even know where Sam Brown's office is! That's a goddamn lie!"

The muscles are working in Luna's jaw, but he acts like he don't hear the disturbance as Burden sits down grumbling. It's then I remember where I seen him before. He's the drunk I slugged on the train when he was harrassing Carl Washington and his colored soldiers. Serves him right, the son of a bitch.

None of Glascock's questions put a dent in Luna's composure. He's cool and smooth as ice. Finally Albert Fall says, "Mr. Glascock, your motion for arraignment on a charge of first-degree murder is dismissed for lack of cause."

It's over. There's some applause in the courtroom, also a few boos from the railroad men. I shake a lot of hands then and mumble thanks at the people congratulating me, but I ain't happy. I'm relieved because I'm off the hook and I was scared there for a while. But Sam Brown's still loose, and me getting off don't bring Cody back. Luna feels the same way because he don't take part in the celebration that night at all. I pass by his office after the party breaks up and find him brooding over a cigar and whiskey, his tie undone and his collar open.

"I come to say thanks," I tell him, leaving the deputy sheriff's star on his desk.

He waves his hand like there's nothing to thank him for, and offers me a drink. "Feeling better?"

"I'm glad it's over."

"Aren't we all."

"You took me by surprise today," I say. "I didn't expect you to go as a witness."

"I couldn't ask the others to commit perjury without taking the same risk myself," he says. "So Dave and I cooked up a reason to put me on the witness stand and help discredit Burden at the same time."

"You did that all right."

"Shows you what a good liar I can be."

"You mean you didn't see him go into Brown's office?"

"I never saw him go anywhere," he says.

Me and Judas

Mountain tells me privately he'll shoot Sam Brown on sight if he catches up with him, but I reckon there's small chance of that. The son of a bitch got clean away and even if he does come back, like Luna says, there ain't enough proof to convict him of anything without Sorenson for a witness. Luna lets Bert Bishop go too, but when he turns up at Gordo Martinez's saloon bragging how innocent he is, one of the deputies beats him unconscious out of pure frustration. Red Holman's there with him, but he cuts out because he don't want more trouble with nobody. You could always count on Red for a coward.

Luna drives me to the railroad station in his buggy.

"I appreciate all you did."

"Wish I could tell you the same."

"What are you going to do now?" I ask.

"They want me to run for mayor."

"Can I help?"

"Don't think I'm ungrateful, Lee, but I'd rather you stayed in Albuquerque, tending to your bank."

"I wouldn't embarrass you, Max."

"Not intentionally you wouldn't, but I do believe I stand a better chance of winning if you stay put."

"What happens now about Sam Brown?" It sticks in my craw, him getting away with Cody's murder.

"Haven't you learned anything?"

"Sure. Next time, no witnesses."

Levi Hennings is wearing a new set of dentures when he greets me at the Albuquerque depot and looks ten years younger than when I left. He talks as much as ever, but he don't spray the world like he used to. Heinz is wagging his tail and looking scruffier than usual. I compliment Levi on his new teeth and tell him to give Heinz a bath before Charlie Bruce comes back.

"Charlie's back," he says, "and he's in a state."

I'm trying to keep the dog from jumping all over me, and having no success. "About what?"

"You. The story's been all over the newspapers, and Wideman was waiting to fill in the rest of the colorful details when Charlie got off the train."

"What the hell does Wideman have to do with it?"

"Far as I'm concerned, nothing. Sorenson got what he deserved. But Charlie still believes he was a respectable businessman or Walt Wideman never would of been partners with him."

"Talk to Luna if he wants to know how respectable Sorenson was. The law in Minnesota's been after him for years."

"That ain't the problem," Levi says as we go into the Harvey House for a drink. The management don't allow dogs, coloreds or Indians in those days, but Heinz sneaks in anyway and curls up under the table before any of the waitresses see him. "Charlie's the problem. He believes Wideman, and he says he's fed up with you playing gunfighter. There's been newspaper editorials here about the violence in Santa Fe, saying we don't want it coming to Albuquerque."

"I agree."

"Except you're the violence they're talking about."

He shows me some clippings and they don't have to mention my name. It's enough to describe a new bank in town receiving deposits at a house of ill-repute, and that one of the bank's senior officers totes a gun and has lately been accused of killing a man in Santa Fe. The editor obviously ain't referring to Charlie, and I can see how this would put my partner in a snit.

Levi orders oysters to go with our beer and when I ask him what else has been going on in my absence, he hands me a telegram. It reads: "IMPERATIVE YOU JOIN ME HOTEL INDEPEN-

DENCIA TAMPICO SOONEST IF ONLY FOR SHORT TIME STOP ALL FEES AND EXPENSES PAID WILL EXPLAIN DETAILS UPON ARRIVAL." Then he hands me two more. The second telegram says, "DON'T LET ME DOWN," and the last says, "WHY DON'T YOU ANSWER?" They're all signed "FORTESCUE."

"What's he in such a sweat about?" Levi asks me.

"The petroleum business," I say.

"Why does Fortescue bother? He's got more money than God."

"It ain't the money, it's the challenge," I tell him. "Opening new frontiers, investing in the country's future."

"Mexico?"

"Fortescue knows what he's doing."

"Will you go?"

"I got to straighten things out with Charlie first."

We amble over to the bank with Heinz sniffing along behind us, but I don't find Charlie. Instead, Brewer's waiting to collect the money Sorenson owed him. He's sitting on a bench in front of the bank, wearing his old white duster and whittling at a stick like a man without a conscience. I tell Levi to get the cash from my account, but I don't invite Brewer into my office. He says, "You still want Sam Brown?"

"Why?"

"Maybe I can help."

"You know where he is?"

Brewer smiles, only on his face it's a sneer. "Utah."

"Is the information reliable?"

"My information's always reliable."

Levi comes with the two hundred and thirty dollars, and Brewer counts it careful before he stuffs it in his duster pocket.

"For a thousand dollars I could set him up for you."

Brewer'd set up his own mother for half of that, but he's reliable in a slimy sort of way. "Brown ain't worth it, Brewer, even if I had it. You're talking to the wrong person."

"Whatever you say, Garland. I'll tell you this much for free. He won't stay away long, so if you want to get him, why not let me help? If we agree on the fee, I know you'll keep your word."

"So long, Brewer."

"I delivered before."

"And you got your money. End of business."

Brewer's looking at me kind of sad and shaking his head. "For a smart man you don't understand much. I'm offering a chance to save your life by killing him before he gets to you."

"If I say no, you set me up for Brown?"

"I didn't say that."

"I already killed one man. You want to be next?"

The bank ain't open for business because it's a Saturday, but Levi hangs around for a while to bring me up to date. Simon Glasinsky is doing so good in his new store, that he's doubled up on his mortgage payments, and Mr. Chavez, the sheepherder, now has deposits totaling over twelve thousand dollars. Sadie Apodaca's still our single best individual client, but Levi says Charlie brought back some new business from his trip, which is mainly the accounts of companies owned by his brother-in-law, Woodrow Sloan. For the first time since we opened the doors, this puts Charlie ahead of me in new deposits, which ought to cheer him up or calm him down or both.

But it don't, because things have already gone farther than I ever guessed, and Charlie don't want me off the hook.

He's been looking for a reason to bust up our partnership for some time, one that puts the blame on me and leaves him in the clear. By taking off after Cody's killers, I give him all the ammunition he needs. It don't matter I wasn't finally charged with murder. My killing Sorenson is enough as far as he's concerned, even if I did it in self-defense, which I didn't.

The truth is we both changed since the days we was humping cattle up from Mexico to sell to the army, when we only had a few thousand dollars capital and Charlie still worked for Sloan's railroad. He was easier then, willing to take risks that could of got him fired, excited as a kid about the cattle drive that almost got him killed. Maybe it was being stabbed by that Mexican that changed him. Maybe it was the money we made or hoped to make. I don't know. But he wasn't the man I started out with.

I changed too, don't misunderstand me. When I met Charlie in Chihuahua, I was on the run from the law and as cocky and reckless as a man could be. If excitement came my way, I'd wade right in. And if it didn't, I never thought twice about looking for it. After Cuba I was more interested in staying alive than making a name. Losing half my friends to fever and Mauser bullets took the shine off a lot of things, and losing Caroline blurred the rest. Why the typhus didn't get me, I don't know. But when I come through all that, I couldn't give a lot of serious attention to making myself over into a stuffed shirt. If I was going to stay alive, I had to be myself, even if it meant losing Charlie's good opinion.

He don't show up at the bank Saturday, but Sunday morning Levi brings a note saying Charlie'd like to see me in his office.

"Why didn't he come himself?"

"Too high and mighty now."

"This ain't the kind of note a man sends his partner," I say. "It's the kind he sends a janitor."

"He's been in the bank all morning with Wideman and the other directors. I dropped in thinking you was there and might want something, and that's when he gave me the note."

"All the directors are there?"

"Except Dave Leahy. He walked out mad as a hornet and I heard him tell Charlie to get another lawyer. When I asked Dave what was going on, he booted Heinz out of the way and said it was nothing he wanted any part of."

"What *is* going on?"

"You better get over there and find out, Lee. They're cooking up something, and I got a hunch it's about you."

When I get to the bank, Charlie's alone, but the air in his office is layered with cigar smoke. "How was your trip?" I ask him, opening the window and pulling up a chair. "Caroline and her family in good health?" He's as solemn as a laid out corpse, although his cheeks are a little flushed. He don't look at me, but plays with some papers in front of him.

"I don't have to ask how your trip was. I've been told." His hair is parted in the middle and plastered down, his high starched collar a little tight because of the extra weight he's put on lately.

"Is that so? Who told you?"

"The newspapers to begin with. And friends here in town."

"Anybody I know?"

"Walt Wideman was kind enough to fill me in."

"I'll bet he was. Did he tell you how his business partners murdered Cody Williams?"

Charlie tilts back in his swivel chair till the springs squeak, shaking his head like he don't believe I'm real. "He said you'd make some crazy accusation like that."

"It ain't crazy and it ain't an accusation. It's a fact."

"Then why isn't the law looking for Brown too?"

"Who says they ain't?"

"Your friend Sheriff Luna in Santa Fe. I talked with him by telephone this morning."

"Looks like you talked with everybody but me."

"I wanted the truth. You've lied to me too often."

"Oh? When was that?"

"From the beginning. You passed yourself off as an honest cattle dealer in Mexico when you were already wanted for murder. If I'd known what you were then, Garland, I'd have never got mixed up with you, let alone permit you to know my sister and cause her so much anguish. Now, it's too late, but I'm determined to terminate any further association as quickly and painlessly as possible."

There it was. My cheeks burned with embarrassment because part of what Charlie said was true. But most of it was self-serving and cheap. I wanted to remind him that I was the one came up with the idea to make us a bundle of cash off the army, the same cash that capitalized our bank. I wanted to say he'd be bones in the goddamn desert if I hadn't found him and got him to that doctor in El Paso. I wanted to ask when I stopped being "Lee" and became "Garland," and what the hell happened to our friendship.

What I said instead was, "What do you want?"

"Your immediate resignation from the bank."

I guess I took a deep breath on that one. I know I walked around the office for a minute before I answered him. "I don't want to be partners with you if you feel the way you do. But it ain't that simple. We own the bank."

"I want you to resign."

"You going to buy me out?"

"I don't have to buy you out."

"Well I ain't about to leave without my money," I say.

"This bank is a public corporation. If you ever bothered to look, you would see that you are only a minority shareholder with twenty-eight percent of the stock."

"Oh? Since when? Who's the majority stockholder, you?"

"Woodrow Sloan."

"That was supposed to be a loan to be paid back as soon as we started turning a profit."

"His investment was secured by forty percent of the shares in the bank. You signed the agreement with me."

"So he can fire me," I say.

"I can fire you," Charlie says, "with his blessing and the approval of the board."

"Which you got this morning."

"Which I have," he says, patting a paper in front of him.

"Suppose I don't want to be fired."

"You have no choice. I want you out now. There's no place here for someone like you. I have Woody's power of attorney and Caroline's so I vote seventy-eight percent of the shares. Any legal steps you may think you can take, I suggest you check with your friend Leahy before you make a fool of yourself."

"I already made a fool of myself when I took your word on the deal with Sloan."

"You signed the paper," he says.

"So I'm out a hundred fifty thousand dollars?"

"You'll find a buyer for your shares. The bank is sound."

"The bank is shit, Charlie, and so are you."

"Insulting me won't change anything."

"Why are you doing this? If you want the whole pie, then why the goddamn theatre? Why not come out and say so? Buy me out if you don't want me around, but why stoop to this?"

"I've had all I want of your posturing," Charlie says. "It's not enough to give the bank a bad name, swaggering around town like a desperado. You still expect to be treated with consideration by decent people after you kill a man in cold blood."

"You call what you're doing decent?"

Charlie's worked himself into a heat by now and he don't intend to leave me any room to maneuver. When I don't say anything to contradict him, he just goes raving on.

"I was hoping you'd resign, but it doesn't matter. Your arrogance knows no limit. You're dismissed from the bank."

"You're serious, aren't you?"

"You may think you own the world, Garland, but you don't own this bank, thank God! This is not some shabby excuse for a courtroom where your corrupt army chums can subvert the law by arranging everything to suit you!"

"You got me all figured out, don't you? Good thing I didn't marry your sister."

"There never was any chance of that!"

"Oh? Why not?"

"Because I nipped it in the bud, that's why."

"I hope you're joking, Charlie." But he's not, and his words bring a lot of little niggling suspicions together that take on a life of their own. "She never got any of my letters, did she? You saw to that."

"Yours to her. Hers to you. I was not about to allow that little intrigue to go one step further than it went in Tampa. I'd sooner see my sister dead than married to a thug like you, and I was right. With some help from Woody Sloan, everything worked out beautifully." He's gloating at me then because he knows this news about Caroline hurts worse than anything to do with the bank.

"Charlie, you're lucky I don't kill you."

"That is your customary solution for people you can't manipulate. But I'm not afraid of you."

I lunge at him behind the desk and lift him off his feet.

"Take your hands off me!"

"You little shit! What did you tell her?"

"Let go of me!"

"You lying, meddling bastard!"

Charlie's a head shorter than me, but gutsy enough, and he's trying to break my grip. I don't know it, but he's already got a Derringer in his hand, and when I don't turn loose of him right away, he pulls the trigger. I hear it before I feel it, a loud pop against my chest.

I back away and look down as he fires again. I'm not wearing my Colt, but even if I was, it never would of crossed my mind to draw on Charlie. I was too astonished and too angry to think of anything but breaking him in two. Then Levi's in the doorway, cradling a shotgun aimed at Charlie, yelling at him to drop the pistol, which he does, saying, "Oh, my God! What have I done?"

I stand there like a dummy, with blood seeping out of a hole in my chest and staining my shirt. My ears ring too, and when I put my hand to my head, it comes away red and sticky. I remember thinking it's going to be funny how my respectable ex-partner Charlie Bruce will have to explain to his respectable friends that he had to kill me to get me out of the bank.

"Hennings, get a doctor!" Charlie shouts.

"Never mind." My ribs are on fire where the hole is, but I don't want to die around Charlie. I walk out of there in a daze. In fact, I walk all the way home and scare the hell out of my landlady, who's just come from church. The sight of her boarder leaking blood all over on a Sunday morning, escorted by Levi Hennings carrying a shotgun, almost unnerves the poor lady. But her doctor tells me I'll live.

Lucky for me, Charlie ain't the deadliest shot in the world, and his little Derringer don't pack much of a wallop. The first shot hit my ribs, but the doctor can't find the bullet. The second shot clipped the top off my left ear and creased my scalp. After the doctor patches me up, he's still worried about getting the bullet out until I find it in my coat pocket. It went in and skidded around the rib and come out again without doing any damage except to the lining of my coat. He says if it'd been half an inch to the right, it would of punctured a lung.

I change my shirt and have a couple of whiskeys with Levi. Once I'm cleaned up, I look okay except for the sticking plaster on my ear. "At last me and Heinz got something in common," I tell Levi, touching the chewed-up ear.

"Charlie Bruce's undying love."

That afternoon I meet Dave Leahy at Bungle's. Killing Sorenson don't hurt my social standing around there. Old Ned's burned up because of the bad publicity in the local paper and says not to judge everybody in Albuquerque by one jackass newspaper editor who's probably a pansy or a Socialist anyway. Argus Haverill looks up from his whiskey to tell me, "You should of shot 'em both, John! Never let one get away!"

"His name's Lee," Ned says.

Argus pushes himself away from the bar and clomps over to peer into my face for a better look. "Ain't you John Potter?"

"I'm Lee Garland," I tell him.

"It figures," he says, spitting a stream of tobacco juice into the spittoon near my feet. "John Potter would of killed 'em both!" On top of being half-blind and crazy, Argus is also drunk so he's making less sense than usual. "No gunplay in Ned's bar," he tells me before he goes back to his drink, "or John Potter will take you out. Here he comes now. Afternoon, John," he says to Dave Leahy, who limps in.

Dave tells me I'm looking well for a man got shot twice in one day, but he wants to be sure I feel as good as I look.

"It only hurts when I laugh," I tell him, "and there ain't much chance of that after what Charlie had to say."

"You going to bring charges?"

"What for? Throwing me out or using me as a target?"

"He might have killed you, Lee."

"But I'm still here and grateful for small blessings. All I want to know, Dave, is how I get my money back?"

Dave sips his whiskey and shakes his head like he don't know what to tell me. "Short of withdrawing it at gunpoint, you don't. At least not right away."

Little by little he confirms everything that Charlie said. I not only been fired, but I been voted out of my own bank and can't do nothing about it except look for a buyer for the stock and hope to recover my investment that way. "I tried to talk him out of it this morning," Dave says, "but he wouldn't listen. I shouldn't say this, but I have the distinct impression he's been planning to force you out for some time and is using the trouble in Santa Fe as a convenient excuse. It was too neat for a spur-of-the-moment reaction and I can't put any other interpretation on it."

"What chance do I have of selling my stock?"

"I'll ask around, Lee, but don't get your hopes up. Any interested party would want some kind of control over a new bank like this. You know how it is with that kind of investment."

"I know now," I tell him.

"Was that your whole capital?"

"I still got six thousand dollars in my account that I aim to draw out first thing Monday morning."

"What will you do, Lee?" Dave asks me.

"Maybe go into the petroleum business down in Mexico."

"Do you think that's a safe proposition?"

"It's got to be a damn sight safer than banking with Charlie Bruce."

"I still can't believe it," Dave says. "Why in God's name would Charlie do this to you?"

"He's done worse," I say, thinking about Caroline. Whatever else the son of a bitch was up to, that part of my life's beyond fixing now that she's married and got a kid. When Dave asks me what I mean, I tell him, nothing, just that I should of seen something like this coming.

"How could you? He was your partner and you trusted him."

"There's a moral here somewheres."

"You had your share of trouble lately." He raises his glass and says, "Here's to Mexico. Who knows? Maybe you'll strike it rich in the oil business."

"What the hell, Dave. Since Cuba I been living on borrowed time anyway. Same as you and the others."

His loud laugh carries down the bar and Argus Haverill says, "That's telling them, John! He gives you any shit, put his candle out!"

That's how those times were. Painful, dumb and friendly. The kids today talk about making statements when they take their stand on the war in Vietnam or the draft or civil rights, and maybe that's what I'm trying to do here, make a statement about myself. It's something I didn't always get right in the past.

Aboard the "Molly Pratt"

I been asked by a lot of people how I made my first million, and I always enjoy giving different answers. I tell a cattleman I made it in beef, or I tell some Wall Street high roller it came from pineapple futures, and if I want to shock a Democrat, I say I made it in politics. My family always assumed it came from the oil business, but that's only indirectly true. My first million was a present, no strings attached, give to me by a dead man shortly after we met. It's the kind of true thing still happened in the West when I was young.

After being shot at twice, chucked out of my own bank and learning the truth about Charlie Bruce, I wasn't in no hurry to see him again. My only idea was to shake the dust of Albuquerque from my boots and put as much space between us as I could.

Levi brought me a thousand dollars cash and a bank draft for fifty-two hundred, which closed out my account. I left the stock shares with Dave Leahy, sent Fortescue a telegram saying I'd see him in ten days, and took the train for El Paso.

Ransom's back with the police department, and bitter because he got skipped over for promotion to sergeant while he was in the army. Instead of a cushy job shuffling papers at headquarters he's out on the streets again bashing Mexicans, a pastime incompatible with his temperament and ambition.

Like a few others from our old outfit, he's bored after Cuba, so he's volunteered to go to the Philippines. He's leaving in a couple of weeks and I tell him he's crazy. The newspapers are full of what's going on there, and now that the Spaniards are gone, it's open season on American soldiers.

"They give me a lieutenant's commission because of my experience," he says, like that's going to exempt him from a bullet.

I wouldn't go back in the army if they made me a general, I tell him, and especially not to fight in the Philippines. "Don't you read the goddamn papers, Ransom? Out there they chop you up with bolo knives, which is worse than Cuban machetes."

"I don't believe that hogwash," he says. "Remember the reporters in Cuba? They made up half the stuff they wrote about us."

"But the other half was true," I remind him.

"Well, I'm going anyway," he says, his feathers ruffled because I don't congratulate him on such a sensible decision. "Somebody's got to defend this country."

That makes me laugh. "Why, them islands ain't even part of America. You got to cross a whole ocean to get there."

"We won them fair and square," Ransom says stubbornly, "and we're going to keep them. They're an American Territory now, just like New Mexico."

"Nothing's like New Mexico," I tell him. "If you'd been born there like me instead of in this godforsaken gopher hole, you wouldn't have to go traipsing off to some little pissant country on the other side of the world to find what you're looking for."

"If New Mexico's so great why don't you stay there instead of running down to Tampico?"

"I'm a businessman, Ransom, so I go where the business is. But I ain't looking for an early grave like you."

"You don't understand, Lee. The Philippines is part of the new American empire. That's what we're building today."

"Didn't you get enough empire-building in Cuba? You need your head looked at."

"What are you and Fortescue going to do in Mexico then, if that ain't empire-building?"

"I won't know till I get there, but for sure we ain't going to get sliced fine by some juiced-up cannibal with a grudge."

"The minute you cross the Rio Grande your life ain't worth a nickel. You know that. You worked there before."

"And made money," I say. "Maybe I'll get lucky again."

Ransom's still got the Winchester rifles I bought in El Paso before the war and wants me to take them. I tell him thanks but they'll be more use to him where he's going. I don't aim to meet any bandits in the petroleum business.

There's only two ways to get to Tampico from El Paso in them days. One's from Juárez straight down the backbone of Mexico on Woodrow Sloan's railroad. The other's by Southern Pacific train to San Antonio, then by overland stagecoach to Laredo, where a riverboat takes you down to Brownsville at the mouth of the Rio Grande. There, you cross over to Matamoros and get the Gulf Coast steamship for Tampico. I'm taking the second route even though it's a few days longer, because I ain't about to put a dollar in Woodrow Sloan's pocket by riding his damn railroad.

That's my first mistake. My second mistake is turning down Ransom's offer of the rifles. But hell, this is the twentieth century, and I ain't punching cows along the Rio Grande anymore with Mexican bandits ready to steal my teeth. I'm a businessman traveling by first-class public conveyance all the way to a major city, so the last thing I need is a rifle. I got my Colt anyway, and that's enough unnecessary weight.

Ransom shakes my hand when I climb into the Pullman and we both laugh at the difference between my trip now and the one we made over the same tracks to San Antonio two years before. "Keep your head down and your pecker in your pants," I tell him.

"You too, Lee. Take care."

"See you, Lieutenant."

It's a funny thing. Ransom and me was never close, just two men who shared a war. But when I'm settled in my seat and the train starts moving, I'm real sad about that farewell. I think he's a damn fool to go volunteering for the Philippines. But he's happy about their making him an officer and doing something he thinks is important instead of busting heads on a El Paso police beat. All that crap he talked about empire-building only proves to me he didn't learn a thing if he's looking for the same kind of trouble all over again. But who am I to say?

What did I learn? Nothing I didn't know before I went. So what's it all about, I ask myself? I thought I had the best life in the world, until Cody's death changed it all. Or did it just wake me out of a dumb dream?

Like Dave Leahy said, Charlie was laying for me a long time, probably since Tampa. But I didn't see it. So how many more times am I going to get bushwhacked before I smarten up? I was no banker even though I learned to dress like one, and I ain't no petroleum businessman now, no matter what I tell people. I'm still drifting through life like a twig on a river, and that's a poor way to get anywhere.

Empire builder! I got sticking plaster on my ribs and a chunk out of one ear, a hundred fifty thousand dollars of worthless paper in a strong box, and the world to make good in! If it wasn't for Fortescue, I'd be as ready as Ransom to go shoot up another island.

As the train lulls me into a half doze, I think I know two things for certain that give me a terrible case of the blues. Caroline's lost to me and Ransom won't make it back this time.

San Antonio ain't changed a bit in two years, but I don't linger because there's too many ghosts. The stage to Laredo goes every day and I just make the connection. It's one of the last lines still carries passengers. Mainly they haul freight and mailbags to connect with the riverboat. The coach is one of them heavy old Studebakers drawn by four mules that takes two days to make a hundred sixty-five miles, riding all night and changing teams every forty miles.

The only other passengers besides me is a harrassed young woman with two children, the family of an army officer stationed down in Brownsville. After the usual pleasantries we don't have much to say to each other. She's too busy with her kids, who are right spoiled and disappointed there ain't no Indians chasing us. I'm in agony from where Charlie shot me because the road's as rough as a razorback and my busted rib's got no more give than the springs on that old stagecoach.

I don't get much rest after we pull into Laredo either, because the Travelers' Hotel there is full up and the army officer's wife and kids don't have a reservation. So I give them my room and stretch out on a sofa in the lobby, which is like trying to sleep on rocks. The riverboat arrives early the next morning, and after a lot of huffing and churning and whistle-blowing around the wharf, they snub her into the pier and load up.

There I see barefoot Mexican stevedores who don't weigh more than a hundred pounds pick up two-hundred-pound loads.

They're all bone and muscle, with a harness like a mule, and before they go for the load they pump their legs up and down double time, never looking up. Then they jog past the freight platform, where a foreman tips a bale or crate on their backs. They never stop moving their legs, just keep pumping right on up the gang-plank to where they tip the load onto the deck and go back for another. It's a trick, the pilot tells me. Easy for a Mexican, but no work for a nigger.

"Why not?

"Too lazy."

"What about a white man?" I ask him.

"Too slow," he says.

In his case I believe it. He's a head shorter than me and as big around the middle as he is tall. A good advertisement for the food on board, I figure.

By nine o'clock we're on our way again in some comfort. The boat's a prehistoric stern-wheeler called the *Molly Pratt* that's been plying the Rio Grande since the Civil War, which is about when she was painted last. My cabin is big and airy, with a brass bed the size of a hayfield. I fall on it and sleep away the morning. The steady drum of the engine helps, and I don't even feel my busted rib pulsing anymore.

I give myself a bath and a shave before I go to the main saloon for lunch. The food's as good as you can expect outside Santa Fe. Steak and eggs, chili, potatoes, ham, chicken and apricot pie. There ain't too many passengers and I get to share a table with the fat river pilot. Between stuffing his face, he's telling me that the river's low right now and he don't know if we'll make the schedule.

"Silting downstream, and there's some bandits working the Mexican bank below San Ygnacio if the Texas Rangers ain't driven them off. The big river's a peril this time of year."

"Is that so?" I say, tucking into a piece of chicken before he nails it.

"It's aggrading," he says, going on to tell me how much water the *Molly Pratt* draws and how they only skimmed over a place called Knuckle Shoal on the trip upstream last week. "The trick is knowing how the drift lies. If you go too far against the Mexican bank you get stuck there," he says, shoveling in the ham and potatoes. "But if you give way too much to avoid grounding, you find yourself sucking wind on our side where the shoal is."

All this talk makes me nervous. "Shouldn't you be up in the pilot house or whatever you call it?" I ask him.

He shakes his head and wipes his brow with his napkin. Like most fat men he sweats a lot even when it ain't hot. "River runs hard and deep until we reach Salado Point," he says.

"So what do you do if you get stuck?"

"Back down and try again. If the *Molly Pratt* can't do it on her own, we winch off. If that don't work, we sit it out."

"How long?"

"Well," he says, casting his eyes over what's left of the chicken and scraping two legs and a breast onto his plate. "This river's like a woman, all quicksand, and changes her mind every minute. If she wants to let you go, she does. And if she don't, she don't. I been hung up on a woman for as short as ten minutes, and silted in for as long as two weeks. Same with the river."

"Two weeks!"

"Don't worry. Room and board's on the company."

"I got to be in Tampico in a few days."

"Then you should of took the train." He reaches for the apricot pie and takes half. There's supposed to be another passenger named Doheny at our table but he's keeping to his cabin. "I reckon he don't have your natural curiosity about the beauty of the river. You want some more pie?" I ain't had my first piece yet, but I'm full anyway, so I shake my head and he takes the other half. "Doheny's in the oil business too," he says.

After lunch I pass the time playing a little poker with three other passengers and lose forty dollars. One's a drummer for a drilling-pipe maker on his way to Tampico like me, one's a Pinkerton detective and the third works for an insurance company. When they ask me what I do, I tell them I'm looking into the petroleum business.

The pipe salesman says, "Wildcatting's as fast a way to go broke as I know of."

The detective says, "There's more deception in oil than any other industry. Riskiest investment there is." I could tell him a few things about the banking business too, but I don't.

The insurance fellow says, "We wouldn't write a petroleum policy at any price."

The pipe drummer says, "Hunting gold in the Yukon's less dangerous."

"Where's the danger?" I ask them, and each one gives a different answer.

"Fire," says insurance.

"Fraud," says Pinkerton.

"Dry holes," says pipes.

"I see you're a risk-taker though," the insurance fellow says when he scoops up another pot after calling my bluff.

"You meet Doheny?" the Pinkerton man asks me.

"No."

"He's a good example. Made a fortune in petroleum over in California, and now they say he's broke."

"Why's that?"

The pipe man deals the cards. "He put it all back in dry holes. He owes my company a hundred and ninety thousand dollars."

"They're all alike," the insurance fellow says, snapping his sleeve garters and taking off his celluloid cuffs before he picks up his cards. "Dangerous and undependable."

Pinkerton studies his hand and opens for a quarter. "He's papered the Southwest with stock in his Mexican company. I even bought some myself, which shows what a dumb son of a bitch I am."

"He won't find oil," the pipe drummer says.

"How do you know?" I ask him.

"Because it ain't there. He's already drilled eleven wells and brought up nothing but water."

The insurance man raises him a quarter and says, "He's impractical. Can't face reality."

"He's a crook," the detective says, "but likable enough."

As the *Molly Pratt* churns through the afternoon, we finally quit the game and the two salesmen retire to their cabins. But I ain't sleepy so I go on deck to watch the broad, coffee-color river pass, with Mexico on our right and Texas on our left. There ain't many settlements along this part, just miles of rocky desert down to the water's edge, with sometimes a clutch of cottonwood or willows on the banks. Every few miles I see a lean-to or a mud hut where some poor devil and his dog keep a lonely lookout over a herd of sheep.

The Pinkerton man joins me and we get to talking. It turns out he was in Cuba too, with a New York regiment, and agrees it was about the worst-run war he ever heard of. He's escorting some crates of silver bars belong to a mining company.

"What about the bandits I hear are working this river?"

"The Texas Rangers raid into Mexico every now and then to keep their numbers down, but they ain't really a threat." He laughs and offers me a cigar. "Until they learn to row and turn pirate, they'll never get near my cargo anyway."

"It sounds like a good job."

"Oh, it was, except this is my last trip."

"Why is that?"

"That insurance fellow sold the mining company a robbery policy, so they don't need Pinkerton's. Protecting their silver with a piece of paper is cheaper than paying me."

"Does that mean you're out of work?" I ask him.

"Hell, no. But whatever job they send me on next won't be as cushy as this one."

He decides to stretch out in the main saloon after a while so I wander up to the wheelhouse to see how the pilot keeps us in the channel. He's been steamboating since the age of twelve, he tells me, with thirty years as pilot on the Rio Grande.

"I guess you know it better than anybody then," I say.

"Nobody can know a river," he says. "The Rio Grande we're coming down ain't the same one I went up last trip."

"Then how do you know where the channel is?"

"Guesswork. Being a pilot is knowing how to guess right."

He's perched on a stool, his big hams almost making it disappear under him, his belly resting on his thighs, sweat pouring off him even though there's a nice breeze through the open windows of the wheelhouse. His assistant, a kid about eighteen, is actually steering the boat with a big spoked wheel while the pilot sips his coffee and gives the orders, a point to starboard or larboard, whatever he wants to keep the boat pointed downstream. Up in the bow is another kid throwing a lead and yelling out the depth of the channel. The deepest it's been all afternoon is nine feet, and according to the pilot, we draw six.

There's a bell rope over the fat man's head and a speaking tube connects to the boiler room so he can signal the engineer how much steam he wants. Two or three times while I'm standing there he stops the engines and we drift as the leadsman in the bow calls out "Seven a half! Seven! Six a half!" The pilot rings the bell frantically and yells into the speaking tube, "Full astern!" until the

Molly Pratt backs down about a hundred yards because he mistook the channel.

He mops the sweat away from his eyes with a greasy handkerchief every couple of minutes and takes down a spyglass to look at something far ahead on the river. "Not much water here," he says. "Couldn't come through at night." The words ain't hardly out of his mouth when the boat shudders to a dead stop that nearly throws me off my pins. He grabs the wheel away from the kid and jerks the bell rope to ring full power astern. After a minute, the *Molly Pratt* backs off the sandbar, shaking and clattering until she's in the channel again, and he points her off toward the other bank before we get stuck a second time.

"I guess I'm distracting you," I say.

"Not at all. We'll be by this soon. You see the big river's just about out of water here. In another fifteen miles, where the Salado empties in from Mexico, she deepens again, and gives us good draft to Mier and Rio Grande City."

We're creeping now, feeling our way, even though the river's wide and looks like it could hold a hundred ships abreast. I don't know how the pilot finds the channel. As far as you can see the sluggish water's flat and dull as a dirty plate, with not a marker or a ripple anywhere. There's a wreck on the Texas side he says exploded and burned back in eighty-five. It's been ages since I seen any sign of life on either bank, and I'm thinking this would be a bad place to be stuck.

We run aground again in half an hour and churn our way off. The pilot curses. "We'll have to hug the Mexican shore."

I don't want to make a pest of myself so I climb down to the saloon, where the army officer's wife is yelling at her kids to stay inside before they fall overboard. The Pinkerton man's dozing over an old newspaper, and the pipe salesman's writing a letter. I wander back to my cabin, thinking maybe I'll take a siesta after all, when we run aground again. The old boat tries to back off, but this time she don't make it. When I go out on deck the pilot's hollering from the wheelhouse to break out cable. We're so close to the Mexican bank you can almost step ashore without getting your boots wet, and a hundred yards downstream there's a clump of cottonwoods they plan to winch off.

Me and the Pinkerton fellow offer to help with the lines while the crew carries them ashore. The pilot tells them to make it quick because if we're not off this bar and into deep water before night-fall we'll have to lay up.

It's hot work handling that heavy hawser, and before we pay out half of it, a fellow appears on deck I never seen before. He ain't wearing nothing but boots and his BVDs, but he pitches right in with me and the Pinkerton man. He's a ruddy-faced, balding dude about forty, on the short side, but built like a goddamn bull.

In fifteen minutes, the line's attached to the trees and the three of us man the capstan while the pilot clangs the bell and shouts orders from the wheelhouse.

The stern-wheel churns the water to a boil, and that rope stretches so taut I think it'll part. But after five minutes of shaking and straining, with great columns of heavy black smoke pouring out of her stacks, the *Molly Pratt* don't move an inch.

"What happens now?" the Pinkerton fellow says to me, after the paddle wheel stops turning and we straighten up from our labors.

"We're worse off than before," the stranger says. "That stern-wheel just piles the mud up under us. A side-wheeler would have been off this bar by now."

"I don't see one around," Pinkerton says real sarcastic.

"Shift the cable to get a better angle!" the pilot hollers. "Stand by ashore!" And he bustles down from the wheelhouse, his great round bulk real nimble on the ladder.

"I'm E.L. Doheny," the red-faced bull says to me, sticking out his hand. "You must be whats-his-name."

"How'd you know?"

"I saw the passenger list. You're not a woman or a child and I know all these other vagrants. What's your business, Mr. . . . ?"

"Garland. It used to be cattle and a bank. But now I'm thinking about petroleum."

"You're on your way to the right place."

"They tell me you're in the oil business."

The Pinkerton fellow hears that and says, "Snake oil's more like it. Don't let him sell you any stock, Garland."

Doheny glares at him and his face gets so red that for a minute I believe there might be a fight. Then Doheny laughs. "Don't pay any attention. Like all ignorant, suspicious men he wouldn't recog-nize a gift horse if it bit him in the foot."

Pinkerton says, "You got grit, Doheny, I'll give you that. If I was in your position I'd avoid Tampico like the plague."

"That's only one of the many differences between us," Doheny says down his nose. "It so happens that Tampico will be the biggest strike of all."

"Is that so? Then why don't you buy back my thousand shares in your Pan-American Petroleum Company? You can have them for a hundred dollars, just what I paid."

"Hold onto them," Doheny says. "Your heirs may like money even if you don't."

"I got no heirs," the detective says, "which is lucky for you, or I'd shop you for swindling women and children." He takes a stock certificate out of his pocket. "Make me an offer, I dare you!"

"He just don't want to get rich," Doheny says to me with a wink. "Did you ever hear of such a thing?"

"Rich? Don't make me laugh!" These are the last words the Pinkerton man speaks. There in the warm afternoon sun, a red hole blossoms next to his nose. He staggers back against the winch and topples to the deck. I'm slow to realize what's happening until I hear the shot. I turn toward the shore and see the fat pilot running for all he's worth toward the boat, yelling, "Bandits! Bandits! Take cover!" He's followed by the two crewmen, one of whom goes sprawling in the mud, face down on the riverbank. The other kid keeps running, bullets kicking up the dirt around his feet, but the fat man turns back to help the one got shot. I don't see who's doing the shooting, because me and Doheny are flat on the deck by now.

Then the army officer's wife runs toward us, yelling for her children until a bullet splinters wood in front of her and stops her cold, a perfect target. I knock her down and drag her into the saloon, where the pipe salesman and the insurance fellow are squatting down behind the sofas. Her children are there too, thank God, and she rushes over to hug them, crying hysterically now.

The pipe fellow's about to wet his pants, but the insurance man keeps his head and starts turning over the sofas and stacking pillows and cushions all around them. My Colt's in my cabin and I get it. I figure the Pinkerton man may have a gun in his cabin too, and I'm right. I find a twelve-gauge shotgun and a box of shells next to the bed.

I make my way to the bow, where the freight stacked along the deck offers some protection. A chunk's gone from the back of the detective's skull and the deck's slippery with his blood, but he's still breathing. Doheny finds a small pistol in the man's pocket and shoves it in his own belt. I toss him the shotgun, but tell him not to use it unless they actually get on the boat.

The shooting lets up for a minute as the pilot drags the kid toward us. Goddamn, he's got *cojones,* this fat man. There ain't much cover I can give him with the Colt, but I peg a couple of shots in the direction of the cottonwoods anyway, because that's where I guess the shooters are.

The sons of bitches let him get all the way to the *Molly Pratt,* where he's standing in water up to his armpits, trying to heave the unconscious kid over the rail. Then before me or Doheny can give him a hand, the bandits open up like a war and riddle the poor bastard. Him and the kid sink into the river and drift downstream with the current, bumping and turning against the bank.

As the bodies reach the clump of cottonwood trees, I see our enemy for the first time. Two of them break cover and slip down to the river's edge to catch at the dead men as they float by.

The range is about seventy yards, too damn far, but I hit things with my Colt before at that distance. When the two Mexicans are both in the water, snatching at the fat man's belt, I shoot.

I miss, but on the second round, one of them crumples and they let the pilot's body go. As the other one starts to scramble up the bank, I shoot again and get him square, but the first one I hit staggers out of the water and gets to the trees.

"Good shooting," Doheny says. "Maybe they'll give up."

"Why should they?"

"Cut their losses."

"One man ain't a loss to them."

"How many do you figure we're up against?" Doheny asks me.

"Ten, fifteen, maybe more. But they only got one or two rifles, which means they'll probably rush us."

"If only we could get off this bar."

"Small chance now."

"What do we do?"

"Wait. Why don't you find that kid and see if there ain't a rifle on board?" He duck-walks down the deck behind the crates while I watch the shore. Sundown is when they'll come.

The Pinkerton man takes a long time to die, his eyes open against the sun, gagging and twitching every little while until he's still. The stock certificate's clutched in his hand, and I stuff it in my pocket with his watch and sixty dollars he's carrying. Then I roll him to the rail because he's starting to draw flies. With a splash he joins the unlucky pilot and the dead kid, who'll probably get to Brownsville before I do.

When Doheny comes back, we rig an awning behind the crates to give us some shade while we keep watch. There's no other weapon on board except a flare pistol from the pilot's cabin. "Our best chance is to swim for the Texas shore after dark," he says.

"For you and me maybe. But what about the others? That woman and her kids don't look like swimmers."

"How long can we hold out here?"

"Depends. If we make it expensive enough for these bastards, they'll be careful and hang back. We got food and water for a week or more. By that time they'll either give up and go away or somebody'll miss us and come looking."

"Then let's see just how expensive we can make it," Doheny says, and we shake hands.

X X I V

Doroteo Arango

Me and Doheny pile up some of the cargo to make a better bulwark on the land side of the boat, and cut the winch line running up to the cottonwood trees. Doheny brings a keg of axle grease from the engine room and we slop it all over the rails on the shore side. Then we do the same thing on the stern with the insurance fellow's help. They'll try to rush us at least once, and I don't want to make it easy for them.

"I told the engineer to keep the steam up," Doheny says, "because there's always the chance of the river rising during the night and us floating off by ourselves."

"Who steers the boat if we do that?"

"The apprentice knows the river."

"We can't count on the river rising," I say.

"But we can count on the steam. Give me a hand here."

I don't know what he's up to at first. We snake out two old fire hoses, one pointing down the foredeck and one toward the stern, with both connected to live steam from the engine room. This Doheny's a first-rate engineer and a fast worker, rigging the connections to the steam pipes, and drilling holes to bolt the nozzles to the deck so they won't leap around once the pressure comes. When he's ready he has the engineer give a short squirt to test each one, and a hot cloud of scalding vapor shoots twenty feet down the deck.

310

The insurance fellow brings coffee and hunkers down with us for a few minutes. He tells me that besides us on board, there's a coal passer and the cook, who's hiding in the hold and won't come out for all his coaxing.

"As long as they stay out of the way."

"When will those bandits come back?" he says.

"Mexicans don't have a lot of patience."

"Can you hold them off?"

"We'll see," I say.

"You aren't scared, are you?" Doheny asks him.

"Course not. I've got plenty of life insurance."

Doheny tells the fellow in that case he's got nothing to worry about, and puts him in charge of the bell rope to signal the engineer for the steam. He's to stay where he can see me in the bow and Doheny in the stern. If either one of us hollers for steam he's to ring the bell and the engineer will turn it on.

As the sun disappears, I tell the woman not to light any lamps, and to stay down behind the sofas no matter what happens. She's real calm now and the kids are quiet, huddled against her while she tells them a story. I drag that goddamn pipe salesman out of there though, before he unnerves the whole family. "We're all going to be killed," he cries, and I tell him if he don't shut up, I'll kill him myself. Then I lock him in his cabin.

The pilot's apprentice is anxious for orders so I tell him to keep close watch on the shoreline and sing out the minute he sees anything. I give him the flaregun too, just in case any boat passes in the night. Then I settle down behind the crates, check my Colt and wish to Christ I had one of Ransom's Winchesters.

Twenty minutes goes by without a sound as the night gets blacker and I see nothing. Mexican bandits are as unpredictable as wolves. If their bellies are full and they got a place to go where there's booze and women, no matter how poor and miserable, they'll pass us by. If not, they'll hang around. I just about got myself convinced they're gone when a scream puts the evening in perspective again.

A bandit's already on deck, looking through a window at the terrified woman. I shoot and miss him, and he fires back, dinging a stanchion an inch from my head, driving pieces of bullet like sand into my cheek. My second shot drops the bastard and I hear him splash. Doheny blasts another one with the shotgun and he staggers back along the deck, blinded by the pellets, his face a pulp. But more are coming over the foredeck, slipping and stumbling in the grease, and hard to see.

That's when the kid in the wheelhouse turns out to be the smartest of us all.

There's a big reflector spotlight up there I didn't even know about, a kerosene lantern with a focusing lense the pilot uses to spot markers and hazards on the river at night. The kid gets it lit after he hears the first shot and points it at the bow, where they're swarming aboard, lighting them up like Christmas, and blinding them. Their grinning, sweaty faces bob in the light not twenty feet away and I get three before the rest leap over the side. I'm pulling a trigger on an empty revolver, but they don't know it. I reload fast but there's nothing to shoot at, and I can't make them out good enough in the water or on the bank.

We're okay for now. Me and Doheny collect the guns and cartridge belts before we dump the other Mexicans in the water. Two dead, two mortally hurt but breathing, and the river will finish our work. My shooting should have been better, but I ain't had much practice in the dark.

I holler at the kid to douse the light, but before he can do it, there's a rifle shot from the shore and the light winks out. There's a whole fusilade then and the goddamn windows in the wheelhouse explode into a million shards of glass. When the racket stops I call up to know if the boy's all right.

"Yes, sir, I guess so," he answers in a small voice.

"Any chance of fixing that light?"

"The lense is smashed."

Doheny says, "Maybe they had enough."

"It ain't over yet. Now they know that there's only a couple of us, they won't give up that easy."

"I'm glad you're here, Mr. Garland, because I can't shoot worth a damn."

He's still in his underwear when he gives me that good news, and I tell him to get dressed while he's got a chance, because his white BVDs make too good a target.

There's only two decent revolvers in the bunch we collect from the Mexicans, a old Navy Colt I give Doheny to keep by his side, and a Webley forty-five I take for myself. I pass another gun up to the kid in the wheelhouse and one to the insurance agent with orders not to shoot unless the Mexicans are right on top of him.

The engineer comes up for air about then, sticking his head out and raising a lantern. I get a glimpse of an old man's face, skinny and bald as a turkey gobbler, before bullets splinter the combing and he tumbles out of sight down the hatch. I don't know whether they killed him or just scared him to death.

I crawl to the hatch on my belly. "You all right?"

"If you don't count broke bones and a burned arm, I'm in the peak of condition," a voice answers me. "Who wants to know?"

"Lee Garland. I'm a passenger."

"Where's the pilot?"

"Dead."

"What are you going to do now?"

"Stop them. Can you keep steam up all night?"

"That's my job, ain't it?"

"Sorry."

"How many guns you got?" he asks.

"Three."

"I can shoot if I have to."

"We'll need the steam."

"You got it. Send the cub down with some food, will you?"

"He's on lookout in the wheelhouse."

"Then send the other one."

"He's dead."

"That bad, is it?"

"It's close," I tell him.

"How many Mexicans you get?"

"Six. Any idea who they are?"

"Has to be Villa. Seen us go aground."

"Who's Villa?"

"The Pinkerton dick can tell you."

"Not anymore. They killed him too."

"Jesus Christ! Anybody alive besides you?"

"There's a woman with two kids," I tell him. "I'd like to put them down with you."

"Pretty hot and noisy."

"Not as hot and noisy as it's going to get up here."

"Send 'em down then. I ain't seen a woman in a month. What did you say your name was?"

"Lee Garland."

"You a shooter?"

"When I have to be."

"Lawman?"

"Petroleum business."

"You know Doheny?"

"He's here with me."

"Ask him when he's going to find oil. I'm a stockholder."

"Not tonight, I guarantee it."

"He couldn't find his ass with both hands."

"He killed a Mexican."

"With what? Talk?"

"Just keep the steam up, will you? And be nice to the lady and her kids."

The children are scared and trying not to be, but the woman's aged a hundred years in a day, poor plain creature, her face lined with fear and worry, and she can't be more than twenty-five.

"It's going to be all right," I tell her, but when she looks at me, the terror in her eyes is like an electric fire. She's the last one to go down the ladder and I catch her by the shoulders before she descends. "You're safe now," I say with all the conviction I can muster. "Do you know who I am?"

She shakes her head.

"Where you from, ma'am?"

"P-p-port Huron, Michigan."

"Back there, maybe my name ain't a household word yet, but around these parts it is. You heard of Kit Carson? Jesse James? Billy the Kid?"

She nods, tiny tears of fear watering her eyes.

"You might say I'm in the same category."

"But they're all dead," she says, with that stubborn kind of logic some females got a talent for.

"Well, I don't like to brag, ma'am, but I'm a better shot than all them fellows put together. I don't even bother to count the Mexicans I kill."

"W-w-what's your name?" she says, trembling like an aspen leaf in an autumn breeze.

"Lee Garland," I say. "Remember it so your kids can tell their grandchildren."

I close the hatch on her and breathe a deep sigh. Doheny's been listening and he says, "My, my. That's as smooth a line as I could invent. You trying to save that woman, Mr. Ireland, or just seduce her?"

"The name's Garland, Doheny. And I'll thank you just to keep your eye on the shore, and never mind the lady."

The hours pass like years as we sit in the dark. A sliver of moon comes up, but it don't give enough light to be a help. If I was them, I'd try again just before dawn, when it's still dark but after enough time has passed to lull us into a false confidence.

The insurance salesman brings more hot coffee. He's a resourceful fellow, and cool in the clutch. Too bad he can't shoot. "Maybe if we gave them all our money," he says, "they'd go away."

"That ain't the way they work."

"No, I didn't think so." He tells me he's got two kids up in San Antonio, where he's from. "You married, Mr. Garland?"

"No."

"Engaged?"

"Not lately."

"Any dependent parents?"

"No."

"Then you wouldn't be interested in life insurance."

I shake my head.

"Ever been up against bandits before?"

"I have."

"Where you from?"

"New Mexico."

"What made you decide to go into the oil business?"

"It's a long story."

"Take my advice. Stay out of it. Pick something secure like insurance. You know how much I made last year in commissions? Over four thousand dollars. You don't find money like that growing on trees. Course, you have to work for it, move around, make contacts. But it's real good security."

"I bet it is," I say, thinking he may be catfish bait before morning because of his secure insurance business.

Security's not something I ever give much thought to. I always wanted the people I love to feel a little independent, at least in a financial way. But even that's an illusion. Tom Isbell used to say the only real security is the grave, but that ain't true either. Graves get robbed and worms eat the bodies.

All my life I heard politicians lie about security; personal, social, national or whatever. And look where we are. A man was safer on the streets when I was a boy than he is today. But national security's the worst fraud of all, and I know something about that, being a victim. It's a typical politician's solution to unemployment, keeping a lot of people busy making bombs and rockets who couldn't get a honest job otherwise, and feeding a herd of tinhorn admirals and generals at the public trough in the Pentagon. National security means taking over good range land like mine to shoot rockets off of, and stealing from the taxpayer to build more when we already got enough to blow up the world.

No, I never cared for that security talk, never believed it. The Communists claim they invented the best kind. Do as you're told, keep your mouth shut and they'll take care of everything. Womb to tomb slavery is what I call that, and any man dumb enough to yearn after it deserves what he gets.

If you ask me, no free man is ever secure. As I tell my grandson Pete when we talk about such things, it's a contradiction in terms, not a matter of degree. A man's either free or he ain't. And if he's free, then he's got to stay on his toes all the time because somebody's always trying to steal his liberty from him with one kind of lie or another.

"Which way do you think they'll come?" the insurance man asks me, as if I got a crystal ball.

If I was them I'd try the stern, so I creep along the deck to tell Doheny to change places with me. I ain't halfway there before a shot rings out, followed by half a dozen more all splintering the cabin wood above my head.

"You all right?" he asks when the shooting dies down.

"Don't worry about me. Did you see anything?"

"My eyes aren't that good," Doheny admits.

I peer into the shadows by the stern-wheel and think I see it move. Doheny says it's just the current, but I can't tell. "Go on up where I was," I say, "and I'll take over here."

Before he can leave there's another fusilade of shots and I see the flashes this time on the shore. Then I hear the creak of the paddle wheel and know it ain't the river. I'm trying to focus all my attention on it, the Colt cocked in my hand, when I hear another noise behind me. I look around, expecting a Mexican, and damn near shoot the pipe salesman. He's standing there, big as life, his derby hat on and a valise in his hands.

"Get down, you goddamn fool!"

"I won't stay here to be slaughtered!"

"Get down!"

"You can't stop me!" He lunges off down the deck and I expect him to be shot to pieces because somebody must surely spot him from the shore, but nobody fires a shot. He slips over the side of the *Molly Pratt* with his case, and I hear a small splash as he drops to the water. Next I see him in the shadows struggling up the bank, dragging the valise behind him. He's as good as dead and I don't understand why they ain't shot him already.

When I turn my eyes back to the stern, the paddle wheel moves again, and this time I see our visitors. At first it looks like four or five, but in a second I see it's a lot more. They come swarming on the deck as I yell for Doheny and the steam at the same time. The nearest one is thirty feet away and I drop him with my first shot. I don't have time to aim, damn it, and I miss the next one. But they're in the open and I'm behind two crates of tools. One of them gets to within five feet of me before Doheny cuts him in half with the shotgun.

I empty the Colt, switch to the Webley and keep shooting, hollering all the time, "The steam, goddamnit! The steam!" There's six or seven of them down already but that don't slow the sons of bitches. When the Webley's empty, I ain't going to have time to reload before they get me in the rush. There must be fifteen more climbing up over the paddle wheel, and they ain't even trying to take cover. "The steam! Goddamn you, Doheny!"

I fire my last round and manage to shove two cartridges in the Colt as they come up the deck, but I know that won't stop them. There's a shot from up in the wheelhouse and all of a sudden the whole deck between me and them Mexicans blazes red. I'm blinded for a second, but so are they, and they freeze like jackrabbits. Doheny takes the nearest two with the shotgun while I shove another four bullets into the chamber of the Colt. The red glow of the flare's still dazzling me when I hear the welcome hiss of the steam and see the hose writhe like a live snake.

A scalding waterfall hits them and they fall tumbling and screaming in the weird red light like souls in the grip of hell. I never seen anything so terrible and so wonderful as Doheny sweeping the deck like a man scything grain.

Once the valve is opened, the pressure can only be kept up for a few seconds because the hose is old and leaky. But it's enough. Before the hose collapses like a limp dick, they're all either dead, dying or gone over the side trying to save themselves.

"God bless the kid with the flare," I say, "but what the hell happened to the steam? That engineer go to sleep?"

"He turned the wrong valve and sent it to the bow. It wasn't his fault. I should have rigged a simpler signal."

The deck in front of us is carpeted with dead and dying men, most of them young and hungry-looking. When one tries to get up with his gun, I shoot him. Another one is so bad burned, his face and chest boiled to a blister, that he's screaming to be put out of his misery. I do him the favor.

We heave them all over the side just before sunup, the dead ones and the live ones alike, after taking up their pistols and cartridge bandoliers. I count fourteen men down and we got enough weapons now to start a small army, but still no rifle.

"That's got to be the end of them," Doheny says, but just as if somebody overheard him, another storm of gunfire rips into the cabin and sends us both scratching at the deck again. "How many of them bastards are there?"

"More than twenty," I say.

"Hell, we killed that many!"

"That's what I mean."

Dawn's breaking now and I'm hungry enough to eat bricks. None of us had a bite since yesterday lunch, and I tell the insurance salesman to see if he can get the cook working again. I remember the woman and call down the hatch to her and the engineer. "It's over for now, but I want you all to stay put." I hear him cackling below as he brags to the woman how we steamed the Mexicans off the *Molly Pratt.*

There's no persuading the cook back to work. He's hid out behind a pile of grain sacks in the hold and he ain't coming out until we get to Brownsville. But the insurance man rustles up scrambled eggs and bacon for everybody. When the kid climbs down from the pilot house I tell him he saved the fight and everybody with that flare.

"I wasn't sure if I should do it," he says, "But when I seen how many there was, I guessed it could help some."

"Can you navigate this boat downriver?" I ask him.

"We got to get off the bar first," the boy tells me.

"The pilot said last night the river might rise."

"It's on the rise now, mister."

"Can you move this tub?"

His eyes scan the bank and he looks back at the deck, caressing it with his hands where we're squatting down behind the freight. "The *Molly Pratt* ain't a tub, mister," he says.

"Whatever you call it. Can you get it out of the mud?"

He shakes his head. "I never done it," he says.

The sun's high by now and it's getting warm and I'm out of patience with him and his steamboat. I grab him by the collar. "Goddamn you! Can you back off this sandbar or not?"

Again he shakes his head. "She won't back off because she's dug in, but if we get enough water we might float her off."

"How much do we need?"

"Not so much if we could lighten her."

"Then let's do it."

"It ain't certain she'll cross over," he says.

My enthusiasm don't last long after I think about it because them crates of tools and silver bars are our only protection against the rifle fire. I tell the kid, "We'll have to come up with a better idea."

Just then, Doheny shouts, "Garland, look!" and points at the cottonwood grove where the Mexicans seem to be holding a meeting.

"How many you make out?"

"Thirty-five, forty. No! More! Christ, there's another crowd riding down to join them."

I'm thinking this ain't a gang of bandits, this is an army. The only satisfaction I get is that a few got rags and makeshift bandages on their heads and arms, veterans of our steam hose, no doubt. I could probably hit a couple with the Colt, but the range is long and I don't want to waste the cartridges. They mill around the brow of the hill for a while before some of them break off and ride toward us. When they get closer, I see they got the pipe salesman in the middle.

They come to within fifty yards of the boat and stop. The salesman's hands are tied and they're leading his horse.

"Mr. Garland!" the salesman calls out.

"I hear you!"

"They want to talk!"

The rider next to him cups his hands and shouts in Spanish, *"Hola,* Lee Garland! Is it you?"

"It's me! Who are you?"

"Remember me? We work together!" I never worked with no Mexicans outside my own family and I don't recognize this son of a bitch. Then he laughs and says, "You remember all right! From Chihuahua!"

The laugh jogs my memory and now I know who he is. The *vaquero* I hired to help bring the cattle we was selling the army. One of the varmints that jumped us at night and nearly killed Charlie Bruce. Doroteo Arango's his name.

"You're running with the wrong crowd, Arango!"

"They're all good boys!"

"What's left of them, maybe."

"Come down and talk."

"We're talking now."

"I'm in a hurry."

"So am I."

"You take things from Mexico!"

"No, we don't."

"Silver from the Mexican people!"

He's a cheeky son of a bitch, I'll give him that.

"We want that silver."

"Come and get it!"

Doheny catches my arm. "What's he saying?"

I tell him.

"Give it to him. Maybe they'll go away."

I can just make out Arango's face under the shadow of his sombrero, babyish, with a short, wide nose, pouting lips and small, cruel eyes. He's mounted on a big, skittish gray, much too good for a bandit, and judging by the silver on his tack and saddle, he's come up in the world since I seen him last. I don't believe he's the leader of this gang, just the man they picked to parley.

The salesman hollers, "They'll kill me if you don't give them what they want!"

"Arango!"

"Yes, my friend!"

"Turn him loose and you can have the silver!"

"No, *hombre!* You got it backward! Give me the silver, I turn him loose!"

"Like I said, come and get it!"

The woman and her kids come on deck with the engineer and squat behind the crates to watch. I wish they'd stayed in the engine room because I don't want them bandits to know we got a family with us, but I can't do anything about it now.

Doheny's at my side the whole time, urging me to give them the silver or they'll kill that poor salesman.

"He's dead already only he don't know it. They won't let him go before they get what they want, and they got no reason to turn him loose if we give in to them."

"Negotiate," Doheny says. "Bargain. Talk."

"It's like preaching to an alligator, Doheny."

"Give them half."

"It won't work," I tell him, but I make the offer anyway.

"Okay!" Arango agrees.

"Leave him out where we can see him," I yell, "and we'll push it over the side. Send your men down to get it. No guns!"

Doheny and me juggle some of the tool crates around and heave a couple of grain sacks on top. Then I break open the silver box and take out four bars probably worth a thousand dollars each. Dull as lead and almost as heavy. I heave two over the side near the sandy bank, and Arango motions a man to dismount and wade into the water after them.

He takes the ingots dripping wet for inspection, and Arango waves his thanks. Then the bastard rides up the hill and sends more men down as I toss the bars in the water. He must be in charge after all because I don't see him report to anybody else, and they all jump to obey his orders. Then I remember how tough and clever he was in Chihuahua.

Most Mexicans lead hard, short lives, because there ain't enough of anything to go around. The majority stay docile as sheep. But put one on a horse and give him a gun and you got a bandit who ain't afraid of nothing because he's got nothing to lose. They feed off other poor devils like themselves, and are a curse on the land.

To be a leader of bandits a man has to be a better rider and marksman than the rest, and a worse criminal. If he's cunning enough, more of his kind follow him because he gets their respect by filling their pockets as well as their bellies. If he's ruthless enough, he'll hold his place because they fear him more than death. I got to admit this Arango is a prime example, because he's got the biggest gang I ever seen and he ain't no older than me. We're in trouble if he don't get the silver now because he'll lose respect if he leaves without it after the beating we give him.

In half an hour, they got a small fortune as I throw the bars over, two at a time. There's six boxes on the boat, but I figure we ought to try again to get our man back before I give them any more. He's sitting on the river bank now while one of the bandits sprawls next to him with his pistol out. When I signal to release the pipe sales- man, one of them rides over the hill after Arango.

While we're waiting, Doheny tells me the river's up some more. Not enough yet, but maybe by afternoon we could float off. "Whenever the kid thinks we'll move, give it a try," I say.

"What about him?" He points to the salesman sitting in the sun, trying to keep the flies off with his hands tied.

"Let's see what they say."

"We can't leave him."

Arango appears again and he don't look too happy.

"We agreed half," he shouts at me in Spanish.

"That's right! Release him and I throw out the rest!"

"Garland, why make trouble between old friends?"

"You ain't done nothing friendly for me yet, Arango! Turn that man loose if you want the silver."

"Garland, old partner!"

"I hear you!"

"Watch!"

He shouts an order to the guy guarding the salesman, who jerks the prisoner to his feet.

"Don't make me kill him, Garland!"

The salesman's wet his pants by now as they drag him over to Arango, who points a pistol at his head.

"Pull that trigger and you get nothing!"

The woman grabs me by the arm. "Give him what he wants for heaven's sake! What kind of a man are you?"

I don't know whether she understands all our Spanish or just put two and two together. But whatever set her off plays right into Arango's hands, because he sees her begging me. "Lady, please. They ain't going to let him go no matter what we do."

"There's always a chance," she pleads, "At least they won't shoot him if they get what they're after."

The kid comes back from the bow where he's been throwing the lead to check the water depth. "I think we might get off," he says, "if we try now."

"Garland! I want an answer!" Arango's grinning up at us, his gun against the salesman's head.

"Let's do it," I tell the kid.

"What about him?" Doheny says, pointing at the prisoner.

"He's a dead man."

The woman cries, "You can't let him die like that!"

"How long will the water hold?" I ask the kid.

"Maybe a week, maybe half an hour."

Arango shoots then, and the report echos up and down the river, shattering the quiet of the morning and scattering crows from the cottonwood branches. I see the salesman pitch over on his face as his hat flies off, and hear the bandit's laugh.

The woman collapses into Doheny's arms, crying for all she's worth, and I swear if I don't do anything else, I'll get that greaser. The range for the Colt is good, but the horse is dancing around, making a hard target of the rider. I take my time, not wanting to miss.

"Next time I really do it, Garland!" Arango shouts, and I see the pipe salesman ain't hurt as they jerk him to his feet again with the rope. Arango's still smiling, waving his gun in the air. "Now I got your attention! What's your answer?"

"Okay, you win!"

"The people of Mexico thank you, Garland! And this little worm thanks you!" He waves an arm at the poor salesman, who's fallen on his hands and knees again, and rides off laughing.

It takes a couple hours of sweaty work, but we pile enough bales and grain sacks to take the place of the silver while we break open the boxes and toss the rest of the bars into knee-deep water for the Mexicans to retrieve. The kid says the river's holding, and by losing the extra weight we've gained another inch or two. He's confident now he can get us off.

When the last silver bar's ashore. Arango comes back and gives the order to release the prisoner. They give him a kick in our direction, and the poor son of a bitch stumbles down the bank into the water, sobbing like a woman. I still don't believe he'll make it alive, but it won't be the first time I misjudged an enemy.

What jars me is the whole thing ain't natural. It's out of character for an animal like Arango to let a man go when he don't have to.

Bandits ain't famous for their gratitude or their mercy, but I'm
happy to be mistaken this time. Still, I'm holding my breath till the
man's safe aboard.

The poor bastard's still whimpering as he splashes to the side
of the boat and hauls himself up. He slips in the grease before he
makes it to the deck and is swinging his leg over the rail when
Arango shoots him. Bullets rip into his back as he gapes in surprise. He teeters there a second, like he's wondering which way to
jump, then falls back into the water. The only sound for a minute
is Arango's crazy laugh echoing over the big river.

I open up with the Colt, but I don't hit him because of his
prancing mount. Arango's the best I ever seen. I doubt even Luna
could put three bullets in a man's heart from a skittish horse at fifty
yards.

The kid gets us off the sandbar finally and we make it to Brownsville after notifying the Texas Rangers at Zapata about the bandits.
They don't catch them because by the time they get to where we
was, Arango and his crowd are a hundred miles away.

When I ask Doheny what I should do with the Pinkerton man's
watch and stock certificate, he says, "I'd hold onto them if I were
you. The watch is worth a dollar and the stock will make you rich."
I buy him a drink while we wait for the steamer to take us to
Tampico. That's when I find out Arango don't go by his own name
no more. He calls himself Pancho Villa now.

XXV

Tampico

What hit me most about Tampico when I first seen it was the sickly sweet smell of decay and putrefaction that reached out over the Gulf long before you got to the harbor. The second thing was the oily slick of sewage floating in the water.

I'm taking in these sights and smells as the steamship slows for the channel, listening to Doheny, who ain't shut up since Brownsville. He sucks in a deep breath like it's French perfume, and claps me on the shoulder. "Tampico, Garland! Isn't it wonderful?" I figure something's wrong with his nose, but I don't say so. In the few days I've known the man, I discover he's a lot smarter than he sounds at first, good-natured, and full of his own special charm.

The sudden loss of a breeze brings on the old feeling of suffocating inside a wet oven like in Cuba. It's the same brutal heat, all right, but the Mexican coast ain't as pretty. No purple mountains and sandy beaches, just miles of swamp and mosquito marsh. Even so, the steamship from Matamoros is such a comedown after life on the *Molly Pratt,* I'm glad to get ashore.

Me and Doheny share a jitney from the customs house to the Hotel Independencia, winding uphill through dirty streets crowded with peddlers, bare-assed kids, mangy dogs and donkeys. It's as picturesque as poverty anywhere. Away from the port, the stink ain't so bad, more like rotten oranges than dead bodies, but it ain't a place to interest tourists unless they're in the garbage business.

All the time, I'm getting a running commentary from Doheny, who never takes off his rose-colored glasses. He's led a active life from the Indian Territory to Arizona, where he fought off a mountain lion, prospected for gold, broke both legs in a fall down a mine shaft and spent a year crippled. That's when he become a lawyer and then learned mineralogy.

He's worth a fortune already from the petroleum wells he owns in California, but he's short of cash because he had a run of bad luck on the first Mexican wells he drilled. Instead of following his own educated nose like he did in California, he listened to some other mineralogist and drilled in the wrong places. Well, he ain't going to make that mistake again, he tells me. Since Brownsville he's been urging me to invest in his petroleum company, but I tell him no thanks, I'm content to stay with the shares I inherited from the dead Pinkerton man.

"Smell it, Garland!" he says, flaring his nostrils and sucking in another great breath. "That's the smell of money!"

Whenever I hear that expression, I think of Doheny and the stink of Tampico because he was right. If you ever been near a oil field or a refinery, you know raw petroleum smells awful. It don't have the nice, clean odor of a crisp hundred-dollar bill except to the man that owns it. While all I could smell was Tampico that morning, Doheny was sniffing millions.

The heat and humidity is like a great weight on the city. Even the palm trees seem to bend under it, and there ain't a breath of breeze anywhere. I'm still wearing one of my wool banker's suits, and Doheny says the first thing I got to do is get linen ones made, like he's wearing. "In white," he says, "because white reflects the heat."

He calls my attention to two policemen who pass us on horseback in front of the old cathedral. Fat mustachioed fellows in khaki uniforms, with sabres clanking against their saddles. "Mexican justice," Doheny says with a smile. "Where were they when we needed them?"

The brown faces of the policemen are like the others in the street, more Indian than anything else, with hook noses and obsidian eyes that take in everything and tell you nothing. They're dragging a prisoner behind them on a rope, a skinny, barefoot devil in baggy cotton pants looks like he ain't had a square meal in a month. His head's all cut and scabby from a beating, and when he stumbles and falls, the policemen don't even look back, just drag him through the dust until he staggers to his feet again.

"They'll shoot him in the morning," Doheny tells me. "Every day except Sunday they clear the jails with a firing squad." He laughs. "With all that practice they ought to be pretty good shots."

When we get to the hotel I see that the gringos outnumber the Mexicans around the veranda, and white linen suits and wide pan-ama hats seem to be the uniform. When I remark on so many Americans to Doheny, he says, "Who else can bring Mexico into the twentieth century, and into the United States as well?"

I remember Ransom and his empire-building when Doheny says this, and I don't take it serious. Inviting Mexico into the union would be like turning a million roaches loose in your kitchen. They'd just be underfoot while they eat you out of house and home.

"We own half the damned place already," Doheny says. "Between cattle ranches, railroads and mines, American business has more money invested here than we do in a lot of states. Once the petroleum comes in big, we'll have to annex the country to protect our interests."

"We'd have to fight the Mexicans for it, I reckon."

"If you call that fighting. Hell, we took the country over once, didn't we? And that was in the forties when old Winfield Scott marched right down to Mexico City. We gave it back like damn fools, but nobody needed petroleum then. Modern times are different."

On the hotel veranda, Doheny meets a dozen men he knows, all looking for oil like him, or backing others that are. I check in and ask after Fortescue, but he ain't around. I leave a note for him and go up to my room, which is half the size of a tennis court, with an electric fan in the ceiling that don't work and lizards climbing the walls. But it's clean, and full of chipped, gilded furniture like a run-down palace.

It's impossible to get cool even with the blinds closed so I shuck my jacket, put on a fresh shirt, and go down to the veranda again. It's as much of a Turkish bath as the rest of the place, but at least there's something to see. I don't know it yet, but the veranda of the Hotel Independencia is the real oil market. All the lease trading and drilling contracts are being negotiated here. Doheny ain't around so I take a table where I can watch.

The language they speak might as well be Chinese. They talk about Billy Joe spudding in on number three and Duane taking over Everett's rig while Floyd got gas so bad it blew him apart. To me a spud is a potato, a rig is a saddle and gas is gas, but I never heard of anybody having it that serious. Maybe Fortescue can translate when he arrives.

Pretty soon I stop listening and just sit over my whiskey, depressed by the heat and the talk and turning in on myself. I don't know what I'm doing here and I can't imagine why Fortescue ever thought I'd be any use to him. I'm a goddamn flop is what I am. The only success I ever had was in the army, except for smuggling cattle over the border. I'm a bust as a banker, a total loss to the only woman I ever loved and a failure to my friend Cody. I couldn't even kill a varmint like Sorenson without leaving a mess for my friends.

I sit there feeling sorry for myself, thinking the only thing I'm good at is shooting a gun, and even then a greaser like Arango can make a jackass out of me. Without that steam hose, I'd be fish bait on the big river now myself.

I don't know what makes me think of Caroline all of a sudden, but I do, and the memory sweeps over me like a dark wave of grief. Of all the things I handled wrong in my life, that's the one hurts the most. I should of gone up to Boston as soon as I was out of the hospital and not listened to Charlie Bruce, not waited. Even if she was already married, I could of done something.

What?

Something, goddamn it.

What?

She married the man. She has his baby.

My Caroline.

Why am I so sure I could of changed things? Because I love her? That wouldn't of mattered to anybody. It's just a condition of my life. Because she loved me. That's what sticks in my gut like a knife. I been mistaken about a lot of things, but not that. Caroline really *loved* me.

As I tell this now, all these many years after, it's still the truth. She also trusted her brother, who convinced her she was wrong. He persuaded her I didn't care because I didn't write, didn't come, didn't call. The same way he persuaded me. Clever Charlie Bruce. If I'd left him to die in the goddamn desert I'd still have Caroline.

"Lee!"

Fortescue brings me back to Tampico and reality. He's dressed Mexican style, in boots and baggy cotton pants, and we clinch in a prizefighter's embrace. For a man who never shows emotion about nothing, every now and then something gets to him. He's relieved that I showed up, and his relief flatters me.

"What happened to your ear?"

"You don't want to know."

I didn't realize until that minute how much I liked this man and missed him. We was never as confidential as I was with Cody or Mountain. There was always a kind of distance between us from the beginning when we had the fight in San Antonio. But there's nobody I trusted more than him, and nobody I admired more.

The thing is we was different, but close. I never worried about him or felt I had to protect him, and he always acted the same about me. I just knew he was on my side, no matter what. I didn't always understand the man, and I often disagreed with him, but I guess that's the mark of a friend. You make up your mind about a person in the beginning and then stick in there no matter what.

He's hired his own carriage by the week, a big black laquered contraption looks like it belongs to a Mexican general. It's drawn by two fine-looking bays, and besides the driver there's another Indian holds the door and climbs up to his perch in the rear. The carriage takes us to a small restaurant, where we eat in a pretty garden surrounded by hibiscus trees and hanging orchids.

He says the food's less likely to put us in the hospital than what they serve at the hotel. Tampico's worse than Cuba for disease. They got all the usual ones, plus a few local specialties like chigger worms, cholera and Mexican spotted fever.

After I tell him about Cody, we don't talk for a while, just sit thinking about so many dead friends. He don't seem shocked about what Charlie Bruce done, and tells me I was lucky to get off so cheap.

"I don't call a hundred fifty thousand dollars cheap."

"You'll make that back in a week here. Tell me about Captain Fall and the hearing."

"He's a good actor, all right, but Luna's the one surprised me. He laid his reputation on the line to help."

"You're the son he never had."

"Remember when he made us form the choir?"

"He bragged about it all over camp."

"Until we wrecked the beer garden."

We go on reminiscing, and if anybody'd been listening, they'd of thought the Spanish-American War was a picnic. I guess it's only human to filter out the ugly parts and make the rest sound better than they was. I mean sooner or later everybody's story has a bad ending.

When I tell Fortescue about the trip down the Rio Grande on the *Molly Pratt,* he says he wishes he'd been there. "So do I. Mexicans was popping out of nowhere like jumping beans."

"You're lucky, Lee."

"So's Arango. He rode off with sixty thousand dollars worth of silver in his jeans, laughing at the world."

"I'm glad nothing happened to Doheny," Fortescue says. "He's the horse we're betting on."

"From what I learned, he ain't won too many races lately."

"It's the first time he's failed."

"Then why keep drilling in Mexico?"

"Once the oil bug bites, you seldom recover. You'll see."

"You got it, too, don't you?"

Fortescue smiles, showing perfect white teeth against his tan. "I suspect I'm in the early stages, yes. It's a little like gold fever. Highly infectious and practically incurable."

"And you're backing Doheny's play?"

"Riding with him. I've acquired three new companies to drill for petroleum, transport it and market the products."

"Where do I come in?"

"I want you to go partners with me and run things here."

"Run what?"

"The drilling company."

"Is that all? For a minute I thought you was asking me to do something I didn't know how to do. But who's better qualified than me to run a little old oil company in Mexico?"

"Exactly."

"Ronnie, I'm Lee Garland, remember? All I know about petroleum is that it comes out of the ground, and I only know that because you told me. I heard them fellows talking on the veranda this morning. They was all speaking English but I didn't understand one goddamn word."

"Is there any other reason not to do it?"

"I got no capital right now."

"I don't need capital. I need a partner I trust to get things off to a good start."

"I'll work for you. But find somebody else to run it."

"You didn't know anything about banking when you started out with Charlie Bruce."

"And look what happened."

"That wasn't your fault."

"Do you understand what I'm saying? The answer is no."

"You haven't even heard my proposition yet."

"I don't have to hear it."

"I need you, Lee."

"You need an expert, not an out-of-work cowboy."

"There are no experts."

"There's got to be somebody better than me."

"Study some maps before you make up your mind."

"Jesus Christ! My mind's made up."

Back at the hotel, he spreads out a bunch of maps on his bed and continues the lecture. What he's showing me is two things. Doheny's leases and his own. They run all over the place to a hundred miles south of Tampico. The dry wells Doheny drilled are clearly marked, and so is another big section twenty miles north.

"That's where he's drilling now," he tells me. "The leases I acquired parallel his sections. If he strikes it rich, so do we."

"Suppose he don't."

"Then we try here," he says, pointing to another place all marked out, farther inland.

That night we go to the same restaurant again, where Fortescue tells me he's already put me down as a director of his companies and president of the drilling outfit.

His stubbornness is enough to try a saint's patience, so I tell him, all right, I'll do it. "But don't say I didn't warn you," I warn him, "because I don't know what I'm agreeing to."

We drink to my new job, which will pay me a salary of twelve thousand dollars a year plus emoluments.

"What in hell are they?" I ask him, dumber than a duck.

"Stock. You'll be a one-third owner of the drilling company, with me holding the other two-thirds."

"But I told you—"

"No investment capital required, old boy. Just your sweat, brains and luck."

"I can't accept an offer like that."

"Sure you can. Call it a loan. If I sold the leases on all those tracts tomorrow I'd be lucky to recover the hundred thousand I've invested. So, let's say you owe me thirty-three thousand dollars, which you can pay back out of your share after you bring in the first well."

"And if I don't?"

"You can pay me in bank stock, since you seem to have more than you want at the moment."

"That's crazy, Ronnie. You're crazy."

"Lee, we'll make a fortune."

"You already got a fortune, if you don't piss it away."

"No chance of that. I can't tell you how pleased I am that you're joining me. It saves changing the company name."

"Why's that?"

"I called it Fortland Oil, after us, the two founders."

"You did that before you even knew I'd show up?"

"I knew I could count on you sooner or later, but I have Charlie Bruce to thank for making it sooner. You would have packed it in with him eventually. Banking never was your cup of tea."

"What makes you think this is?"

"Everything I know about you."

"Fortland Oil, huh?"

"Like it?"

"It's better than Gartescue," I tell him.

After supper we visit Tampico's best sporting house for a little exercise, a white frosted mansion on a hill that's lit up like Christmas, with electric lights strung on all the palm trees in the garden. Aside from getting off a couple times on a pretty little Spanish girl who reminds me of Rose-of-Sharon Moriarty, I drink a fair amount of whiskey, and the next morning got a head like a fire gong.

But Fortescue's banging on my door at dawn, saying we're off to look at where Doheny's drilling next to one of our leases. It's about twenty miles from the city and takes us six hours to get there in the carriage. I sleep the whole ride under a mosquito net, but by the time we arrive I'm not feeling any better.

The place is just a clearing in the middle of the jungle, with a bunch of corrugated-iron huts and a wood tower sixty feet high. Doheny's on the drilling platform dressed in white linen suit and puttees, but he comes down, waving a welcome.

A drilling rig is one of the noisiest machines a body can imagine, and in the old days they was even noiser than today. They didn't have diesel engines yet, but old steam engines that used thousands of gallons of water every day and tons of firewood to heat the boiler.

Doheny struts over to shake hands, a broad smile on his face. It's hard to hear over the whining and screeching of the rig, and the banging and clattering of the steam engine. "This is it!" he shouts. "We're only down a few hundred feet, but Tampico Twelve will make the Pan-American Petroleum Company!"

"Can you smell it?" I holler over the racket.

"Damn right! The core samples I got so far confirm everything I suspected. Come on, I'll show you."

He leads us away from the rig, past drilling pipes stacked around the clearing like jackstraws, to an open tent he uses as his office, where the noise ain't so bad. Mexican laborers chop firewood for the steam engine, while donkeys lug barrels of water from a nearby stream. The only gringos around beside Doheny are a couple of sweaty roustabouts with torsos like dray horses, working up on the drilling platform.

Under the tent awning is a table covered with chunks of dirt and rock, each one about three or four inches in diameter. These are the core samples Doheny's raving about, and according to him, the order they come in from the drill is what indicates petroleum below. Or not. Between the tropical heat and my hangover, I can barely focus on the table, let alone learn the oil business.

"How deep will you have to go?" Fortescue asks him.

"Hard to say. By the tone and consistency of these calcareous concretions we should be running into porous glutius maximus before long." That ain't really what Doheny says, but that's what it sounded like then to a ignoramus like me.

The more I listen, the more depressed I get, until I decide to back out of Fortland Oil as soon as we get to the hotel, even if Fortescue does have to change the company name.

But I don't reckon on his unreasonable optimism. He's one of these men only has to think up a thing to be convinced it exists. If he believes I can learn enough about petroleum in a few days to drill a well, then he won't take no for an answer.

All the way back to Tampico, we argue about it. But he's got an answer for everything. When I say I don't know the first thing about a steam engine, he says I don't have to, he's already hired a stationary engineer who does. When I tell him I wouldn't know where to set up a drilling platform, he says that don't matter either because he's negotiating now with a fellow who does.

"And all that muck on Doheny's table? Them core samples? They all look the same to me. I couldn't learn the stuff he was talking about in a hundred years."

"We have a mineralogist for that," he tells me. "All you have to do, Lee, is what you do best. Ride herd on the whole works. It won't be simple, but it's safer than what you did in the army, and easier on your nerves than playing banker with Charlie Bruce."

That night Fortescue holds court on the hotel veranda while I listen. There's a dozen slickers who know he's a millionaire investor, trying to sell him oil leases, and another bunch offering stock in their so-called oil companies. Tampico at that moment is like a racetrack. The odds vary by the minute, favorites come and go, and a lot of money changes hands.

One thing I gather from all the talk is that practically nobody except us is betting on Doheny. But that don't seem to bother Fortescue. In fact, it mainly amuses him. I hope maybe he knows something I don't know, but I doubt it. He's just figuring Doheny's been lucky before, so he will be again.

I start my career in the petroleum business the next day, and hotter, dirtier, sweatier, more bug-infested work I never done, not even in the army in Cuba. Fortescue decides to drill on a lease we own less than a mile from where Doheny's Number Twelve hole is going down. We run an office at the Hotel Independencia, but I spend my time out on the site or running back and forth, making sure we get what we need.

He's found some competent men, Texans mostly, but hard workers, and a bunch of Mexican peons for the heavy labor. A spindly-looking fellow named Luke Sawyer hires on as tool pusher, which is the most important job on a oil well. He's the expert who decides what cutting tools to use and what size pipe and casing to put down and how to keep mud and water circulating so the drill don't overheat. Luke's from Pittsburgh and he's been drilling oil wells around Pennsylvania since he was a kid: a wirey, cadaverous little guy with a walleye and three fingers on his right hand, who's worth ten of anybody else.

In two weeks we're drilling and I learn quick enough to bullshit with the best of them on the hotel veranda if I only had the time. My days start before dawn and never end until midnight, but I got a case of oil fever myself by now, so it don't matter.

Whoever said you only find oil in godawful places was right. The Fortland Oil Company's Number One well is in a worse place even than where Doheny's Number Twelve is. All around our clearing is the ugliest, most malignant jungle a man can imagine. At sunrise, black clouds of dum-dum flies swarm out of the green bamboo. Ants the size of grasshoppers crawl over everything, and the sons of bitches bite right through bootleather. Trails have to be hacked out fresh every few days, and where little patches of leafy sunlight break through the tree canopy overhead, you're most likely to see a fat, slick snake sunning his venomous coils. The stink of leaf mold and rot is every place, and the mosquitoes work twenty-four hours a day. But more than that is the vomity smell of gas, which seeps through the jungle floor and permeates the air. In certain places, you can light it without setting fire to the damp carpet of rot.

Anything happens to you here, the jungle eats you. Flesh, bones, hair, clothes are all gone, swallowed up and digested by this great dark, rotting rain forest in a week. Steel drilling pipe turns to rusty scrap iron almost overnight unless it's used. Men get sores, infections and fevers from nothing. The mortality in burros is astronomical and the turnover in personnel is high because most men can't take the heat and the hardship.

The days and weeks go by until we hear Doheny's lost the Number Twelve hole in quicksand. But that don't faze him any and he goes off to drill in another place. We're at five hundred feet with nothing to show for it, drilling between twenty and thirty feet a day with a cable rig, but in my ignorance I ain't discouraged. That's the oil fever. Every day the mineralogist peers at wet sand and fresh core samples like a gypsy reading tea leaves, but he don't see no oil.

Doheny's new site is on a rise only about two thousand yards from us, but he's as enthusiastic as he was about the last one.

"Thirteen is my lucky number," he tells me. "I'll bet a thousand dollars I'll spud in before you do. And another thousand says it's a pressure well!"

"Why do you think that?" I ask him.

"The geology of the slope," he says. "I'm on the cusp of the salt dome and you're off to one side."

Fortescue takes the bet and we all go back to work.

Exactly one month to the day after Doheny starts on his Number Thirteen hole, he collects. He hits a pressure pocket all right, with less than fourteen hundred feet of pipe in, although even he don't know it at first. One morning drilling mud comes flowing up over the rotary table of the rig and then into the derrick, covering the crew and the tools. Then the well quiets down for a minute. Doheny's having breakfast nearby when he hears a rumble and a screeching, and a salt water geyser comes out of the earth that takes the top off the rig and spouts a hundred feet above the jungle. I'm on our own rig when it happens, and we all stare.

The big danger is fire. You can smell the gas everywhere now, and any spark can set it off. The whole jungle's full of it, while the trees and vines are crusted white from the salt water.

Behind the water comes the oil at last. First a greenish sludge, then a black gusher that takes the crown block off the top of the rig and sprays the jungle for hundreds of yards in all directions. We rush over for a closer look and see Doheney laughing and jumping around with that limpy gait, his white linen suit black and slimy, and his face like a minstrel show clown's.

I bring our crew to help throw up small damns and levees to contain the oil so it ain't lost, but it's two weeks before Doheney gets the well under control, and by that time the place is a petroleum lake.

He's a genius, no doubt about it, and he designs an apparatus called a Christmas tree, which is a huge T-shaped valve system that deflects the oil stream from vertical to horizontal and then slowly closes it off. Doheny's lucky and there ain't any fires. He estimates the well will put out a record forty-five thousand barrels a day, so his main problem now is to get a pipeline built to move the oil to the coast.

We lose our own hole a few days later and start again closer to Doheny's Number Thirteen well. After only six weeks of drilling, we spud in too, and the Fortland Oil Company is finally in business as a petroleum producer.

What all this means to me I don't get right away because there's so much hard work I barely have time to think. I know I'm rich, but I really don't do any figuring to see just how rich. Doheny's Pan-American Company is going to be partners with Fortland Oil on the pipeline construction, so Fortescue goes up to Texas with Doheny to arrange it, leaving me on my own to deal with the engineers and geologists, bully the competition and buy off the Mexican governor. Luke Sawyer, our tool pusher, is the biggest help. Without him I never could of done all I had to do. I triple his salary and promote him to drilling superintendent because by now we're getting ready to put down a lot more wells in order to exploit the new field.

Our discoveries bring in more wildcatters than ever and puts Tampico on the oil map for good. Every tinhorn, two-bit chiseler for a thousand miles turns up on the veranda of the Hotel Independencia that year, and a lot of solid, serious oilmen as well. One day, for the first time since I arrived in Tampico, nobody's talking about oil because we hear President McKinley's been shot by some crazy anarchist. According to the news he's just wounded. Then, three days later he dies and Colonel Roosevelt's the new president of the United States.

Me and Fortescue are drinking the colonel's health when Doheny joins us to say if I want to sell him back my shares in his Pan-American Company, he'll buy at a thousand dollars.

"I don't know," I tell him.

"Per share," he says.

"Are you serious?"

"I'll give you the check today."

I didn't take him up on it even though it would of put a hundred thousand dollars in my pocket. Instead I stayed with the stock on account of his gusher, and in a few months it was worth ten times more. That's how I got my first million, as a gift from that unlucky Pinkerton detective who died believing Doheny was a fake.

PART

3

XXVI

Settling Down

I brought Mountain down to help Luke Sawyer, and he took to
drilling like a calf to the tit. Ben Butler's widow didn't need him
anymore because she was getting married. Levi quit the bank too
and came with us as chief bookkeeper, with old Heinz still nipping
at his heels. Levi tells me Charlie Bruce is doing okay, but not as
good as when I was around, which gives me a certain pleasure.
Sady Apodaca took her money out after I left, and so did most of
my other Old Town friends.

I'm hustling between the oil field and the Hotel Independencia,
and it's clear we got to find bigger quarters. I never do bother to
collect my salary because within six months my share of Fortland
Oil's already making me nine thousand dollars a day with only two
wells in production. Besides the million my Doheny stock is worth,
the money's piling up in New York like a blizzard, all thanks to my
friend G. Ronald Fortescue and his persuasive optimism.

By the end of the year we get the pipeline and four more wells
on stream. People are drilling all around us, and most of them are
striking oil. The jungle's nearly disappeared and been replaced by
a man-made forest of derricks and shacks. Although Doheny was
right about where to drill, even he didn't guess it's the biggest oil
puddle ever found, and we're smack at the center of it. There's so
much oil pouring out of the ground by the end of nineteen-o-three
that they call the place Black Gold Lake.

341

Fortescue's working as hard as I am, running between New York and Galveston, never staying in one place for more than a week because so many things have to be done to move the oil to market.

We set up new headquarters in a old mansion we buy on the outskirts of the city, and build our own port facility where the pipeline reaches the harbor. The funny thing about all this is that the Mexicans hardly figure in the picture except at two extremes. The governor, mayor, port captain, police chief, local army commander and a hundred other officials count on us for the *mordida,* an old Mexican custom we call bribery. No rock gets turned, no well gets drilled, no tanker anchors in the harbor without the *mordida.* Then there's the higher-ups in Mexico City, the big bandits like old Diaz himself, the president, whose take is already in the millions.

At the bottom of the pile are the thousands of Indians who get work all of a sudden, families that was starving before we brought the oil in. We put food in their bellies and pesos in their pockets, and if the jails ain't exactly empty, they ain't filling up as fast as they used to. I don't see so many poor devils being dragged through the streets anymore like that first day with Doheny.

But oil is mainly a Yankee operation, with just a few English and Germans out to make a buck like us. Within two years, over six thousand Americans are working out of Tampico. All the transport, supplies, food and oil-field support is in the hands of the gringos. Mexicans ain't lazy, so why do they sit back and let us take over their country like that? Since then I been all over South America, seen the same story everywhere, and always asked the same question.

The only answer I come up with is that Spain stuck them with a lot of backward institutions like a self-serving church and a tyrannical type of government. Most of them countries didn't even fight for their independence like we did, even though they all pretend that's what happened, and lie about it to their kids. They got their freedom cheap when Napoleon took over Spain, and they spent their time since then squabbling about who'll be in charge of each country instead of holding elections like normal people. They been crippled by every goddamn antidemocratic, anticapitalist, antiprogressive, antisocial notion they inherited from them priests and kings who left them with no sense of justice, no sense of time and no sense of responsibility. And at the top, the rich ones got no sense of work either, except that it's something you leave for the poor peons at the bottom to do.

We get our first visitors from home when Emma Fortescue shows up with Honora Stockton to spend Christmas. I wasn't expecting Nora and I must of looked pretty dumb when she steps off the boat, because her smile fades fast and she says, "Lee? Don't you know me?"

I say, "Sure, Nora. I'm just surprised to see you here."

"Emma didn't tell you?"

"Not a word." Fortescue's laughing because Honora Stockton is a surprise and Emma's beaming like she just made my Christmas and they all assume my disappointment is confusion. Except Nora, poor girl. She knew I had another face in mind. Women sense them things like horses smell snakes, but she's too well-bred to let on.

I ask her about people we both know in New York. She sees Knoblauch and Mitchell at parties from time to time. Knoblauch's getting married, and Mitchell's got himself an Italian girl friend, an opera singer who don't speak English.

"Since when does he speak Italian?" I ask her.

"He doesn't," she says, laughing, "which is probably why they're so much in love."

"And what about you?"

"Oh, I soldier on, Lee. Dear Emma's still trying to find me a husband. She's disgusted with most of the eligible men in New York and thinks I might have better luck here."

"That's silly. You could have anyone you want."

"But I don't want just anyone." She looks at me and laughs again, a pretty, musical laugh and one of the main things I always liked about her. "You should see your face. Don't worry, Lee Garland, you're safe. I crossed you off my list ages ago."

"Why?"

"Because your heart belongs to someone else."

"Not anymore."

"Oh? Then are you a potential suitor for my hand?" She's looking at me like a pixie and holding her wrist up, la-de-da, which makes me laugh. She's laughing at me too behind her eyes, but I know she's also half serious, so I'm wary. She was always bold as brass, Honora, not a shred of modesty the way most girls was taught those days. Spending time around Emma I ain't surprised. It was still an age when a well-bred girl like Caroline would blush and hide behind a fan, but not Honora. She used her fan the way Luna used his riding crop, stabbing the air to make a point when she was excited, or sticking it in your ribs to get your attention.

She was prettier than I remembered. Wonderful white teeth when she smiled, which was often, eyes that danced when she laughed or were solemn and sometimes eager, but seldom sad. Nora had a sharp sense of humor, and an even sharper tongue. She was her own worst enemy with men, and I'm probably the only one really ever bothered to notice her intelligence. I have to admit there could be worse fates than being hitched to a woman as bright and pretty as Honora Stockton. She and Emma are like royalty riding in Fortescue's big lacquered coach, and Tampico society trips over itself inviting them out.

When Al Fall shows up on business, him and Doheny compete for Emma's attention. Fall's left the bench and switched to being a Republican. He's here now to tap us for political contributions, but the reason he stays nearly three weeks is Emma Fortescue.

I don't know it then, but this chance meeting would change all our lives in the years to come. My own association with him, which began on the battlefield in Cuba the day Ben Butler was killed, lasted more than forty years until he died. Fortescue and him stayed friends a long time too, but that friendship didn't survive the trouble Fall got into during the Harding administration. Emma and him was a different story, a love story that started in Mexico and didn't end until she died.

Looking back on it, I should of known what was going to happen between them almost from the first, but I was too busy thinking about myself. Emma was old enough to be my mother, after all, and Al Fall was an important figure in New Mexico politics. It don't cross a young man's mind that a middle-aged judge can fall in love or that a respectable matron like Emma Fortescue would risk her reputation by climbing into bed with him, but that's what they both done, and quick as rabbits too.

I learn that Al Fall is an expert on mineral rights because he handled quite a few legal cases involving the mining companies. When Fortescue says it's the first time he ever seen his mother interested in the oil business, she tells him it's the first time she ever heard it explained in such an exciting fashion by such an interesting man.

There was something about that season and our mood that was

made for romance. I even found myself with a crush on Nora that turned our friendship into something more serious.

It started one day when I took her riding along the beach at Medano. After a good gallop, we picnicked on a little sandy hill, the only two people around for miles. She's telling me about a novel she'd read called *House of Mirth* that don't sound funny to me at all, but sad. We're watching the ships through the golden haze of Tampico harbor, and Nora looks so beautiful with her hair pinned up that I put my arms around her and kiss her.

My reward is an Honora Stockton I didn't know existed. She don't melt into my arms, she explodes with a passion I wasn't use to, except for when I knew Caroline so long ago. I explode right back and we go groping and kissing near to exhaustion.

During the days that followed, I had to go to Tuxpam, a place about a hundred miles down the coast where we was drilling in a new field, and Honora was on my mind a lot. In fact, I could hardly think of anything else, remembering the sun glinting in her hair, her scent of lilacs, and the cool, sweet feel of her mouth. I really liked her and was glad she come along with Emma.

Sometimes we go out alone and other times with Fortescue or Emma and Judge Fall. The subject of marriage comes up again one evening when she and I are at a Viennese restaurant in Chijol, listening to Straus waltzes while we hold hands and sip wine. She's wearing a pretty white lace Mexican frock I tell her looks like a wedding dress.

She throws her head back and laughs. "Lord in heaven, Lee, do you think I'll ever wear one?" The question stumps me, so she squeezes my hand and says with her clear, honest eyes looking into mine, "Now you'll think I'm pressuring you and I'm not. I love you. You know that by now. But you don't have to marry me. I'm yours whenever you want."

We spend part of that night in my room and she's as juicy and firm as a fall apple. The next morning over breakfast, I propose.

"Thank you, Lee, but no, thank you," she says, and I nearly fall off the chair.

"What do you mean, no?"

"Shall I say it in Spanish too? No."

"Why not? What did I do wrong? I thought—"

"Nothing, darling." She touches my hand gently. "I'm deeply honored, but you're under a spell right now. If I had an ounce of

sense I'd take advantage of you and accept before you change your
mind, because it's what I really want. But I can't do that, and don't
ask me why."

"Of course I'll ask you why."

"Please."

"You owe me an answer."

"I told you why. You're still in love with her."

"She's married and has a child."

"I don't want half of you, so it's no, with regrets."

"The offer stays open, Nora. Think about it."

"I've thought of nothing else since we met."

Who understands a woman? I wanted her more than ever when
she turned me down, yet I knew in my heart she'd seen clear
through me about Caroline. God knows what it cost her to lay it
on the line like that. But I'm nothing if not persistent, once I get
the bit in my teeth. I draft Emma as my willing helper, and even
Fortescue, who thinks the whole thing is funny as hell. He says
Nora and me got things backward as usual. I wasn't expected to
propose but she was expected to accept, and not the other way
around.

But I plunge ahead and order a ten-thousand-dollar diamond
ring from Tiffany. I would of spent a hundred thousand but Emma
says that big a ring would only be vulgar and I have a lifetime to
give her jewels.

The president of Mexico visits Tampico to see the new oil industry, and to check on his cut, and the governor of Veracruz Province
throws a party in his honor. Diaz is fat and old and he's been
around as president for thirty years, but he's still got a strangle-
hold on Mexican politics. Most of the troubles that would bring
down his government and start the revolution there was still eight
or ten years in the future.

The governor is a sociable fellow and a friend of mine due to our
mordida connection, so me and Fortescue are on the guest list. His
palacio don't have electricity yet, but it's lit with ten thousand
candles that night and looks like a wedding cake. We turn up in
white tie and tails with Emma and Nora, and get presented to Diaz
with about five hundred other people, him sitting on a gilded
throne with a big sash across his belly, drooping white mustaches
and beady little Indian eyes that don't miss a trick.

Just before the fiesta, I ask Nora for the tenth time to marry me and she laughs and says she'll think it over. It ain't quite a yes, but it's a far step up from her original no. There's a lot of money showing that night. Jewels and gowns from New York and Paris on fat little wives and sleek mistresses, but nobody draws more attention than Nora in blue satin and pearls as we go sashaying round the dance floor. Every Mexican general in his peacock uniform is anxious to kiss her hand and give her the eye.

What she don't know is that our engagement will be announced tonight, it being Emma's theory that she really wants to marry me and it's time to stop fooling around because they're due to return to New York soon. Fortescue tells the governor, who tells the president, who will make the formal announcement himself.

He's got some other political decrees to read out first but when he finishes, he takes off his spectacles as the governor ushers me and Nora up to the throne. The room's quiet as church, and hundreds of guests are wondering what's up. Nora's looking at me expecting a translation because her Spanish ain't up to much.

Diaz rises, takes us both by the hand like an old grandfather and says how much pleasure it gives him to announce the intended marriage of his good friend Senor Lee Garland to the beautiful Senorita Honora Stockton of New York. I slip the engagement ring on Nora's finger before she knows what's happening. There's a thunder of applause because everybody likes a romantic gesture, especially from a president. He kisses Nora on the cheek and embraces me while the governor offers a toast and the band strikes up a wedding song.

Nora's staring at the ring in amazement. "Did he say what I think he said?" And tears start at the corners of her eyes.

"He did."

"But I haven't said yes yet, have I?"

"This is Mexico. Back out now, and they shoot you."

"Oh, Lee!"

So that's how it happened. And I can truthfully say she made me real happy that night. We set the wedding date for June in New York because Emma convinces her she'll need six months to get everything ready, and I'll need it to build us a house outside of Tampico. On the fifteenth of January I see her off on the steamer, and me and Fortescue go back to work.

The well in Tuxpan comes in over the holidays, opening a new field, and we're off on another project with Doheny to build a tank farm across the Panuco River from the city. I should of been triplets in those days. Fortescue too. But I've always found the more I have to do, the more I get done. The governor sells me a choice piece of land on the Laguna del Pueblo, where the air is better and the mosquitoes fewer, and where the stench of Tampico harbor don't quite reach.

The tank farm gets built, and I receive two or three letters a week from Nora. All are in her firm legible script and there's no better way to know a woman's character. By May the house is finished, a ten-room hacienda built around a patio, with stables, servants' rooms and a coach house on one side. I order a twelve-cylinder Pierce-Arrow saloon car as her wedding gift, and a diamond necklace. Lee Garland is settling down at last. My passage is booked on the steamer to New Orleans for May, then the train to New York.

The week before I'm supposed to leave, a sleek steam yacht sails into the harbor, and at a dinner the governor gives, I meet the owner. He owns the railroad here as well as silver mines over in San Luis Potosi, but I'm the only one who knows he also owns Caroline. After nearly five years of imagining Woodrow Sloan as some kind of evil old coot, I'm a little startled by the reality.

He's roly-poly and balding, but kind of baby-faced, which makes him look no more than forty, with pale blue eyes, a girl's skin and a gentleman's manners. He says he's heard a lot about me from Doheny, who considers me the boy wonder of the petroleum industry. As far as I can tell he don't connect me with Charlie Bruce, or with Caroline.

But why would he? A man like him has more business and financial interests than he can count, let alone remember a little pissant bank his brother-in-law runs in Albuquerque. He's here to talk about extending his railroad line south to Mexico City, a route that interests us, because it could go right by our new Tuxpam oil field.

The governor treats him like a foreign prince, because a railroad through the province will make him rich in a year. Before the evening's over, we're all invited for lunch on Sloan's yacht the next day. I want to ask if his family's with him, but I don't. We're having a last brandy with the governor when a hell of an explosion jars the windows of the *palacio,* and a sudden glow appears across the river where our tank farm is. There's nothing else in the vicinity can make a bang like that, and I know all of a sudden our luck ran out.

It takes Fortescue and me an hour to get there, and we can feel the heat a thousand yards away. One blazing tank has collapsed, and the way the wind is coming off the harbor, the flames are lapping at a second tank like a giant blowtorch. The lost tank is already a huge twisted, buckled mess, and there's nothing anybody can do except let it go and hope the heat don't ignite the other one. The men are doing what they can, soaking the sides of the second tank with water, but already the heat is so fierce, they can't get close enough, and the water from the hoses turns to vapor when it strikes the hot metal.

Our superintendent Luke Sawyer shouts at me, "We've got to take those people out, Mr. Garland, or someone will get killed!"

There's half a million dollars worth of oil at stake, but he's right. The hoses ain't helping much. One way or the other we probably lost the oil anyway, and there ain't no sense in men dying for nothing. Fortescue orders one crew back while I head for the other one closer to the tank. Already I see some of the men's faces red and blistered, and their eyebrows singed just from being so near the heat, even though they're all soaking wet themselves.

Luke Sawyer says, "It's a lost battle, Mr. Garland!"

"Get out! Leave the hoses! That goddamn thing can blow any second and take us with it!"

I'm herding them ahead of me, with my back turned to the fire when the gas lets go like a volcano. The noise is kind of slow building, like heavy artillery or a gusher coming in. I hear it and then I feel it, like the hot wind of hell on my back. I see Sawyer crumple and I throw myself to the ground, face down and that's the last I remember of that night.

Five men were killed, including Luke Sawyer. Fortescue wrapped himself in wet burlap sacks and charged back into the heat to drag me out. Otherwise I'd of joined the others and been just another cinder. I was lucky, falling face down in the sludge, but I still wound up with third-degree burns on my back and legs, and lay half-conscious for a couple of days. They took me to the Tampico hospital, where the doctors just shrugged. I'd infect and die of the burns, they said. Fortescue himself wasn't much better off, and bore the scars on one side of his face until he died.

What I couldn't even guess then, thank God, was that this was only the beginning of my bad luck. A string of misfortunes plagued my world immediately afterward that left me bitter and demoralized for a long, long time.

The irony is I owe my life to Woodrow Sloan as much as Fortescue. Sloan takes me aboard his yacht and brings a French doctor from New Orleans who's an expert on burns. The pain goddamn near kills me because they plaster me with petroleum jelly every day like a basted turkey, and then peel off the dead skin each morning.

The tank farm burns a month before the fire finally dies out, and Levi calculates our loss at over two million dollars, half in petroleum and the rest to clean up the mess and rebuild the storage area from scratch. For quite a while, however, that's the least of my problems because I'm in too much pain. But I don't infect, and little by little I begin to heal. The wedding's postponed and we leave it that as soon as I'm well enough to travel, we'll be married as planned. Mountain, God bless him, never leaves my bedside, and Sloan's yacht is as comfortable a hospital as anyone in my condition could ask for.

While I'm slowly recovering, Sloan travels inland to visit his mines and railroads and whatever else he has scattered around Mexico, so I rarely see him. Then one day, I have a dream that Caroline appears, looking exactly as she looked five years ago. "Hello, Lee," she says. "How are you feeling?"

Except it ain't a dream. I'm awake and lying out on the deck on a chaise lounge, trying to read Colonel Roosevelt's history of the Cuban campaign. Mountain's there as usual, but fades into the woodwork as soon as she appears.

"I'm okay, Caroline." Like we seen each other yesterday.

She gives me a little smile and a shrug, which in a woman can mean anything. "Are they looking after you?"

"Spoiling me."

"Well." She sits there primly, her hands on her knees, the half smile still on her face, kind of staring at something in the middle distance.

"I'm real glad to see you again, Caroline."

She gives me a tiny nod, still smiling, but forced. "You're awfully thin," she says, looking at me as I look back. I'm thinking my God, what I lost! I don't even remember Honora at that moment.

"Lee?"

"Yes?"

"May I ask you a question?"

"Anything you want, Caroline." I still don't believe this is happening, that she's next to me and not a thousand miles away.

"Remember Tampa?"

"Every minute of it."

"Why did you change your mind about me?"

"I never changed my mind about you."

"But you never wrote, never answered my letters."

"I did write. Letters you never got. Charlie admitted he stopped them because you were already married. But I never got one from you before or after."

"Charles mailed all my letters to you. . . . Or said he did. I had no idea." Her eyes well with tears as she tells me this. "Charles convinced me I was being vain and foolish for thinking you loved me, and that I was not the first woman you had abandoned."

"Did he tell you who they were?"

"He mentioned a girl called Rose Moriarty."

"Rose-of-Sharon? I don't believe it!"

"That was her name."

"She was a Mexican girl who went out with a friend of ours. We all knew her. When I talked to Charlie in New York he said you didn't want to see me."

"He told you that?" She's trembling and shaking her head with her eyes pressed closed, sort of holding her breath. "He said you never wanted to see *me* again."

"Caroline, I telephoned from the hospital and talked to Charlie. I wrote and wrote. He said you'd met someone else and it was all over with us. You were married to Sloan. So there I was."

Tears are streaming down her face now like she's in pain, and one hand pressed against her mouth, as if she can't stand to hear any more of this. "I'll never forgive him," she says, "as long as I walk this earth I'll never, *ever* forgive him! He owed you his life and his fortune, and he repaid you by destroying us."

"You really did want to see me?"

"I waited and waited, Lee."

"Then why did you marry Sloan?"

"I loved you. But after what Charles told me there was no other way. I had to marry someone."

"Why not me?"

"I believed Charles."

"Instead of believing in me."

"But I'd heard nothing and I was desperate. And Charles was the only person I trusted."

"I trusted him too."

"My own brother! I knew I was right in loving you."

"Then why didn't you wait a little longer, Caroline."

"I couldn't."

"It wasn't the end of the world."

"It was the end of my world, Lee."

"A month or two wouldn't have made a difference."

"I couldn't hide it any longer."

"Hide what?"

"Your child, Lee."

XXVII

Love and Marriage

On the dresser in my bedroom are four family pictures. One is of my grandson Pete when he was about ten holding a two-pound rainbow trout he caught here at Eagle Nest. One is my little daughter Emma when she was four or five. One is of Caroline and me taken in Washington during the First World War. And the other, also from that war, is of my son Matt in his flying clothes, standing by his airplane.

Matt, when I meet him for the first time in Mexico, is five years old: a bright, chirpy little fellow with his mother's green eyes and my blond hair. I was in shock for a few hours after what Caroline said, listening to her tell how that scheming bastard of a brother blighted everybody's life with his lies. The truth kindled a rage in me I hadn't felt since Cody Williams was murdered. If Charlie Bruce had been anywhere close right then I'd of killed him with my bare hands. After Caroline discovered she was pregnant, but before anybody else suspected it, she confided in her brother, threw herself on his mercy so to speak, and hoped for the best. As she said, I wasn't around, and she had nobody else to turn to.

Charlie's reaction was predictable enough; moral outrage and condemnation, the self-righteous prig telling Caroline he had a whore for a sister. Then, while she's contemplating suicide and he's checking out the cost of backstreet abortions, Woodrow Sloan enters the scene.

Charlie had worked for the man's railroad since he graduated
from Harvard, and they were social equals, if not exactly on the
same dollar level. Sloan invited him and Caroline to spend Marble-
head Race Week aboard his yacht. Sloan had known Caroline since
she was a child, and even though he was twenty-five years older,
wanted to marry her.

According to Caroline, when Charlie realized Sloan was serious,
he nearly fell down trying to hurry things along, sucking up to him
and spending his own money to buy her fashionable dresses to
ensure she got all the attention at Sloan's parties. As long as he
didn't guess about her condition, Sloan was the perfect, elegant
solution to everybody's problem. Poor, pregnant Caroline would
have a husband, her baby would have a father, and helpful Charlie
Bruce would acquire a rich and influential brother-in-law.

I was still traipsing through Cuban cane fields at that time, or
lying feverish on a hospital cot, so I didn't figure as part of the
problem except to Caroline. She said she prayed right up until the
night before the wedding that I'd turn up to save her.

After meeting Caroline again in Mexico and finding out about
our little boy, I was still crazy in love with her, willing to do
anything to be with her, as desperate as I ever been in my life. And
the idea of having little Matt for my son was the best thing I could
imagine.

The funny part is we never made love but only talked for hours
and hours. I still had a fair amount of pain in my legs from the
burns, but the rest of me was ready. All I wanted was to hold her
and bed her and never let her go.

"No, Lee."

"You love me."

"I've never been in love with anyone else."

"Then?"

"Woodrow knows Matthew is not his."

"How did he find out?"

"That's where all of Charles's plans should have collapsed," she
said, "because he was unaware of something vital about Woodrow." We were on the deck of Sloan's yacht when Caroline told me
the man's secret, leaning against the rail and watching the sun set
over the Panuco River.

"Whose child does he think he is?"

"He has no idea. Aside from you, Charles is the only one who knows."

"Get a divorce and marry me now."

"You don't understand. I thought I was clever enough to fool Woodrow, but when Matthew was born, he said, 'I know the truth, Caroline, and it doesn't matter, so put your mind at rest.' The subject has never been mentioned since."

"But surely Charlie didn't let on."

"The baby had to be someone else's, Lee, because Woodrow cannot father a child. That was something my scheming brother never suspected when he thrust me at him. Since then, in spite of his knowledge about me, Woodrow has been a considerate husband. So you see why I could never ask him for a divorce."

"What about us?"

She cries as she answers me. "There is no us, Lee. My ambitious brother did his work well. Matthew believes Woodrow is his father and I'm lucky to have such a man to look after us both."

"Caroline, we love each other and Matthew is ours. You can't stay with Sloan now."

"Lee, I'm tied to him by something stronger than any marriage vow. Another man would have put me in the street knowing what he knows. But he saved me, and I couldn't leave him now, even for you."

"You can't waste your life working off a debt like that."

"It's not a waste if Matthew is happy. I'm sorry, darling." She clings to me for a long time and I hold her. Then she breaks away and wipes her eyes and looks at me and cries some more. It's like we both got our wires crossed somewhere. I mean I don't criticize Caroline's values, I never did. But what she's doing ain't right no matter how I try to see it. She says Woodrow Sloan saved her from shame and the gutter, probably from killing herself and Matt too, before he was even born. Okay. But that don't mean Woodrow has to be a permanent fixture in her life now that I'm here and the truth is known.

"You still could of waited," I tell her.

"Only a woman would understand," she tells me.

"But that ain't your position now."

"Lee, I can't change things."

"What you're saying is you don't love me enough to change

things. Or you'd leave him now," and she starts to cry again and I take her in my arms and neither one of us makes a lot of sense.

"I want to, my darling. Believe me, I do."

"You're mine," I tell her. "You always were." She hugs me tighter and can't stop sobbing, but she don't change her mind because she is the most stubborn woman ever lived.

A week later she sails away with my little boy and they disappear from my life as if they had never been there. I said and did everything I could to make her see how wrong she was, but it was no use. To her way of thinking, she had an obligation to Sloan, even though she loved me. Maybe what she did wouldn't make a lot of sense today because people got different standards, but she did it because she felt she had to. I loved her even though I wanted to pick her up and shake her. I never loved anybody like I did Caroline. Not in the beginning, not then and not now.

But I had to live with this new knowledge too, so I sulked and grumbled and turned the whole thing over in my head for a while. I just about made up my mind to follow her back East and keep up the pressure until she gave in, when I woke up one morning and decided not to. Nothing special happened except maybe the smallest niggling suspicion that maybe she didn't love me enough. Even when I said it, I didn't believe it. If Caroline wanted things this way, she had her reasons, and I'd be better off getting on with my own life and forgetting her, and maybe the best way to do that was with Nora.

It was dumb, looking back at it, but I couldn't think of nothing better to do than to get together again with her, and sooner or later that meant I'd go ahead and marry her. Before the tank farm accident, and before Caroline turned up with Matt, I had chased her hard. I had convinced her against her better judgment, bought the ring and built the house in Tampico. If Caroline felt an obligation to Sloan, as the time passed I felt something similar toward Nora. Guilt mainly. Guilt if I jilted her and guilt if I went through with getting hitched.

I was as nervous as a dog with the trots, trying to convince myself that marrying Nora was the right thing and never quite managing to do it. I dragged my feet, using first my injuries and then my work as an excuse for not doing it, always hoping if I stalled long enough Caroline would change her mind and leave Sloan. But the months went by and it didn't happen.

Nora and me tied the knot in October of nineteen-o-four, more than a year after my encounter with Caroline, who I even telephoned when I got to New York just before the wedding. If she'd given me half a hope, I'd of dropped Nora, cancelled everything and run off with her. And I'd of done it knowing Nora was already pregnant. That's the kind of man I was then. But Caroline asked me please to stop torturing us both.

The wedding was at the Grace Episcopal Church and Emma give us a big reception afterward at the Fortescue house. They used to talk about the New York Four Hundred in those days, meaning the high society, the old families. But there was more like a thousand of them, and they all showed up at the party, plus my friends from the Rough Riders, half of Wall Street, and the president of the United States. Roosevelt's daughter Alice was a friend of Nora's from school and one of her bridesmaids, and Fortescue stood up as my best man.

At the reception, Roosevelt toasted Nora, who he had known since she was a kid visiting his summer place out at Oyster Bay, and said some nice things about her beauty and poise that made me proud to be the bridegroom. Then he turned to me and Fortescue and said with a wink, "Thanks for making me president, boys." Everybody knows that what made him president was the crazy anarchist who shot McKinley and left the job open. But the colonel always liked to say it was the Rough Riders that was responsible for his political career, that he never would of been elected to anything if we hadn't made him famous.

I always figured it was the other way around. He invented us, and we just had to live up to his good opinion. Like kids with a proud father, we just tried harder to please him so he wouldn't think he'd been mistaken. I think that's why he was a good president and a great leader, because most Americans felt that way about him, and tried harder. He had such a high opinion of his country and the people in it, nobody liked to let him down.

While he was telling stories about the war at the reception, and making me look ten feet tall, I was thinking maybe, just maybe, I could be happy without Caroline after all. Nora had never looked more beautiful, I was surrounded by people who loved me: Fortescue, Knoblauch, Mitchell and my surrogate mother Emma, who smiled and shed a tear every time I looked at her that afternoon.

We got a fortune in presents, enough silver and crystal and

porcelain to outfit a palace. Levi Hennings probably spent three month's salary on the chair he sent us from Mexico, made entirely out of cowhorns, while my generous partner Fortescue gave us a block of stock in Fortland Oil worth a hundred thousand dollars when the market closed the day of the wedding. Mountain came all the way East for the ceremony, and Emma somehow got the tailor to cut and sew him a monkey suit in two days. I made him chief usher at the wedding and he even wore shoes in honor of the occasion.

Knoblauch showed up with his wife and Mitchell brought his Italian girl friend, a soprano who was singing at the Metropolitan Opera. He was producing his own moving pictures by then and making more money than he did as an actor, but when the colonel asked him how he liked what he was doing, he just shook his head and quoted something from Shakespeare that made Roosevelt laugh. By that time, we'd drunk a river of champagne so everybody was pretty relaxed.

"What would you rather be doing?" Fortescue asks Mitchell.

"You want to know the truth?"

"Whatever you want to tell me," Fortescue says.

"Since we returned from our great adventure," Mitchell says, looking from Fortescue to the president, to Knoblauch to me, "I have been seeking another like it. Without success."

"Try marriage, like Lee," Roosevelt says, and we all laugh.

"Or the Philippines," Knoblauch says, "like Ransom. On second thought, better not. Look what happened to him."

"What happened to him?" Fortescue and I ask, not knowing.

"He was killed," Knoblauch says.

I'm shocked but I ain't surprised. Somehow I knew I'd never see him again after we talked on my way to Tampico. I'm thinking, there, but for the grace of God and my old partner Fortescue, I might of gone. "He was real proud to be an officer," I say to the others. "Real proud."

"Who was Ransom?" Nora asks us.

"A friend we lost in the Philippines," Knoblauch says.

"Did he leave a family?"

"A wife," I tell her.

"You should write her, Lee."

"And say what?"

"That you're sorry. Poor woman."

Mitchell says, "Remember the time we stole his pants?" and Roosevelt's laugh booms above the guests in that vast ballroom.

"In the middle of a battle in Cuba," he explains to Nora, "your husband and his friends stole Corporal Ransom's pants and he had to report to me in his long johns."

Nora says, "I've heard so many amusing stories, I wonder when you ever found time to fight the Spanish."

"Oh, we did, my dear," Roosevelt says, "and when we did, we were formidable indeed."

"We were more afraid of you, Mr. President, than of the enemy," Fortescue says.

"Me?" Roosevelt cries in mock surprise. "I thought it was Captain Luna you feared, particularly after your failed singing careers in San Antonio." That reference naturally calls for some more explanations to Nora, and we all wind up laughing like fools, the president more than anybody.

The party's a success even if I did go to the altar with more guilt in my heart than most murderers carry to the gallows. But I never let on to Nora. She was beautiful on that day, as brides are supposed to be, and proud and happy, and kind of fragile-looking. Making a little joke, she thanked me for saving her from spinsterhood. Then she shocked me at the most romantic moment of all when I kissed her after cutting the wedding cake, by whispering something in my ear.

Brides are supposed to blush, not bridegrooms. I never heard anything like that from a woman outside a whorehouse, and even there not often because whores pretend to be delicate around clients. While I feel the heat flood my cheeks, Nora is smiling back like I'd imagined her words instead of hearing them, and I walk out of the reception with my crotch in a state of some excitement. What she said was, "I want your cock," and at the beginning of the century, nice girls weren't supposed to know what a cock was.

Honora knew and so did I, and we put mine to good use. To my surprise, I liked being married and I liked being fussed over. I rolled and wallowed in sex like a pig in paradise because Nora was as excited and excitable as me, as good as any fancy girl I ever knew once she got the hang of it, and ten times as pretty. A funny thing. She seemed to get prettier after we was married, and gentler too, and calmer. Everybody said so.

From the wedding day onward we made love until we both was

sore and chafed and laughing and out of breath, and then we made love again. Sometimes it was like a wild sport with her riding me, bouncing and about to break it off at the root. Other times I just speared her into the pillows as hard and rough as I could while she moaned and whimpered and begged, and came maybe three or four times in a row. And sometimes we'd do it so soft and tender, we'd just come with a sigh and doze off in each other's arms.

I loved Nora, but I still wasn't in love with her and she knew it. How she knew, I don't know, because I never said so, and I spent a lot of effort trying to convince her otherwise. But she was a sensitive woman. I'd catch her watching me sometimes with a sad look in her eyes, and once in a while she'd get teary for no reason, even when it wasn't her time of the month. If I asked her what was wrong, she'd just smile and shake her head. But I knew.

She had me and she didn't have me, and that's the way it would always be between us. She was deep in love and I wasn't. Caroline was always there in my eyes even if she wasn't in my life. I don't understand it today, a thousand years later, like I don't understand a lot about the world. Do people always fall in love with the wrong people? I guess it's common enough because that's what most of the love songs are about. There I was with a beautiful, intelligent wife who fit me perfect, who loves me to death, while inside I'm still pining for a woman I barely knew a week in Tampa and seen only once in five years.

When I tell this to my grandson Pete, he laughs and says, "Lee, if there's one feeling in the world God meant to be spontaneous, nonsensical, capricious, disruptive, erratic, astonishing and totally unquenchable, it's human love. And that is not a medical opinion."

I guess he's right. I'm supposed to be teetering at the lip of the grave for the last twenty of my eighty-nine years, and Caroline's been gone awhile. But my cock still stirs when I think of her, and that ain't my prostate acting up. I love her and still feel the emptiness, the unquenchableness Pete talks about. I still feel that, all right.

Nora and me honeymoon here at Eagle Nest. We ride and walk and make love and eat tons of good Montoya food. At last my foster father's making more money than he ever dreamed of, selling polo ponies to Fortescue's friends back East. The Montoya's are glad to see me married and settling down, and they all like Nora.

I solve Hernan's problem with the Holmans when I buy their ranch through a blind company Dave Leahy sets up. It's so slick, Ernie Holman don't even know I'm the new owner. After I killed Sorenson, and Sam Brown left the Territory, things started winding down for Ernie. Walt Wideman wasted no time pulling out of their partnership. Red went to jail for check forgery, which surprised me because I didn't know he could write. And Bert Bishop dedicated himself to his career as a drunk.

Some time before we do the deal, Ernie transferred his timber rights to the company he was partners in with Walt Wideman, Sorenson and Sam Brown. Wideman signs off okay when Dave pays him a couple of thousand dollars, but Brown's whereabouts are unknown. When I tell Dave to track him down, to offer a thousand dollars for information on him, he don't believe I want him just for timber rights.

"How do I know you won't finish what you started?"

"Find him, Dave, and don't worry about that. I'm living the good life now. Why would I risk it to settle an old score?"

"You tell me."

"Don't anybody believe me when I say I'm through with all that? I don't even carry a gun anymore, just pencil and paper to keep track of all the money I'm making."

Dave says he'll do what he can.

Me and Nora spend some time in Santa Fe with Luna. He's the mayor now, and thinking about higher office. He's as tough and dry as ever, and joshes me about striking it rich, but he's proud as a new father, too. He falls for Nora and gives her all kinds of advice on how to keep me in check. "I never could do it," he tells her, "but I'm not a woman."

One evening over dinner, Luna says some friends in the National Guard got a full report on Ransom's death. "They mutilated him before they beat him to death. The sort of thing Indians sometimes did around here."

"Alfred S. Sorenson wasn't no Indian," I say.

"Point taken," Luna answers me.

Nora's horrified by all this talk, but I'm not, because the papers have been full of atrocity stories about the Philippines for a long time. I try to bring the conversation to a lighter level by telling Nora it was Ransom left the wrist irons unlocked the time Luna arrested me in El Paso.

"*Arrested* you?" Nora says, real curious.

"It's a long story," Luna says, "and it put me off chicken soup for life."

"What on earth are you talking about?" Nora asks him.

So I let Luna tell his version of what happened on the train that time him and old Rufus Barry come to bring us back for trial.

"But what had you done?" Nora asks me.

"Nothing."

"He was wanted for murder," Luna says.

"I was innocent and you know it."

"True. That time you were," Luna says.

"Then why did you have to escape?" Nora says, looking from him to me. "I don't understand. Was there more than one murder?"

I'm thinking we went a little too far bringing up so much ancient history, because some things ain't easy to explain socially to a woman unfamiliar with the critical details, even if she is my wife. But Luna half-excuses himself by saying, "It wasn't always Lee's fault. Those were violent times."

"And a lot of mistakes were made," I tell her.

"Then you didn't actually kill anyone," Nora says.

"Me? Kill somebody? Me?"

"I didn't think so," she says, satisfied.

A few days later, when Dave Leahy comes to see us off at the railroad station in Albuquerque, he takes me aside while Nora is checking hatboxes and trunks with the Pullman porter. He has some news he didn't want to tell in front of her.

"We found him."

"Sam Brown?"

"Over in Utah. The money you offered helped."

"Nice work."

"Tom Isbell tracked him down."

"Did he get the release on the timber?"

"Not exactly."

Nora's beckoning me from the train and the porter's waiting by the steps as the conductor calls, "All aboard!" Dave puts his hand on my arm and says, "He was in jail over there, Lee. Awaiting trial for grand theft and a murder."

"What do you mean 'was'?"

"He escaped."

"Where's Tom staying?"

"At the Joseph Smith Hotel in Salt Lake. Shall I telegraph him to come on back?"

"Not yet. I'll think what to do and wire Tom from El Paso."

"Don't plan on going there yourself."

"I told you not to worry about that."

"But I do worry because I know you."

"I wouldn't do it."

"I don't believe you, Lee."

I stand there in the clear New Mexico air, my beautiful new wife waiting for me in the Pullman, and I try to come up with a more convincing answer for Dave Leahy. Soon I'll be a father, with all the responsibility that goes with it. But right now memories tumble through my mind. How much I loved Cody Williams and how much I feared and hated that bird-legged bastard Sorenson. I remember my rage when I killed him and my shame when I realized how I ruined Luna's case against Sam Brown.

"The truth," Dave says when he sees me pondering.

"Lee!" Nora calls, scared I'll be left on the platform and she'll wind up on the train by herself.

"I don't know," I say.

Dave just looks at me. "You've got half a mind to do it, don't you? Go over there in Utah and shoot him, even married and living the good life and all. Offer a bounty, but stay out of it."

"Dave?"

"Yeah?"

"It'd be right."

"Right for who, Lee? Cody? He's dead."

"What about justice?"

"Leave that to the Mormons. They'll get him and they'll hang him." He gives me a good-natured shove toward the train. "Don't keep that lovely lady waiting, and for God's sake, take care, cowboy."

"You too, counselor."

"Lee!" Panic in her voice because the train is moving.

I catch it okay and settle in for the long ride, my mind a real tangle, knowing what I want to do and yet trying to use my common sense. I'd be a liar if I didn't admit to feeling cheated. I don't think about Sam Brown that much anymore, but I always cherished the hope that it'd be me who'd kill him, just to round things out.

Should I go join Tom Isbell? Or send him money to hire as many shooters as he needs to track the son of a bitch down and kill him? Or just give the Mormons a big reward to do it for me. "Christ, who knows what's right?"

"What did you say?" Nora says.

"I didn't say anything."

"Yes, you did. I distinctly heard you say something."

"Thinking out loud, I guess."

"About what?"

"You and me. The baby coming. You know."

"With that face? You look as if you could kill someone."

XXVIII

The Regulators

"Here's what we do," Tom Isbell tells me when we're sitting across from each other, sipping bootleg whiskey in his Salt Lake hotel room. "We show them Regulators the color of your money and let them go after him." On the pretext of some urgent business with the Latter Day Saints, I left Nora in El Paso and come up here. She didn't like it much, but this early in our marriage, she's willing to forgive anything.

"What's this fellow's name?" I ask Tom.

"Wayne Webster. He's captain and his brother's chaplain."

"The Regulators sound like the army."

"Except the chaplain's more important than the captain. These are funny folks, Lee. They see things different from you and me. You know anything about their religion?"

"Sure. They can have all the wives they want, but no tea, coffee or hard liquor. And they're tight as tree bark about money."

"The main thing is they're fanatics. They believe some angel called Moroni give them the exclusive answers to everything there is to know about God, and they hate anybody don't agree with them."

"That don't sound much different from any other religion."

"The Regulators got members in every county, like the Ku Klux Klan. Anybody they don't like, which mainly means non-Mormons, they tell to move on. Years ago the army had to intervene here and hang a few after a bunch of them massacred a whole wagon train of settlers who wasn't Mormons. They even slaughtered the women and children so there wouldn't be no witnesses, and then tried to blame it on Indians."

"And we're going to cuddle up to them?"

"They want Sam Brown as bad as we do."

"That ain't possible, Tom, but it don't matter."

What Tom tells me is he met with the Webster brothers before he wired Dave Leahy, and again after I telegraphed from El Paso and told him to offer a five-thousand-dollar bounty for Sam Brown. Although they been looking for the bastard since he broke out of jail, the bounty money made the Websters prick up their ears and concentrate harder.

The next day we take the Union Pacific train south to Cedar City, Utah, which ain't a city at all but just a single dusty street with a lot of presumption. It ain't far from where Brown's said to be in the Wah Wah Mountains with a bunch of road agents and murderers like himself. Wayne and Hershel Webster are two peas from the same pod; gaunt, leathery fellows with eyes about an inch apart, humorless as death. Hershel's the talker, which don't mean he says much, just that Wayne don't open his mouth hardly at all. We shake hands on the station platform, stroll over to a spot of shade, where I sit on a wagon tongue and Hershel gets right down to business.

"How do we know you'll pay five thousand dollars?"

"I'm rich. Didn't Tom tell you that?"

He just looks at me, measuring. "This Sam Brown fellow killed an Apostle of our faith, but none of the brethren's offering five thousand dollars for him. Why do you want him so bad?"

"He also killed a friend of mine."

"Worth so much money? We don't know you, mister."

"What you mean is you don't trust me to come up with the five thousand, and you want a guaranty. Is that it?"

"I mean we don't know you."

"I'll wire the funds to the Deseret Bank in Salt Lake today. With instructions to pay out on Mr. Isbell's authorization."

"Dead or alive. That's what the Indian said."

"Tom Isbell told you right."

"If we get him and he don't pay," Hershel says, "neither one of you better hang around Utah long."

I laugh.

"You think we ain't serious?"

"Serious people don't threaten me, boys. How far away is this place he's at?" When I look hard at Wayne, he looks at his brother, and Hershel shrugs. "A day, maybe two."

"Get him and you get paid."

"There should be something up front," Hershel says. "It'll cost money for men, horses and food."

"How much?"

Wayne speaks for the first time. "Five hundred dollars."

"Tom already paid you a thousand."

"That money belongs to me and Wayne," Hershel says, "because we told the Indian where Brown is. The five hundred would be for expenses."

"Wayne and Hershel can deliver," Tom Isbell says. Then aside to me he adds, "Most of these Mormons are honest to a fault, Lee, and they keep their word even if they are greedy."

"I'm glad you told me. Because every minute we sit here jawing, Sam Brown's closer to freedom and they're farther from the money. All right, I'm in for the five hundred, but let's move it."

Over the next two days, nearly a hundred Regulators turn up in Cedar City from miles around, some on horseback, some by train, all armed with rifles and good revolvers. The local sheriff runs out of deputy badges after the first dozen, but he swears the rest in anyway because vigilantes are illegal in Utah, and these Mormons are scrupulous about staying inside the law.

It's the biggest posse I ever seen. In addition to a number of bishops and elders of the church, it includes a county tax assessor, an undertaker and a justice of the peace. Besides Sam Brown, they hope to capture a marauder called Louie Clegg, the Harmon brothers who was horse thieves and a fellow named Bateman they say strangled his wife over in Provo. Bateman and Clegg was the only Mormons, but Hershel Webster said it won't help them because they was long since lapsed in liquor and unnatural vice.

According to him, the whole crowd plus a dozen or so other malefactors are at a ranch belongs to Clegg. Hershel Webster tells me some are leftovers from the old Hole-In-Wall gang used to raid into Arizona and Colorado and hide out in Utah. The Regulators never bothered them as long as they steered clear of Mormon society and done their robbing on an out-of-state basis. But now that Sam Brown killed one of their Twelve Apostles, they want him bad, and they want them lapsed Mormons bad too, especially the one murdered his wife.

At dawn of the third day, when my patience is running thin, the Regulators muster on Cedar City's one street in the freezing cold with their heads bowed for half an hour while Hershel Webster leads them in prayer. Then Wayne barks a command and they mount up and move out in two long columns, smooth and disciplined as cavalry.

Tom Isbell and me tag along at the rear. He intended going alone and I'm overdue in Tampico, but I can't turn around after coming this far. We take food and fodder for five days, and I hire extra horses. Tom's bundled in a mackinaw and I'm wearing a sheepskin coat against the cold. We bring a couple of bottles of Bourbon along to fortify ourselves. It's November, and in that part of Utah the nights are icy even though you can sweat at midday.

For a while I ride beside Hershel Webster and I ask him how Sam Brown broke out of jail.

"The stupidest way possible," he tells me.

"It would have to be, knowing him."

"I mean stupid on our part," Hershel says. "Only one guard was on duty at the jail and he was new. When he brought the food trays, he had to open the cell door to pass them in. He was careless. Brown's cellmate hit him with a shoe while Brown got the keys. Then they beat the poor sinner unconscious."

"Why would Brown hang around Utah if he knows your Regulators will come after him?"

"From what I heard, he ain't famous for his brains. Or common sense."

When I ask him why Wayne needs so many men, he says Clegg's ranch is in a canyon with as many side exits as back and front, which is why the outlaws use it, and all them holes got to be plugged.

"How'd you know where Brown was?"

"People talk."

It takes us a long day to reach this canyon, and another day of sending men off in groups of five or ten to block the exits from Clegg's place. By that time, our main body is down to about fifteen men, including Tom Isbell, me and the Websters. We camp a mile from Clegg's ranch under an awesome red sandstone bluff. It's beautiful country around there, all pink and yellow cliffs carved by rivers that dried up a million years ago. Some of the colors seem to glow like live coals from the reflection of the setting sun.

The Regulators don't talk much among themselves, but pass the time looking after their horses, reading their Mormon Bibles and oiling their guns. They take turns standing watch and just before dawn bring in a kid they catch near the ranch house. He's a sullen piece of work, but he confirms there's less than twenty men bunking at the Clegg place and they ain't expecting us.

"They're mostly drunk," the kid says.

Wayne Webster shakes the others out of their blankets, and they get their gear together. I'm impressed with the way these boys start out, slick and quiet, without the usual lollygagging cowboys are fond of on the trail. Hershel leads everybody in a prayer again and says, "We'll breakfast, God willing, when the Lord's work is done. Amen."

The men move like gray ghosts against the dawn as we surround the house. When I ask Wayne Webster how he's going to force Brown and the others out, he says, "Easy. Torch the place."

While the rest of us take up positions with our rifles to cover the doors and windows, two Regulators break out cans of kerosene they brought from Cedar City. Others, quiet as Indians, drag hay bales from Clegg's barn, bust them open and pile the hay against the walls. Before they get the kerosene poured and lit, the front door bangs open and a big, beefy fellow with a beard comes out on the veranda. He's barefoot and dressed in dirty long johns, still rubbing the sleep out of his eyes with one hand while he fumbles for his cock with the other. Behind him a woman appears in the doorway and reaches around him, laughing and grabbing after his tool. "Louie, honey, come back inside. I ain't even started!" But he's trying to push her away.

Then simultaneously they both see they got company. The one in his BVDs freezes in a yawn and don't lower his arms, while the woman raises hers as soon as she sees a dozen rifles pointed at her. Wayne Webster steps up to the big fellow, tilts his chin with his rifle barrel and says in a low voice, "The others all asleep?"

He nods, wide awake now, eyes darting from one to the other of us, a little bewildered, but calculating his chances. One of Webster's men ties his hands behind his back while another one grabs the woman, slams her hard against the veranda railing and binds her hands in back too. That's when I see she ain't a woman at all,

but a man in a dress and a shawl. One of the Regulators says it's
Bateman, the wife-killer, wearing his victim's clothes.

Five of the men we catch are wanted for capital crimes in Utah,
including Sam Brown, who is jarred out of his sleep by Hershel
Webster's boot. Ten more are wanted for lesser infractions, and
these are roped together by the neck like goats and shoved into
Clegg's main corral, where rifle-toting Regulators guard them.
When one of them trips and falls, he drags the others down in a
cursing pile, choking in the dust. That's when a hardcase we
missed in the outhouse tries a dash for his horse and runs straight
into the arms of Wayne Webster.

Wayne gives the man a shove that sends him spinning toward
Hershel, who grins and says, "Go on, get! God will never give you
another chance like this." The man hesitates, not trusting his good
luck, but then he takes off like a rocket toward the horses. "Oh,
Lord!" Hershel begins in a prayerful bray, lifting his eyes to
heaven. "Receive this sinner's spirit into your arms, and grant him
your infinite mercy. It is for thy Kingdom, O Lord, that I do this!"
Then he raises his rifle and pumps two bullets into the man's back,
dropping him just as he reaches the horses.

When Sam Brown recognizes Tom Isbell, he let's out a growl of
rage. "There ain't no warrant out on me in New Mexico!"

"Who said there was?"

"Then you got no right. You ain't even a deputy."

"Neither is Lee."

When he sees me for the first time, he don't say nothing, but he
don't have to. His red-veined, evil eyes say it all. Here's a man as
mean as any villain I ever knew, who's been stealing and bullying
and killing since he was a kid. But he's grungy-looking now, trembling like a distempered dog.

The braggart's gone out of him too, yet the eyes tell you he's all
the more vicious when he's cornered. Hershel Webster says he got
fourteen dollars when he stabbed the Apostle to death. The
Regulators know this because the victim lived long enough to
identify him.

So life has treated Sam Brown hard since Jake Williams killed his
brother Arnold. None of his bold schemes has worked out, and not
even his little murders pay enough to keep body and soul together.

"If I didn't know better," Tom Isbell says, his broad Indian face creased in a grin, "I'd almost feel sorry for him."

"Just remember Cody and you won't."

There's another prayer meeting after all the excitement dies down, and a couple of the prisoners are cut loose from the corral and put digging a grave for the one Hershel Webster gunned down. Then four or five of the Regulators cook up a big breakfast, while another bunch starts dismantling part of Clegg's barn and using the timbers to set up a gallows tree. Once again I marvel at the implacable efficiency of these men. No jokes, no kidding around, always dead serious, but they know how to do everything, and do it fast and well. I say to Tom I wouldn't want to get on their wrong side, and he agrees.

While all this activity's going on, the other Regulators are trickling in from where they been guarding the approaches to the ranch, and pretty soon most of them are assembled. Somebody drags Clegg's kitchen table out to the veranda and one of them brings a big ledger from his saddle bag. By late morning they're ready.

The justice of the peace takes charge then. He's a little bandy-legged fellow with rosey cheeks, spectacles and no hair, and wears a fixed kind of know-it-all smile like he faced up to every adversity and won because God was on his side. He calls the men to order, declares his court legally constituted and open for business and reads the names of the men we collected that morning who will now be tried.

Wayne Webster ticks off the first twelve Regulators nearest the judge and they are sworn in as the jury. The lesser charges are dealt with first. When the justice of the peace don't know what a man's crimes are, he asks him.

One kid whines, "I didn't do anything. I'm innocent."

"There are no innocents here," Hershel Webster says.

Then the judge tells the kid, "Consorting with known criminals, aiding and abetting fugitives and lying to this court are all crimes in the state of Utah. How do you plead?"

"Not guilty."

"Gentlemen of the jury?"

The twelve Regulators say, "Guilty," and the justice of the peace says, "One year on each charge to be served consecutively," and they throw the kid back in the corral with the others.

Three years in jail just for being on the Clegg ranch? Before I can make any comment to Tom, he whispers, "Don't say what's on your mind. Just look like you approve."

Finally they drag the Harmon brothers up and the judge says they're charged with sixteen counts of horse theft, how do they plead?

The Harmons are solemn, handsome men in their early twenties, not hard-looking at all. But according to Hershel Webster, who now seems to be the prosecutor, they got a long reputation as cattle and horse thieves, and already served time in the Utah penitentiary.

The younger of the two says, "We're not guilty, sir."

"Sixteen counts," the little judge says, shaking his head but with his smile always in place, "and each one punishable by death."

"Sir," the elder one says, "we didn't steal those horses."

"That's what you'd have us believe, naturally. Because of your youth, and because we can't hang you sixteen times, the court is prepared to show mercy and only try you on one count of grand theft." He peers over his eyeglasses at the other Regulators posing as a jury and asks them, "How do you find the defendants on that count?"

"Guilty."

"Sentenced to be hanged by the neck until dead," says the little judge. "Next case."

There's some arguing then over procedure between Hershel Webster and one of the other Regulators. Hershel says Clegg and Bateman should be tried separately for their killings, but the other fellow says, "Try them together for sodomy and we'll gain time." The judge agrees, so the two men are shoved in front of the group.

Clegg is as surly as he is ugly, a great pig of a man with thick moist lips, a huge gut and bulging, bloodshot eyes. Bateman, the wife-killer in women's clothes, is young and skinny, very coy and feminine in his movements, but with a two-day growth of blond beard and all battered now around the face where a Regulator worked him over.

"Sodomites, how do you plead?" says the little judge, his smile pursed into a sour smirk.

Clegg, who seems to know most of the men present, says, "What difference does it make?"

"Guilty or not guilty?"

"Shit!" says Clegg, and lets go a stream of tobacco juice at Hershel Webster's feet. Young Bateman looks scared, but is trying to maintain some kind of dignity, which ain't easy for a man in a dress.

They're both sentenced to hang with the Harmon brothers, and when the little justice of the peace announces this, Clegg's bravado fails and it's him breaks down and begs them not to kill him, crying and pleading like a baby. When they shove Bateman past me toward the corral again, he's trembling and he's pale enough for a woman, but he don't crack like his boyfriend.

"They saved the worst for last," Tom Isbell says as they prod Sam Brown up to stand before the table on the veranda. The sun is high by now, and most of the Regulators have shed their coats and slickers and are fidgeting around, anxious to get things over with. But the little justice of the peace ain't in no big hurry. He says Sam Brown's charged with the most heinous crime of all. Worse than horse theft, sodomy or ordinary murder.

Then Hershel Webster works himself into quite a state, describing the saintliness of the Mormon Apostle Sam Brown killed. He quotes from *The Pearl of Great Price*, which is one of the Mormon's holy books, and he quotes from the Bible. He also talks a lot of Mormon mumbo jumbo that Tom Isbell explains for me later on the train because he read up some about their church.

I remember one thing because the names was catchy, even if the story's farfetched. This dead Apostle was their great authority on two sacred pebbles called *Urim* and *Thrummim*, which the first Mormon had to put over his eyes to translate the word of God from gold tablets he found in somebody's barnyard. I guess that tale ain't any harder to swallow than the virgin birth, but it's funny what some people take serious.

So killing an Apostle is about the worst crime these Mormons can think of, and when Hershel Webster finally winds down after haranguing Sam Brown for twenty minutes, he says, "The law does not provide a punishment severe enough to fit your crime. All we can do is hang you, and that, God willing, is what we shall proceed to do right now."

But the little justice of the peace whispers in his ear until Hershel scowls at Sam Brown and says, "How do you plead?"

"Not guilty."

"And how do you find him?" Hershel asks the jury.

"Guilty."

"All right, sentence him," Hershel says to the judge, "and let's get on with the hanging."

What they rigged for a gallows tree was two crossbeams from Clegg's barn, set on a couple of posts about twelve feet high. There was no need to build a scaffolding. They just back a wagon under the crossbeams and rig five nooses. Because there ain't room for all five on the wagon at the same time, Wayne Webster decides they'll hang the Harmon brothers first, then Brown, Clegg and Bateman.

They lead the two horse thieves out and help them mount the wagon. Both men are cool and calm, and if they are afraid to die they don't show it.

The elder one says, "We're not too heavy, you know. Is the drop high enough for our weight?"

Wayne Webster says he believes it is. He binds their eyes with handkerchiefs while Hershel prays over them. Neither brother has anything to say. The wagon lurches out from under them, they bounce a couple of times as the beam bends a little and then they're still, twisting a little in the warm noon sun.

When they bring Clegg, they have to half drag, half carry him. He's still crying and pleading for his life. He's sorry for what he done, he says. He'll do penance, he'll make up for it, he'll do anything if they let him live. "Please God have mercy!" he cries as they wrestle him up on the wagon. He only stops struggling when they get the noose around his neck, because he don't want to hang ahead of time. Bateman's still white and trembling but cooperative as they slip the noose over his head and draw it tight under his chin. He asks if he can have his hands free and Wayne Webster says, "It won't help you."

"Please," he says, so Webster cuts the ropes from his wrists.

Sam Brown stumbles as he mounts the wagon, and calls out to me in a hoarse croak, "Don't let them do it, Garland! You know me! I gave you work, helped you when you was a kid! Garland! Talk to them!"

I don't answer him, but I don't take my eyes off him neither as Wayne Webster fusses with the noose until he's got it tight. Luna was right when he said vengeance is best served on a cold plate. Sam Brown's hanging can't bring back my dead friend, but it puts paid at last to all the old anger and frustration.

Why would he think I'd help him even if I could? What a strange notion to enter his head. Yet it enters mine too. I remember the last hanging I seen, when Cody asked them vigilantes to put that poor dummy out of his misery. Just seeing the noose go around Sam Brown's neck suddenly seems to be enough revenge, and if I could of, I would of said, okay, that's it, no need to carry it through to the end. Shows how pity can get the better of your good sense. If ever a villain deserved to hang, it's Sam Brown, and even though I don't relish any man's pain, I got to see this through for Cody.

They tear off part of Bateman's skirt to blindfold him, and when the three are ready, with Clegg still whimpering, the Regulators whip the wagon out from under and they step into eternity. Bateman grabs Clegg's hand in the last second and they stay together like that in death, their necks snapped by the drop.

Sam Brown gets one arm loose as he goes off the wagon and jams his fingers up between his chin and the rope, so he takes longer to die. Tom Isbell and me go off a ways for a swig of bourbon to get the bad taste out of our mouths.

The Regulators torch Louie Clegg's house and barns after that, and leave the five bodies hanging for the buzzards. The trial is recorded all legal back in Cedar City with the names of the jurors and the verdicts and the date and place of execution. The other prisoners are either sent up to the penitentiary or confined in the county jail.

Tom Isbell accompanies the Websters and three other Regulators to the Deseret Bank after I leave Salt Lake, and pays them their five thousand dollars. He told me later that Wayne Webster also hit him for the thirty cents he spent on soap he used to grease the ropes.

I Take a Mistress

Memories keep an old man alive. They're better than books or television even if you can't always trust them. I remember being happy in Tampico after I came back from Utah because I had everything a man could want. Except what I wanted.

For the first couple of years nothing changed except Nora lost the baby she was carrying when we married, got pregnant again and gave birth to a girl we named after Emma Fortescue. Little Emma was a chubby, active child with blue button eyes and a smile that lit up my world. Before she was three she chattered like a bird in two languages, all mixed up, but we understood her well enough. Then we had Ben, who I named after Ben Butler.

By that time some of the novelty had worn off the marriage, although we got along okay and kept each other entertained in bed three or four times a week. Fortland Oil surpassed all my expectations, and Fortescue's too. The company is a money machine and not just in Mexico. The year little Ben was born we moved drilling rigs into the Permian basin around Hobbs, New Mexico, and with the usual Fortland luck, we spud in for ten thousand barrels a day on our third hole. Fortescue is spending a lot of time in Santa Barbara and Houston now, while I'm running between Tuxpam and New Mexico on a regular basis.

I don't mind the time away from Nora so much, because like I said, some of the shine has worn off our romance. And I don't really miss Baby Ben either. Tiny babies ain't as interesting to a man as they are to a woman. But I curse every minute I have to spend apart from Little Emma because she was my big love.

She cried when I went off to work and hugged me when I came home. I pampered her something terrible, yet she was never spoiled because her nature was too good and cheerful. She loved her Mommy and her baby brother, but she loved her Daddy most. When I went on trips I always brought back something for everybody, but the special presents were for her. Nothing thrilled me more than to see her bright smile under a halo of golden curls when I come in the door after being away for a day or a week. "Daddy! Daddy! Daddy! Mommy! Daddy's here!" I was the present she was really waiting for and I never disappointed her. I think Nora was even a little jealous, but she got around it by saying, "Lee, you're playing favorites. Little Ben is glad to see you too, even if he can't tell you about it."

Ben was still in a crib when the Diaz government collapsed and the Mexican Revolution flared up. If ever there was a recipe for chaos and terror it was in that place at that time. Fortland Oil was in the middle of it, and I didn't like leaving Nora and the kids alone once the troubles started. But by that time the company had grown into something of a power in Mexico, so I hired a small army of guards to protect our installations and our families.

The problem was who to put in charge. I thought of Mountain first, but there's a certain amount of administrative work in that kind of thing that he just wasn't equipped for. What I needed was a man who spoke Spanish, who I trusted absolutely and who had army or law-enforcement experience.

"Tom Isbell," Mountain says, and he's right. Except Tom ain't an easy man to find. After we saw Sam Brown off, Tom tried for a while to make a living selling insurance in Albuquerque, but his being Indian put some people off, and besides that he was a terrible salesman because he didn't really believe in insurance. Then he disappears and I hear he's on the road with Buffalo Bill's Wild West Show.

I chase him all over North America by telegram without getting an answer, and nearly give up. Then when me and Fortescue are in New York to sign some oil contracts, I see Buffalo Bill's show is on at the Hippodrome. We go to the Fifth Avenue Hotel before the show and find Tom sipping whiskey in the bar with Mitchell.

The first thing he says is he's been meaning to answer my wires but between one thing and another, he didn't quite get around to it. When Fortescue says we come all the way from Mexico looking for him, he almost dies from embarrassment for causing us such an inconvenience. He ain't sure he wants the job but he's tired of playing cowboys and Indians in a circus tent. Mitchell says he'll take it if Tom don't.

"A famous actor like you?" Tom Isbell says. "Why?"

"The same reason he went to Cuba," Fortescue says. "Adventure."

"Everyone knows I went to Cuba for the money," Mitchell tells us with a wink.

We take in the show that night with Knoblauch and his wife, and watch Tom Isbell and some other Indians in full regalia attack a stagecoach, whooping and hollering like they really mean it. At the intermission Buffalo Bill Cody himself makes an appearance. He's a distinguished, elderly gent with long white hair and dressed in white fringed buckskins. To our surprise he calls out our names as Rough Rider heros of the Spanish-American War, and has the spotlight pick us out of the crowd. There's loud applause and we doff our hats like celebrities.

When we're all having a champagne supper after the show, Fortescue says to Tom, "What about an answer? Are you coming to work with Fortland Oil or not?"

"On one condition."

"Name it," I say.

"Mountain Moore's my partner."

"You got him."

They made a good pair. Tom Isbell had the experience and authority, even if he was just average size and Indian, while Mountain had the biggest muscles in Mexico. Within a year I added a hundred more men, most of them American police veterans or ex–Texas Rangers. We were lucky at first, because the fighting and looting was in the north and west, and not on the east coast where we was. But as the revolution spread, the violence finally reached us. Roaming bands of deserters who called themselves soldiers, bandits and police preying on the nearby rail lines, or the regiment of one general fighting another.

I was rich enough by then to pack it in if I had to, but I considered it a matter of principle to hang on, like I been doing all my life. Like I'm doing now.

Americans had two billion dollars invested in Mexico in those days. Most of it belonged to people like Woodrow Sloan, but a few millions belonged to me and Fortescue. Our Tuxpam field alone was generating revenues for Fortland Oil of more than four hundred thousand dollars a week, and neither me nor Fortescue was about to give up one penny of it. We never thought of ourselves as exploiting Mexico. Hell, the oil was there and we found it while the Mexicans was content just to look on and collect the *mordida*.

We'd been working our tails off ever since we set foot in the country, not just getting rich, but building an industry that didn't exist until men like Doheny and Fortescue came along and invented it. It was them that first chartered tankers to carry the oil direct to the East Coast and organized a chain of filling stations to market our products. Between them they built refineries that were running twenty-four hours a day. It was them, with Levi's help, who kept track of all the money and kept the profits rolling in. We was developers, not exploiters, and proud of it.

And all this while Mexico's falling apart. Madero, the fellow who followed old Diaz as president, was a weakling and a dreamer who tried to please everybody and got himself assassinated by the one who came after him, Huerta, a real piece of work, a vicious son of a bitch who killed anybody got in his way.

By the end of nineteen and eleven, the chaos is near complete. My friend the governor's gunned down in the garden of his residence and gunfire on the streets of Tampico is a regular thing. I tell Nora it'd be better if her and the kids move up to New Mexico until things settle down, but she says she'll stay where she is as long as I do. Four of Tom Isbell's men are on duty all the time at the house, so the family's safe enough, but our social life grinds to a halt. No more going out to parties and dinners because nobody's giving any more parties and dinners. Most of the American families are pulling out, with the men sending their wives and kids ahead, and then following them.

In the summer of nineteen and twelve I finally move Nora and the kids to a beach house at Miramar, six miles north of where the Panuco River empties into the Gulf and out of the way of the revolution. It's pretty, and a lot cooler and healthier than where our house was in Tampico. Little Ben had been sick a lot that year and Nora was worried he'd get one of the summer fevers that was so common, especially among children. He was kind of a scrawny, weak little boy anyway. Not healthy and strong like his sister.

By then the city's swarming with troops and even with Tom Isbell's guards around, there could be trouble. Some of these so-called revolutionary soldiers would just as soon shoot you as look at you. And they wasn't particular about age or sex. They'd rape a woman or kill a kid for no more reason than the hell of it.

I commuted between our Tampico office and the beach house in a Model-T Ford, and tried to spend as much time with Emma and little Ben as I could. The boy had lost some of his frailness and put on a little weight after they'd been there a few weeks. He got some color and his appetite improved with the sea air. But he remained as serious and quiet as ever, and never seemed to find the fun in life little Emma did. She flourished around the water. She loved the beach and the birds. She collected stones and shells and driftwood. She ran and played and shouted and jumped like a regular little tomboy, and she loved her Daddy. Those blue, blue eyes followed me everywhere, and it was easy to see she would be a beauty like her mother some day.

Funny thing about kids. I mean Emma was a love affair for me from the beginning, and Matt, when I got to know him, was another. But Ben and me never quite learned how to deal with each other. I couldn't seem to get close to him no matter what I tried. I mean, when I threw Emma in the air and caught her, she laughed and screamed and wanted more. When I tried the same thing with Ben, he'd cringe and start to cry until I put him down. Nora said he was afraid of me, but even she didn't know why. Maybe it was my rough ways, or because I spoiled Emma, I don't know. There wasn't no psychologist around in those days to tell you what you were doing wrong.

Anyway, that summer started out to be one of the best. Nora was teaching the children how to swim, and they spent hours every afternoon splashing around the surf. We were a happy family on those hot, hazy days, building sand castles at the water's edge. I was a little critical of Nora because she was so free and natural with the kids and I'm a real nervous Nellie. She'd let Emma swim way out beyond her depth and I feared the undertow. I remembered them poor devils drowning when we landed in Cuba.

But Nora was a powerful swimmer and there wasn't any danger as long as she was watching. "You can't raise them in cotton wool, Lee," she said, "even though you'd like to." Then she'd dive in and circle little Emma like a dolphin and the two of them would come out of the water laughing and dripping and making fun of Daddy. I can still hear my daughter's high, piping voice calling, "Daddy! Daddy! I saw a fish jump!" That summer's haunted me all my life, like a beautiful dream that turned into a nightmare.

A few of Caroline's letters from that time are in front of me, some so brown and faded they're barely readable. One carries the date in her strong, clear handwriting, September 14, 1912. "My darling," it says, "I count the days of our separation as a prisoner marks off his sentence. I must discover more urgent business in Albuquerque to get me through the year."

Another, dated a month later, says, "Lee, do you like this new style or is it too daring? I'm thinking of having Madame Lefevre copy it in a crushed silk velvet. Shall I do it in black or burgundy?" Attached is a page from a fashion magazine showing an evening gown with kind of a low front. I remember her in that dress. She wore it to the inaugural ball in Santa Fe when Luna became governor, her hair swept up, her tits squeezed a little together and her throat sparkling with Woodrow Sloan's diamonds. She was my mistress by then, and this is how it happened.

Dave Leahy writes that Sloan is willing to pay two hundred thousand dollars for my old bank stock. I can't believe he would give me a profit like that of his own free will, so it's got to be some scheme of Charlie Bruce's. But I'll take the money. I go up to Albuquerque and ask Dave what's behind it.

"Mrs. Sloan," he says.

"Caroline?"

"The offer came from her, although she's speaking for her husband and has his power of attorney."

"It don't make sense, Dave."

"It does if you know the background."

"I know the lady."

"She hasn't spoken to her brother in a long time because of a family feud, and she'd like a way to get back at him."

"I can understand that."

"Mrs. Sloan calculated correctly that the best way to hit Charlie where it hurts would be through his pocket, and that meant finding out more about the bank."

"Which is where you were helpful." I smile at him. Dave had been representing Caroline on the board at the bank since she stopped speaking to Charlie.

"When I told her about your stock shares, she saw a way to get at Charlie and put money in your pocket at the same time. I gather you two were more than friends once."

"She tell you that?"

"She didn't have to, Lee. I see the way her eyes light up every time I mention your name."

"Charlie won't sit still for this."

"What can he do?"

"He knows if my shares pass to Caroline she could fire him any time she felt like it, so he's got to do something. Come up with a better offer or persuade Sloan to change his mind."

"He can't stop the sale."

"Charlie's smart and he's devious. He's also desperate."

"What do you care what he does? Grab the money and run."

"It ain't like him to take a loss lying down. He must have a round or two he ain't fired yet."

Me and Dave are having a drink in Bungle's bar when Charlie walks in, obviously looking for us. I haven't seen him in years and didn't plan to see him now because Dave is managing everything, but it's impossible to avoid the man in a public place.

"You're looking well, Lee." He stands up to the bar like he just seen me yesterday and nothing ever happened between us. Then he says, "I owe you an apology."

"Is that so?"

He's kind of flushed looking and fatter than ever. Sitting in his banker's chair must agree with him. He says, "I don't know what came over me that time."

"What time was that, Charlie?"

"The day of our unfortunate misunderstanding," he says.

"Are you talking about the day you shot me?"

"A terrible thing."

"Not as terrible as some other things you done." I turn my back on him.

"Lee," Charlie says, "we have to talk."

"No, we don't."

"I thought we could have a drink and sort things out."

I look at him like he's crazy. "I'm real fussy who I socialize with, Charlie, and you ain't on my dance card."

"I understand how you feel, Lee, but I thought enough time had gone by to bury the hatchet. Men of good will should be able to reconcile their differences after so many years. I am truly sorry. Can't we shake hands?" He sticks out his hand, then drops it at his side when I don't take it.

"I have a business proposition for you," he says.

"Here it comes" I tell Dave

Charlie hems and haws and shuffles his feet, and I enjoy his discomfort more than my drink. "Can't we talk privately? It's rather personal." He's looking at Dave when he tells me this.

"Anything you got to say, you say in front of him."

"Lee, you don't need the paltry little profit you'll take from selling your shares to Caroline. You're a rich man."

"No thanks to you," I say.

He takes a deep breath before he says, "I've done a good job of running the bank, if I do say so myself. It's prosperous and it continues to grow. But the time has come to capitalize on a larger scale with a new stock issue, and well, I'd like to offer it to you."

"Why me, Charlie?"

"Your oil company's drilling in the Territory now, around Hobbs. You need a good, solid bank in New Mexico."

"I got one."

"I mean control of one, Lee."

"What will you do with Woodrow Sloan?"

"He has many more important interests. Remember, Lee, he only invested in the bank as a favor to me."

"I thought it was a loan, Charlie."

"Well . . ."

"How come you're so generous all of a sudden?"

"Lee, after my inexcusable behavior, I owe you something. I know you may find it hard to believe in my sincerity, but I was wrong about you and I admit it."

"Amazing how a man's conscience catches up with him under pressure. Between a rock and a hard place, are you, Charlie?"

"I deserve your sarcasm, but I am telling the truth. This really is partly a way of clearing my conscience."

"If pigs grew wings, Charlie, I might believe you. But you and I both know you're full of shit."

He looks around to see if anybody heard me insult him. Always careful of public opinion, old Charlie. Then he gives a weak laugh and says, like we really understand each other after all, "It's also sound business, Lee. You have the capital and I don't. I offer a low-risk investment with a guaranteed high-yield return."

"I'll say one thing for you, Charlie. You don't lack nerve. How much money you after?"

"About a million dollars, Lee. In your financial circumstances, chicken feed."

"And you'd wind up working for me."

"In a sense, I suppose you could say so."

"That's real funny, Charlie."

"Can I count on you, Lee?"

"If I didn't know you better, I'd swear you lost your mind or else this is your idea of a great joke."

"I'd like an answer as soon as possible."

"You can have it right now. No."

"You haven't given it serious study, Lee. Dave has all our annual reports and profit statements. It could be an important acquisition for a firm such as yours and Fortescue's."

"Charlie, I really doubt your sanity. There's no proposition you could make I'd be interested in, short of killing yourself. Face it. You're a stiff-necked, greedy little shit."

"I don't have to listen to that, Garland."

"Correct. But that's the only kind of conversation you'll get from me as long as you insist on hanging around."

"Success hasn't changed you," he says, his face screwed into a real mask of fury by now. "You're the same poor, ignorant, vulgar misfit you always were."

"Wrong, Charlie. I'm a rich, ignorant, vulgar misfit now."

Afterward, when me and Dave Leahy finish laughing, we talk over Charlie's offer. If anybody but him was behind the deal, I'd grab it, because control of a little bank like the Southwest Century could be real useful to Fortland Oil's expansion. But I trust Charlie Bruce about as much as a water moccasin.

"Lee," Dave suddenly says, looking at his watch, "I've got to be at the Santa Fe depot in fifteen minutes. The lady's arriving to terminate the stock purchase."

"Caroline?"

"It's no coincidence," Dave says, "that she's coming while you're here."

"Why didn't you tell me?"

"Because she asked me not to, and I always respect the wishes of a client."

If the King of France, the Sheik of Araby and maybe a couple of Popes showed up in Albuquerque all at the same time, they couldn't attract more attention than Caroline does with her private railroad car, Daimler touring sedan and liveried servants.

I'm on the station platform with Dave when the train pulls in and she steps down in a gray, ankle length Paris gown and a lavender hat with egrets nesting in it. Women carried parasols in them days and she's got a silk one that matches her hat.

Nobody had a better sense of her effect on a place than Caroline. But she only exploited it when she was bored or didn't like the people. Most of the time she looked at the world as if it was a private joke she'd let you in on when she could.

Her smile made you want to hug her, which is what I did. "Lee!" she says, standing back to get a good look at me. "Oh, Lee!" I can't take my eyes off her, because if anything, she's more beautiful than the first time we met, and she's real happy to see me. She tells me our son Matt is twelve now and taller than she is. She didn't bring him with her because he still has school. She also whispers that having him around is the next best thing to having me, and my heart melts.

While Caroline's railway car is being shunted to a siding, I just bask in the joy she brings. I never knew nobody with more enthusiasm, or more talent for enjoying life. Whatever was ordinary or commonplace always took on a new dimension when she was around. She was one of the smartest women I ever met besides Nora and Emma Fortescue, but she never stopped looking and asking. Yet behind all that curious need was a kind of sad inner awareness, like Caroline never quite found out what she wanted to know, or found it out early and was sorry.

Already there's a crowd where the Daimler's being rolled down to the street. The car's about three times as long as a horse, and painted a dark green. Nobody in Albuquerque ever seen a automobile that big. It takes four roustabouts to pull it with Caroline's mechanic-driver at the wheel, wearing a matching green uniform and yelling at everyone not to knick the paint.

There's always a few old Navaho braves in velvet shirts and long hair hanging around the railroad station, selling rugs and trinkets, and for a dime they'll let you take their picture. In them days the Kodak camera had just become popular and nearly everybody who could afford a vacation carried one.

Caroline asks me what I think of people who run around trying to record their lives on photographic film.

"I never thought about it, but I guess it's harmless."

"Like embalming," she says. You could always count on Caroline to come up with something like that. I never been able to look at anybody taking a snapshot since without remembering it.

"At least the Navaho can use the money," I say.

"Are they so poor?"

"Not compared to the Apache. There's nothing more pitiful than an Apache."

"They killed your family," she says, remembering what I'd told her years before, "yet you feel sorry for them. Why, Lee?"

"You would too, if you seen them. A horned toad lives better than they do. They're poor lost devils."

And so it was small talk about Indians that bridged the years of separation and let us look at each other in a way I didn't think would ever happen again. The truth is, we were shy at first. I was almost tongue-tied, even though I'd rehearsed a thousand speeches in my daydreams. She suggested we have tea, and we went into the Harvey House after Dave Leahy took a discreet leave.

For a while the only sound we make is the clink of teacups against saucers. Caroline stares out the window for a long time and I think she's going to comment on the Albuquerque air or the New Mexico sunshine. Instead, she turns back to me and says, "I've never loved anyone but you, and God knows I've tried."

When I can't think up an answer that don't sound simpleminded, she puts her hand over mine and smiles. "Are you happy with Nora?"

"She's a good wife."

"I was wrong to stay with Woodrow, but it's too late now."

"How do you know that?"

"Would you leave Nora and your children for me?"

For seven years I been convinced that's exactly what I'd do if Caroline ever crooked her finger at me again. But now that she's asked the question and wants an answer, I ain't sure. It's a measure of the perversity in a man. Nothing would make me happier than to have Caroline back, and our son Matt with her. But I'd die before I'd give up little Emma. So I guess that's my answer. Before I can open my mouth, Caroline squeezes my hand. "I'm sorry, Lee. What I asked was terribly unfair. I wouldn't like your answer either way."

"Maybe there's a middle ground," I suggest without really believing there could be.

"Why don't we see if we can find it?" she says.

That night I go to her gilded bed in the railway car and we make love as fierce as the first time on the beach in Tampa. We lay in each others arms for hours without sleeping, just letting our skin touch until the excitement draws us together again and again. And every time I start wondering out loud about what we are going to do, she lays a finger on my lips and says, "Shh, my darling. It will take care of itself."

"I can't leave you again," I say, knowing that's exactly what I'm going to do.

"Now it will be different."

"Not if we're apart."

"But we won't be apart, ever again, even though thousands of miles may separate us."

"That's crazy, Caroline."

"Our love is crazy, Lee, but we've both been faithful to it."

"I wasn't. I married Nora."

"But you never stopped loving me."

"Never."

"You see?"

We stay three days in Albuquerque and then spend ten more days in her railroad car, talking and coupling all the way to Brownsville. She was as determined as I was to see all we could of each other, but she was also resigned to remaining Sloan's wife and avoiding any scandal. Otherwise there was no longer anything to keep us apart except distance.

I finished the business with Charlie before we left Albuquerque, or rather Caroline finished it for me. She didn't throw him out as he expected. Instead she elected herself president, reduced his title to manager and cut his salary to a fraction of what he'd been paying himself. A better man would of resigned and gone elsewhere rather than endure the humiliation, but not Charlie. He hung on with the bitter hope that one day he'd get even, but he never did because Caroline was too quick for him.

She refused to vote dividends no matter how much money the bank made, so for a long time Charlie was left like he'd left me. Not exactly destitute, but with a twenty-five percent interest in something he didn't control, couldn't sell and didn't make enough off of to live on. Eventually, I bought out him and Sloan, and Caroline and our son Matt wound up owning the bank.

When was that? I think around nineteen and seventeen or eighteen when I was in the army again and so was Matt. I look at the picture of him awhile before I go poking through the files and letters. Jesus, the things old people accumulate. I got to have a good fire one of these days and burn a lot of this junk. A shopping list from April 14, 1921. Now why in God's name would I keep that? It's on the monogrammed paper that still smells faintly of Caroline and it's in her writing. Then I see she's written on the back of it too. "Dear Mr. Ambassador," it says. "I shall be delighted to accompany you to the president's reception tomorrow evening if you take me to bed the moment we return. I love you. Caroline." That's why I kept it.

The reception must of been the one Harding invited us to at the White House after he named me ambassador to Mexico. I was forty-two years old and we were both still trying to get over the tragedy in our lives. Mexico helped, but it didn't cure the sadness. Nothing ever did.

X X X

Death in Mexico

That summer of nineteen and twelve was a scorcher, humid and heavy with hardly any thunder showers to cool things down. The revolution heated up too, and I was glad I'd moved my family out of the city. We even heard talk President Taft might send marines down to protect American interests. Nora and the kids spent most of their days splashing around the water's edge to stay cool, because even the beach house was an oven, while I was mainly running back and forth to Tuxpam, dodging rebel armies.

In August I managed to spend ten days with Caroline back in New Mexico, where we was drilling on our new leases. She was using the bank as an excuse to travel West and nobody except some of the servants was wise to what was going on between us.

I was in her railway car one lazy, hot afternoon in Hobbs, when a telegram from Tom Isbell arrives saying a rebel general has taken over our Tuxpam field and wants two hundred thousand dollars to clear out. I authorize the payment and return to Caroline's arms. Then another telegram comes saying the rebels now want half a million. That was steep, but we could still afford it a lot easier than having them around.

I telegraph Fortescue in New York to call President Taft and get a formal protest filed with the Mexican government, even though it's probably a waste of time. If the government had any real power down there, this kind of thing wouldn't happen in the first place.

When I tell Caroline what's going on, she says, "You have to go back, Lee. I understand." We had planned to spend a couple of days exploring the Carlsbad Caverns, but decide there will always be another time. Having made up my mind, I'm sitting on her bed half naked, pulling on my britches while she's running her fingers over my back.

"I ain't going nowhere if you keep that up," I tell her.

"Then I'll stop."

"No, keep it up."

She laughs and when she jumps up, I grab her in my arms. She's wearing one of them filmy peignoirs, and God she was exciting to hold. I got a hard-on like a barber pole from her tickling, and it just slides in easy between her legs because she's ready. "I want it, I want it, I want it!" she's breathing in my ear, her tongue and lips trying to swallow me.

"You got it," I say as it goes in and I lift her off the floor on my cock. I even feel something stirring down there right now thinking about Caroline's little honeypot and remembering how sweet it was all them years ago.

Funny part is we're screwing like two beavers standing up. I mean I'm standing while she's riding me now, with her calves locked around my waist, her hands behind my neck, and my britches down around my ankles. That's when the door opens because we forgot to lock it, and her English butler's standing there. Like a damn fool, I take a step to shove him out, which trips me up and sends us sprawling on the carpet. I'm still inside Caroline and she's looking upside down at the butler over her head when he says, "Excuse me, mum. I thought you'd gone out," and backs away, closing the door like nothing happened.

"Now what?" I say.

"Finish what you started," she gasps, grinding against me harder than ever.

"What about him?"

"You're all I can handle at the moment," she giggles.

But it takes me a while to recuperate from the shock. I can still see that fellow standing there in his white gloves and cutaway coat, not a wrinkle of surprise on his face, like he sees people doing it on the floor every day, It's something they learn as kids, the English, not to show emotion. I seen it in France in the First War, their dead piled up like cordwood, and the wounded muttering things like, "Good show!" or "Bad luck, mate!" or "Chin up!" They never shed a tear or cursed even when they was shell-shocked so bad they couldn't hold their cigarettes. Funny people, the English.

"Will he talk?"

She shrugs. That night I say good-bye to Caroline and spend most of the next five days riding Woodrow Sloan's railroad back to Tampico. The train jerks to a stop every thirty miles where bandits or rebels have blocked the rails. Twice we're delayed by Federal soldiers who drag a few Mexicans off and shoot them by the side of the tracks to impress the other passengers. As we approach Tampico finally, smoke's curling up over the horizon where rebels have set fire to a depot belonging to Doheny's company. Mexico was no place for the fainthearted.

What I find when I get to Tuxpam ain't promising at all. Four of our security guards was killed and seven wounded in the fight with these rebels and we can't take our oil field back by force because these bastards outnumber us twenty to one. The American consul tries to talk to their leader, but he only wants to see our money. The consul's the one tells me a formal protest has been delivered to the presidential palace in Mexico City and they've promised immediate action.

That's a joke. Most of the regular troops are busy fighting rebel armies in Chihuahua and Guadalajara, and even though Mexico City guarantees to send soldiers immediately, hell could freeze before they do. So I either negotiate with the bandits who've taken over our property, or it's going to cost Fortland Oil about two million dollars a month in lost revenues.

Levi sets up a meeting in Tuxpam for the next day, and me, Tom Isbell and Mountain ride out to talk business.

They've occupied our administration building as their headquarters and the place is alive with soldiers. Tom estimates fifteen hundred, and we see three machine guns and two artillery pieces besides their rifles and sidearms. What they don't have, according to Levi, is food, and Fortland Oil's been feeding them for the last ten days because they threatened to burn a rig.

I expect to meet some potbellied greaser with long gray mustaches and a sabre dragging on the ground, but the general who receives us ain't like that at all. About thirty, he's as thin and white as a bleached bone, with short-cut hair, a moth-eaten goatee and the deep-sunk, suspicious eyes of a real fanatic. He's wearing a faded khaki uniform with one of them big German automatics in a shiny black holster, and chain-smoking American cigarettes he stole from our commissary. He introduces himself as General Romero, and the pistol ain't the only German thing about him.

Standing next to him is an officer looks like Kaiser Will, with dagger mustaches, a monocle and a tailored uniform so trim he surely can't sit down without taking it off. He's even uglier than Romero, with a pockmarked face, little piggy eyes and a shaved head. He says in funny English, "I am Major von Witte, chief of staff and interpreter. At your service, gentlemen." His heels click together as he makes us a little bow.

I explain we don't need no interpreter because we all speak Mexican, but this von Witte hangs around anyway and his boss don't seem to mind.

Romero gets right to the point, and the price has gone up again, this time to a million dollars. "We can't pay it," I tell him, without sitting down.

Holding his cigarette between his teeth, and looking straight at me as the smoke drifts up past half-closed eyes, he says, "I know you are stealing from Mexico. Major von Witte has examined your records."

"But he hasn't examined my expenses," I say.

"I can set fire to everything."

"We're insured, General, and troops are on their way."

Romero smiles at my great sense of humor, but he don't say anything. His mouth is too wide and thin, and looks like a shark's. The German says, "Mr. Garland, the general is willing to negotiate if payment is immediate."

"A million dollars is out of the question."

"For your safe return to Tampico?"

"So that's how it is."

"That is how it is."

"And if I don't pay?"

"You remain with us until someone does."

I've done some dumb things in my life, but walking into that rebel headquarters when they had me by the short hair is near the top of the list. Like Luna used to say, I was so cocky—hubris he called it—that it never crossed my mind anything could happen. This von Witte is all of a sudden real friendly and offers me a drink of my own whiskey. He says there's no reason why we shouldn't be released the next day, if the money arrives.

"No money will come unless I bring it," I tell them.

And the general says, "Send someone with your instructions. I'll give him an armed escort."

"If you want it in silver," I say, "it has to come from San Luis Potosi by train. It will take many days and weigh tons."

"So you agree to the million dollars?" Romero says, his shark's smile in place again.

"Do I have a choice?"

At that point Levi has another suggestion. Instead of sending a trainload of silver down to these bandits, let's propose an irrevocable draft payable to General Romero at any office of the Chase Bank, which is where we do business.

We spend a sweltering afternoon arguing the matter. Because Romero has to pay his troops in hard money, I finally agree with von Witte to get forty thousand dollars in silver immediately and the rest in bank paper Romero can draw on later to finance his revolution. What I know, but Romero don't, is that the minute we get out of this place those bank drafts won't be worth two cents, because the code Levi will use when he requests them will make them revocable on my say-so.

In the end, I stay with Tom Isbell while Mountain and Levi go back to Tampico. The general's occupying the quarters I usually use when I'm in Tuxpam, but the German turns over his rooms to me and Tom. This is no act of generosity. We're easier to guard that way. My chances of getting away are slim because all fifteen hundred rebels know who I am by now. My height and my blond hair stand out too much.

Nothing's more depressing than a huge oil field shut down, with all the derricks idle. I pass the time going from rig to rig and talking with the handful of employees they kept prisoner after they took the place over. The workers think things will get better in a hurry now that the boss is here, and I try not to disabuse them of this notion because I want to keep their spirits up. Walking around gives me a chance to see how the rebels are armed and organized, which don't help my confidence either. Mostly they got modern Enfield rifles and no shortage of ammunition. They stay pretty clean, don't drink much and show better discipline than your average Mexican soldier. I calculate it's probably because of this fellow von Witte, who I see drilling them every day.

I wonder what a German officer's doing in a rebel camp, and I figure he probably got kicked out of the German Army. What I don't know then, and nobody knew, is that there's Germans like him scattered all over Mexico as part of the Kaiser's policy. That crafty old bastard was already planning to go to war with France and England, and knew he'd have to fight America too, sooner or later. So he wanted Mexico on his side, whoever won the revolution.

I got cigars and whiskey and Tom Isbell for company. Three days pass with no word from Levi, and I'm beginning to wonder if there's a hitch in our plan. On the third night von Witte invites us to play poker with him and some of the other Mexican officers. I go along but Tom stays in the room still trying to come up with a good escape plan. I don't tell him he's wasting his time because he feels bad about letting me walk into this trap. As chief of security, he says, he should have kept me out of trouble.

The general don't show for the poker game, because according to von Witte, he's entertaining a lady friend. Most of the others seem to be afraid of the German because of his influence on Romero. By two in the morning, I'm winning a few pesos and everybody's drunk. Von Witte is uglier than usual in the flickering light from the kerosene lamps. He's also drunker than the rest, his starched tunic hanging open and spotted with spilled booze and sweat.

He's a lousy cardplayer and after losing two hundred pesos in one pot, he throws down his cards and says he don't want to play anymore. I figure the night's over, but the German lays an unsteady hand on my arm and says, "Now we play a man's game, ya?"

There's some nervous laughter as he staggers around the table, looking at each one of the officers. Only one young captain looks back at him. His skin's dark as an Indian's, but he's got clean, handsome features, and trouble lurking behind light blue eyes. The German stops in back of his chair and runs his hands inside the captain's blouse, massaging his chest in a overfriendly way. Then he leans down like he's going to kiss him, and comes up waving the captain's revolver, grinning like a lunatic. For a second I think he's going to shoot the man, but instead he dumps the cartridges on the table. He has some trouble putting one back and closing the cylinder before he spins it, cocks the gun and aims at me. I feel my balls rocket into my guts but I don't flinch. I'm looking at the gun barrel wavering back and forth, and all I can hope is he'll hit an empty chamber.

Click!

I breathe again.

"Bravo, Senor Garland!" the son of a bitch says. He looks around drunkenly and cocks the pistol again. One fat, middle-aged officer starts to push himself away from the table, and von Witte shouts, "Everybody plays!"

"But, Major," the officer protests, and the German points the gun at him and pulls the trigger. Another click as the fat fellow sags white-faced in his chair. I'm thinking that unless this madman passes out soon, somebody's going to get hurt. I didn't come down here to play Russian roulette, but it looks like I'm included in the fun whether I like it or not.

Only it ain't Russian roulette, it's Mexican roulette. Like most Mexican pastimes it gives you a chance to kill somebody before you get killed yourself. The German spins the revolver on the table and it points to a scared young lieutenant who picks it up like it's going to burn his fingers. He twirls the cylinder, cocks the pistol, takes a deep breath and throws it in the air. It strikes the middle of the table and the hammer clicks home, again on an empty chamber. Too bad because the gun was pointing at von Witte. He laughs and picks it up, repeating the procedure. Again it lands with a click, this time pointing at me.

With the gun in my hands, I entertain the idea of making a break for it. But with one bullet I wouldn't even reach the door. I spin the cylinder, cock the pistol and toss it.

BOOM! And everybody ducks. The bullet slams into the wall between the blue-eyed captain and the petrified lieutenant. The captain smiles as he picks up the gun while the others laugh with relief and everybody pays me ten pesos because it was a live round but harmless. One of the officers tells me the game ends only when somebody gets hit. The whiskey bottle goes around again and the captain tosses the pistol.

For an hour this craziness goes on, and as much as I have to drink, I never had a clearer head. Every time somebody throws that damn pistol in the air, enough adrenaline pumps through my system to sober an elephant. I'm pouring a whiskey when the gun falls on another empty chamber, this time pointing at the fat officer who didn't want to play. He picks it up and his hands are trembling so bad he can hardly pull the hammer back. The German sees this and taunts him for being a coward.

"Go on, throw!" von Witte shouts, saliva spraying from his ugly mouth, the veins standing out on his shaved head as he leans over the table. We all tense again as the fat fellow tosses the pistol in a small arc and it lands with a *BOOM!*

The shot couldn't of been better aimed if the fat officer had been trying. It blows away part of von Witte's hand, which was holding his whiskey glass, and goes into his head from under the jaw. He jerks backward a step or two before he falls, blood pouring from his mouth.

The silence that follows lasts maybe a minute, and at first nobody moves toward von Witte.

Then the blue-eyed captain begins to laugh. Lightly at first, but it gathers force until he's almost doubled up with tears and trying to catch his breath. The others laugh too, and soon they're clapping the fat officer on the back and drinking his health. I mean they break out another bottle of my whiskey and slop the booze all around, and the fat fellow's grinning like he's the biggest hero of the revolution. It's their own relief they're drinking to. I never seen a bunch of men so terrified of anybody as they were of this von Witte, and now they know he's in no condition to bother them anymore.

The German ain't dead yet, but sort of twitching and moaning, convulsing on the floor with his eyes open, and his arms and legs jerking like a spastic. The captain rises, picks up his revolver and loads it. He takes three steps to where von Witte is, kneels down and fires a round into the German's ear.

As he holsters the pistol, he says to the scared young lieutenant, "Go tell the general." The kid makes his way to the door, gripping the chairbacks all the way to support himself because suddenly he is very drunk.

I could of walked out of there then, because none of them paid any attention to me, but I didn't see how I'd get past the sentries around the perimeter fence.

I go back to the room where me and Tom Isbell sleep at the end of the building. The guard's dozing outside the door. I step around him, expecting to find Tom, but the room is empty. That don't make a lot of sense because the window's barred on the outside, so he has to be in there. When I go back to prod the guard awake, he rolls over with a bloody hole between his shoulder blades, as dead as Major von Witte.

It seems Tom got away by himself. My mind's racing a mile a minute as I take the Mexican's revolver and gunbelt. Do I stay and risk what General Romero may do to me in the morning, or do I run for it? They probably won't shoot as long as I'm worth big dollars. But it's dark as pitch out there and it might just happen by accident. On the other hand, I got a six-shooter in my hands and a belt full of bullets. I'm young, I'm fast, I'm full of fight, and it ain't in my nature to hang around waiting for somebody to find a dead guard and come after me.

While I'm debating exactly which is the best direction to bolt in, there's a hell of an explosion a few hundred yards away on one of the shut-down rigs. I watch the night sky light up as a huge sheet of gas flame billows from behind the nearby buildings.

My first thought is that the goddamn rebel general's decided to torch the place after all. Then I see soldiers come running and tumbling like mice, most of them half dressed and half asleep, and I realize nobody knows what's happened so it had to be an accident. Probably one of the terminal valves was badly shut down and an accumulation of gas at the wellhead caught a spark. But before I can get used to that idea, another big bang lets go and then a third explosion farther down the field, and I know I'm not listening to a coincidence.

Move your ass, Garland, I tell myself. If you got a chance of getting out of here, it's right this minute in all the confusion. Tomorrow's time enough to puzzle out the cause. I start for the perimeter fence with my hat brim down and my shoulders hunched, glad to see most of the soldiers are heading in the direction of the fires. For a couple hundred yards I'm okay. They're too panicky to pay me any attention, and luck is with me because by now the front gate's shrouded in heavy black smoke drifting from the nearest burning rig.

But it don't work. Three Mexicans in a Model-T truck pull up alongside me. One of them with a rifle hops out right in my path, and I draw. But it ain't a Mexican, it's Tom Isbell in a rebel uniform.

"What the hell!" I say.

"Lee, into the back! Quick!"

I stretch out in the flatbed of the Model-T and the driver guns the motor as we go careening toward the gate. He crashes right through and there's some shots, Tom shooting from the truck cab, and three or four bullets slamming into the boards around me. But in a minute we're out of there and bouncing down the Tampico road. A mile or so later, we stop and I get into the cab, laughing, while Tom climbs in back. The driver turns out to be Mountain Moore and the one next to him is a girl.

I ask him, "What're you doing here?"

"Fortescue's idea. He sent dynamite instead of money."

"So it was you knifed the guard. I might of known."

"Damn good throw too. While I went looking for you she was sucking the general's cock. She ain't as young as she used to be, which is why his concentration wandered and he nearly got me." He shows me a bloody gouge where a bullet creased his forearm. "Say hello to Mr. Garland, Rosie."

I take a second look and see she's a little the worse for wear since the last time we run into each other, but it's Rose-of-Sharon Moriarty all right, no mistake about that.

"Sorry to blow the wellheads, Lee," Mountain says, "but I had to get their attention before we could get you out of there."

When I ask Rose-of-Sharon what she's doing in Tampico, she gives me her typical answer. "It's where the money eez, Garland, don't you know?"

"Did they run out of money in Texas?"

"The Texans deported her," Mountain says, "because she couldn't learn their language. No more fooky-fooky for them."

"Very funny. Weethout me tonight, you would be one dead duke." She lights a cigarette and gives my knee a squeeze as we bounce along the road.

"That's duck, not duke," Mountain says.

"Anyway you're not dead," she says in Spanish. "Like Romero."

"Well, she did a hell of a job," Mountain admits. "It was her idea to keep old Romero occupied while we went looking for you."

"I do it for Garland," she says.

"I appreciate your sticking your neck out," I tell her.

"More like her tongue. She'll cost you, Lee. Watch out!"

"Not as much as them rebels would of."

We roll into Tampico a little after sunrise and I go by the Fortland Oil Building to clean up and change before driving out to the beach house. One of the guards brings me some hot coffee as I strip off my shirt, and Levi's waiting when I walk into my office.

"That's one million we won't be paying," I tell him, "even if they burn Tuxpam to the ground."

"Lee, sit down."

"I ain't tired, just mad as hell at myself."

"Lee, I got something to tell you."

There's a special quaver in his voice that tells me this ain't just ordinary bad news, it's worse, like when he told me about Cody. I put the coffee cup down and look at him.

He turns away and I see he's starting to cry.

"What is it?"

"I ee . . . I'm awful sorry . . ."

"What is it, goddamn it! Something happen at home?"

"It's little Emma, Lee."

"What's wrong? What is it, Levi! Is she sick?"

"I'm sorry, Lee."

"No!"

"Yesterday afternoon. Nora tried to save her but she was too late. Poor little darling drowned in the sea."

I am numb with disbelief. My little Emma dead? Impossible! Daddy's little girl gone swimming on a summer afternoon? Gone forever? *Daddy, Daddy, Daddy! I saw a fish jump!* Oh, my baby! My poor, poor, poor little baby!

I want to die.

XXXI

Seeds of Doubt

I don't remember too much of what happened in the days that followed. There was the funeral, and I looked on her tiny body in the casket, so frail she seemed now with her eyes closed, her cheeks pale as porcelain and her blond curls streaked platinum from the summer sun. She was six and we buried her in a satin party dress she loved. Nora held up okay until it was over, then collapsed in her room and I called the doctor. We didn't say a word to each other the whole time, didn't embrace, nothing.

I didn't want to blame her, but I suppose I did in a way, although never as much as she blamed herself. I stayed drunk for a month, couldn't eat, didn't work, tried not to think, just numbed myself with booze and wept, and sobered up and wept again. There's no wound so deep as the death of a child because there's nothing worse in this world. Nothing. The despair you feel has no bottom, and the anger has no place to go.

Nora came out of her own grief slowly and with a lot of help from our son Ben, but we wasn't a family anymore without little Emma. It was me alone and Ben with Nora. I even found myself thinking the worst possible thoughts, resenting that little boy because he was alive and my Emma was dead.

As the months passed, I made excuses to be away as much as possible. When Nora finally said she wanted to get away too, and take Ben to New York, I had no objection. We both knew it was the end of the marriage, but I didn't care and I guess it was easier on her. She had enough trouble handling her own guilt without having me around thinking all the time if she'd been more careful, or if she'd done this or not done that or got there sooner, our little girl would still be alive.

I couldn't go back to Caroline at first, but she was the one pulled me out of it finally. She and Matt. I had to be in New Mexico a lot, with our new Hobbs field coming in, and when she traveled West for Luna's inauguration as governor she brought Matt with her. I had promised Caroline not to tell him I was his father, at least until he was grown, but he was sprouting into a man already, tall and lanky, and the resemblance was obvious to other people even if he didn't seem to notice.

I brought them up here to Eagle Nest where we spent some days riding Hernan's horses and stuffing ourselves with Mama Montoya's Mexican cooking. Matt was a natural rider and a good shot with a rifle. I taught him how to throw a rope and showed him Ben Butler's kindly style of breaking mustangs. In the evenings, we played seven-card stud for pennies, or sat around telling tall tales. He had as much fun as any healthy fourteen-year-old can have in the West, and so did I just watching him.

When we went deer hunting he bagged a twelve-point buck with a clean neck shot from four hundred yards. Damn, I was proud of that boy! He had his mother's enthusiasm for life, and her good nature too, not spoiled in spite of all the money he was used to, and game for anything.

On the way back from our hunt, packing his deer on a spare horse, we stop at the cabin where me and Mountain passed the winter sixteen years before. It's freezing cold so I build a fire in the hearth. Hernan kept the place stocked with staples for when he hunted here. I find coffee and sugar and we sit in front of the fire, eating the corn dodgers and enchiladas Mama Montoya packed for us before dawn.

I tell Matt about the time the wolf nearly had me for lunch and he says, "Weren't you scared?"

"Never been scareder." I open my shirt and show him the scars where the lobo tore my arm and shoulder.

"Gosh! How old were you?"

"A little older than you."

"Were you on school holidays?"

I laugh. "I was on a permanent school holiday."

He's gaping at the scars and when I tuck my shirt back in he points to another dent in my ribs and says, "Is that a bullet hole?"

"It is."

"Gosh! From the war?"

"No. A fellow shot me in an argument once."

"Did you kill him?"

"I should of, but he wasn't worth killing." I don't tell him the fellow was his Uncle Charlie.

"Gosh! How many men have you killed, Lee?"

"One."

"Only one?" He's disappointed. "What about in the war?"

"That don't count," I tell him. "In a war you're just trying to stay alive, and killing the enemy is one way to do it."

"Why did you kill the man?"

"He murdered a friend of mine."

"Then he had it coming."

"I guess he did."

"Did you shoot him in a gunfight?"

"Yes," I lie, and realize when I tell my own son what I done, that I'm ashamed of killing Alfred S. Sorenson after all these years. For the first time I feel real guilt when I look at that boy's face and wonder what he would think of me if he knew the truth.

"Lee?"

"What?"

"Mr. Doheny told mother how you and he slaughtered a whole lot of Mexicans once on the Rio Grande. Is that true?"

"We got a few."

"He said it was Pancho Villa's army."

"It was him all right, but he was just a bandit."

"How many did you kill?"

"Why are you so interested in a thing like that all of a sudden? Killing men is nothing to be proud of."

"Then why did you do it?"

"Self-defense. They attacked us."

The boy sips his coffee and looks dreamily into the fire. "I wish I'd been there. I wish I could do the things you've done."

"You'll do your own things when the time comes. Don't be in too great a hurry."

He says sadly, "I'll never lead a life like you."

"You'll lead your own. It'll be different because the times are different."

"I don't mean that. I have to finish school, and Yale, I guess. Then into business. There's nothing exciting about that."

"Don't be so sure."

"I'd rather stay here or fight in Mexico or something."

"Don't tell your mother that."

"Oh, she knows me," he says. "She wouldn't blame you."

"Get your education. You got lots of time to find excitement."

"Did you know my mother before I was born, Lee?"

"We go back a long time."

"Before she met my father?"

"That's right."

"Why didn't you marry her?"

"We were hardly more than kids, Matt, and I was going off to the war in Cuba."

He's real thoughtful for a while before he says, "I wish you were my father. Then I could do what I want."

"What makes you think so?" I try to make light of it. "I'm one tough son of a bitch when I put my mind to it."

He smiles and shakes his head, like I can't fool him.

"Your father's a fine man, and he's interested in your future," I hear myself tell him. "You don't want to grow up ignorant like me."

"Nobody knows more about everything than you do."

"Some things maybe. But I never had an education."

"You didn't need one. You always did what you wanted and everything worked out perfect."

"Not so perfect, Matt."

"You're rich," he says.

"That ain't everything."

"What would you want right now, Lee, that you don't have?"

I look at him, this son I love, and think of Caroline waiting for us back at Eagle Nest, and I can only answer the truth. "Nothing, Matt. Nothing at all."

"So, you see?" he says, like he won the argument.

That evening after I help him skin the deer and he goes off to bed happy and exhausted, I sit on the patio with Caroline, holding hands and sipping a whiskey before we turn in.

"You're his hero," she says to me.

"Every kid needs one."

"Did you?"

"I had two. Ben Butler and Luna. What about Sloan?"

"Woodrow has always been good to Matt," she says, "but I'm afraid each is a bit of a disappointment to the other. Woodrow would prefer a certified public accountant for a son, and if Matt could choose his father, he'd choose you."

"He don't have to choose. He's got me."

"Do you think we're doing the right thing, not telling him the truth about us?"

"That's a funny question coming from you, Caroline, since it was your idea in the first place. I always thought you were mistaken, but now that it's gone on so long, I ain't so sure. When we do tell him, he might hold it against us."

"Lee, don't say that."

"I think I would if I was him. I'd feel cheated."

"And you think I cheated him?"

"You know they say good intentions pave the way to hell."

"I could not have done otherwise, Lee."

"Then don't ask me if I think you did right."

We don't say anything more for a long time, but then Caroline gets up and walks around behind my chair, letting her hands run over my shoulders and down my chest. "Do you think we'd still be in love if we'd been married all these years?"

"What've you been drinking, Caroline? Tonight you're full of tough questions."

"Is that a tough question? Yes, I suppose it is."

"It's an easy one." I take both her hands in mine and she leans down to kiss me. "I fall in love with you all over again every day," I tell her, "in spite of your contrariness. And every day I like it better. Ours is some love story, all right. Two idiots pretending to be smart people."

"Do you think the time has come, Lee?"

"The time came long ago. You want me to talk to Sloan?"

"I'll do it," she says finally. "I owe him that. And I'll tell Matt as well."

We leave it at that and the rest of the time we're a happy family. Caroline don't say nothing to the boy yet because she wants to talk first with Woodrow Sloan when she gets back East.

The last few days we spend in Santa Fe as guests of Governor

Luna. Me and him are having a drink in the privacy of his office one afternoon before we all go to dinner to meet his new wife, when he says, out of the blue, "The boy's yours, isn't he?"

I nod.

Luna's standing by the window, looking out at the plaza as the last rays of the sun light his profile. He ain't changed much physically over the years, a little gray maybe, but just as lean and starchy. Only he's mellowed. Politics in a place like New Mexico does that to a man of his quality. The deals and compromises necessary to run a state government don't come natural to Luna because of his honesty and his inflexible disposition. On top of that, New Mexico is a new state then, feeling it's way in the Union, and Luna stands for the Hispanic minority that's mainly poor, don't speak English and think he's a god. It's the god part he finds hard to handle. The old adobe governor's palace is crowded every morning with humble petitioners who don't understand why he can't grant all their little wishes, so he has to spend a lot of time explaining how democracy works.

Meanwhile he's surrounded by professional politicians like Al Fall, who helped put him in office, and they got their special needs and constituencies too.

"You want to tell me about it?" he says, meaning about Caroline and Matt.

So I do tell him, from that day on the hotel veranda in Tampa when Caroline threw herself into my arms and Luna suggested we find a private place to talk, down to our present dilemma.

"All that boy has to do is look in a mirror and know he's your son," he says when I finish. "He's the image of the kid I once saved from Alfred S. Sorenson."

"Well, Matt don't know it yet."

"How do you think Mr. Sloan will take the news? You're a big fish now, Lee, but he's still a great deal bigger. Does he know what's going on between you and Caroline?"

"I don't think so."

"Maybe he knows but doesn't care as long as you're discreet and keep things this way. On the other hand, maybe he'd care a whole lot if you made a public fool out of him."

"Not much he can do either way."

"The only thing has more fury than a woman scorned," he says, "is a rich and powerful man made to look ridiculous."

"Why would he want to make trouble?"

"Put yourself in his place."

"What can he do?"

"What can't he do is more like it. With his resources?"

"That don't scare me off, Max. I got more money than I know what to do with."

"Not his kind of money."

"It ain't a factor, Max. Believe me."

"Suppose he decided to put you in the poorhouse."

"You know what I'm worth?"

"Five or six million by now, I reckon."

"Try fifty."

"Well, congratulations. I'll expect a bigger campaign contribution next election. But don't get cocky, Lee. Woodrow Sloan is one of the richest men in the country, besides being an intimate friend of President Taft's. He could wreck your relations with the Mexican government or screw up your financing with the big Eastern banks if he decided it was worth it. I wouldn't want him for an enemy."

"Caroline and me can't go on like this any longer."

"What about Nora?"

"We'll divorce. She's well off."

"I hope you know what you're doing."

"Whether I do or not, I'm going to do it."

"What I like about you is you never change," Luna says sarcastically. "Everyone grows older and wiser except Lee Garland. You'll still run any risk to get what you want no matter what the odds. But your confidence in people like Sloan may be misplaced."

"I got to be with Caroline."

"That's something else I want to talk about. I don't know how much time you'll have for her in the next few months."

"Why?"

"I have a job for you."

"I got a job."

"I need you."

"A political job?"

"You could call it that."

"Doing what?"

"Soldiering."

"Are you serious?"

He hands me a fancy parchment all made out in my name, commissioning me a captain in the New Mexico National Guard. When I ask him what it's all about, he says he wants me to take off from Fortland Oil for a month or so and command a detachment of New Mexico cavalry on duty along the border.

"Why would I want to do that?"

"As a favor to me."

"Fighting Mexicans?"

"Scaring Mexicans. Villa's people are raiding across the Rio Grande lately on a regular basis, taking horses and cattle and anything else they want. I promised to put a stop to it."

"Why not Dave Leahy or somebody else with experience?"

"Dave can't sit a horse since he was shot in Cuba, and you have the experience."

"I wasn't an officer and that was a long time ago."

"You know Villa and you know the border."

"I can't leave Fortescue in the lurch. I'm sorry, Max."

"I've already talked to him and he agrees you'll do your oil company more good going after these bandits than working."

"Is that a recommendation or a criticism? Don't tell me. I'll ask Fortescue."

"You've waited fifteen years for Caroline. A couple of more months can't hurt you."

"Are you kidding? They could kill me."

That evening over roastbeef in the dining room of the Exchange Hotel we keep Matt, Caroline and Luna's bride in stitches laughing at our yarns. To hear Luna tell it, the only real war in Cuba was between me and him, and the Dons was just a nuisance we had to put up with while we fought each other.

Matt's tucking into his second plate of huckleberry pie when Luna's secretary appears with a telegram, which Luna reads and passes to me as the women and Matt watch with curiosity. It's from the mayor of Mimbres, New Mexico, a dusty little border town where a band of Mexicans just swept through and stole forty horses, shot two citizens and trampled a child to death on the main street.

"There you have it," Luna says, and we talk about how soon I can leave. Caroline don't like the idea at all, and Matt naturally wants to come along with me. Luna says this raid on Mimbres changes the basic plan he had in mind. What he talked about

earlier was mounting National Guard patrols along our side of the
border for a couple of months. But what he wants now is a reprisal.
Such a thing is totally illegal and we both know it. No governor has
the right to call up state troops for an invasion of a foreign country.
Circumstances, however, determine his course of action. If the
United States Army can't protect New Mexican citizens, then Governor Luna will. He says, "Those bastards have to understand they
can't rob and kill here without paying a price."

I'm sworn in the next day and go on temporary active duty. This
don't mean I head right for the border because there's a lot to do
in Santa Fe first. Half the unit I'm in charge of is already billeted
in Columbus, about ten miles from Mimbres. But the other half is
assembling in Santa Fe: two hundred thirty men. A few are veterans like me, but most are youngsters, and just as eager and full of
spirit as we were when we went to Cuba. They don't know yet what
Luna's got planned, but I can tell them it ain't going to be a piece
of cake.

We're going to high desert country where food, fodder and
water won't be under every tree because there ain't any trees. Just
rocks, cactus and Gila monsters. And to catch the greasers, we got
to be as fast on our feet as they are, and maybe a little faster. At
the end of ten days we embark by train for El Paso with horses,
mules and baggage.

Caroline hitches her private car on the train and Matt rides with
me in one of the troop coaches. They'll continue east from El Paso,
but Matt's almost as thrilled as if he was part of the expedition,
talking with the soldiers and joining in the spirit of the thing.

He begs me to take him along and I have to be careful how I
answer. I can't say a military campaign is no place for a fourteen-
year-old kid, because he ain't an ordinary kid and he knows it. He's
a first-rate rider and a sure shot, and he's got most of his growth
already. Even if he's a little uncoordinated and got no beard, he
can pass for seventeen and looks no younger than some of the
soldiers in the detachment. I put him off by saying this won't be
his only opportunity. The chances are we'll be living with this
border problem for some years to come and I promise when he's
a little older, maybe after he's finished school and it's okay with his
mother, I'll take him along.

That don't quite satisfy his lust for adventure, but he stops
badgering me. What I remember about that conversation was how

grown up he was for his years, like I was at his age. And I remember something else which probably had to do with my losing little Emma as much as it did with Matt and Caroline. I remember the awful fear I had that I could lose them too, the kind of terror that only comes when a man knows so much love and happiness.

Our two-month campaign against Villa turns into six months of frustration. We never really have a chance at him because every time we get word on where he is, he's skipped by the time we get there. If we marched by day, the dust we raised could be seen for miles across the dry alkali flats, and if we rode by night they was sure to hear us. An army on the move clinks and rattles like an old car on a rough road, and we was no exception. The noise of cups, carbines, canteens and harness jingling was our surest advertisement.

It was only on small patrols of ten or a dozen men that we made any contact, and then my people couldn't stand and fight because they was usually outnumbered. But we did have a few brisk skirmishes, and it was in one of them that I renewed my acquaintance with that scoundrel Doroteo Arango, or *General* Pancho Villa, as he was calling himself by then.

I had taken a detail of eight troopers to the mouth of a canyon about ten miles from our main camp to show them how to set up an ambush. We didn't really expect anybody that night, but there was a good chance we'd catch a party of Villista bandits passing the next day because we knew they used that trail. We was carrying our regular weapons plus a light mortar, which two of my sergeants were real handy with. They had about a dozen rounds of high-explosive ammunition and knew how to drop them in a small circle from a two- or three-hundred-yard range.

By ten o'clock we're looking down on this narrow draw, me and my mortar experts on one side, and five troopers with rifles hidden among the rocks of the canyon wall across the way. It's damn near a perfect setup. There's a high half-moon throws a little silvery light on everything, and I've arranged to signal by flares. We can blow hell out of anything passes through this bottleneck at no risk to ourselves, and the men on the other side are under orders not to open fire until I do. The horses are tucked out of sight as we settle down to wait.

The night drifts by real quiet, and a few minutes after dawn, when I'm in a half doze, dreaming about Caroline, one of the sergeants tugs my sleeve and points. Entering the draw is a bunch of men riding four abreast, taking their time, talking among themselves. Through the binoculars, I count sixteen, and in the middle of the first rank I see the familiar face, relaxed, chewing on a chicken leg. He's aged since we last met on the Rio Grande, put on a paunch from too much high living.

I pass the binoculars to the sergeant. "See the fat one in front, second from right, eating his breakfast?"

"General Villa?"

" 'General' my ass."

"He don't look like he'd hurt a fly," the sergeant says.

"No, he'd just pull the wings off it."

"What do we do, sir?"

"Stand by."

The riders get closer until they're nearly in the draw below us, well within range. The mortar's in position and my men are only waiting for the signal to fire. But I want them bastards all the way into that canyon, so when we open up, not a soul will get out alive.

It's then that Arango reins in his mount and looks up at where we are. There's no way in the world he can see us in these dim, early-morning shadows, but he sits his horse real quiet, picking his teeth and wiping a sleeve across his mouth. He turns his head real slow, one way and then the other, looking up like a coyote sniffing the wind, and I get the definite feeling he knows we're here. The son of a bitch always had a sixth sense about danger, which is why he stayed alive so many years. But he was smart too, and saw the possibilities for ambush in that canyon as well as I did. And once he saw them, he decided to turn around and take a longer, safer trail.

The instant I see what he's going to do, I shoot a flare and tell my boys to open fire. If we can't get them all, at least I'll spoil that bastard's breakfast.

The first mortar round is long, and strikes about fifty feet behind them, but the explosion panics their horses. They're rearing and milling around in total confusion when the second round lands practically in their laps. This time one of the animals goes down flailing and screaming, but it's impossible to tell through all the smoke and dust if we got Arango. My troopers open up with their rifles from the other side of the canyon, but they don't have clear targets either, so it's all a matter of luck if they hit anybody.

The noise is something fierce as the explosions echo off the canyon walls, but not until several minutes after the last shellburst does the air clear enough to see how much damage we done. Four horses are down, three Mexicans are dead and one wounded. The rest peg a few shots in our direction before they take off lickety-cut, with Pancho Villa Arango leading the pack.

Even though we didn't get that murderous son of a bitch, the near miss helps relieve the frustration I've been feeling up to then. Hunting him was like squeezing grease. Every time we thought we had him, he gets through our fingers. To complicate everybody's life further, Luna's in trouble with Washington for allowing us to cross the border, even though I deny we ever did.

After Colonel Roosevelt and the Bullmoosers lose the presidential election to that nitwit Wilson, the new Democrat administration decides to cuddle up to the Mexicans. That was just the first in a long list of mistakes the Wilson crowd made in foreign affairs. Jesus, if ever there was a worse collection of pussy-footing, inept, hymn-singing jackasses in charge of the government than them Wilson people, I don't know who they might of been. From their Mexican policy to their insane "Help the Allies but Keep out of the War" policy, to their fourteen points and League of Nations, they was about the most naive, puritanical, dreamy-eyed, feather-minded bunch of pissant bureaucrats any political party ever turned loose on the American people.

There's nothing more dangerous to a nation than a do-gooder with power. Give me a smoke-filled room of political cynics any time and keep your Sunday-school teachers. The world's too harsh a place to let the pantywaists decide who's going to live and who's going to die. But when it does happen it can have results that are sometimes as funny as they are stupid.

After our raid down into Chihuahua, and the partial success of our little ambush, the lieutenant in charge of the regular army detachment at Columbus gets orders to stop any National Guard units from going into Mexico. When I ask him how he proposes to accomplish this, he's embarrassed.

"Them bandits raid our farms and ranches," I say, "kill grown people and children in an American town, and you tell me the regular U.S. Army's going to protect *them* from *me?*"

"I'm sure it won't come to that, Captain."

"That'd give the greasers a laugh. Americans fighting Americans

to save Mexican bandits. They think we're sappy enough, without
giving them any more proof."

"The Mexican government says it will clean it's own house and
has formally protested your incursions into its territory."

"How long you been here, Lieutenant?"

"Two months."

"Then you ought to know there ain't any government in Mexico,
just a bunch of self-styled generals fighting one another."

"Sir, I have my orders. I'm to defend the border and protest
directly to the nearest Mexican military commander if there are
more bandit raids from their side. That is the limit of my authority,
apart from keeping you and your men on our side of the river."

"Do you know who the nearest Mexican commander is? 'General' Villa he calls himself, and it's his men raided Mimbres."

"As I said, sir. I have my orders."

"Well, you better be careful how you carry them out, son, because my men outnumber yours four to one." I telegraph Luna
about the army's attitude and he wires back to stay put for the time
being. A couple of weeks later we're ordered back to Santa Fe and
inactive duty. I'm frustrated and angry, but not at Luna. Our presence stopped the raids for awhile even if we didn't catch anybody,
and now President Wilson's decided Villa's on our side because
he's buying most of his guns in El Paso. I guess the Mexicans figure
there's no percentage in antagonizing us further while they still got
each other to fight.

In Tampico things go from bad to worse. After Mountain killed
that General Romero, another greaser took over his army. We
didn't pay them anything and they didn't wreck our Tuxpam field,
but the lost production hit our pockets hard. The sons of bitches
finally fight a battle with federal troops and lose, which is maybe
worse than if they'd won, because for weeks after that, bands of
armed men roam the countryside, killing and looting around Tuxpam, while the "victorious" government soldiers stay drunk in
Tampico.

By that time, Fortland Oil has hired another sixty guards, most
of whom I handpicked from the men who soldiered with me along
the border. Tom Isbell is practically a general in his own right now,
supervising close to three hundred of these fellows with Mountain,
and the expense makes Levi Hennings wince. But it's worth it
because they keep us in business while things fall apart.

Caroline writes to me regular, and Matt too, and I'm desperate to see them again. She tells me she's talked to Sloan, but she don't tell me what his reaction was. She says it's a long story and best told in person as soon as I can come East, but not to worry. So I worry. I don't want her coming to Tampico under any circumstances, but it's months before things settle down enough for me to get away, and then it's only to El Paso when I get her wire.

Sloan's on business in Mexico because his railroads are being used by both sides of the revolution without any revenue coming in—that's the early summer of nineteen and fourteen—and because his mines aren't producing much either. Caroline comes to El Paso, expecting to have the whole thing out with him after seeing me. She brings Matt, but she hasn't told the boy anything yet.

It's a grand reunion. She takes the biggest suite in the Shelton Hotel and we three have dinner downtown the first night. Across the river then, Villa's army is occupying Juárez after whipping government troops and taking over most of Chihuahua.

Matt loves the story of my time on the border, even though I try to make it sound duller than it was. He's grown another two inches and there's peach fuzz on his chin now. He tells me about his own successes in track and hockey, and how he won a prize that year for a paper he wrote about me and Eagle Nest. He reminds me of my promise to take him the next time Luna needs any services on the border, and Caroline gives me a mother's look that could wither a prickly pear.

After Matt turns in, I slowly undress Caroline. As I run my hands over her and feel her cleave to me once again I know I'm back where I belong. We're both so horny we don't even get all our clothes off before we role onto the bed squirming like a pair of teenagers. She says I'm impossible, that I can't love her as much as I say I do if I let three months turn into nine without seeing her, and I try to explain about bandits and Luna and the damn Mexican Revolution. She kisses me and says, "You'll never change and I really don't want you to, but we must get a better grip on our lives, Lee, if we're ever going to share them with each other."

I'm dying to know what she told Sloan and what he said, but she keeps me in suspense until we're laying there in the dark much later, naked and sweaty after making love for about the third or fourth time, and content for the moment in each other's arms.

"He won't hear of it," she sighs finally, "and I don't know what to do."

"He's got no choice," I say.

"When he refused to give me a divorce, I said I'd leave anyway."

"Did you tell him about me?"

"I didn't have to. He already knew."

It's like Luna suspected. Sloan didn't get where he was in the business world without a good spy system, and they reported to him the first time Caroline and me fell into bed together. I remember the time the butler walked in on us and wonder how much Sloan was paying him on top of what Caroline gave the man. He could of been photographing us the whole time with a Kodak and passing the pictures on to Sloan.

"He told me he didn't object to my taking a lover because he could never be a proper husband to me, but he insisted the marriage must continue as it is. If I choose to leave him in spite of this, he'll cut me off without a penny."

"It doesn't matter."

"And he'll keep Matt."

"That's up to Matt."

"Not yet it isn't. Matt's only fifteen, and until he turns twenty-one, Woodrow has complete control over him."

"And if Matt decides to come with us?"

"Woodrow will disinherit him."

"I'm a rich man, Caroline. Whatever I've got is yours and Matt's as well. You don't need Sloan's fortune."

"It's not that at all, darling. It's simply that I've never seen Woodrow in such a fury. He's normally a very steady person. Stiff, but willing to listen to reason. Not this time. He said if I ever considered abandoning my position as his wife and taking Matt away, he'd ruin us all."

"And you're afraid of him."

"You have no idea how enormously powerful he is, Lee. And vindictive too. I've seen him drive competitors into bankruptcy in order to take over their assets. God knows what he'll do to you."

"He can't do anything to me."

"He can do what he wants to anyone he chooses."

"Come on, Caroline. I'm not afraid of Woodrow Sloan."

"He's one man you should fear, darling."

"What's the alternative?"

"To go on as we were. He'll allow me all the freedom I need as long as we don't appear together in society. He's traveling at least six months of the year anyway and I no longer accompany him. It isn't the happiest arrangement, but we could manage it, Lee, at least until Matt is a little older."

"Suppose I talk to Sloan."

"He won't listen. I know him."

She was right about most of what she told me. But Sloan was willing to listen. I crossed into Villista territory the following day and rode a troop train that took forty hours to get to Chihuahua city, where he was holed up in a huge suite at the Victoria Grande Hotel. Right away he offered me a drink in that thin, high voice he has, asking me how the Tuxpam field was doing.

"I didn't come here to talk business," I tell him.

"A social call then?" he says. Most of his hair's gone, and the baby face I remember is lined and crinkly like parchment.

"Caroline told me she spoke to you."

He don't say a word, and I notice for the first time that he don't have any beard, I mean none at all, like a woman, but his eyes are as hard as little stones when he looks at me, and I'm wondering who does he remind me of?

"We want to know what you plan to do."

"Do?" he says with a puzzled frown. "About what?"

"Caroline and me."

"Don't tell me you crossed war-torn Mexico to talk about your tawdry pursuit of my wife." He's got big hips, small shoulders and fleshy pink hands that look like they been in water too long. He passes me a tumbler of whiskey and perches on the arm of a sofa where he can look down at where I'm sitting. When I once described to Pete how Sloan looked then and how he couldn't function as a man, Pete said it sounded like a glandular problem, but I don't remember which gland.

"She wants a divorce," I say, laying it out. "She's told me you won't give her one and that if she leaves you, you'll make things hard on her and the boy."

"Indeed," says Woodrow Sloan. He gets up and walks around the room, holding his glass in both hands and nodding to himself like he's deep in thought. "I'll ignore your intrusion into my personal affairs for the moment because you seem to be under the illusion you have some rights here. We'll get to that, of course, but first I want you to be as accurately informed as possible." He don't look at me, just keeps circling the room slowly, and I'm still trying to think who he reminds me of. When he stops finally, and watches me over his drink, I remember. He reminds me of Alfred S. Sorenson. Not in looks so much as texture, with his wispy fringe of hair, crinkly, pink skin and tinny, high-pitched voice. "Just how well do you know Caroline, Mr. Garland?"

"What's that got to do with it?"

"I've known her since she was a child. She has a vivid imagination, a taste for romance and a keen interest in her own comfort. Do you know the story behind our marriage?"

"Maybe I know it better than you."

"I doubt that."

"I know you're not Matt's father."

"And you're going to tell me who is?"

"I don't think I have to."

"Of course you don't. For reasons that don't concern you, I was unable to father a child of my own, but that is really beside the point. Matthew is legally my son and that's the end of it. And Caroline is my wife, and that's the end of that, too. I asked how well you knew Caroline for a reason. You may think you alone exist for her, Mr. Garland, as her lover or stud or whatever you call yourself, but you are one among many."

"Just a goddamn minute, Sloan!"

He raises a wrinkled pink hand as he circles away again to put some space between us. "That shocks you, does it? Good. One illusion less. Caroline is not the innocent prisoner of this marriage you seem to believe. In fact it is she who insists on continuing it because she requires the protection it offers in order to pursue her erotic adventures with other men."

"That's crap, Sloan, and you know it."

"I indulge her as long as she doesn't embarrass me."

"Give her a divorce, or I'll be the one who embarrasses you."

He smiles at that, but not because he thinks it's funny, just ridiculous. "Try to understand one thing, Mr. Garland. In no recent conversation with Caroline has she even mentioned you, although I've known about your relationship since it started. Nor did we ever discuss the possibility of a divorce."

"That's a lie."

"Caroline's the liar. She is a vain and selfish woman dedicated to her own pleasures and interests. Don't you see how her mind works? She thinks quickly but not deeply, although she has moments of perception that give her a reputation for sharpness she doesn't deserve. She's had you fooled for years."

XXXII

Matt Finds Out

I knew the son of a bitch was lying, knew it in my heart, but he succeeded in one thing. Whether I liked it or not, he had planted the first niggling suspicion I'd ever had about Caroline. I didn't believe it about her having other men. But I did wonder if he wasn't telling a half-truth when he said she was as responsible as him for wanting to keep their marriage going.

So the only thing I accomplish with Sloan is to unsettle my own mind. Back in El Paso, she says nothing to Matt and persuades me to carry on as things are for the time being.

Oh, Caroline, what fools we were to drift like that, to let so many years pass! I don't know why I let you talk me into it. A month here, a week there, sometimes with Matt and more often without him because school or friends or Woodrow Sloan always intervened.

By nineteen and fifteen our wells around Hobbs and Artesia, New Mexico, were producing as much as the Tampico and Tux-pam fields, and Fortescue and me were recovering some of what we'd lost because of the Mexican trouble. I was back and forth to New York, where I saw Nora and my son Ben, who turned six that year, a week after our divorce decree. A serious little boy, very polite and well brought up, but a stranger to me, and that's how we remained for years.

Business took me to Washington because of war contracts to supply oil. Al Fall was in the Senate by then and a great help to

418

us. Fortescue's father had died the year before, changing Emma from merry wife to merry widow. While Nora and my son Ben lived in the Fortescue New York mansion, Emma leased a Washington town house, and directed her extraordinary energies into Al Fall's political career. His wife stayed in New Mexico, and he kept discreet bachelor's quarters in the capitol, but if you wanted him any time after six in the evening, you usually found him at Emma's.

In the autumn I returned to duty with the National Guard, this time as a lieutenant colonel on the staff of General Funston, who had charge of keeping peace along the border. Once again Pancho Villa was the cause, and once again I did it as a favor to Luna. The Villista raids had escalated over the past year until the whole lower Rio Grande valley was living in terror.

At Doyles Wells, near Hachita, New Mexico, in January of nineteen and sixteen his men kill four cowhands and burn several farms and ranches. Over in Texas they strike in a dozen more places, taking what they want, and robbing and killing. In Glenn Springs four soldiers, three civilians and a child are gunned down by the bastards. And while Doroteo Arango laughs up his sleeve at us, President Wilson dithers in the White House, writing letters to the German Kaiser, asking him to please stop encouraging the greasers in their depredations.

About this time, when I'm based in El Paso but moving around to inspect the garrisons of the border towns, I get a telegram from Caroline, who's up in Alburquerque, saying Charlie Bruce dropped dead. Needless to say, I wasn't too broke up about his passing. Caroline cried a little when she joined me in El Paso, remembering the brother she once loved, but she's mainly upset about something else.

"Have you seen Matt, Lee?"

"How could I see Matt if he's at Yale?"

"He's here. In the army."

"Our Matt?"

"You've got to find him!" Matt is seventeen by then, and he dropped out of college to join up without telling anybody. After a two-day search I track him down in a machine gun company at Fort Bliss. He's tanned, lean, fit and happy as a bird.

"Hi, Lee, Colonel, sir." His smile lights up his whole face when he sees me, and we throw our arms around each other. I tell him his mother's having a conniption fit because of what he done. "But

I told her I was going to do it," he argues. "I don't know why she's so surprised."

"When did you tell her? She didn't know a thing."

"Ages ago at Eagle Nest. Don't you remember?"

I get him transferred to my detachment and assigned to my headquarters when we move to Columbus. At least that way I can keep an eye on him and see he stays out of trouble.

Caroline ain't happy about either of us being in the army, but I make her see it's only temporary, and my having Matt with me is the best arrangement we can invent under the circumstances. He's as stubborn as she is or I am, and determined to prove himself. I'm just trying to cover his ass while he has his great adventure. I can't bear for anything to happen to that boy any more than his mother can, so I don't intend to let him out of my sight. The day we say good-bye to Caroline, she can hardly speak for the tears, but she says, "Lee, I hate you at this moment," and she looks at Matt and adds, "I hate you both."

"You're just jealous, Mother," Matt says, grinning, and that starts her tears again.

I put my arms around her without thinking about Matt being there and say, "Don't worry, darling. We'll look after each other."

Early in March we're receiving reports that Villa's lurking just over the border, first in one place, then another, but most of them turn out false. Until one day a Mexican cowhand working for an American cattle company tells one of our patrols that he's camped with five hundred men forty miles southwest on the Casa Grande River. Another cowboy confirms this story and I decide to go after Villa again myself.

I take two troops of cavalry and one machine gun, but leave over a hundred men in camp at Columbus. Matt wants to come, but as we're preparing to leave, he wrenches his knee when he's thrown from a spooked horse, and can't ride. He's one dejected kid, but I tell him there'll be other chances for glory.

We spend all day getting to the Casa Grande, but we don't find any Villistas, except where they was camped a few days before. I split the two troops, make a wide circle on both sides of the river, and come up with nothing. After another day of chasing my tail, I realize we been misled again, and give the order to turn back. That's the ninth of March when a courier arrives from Columbus with terrible news.

At four o'clock that morning, Villa crossed the border just west of Columbus with six hundred men, attacked our main camp and burned the town. The son of a bitch knew what he was doing, all right. He'd sucked me into marching all around the countryside while he hit us where it hurt. It didn't take a genius to figure that the cowhands who gave us the Casa Grande story were his men, and that he had others planted as spies in the town as well.

The worst part of the long ride back was the worry about Matt. All the courier told me was that we'd suffered twenty dead and wounded, but not who they were.

When I get within sight of the town, I see Lieutenant Castleman riding out to meet me. I rein up and wait, mumbling to myself, please God, don't let my boy be one of the dead.

Castleman throws me a smart salute, and I ask what happened, needing to know, but not wanting to. "Eight killed from our detachment, sir, and eight civilians. Seven men wounded, but we counted sixty-seven enemy dead." He flashes me a big grin and adds, "We really gave them a hot time, sir!"

"Who did we lose?"

He hands me a list and my worst fears are realized when I see Matt's name on it. First my little Emma, now him. How do I tell Caroline?

Then Castleman says, "That's everyone, sir. Killed and wounded."

"Sloan, Matthew?"

"Wounded, sir. Sorry. The casualty list should have made that clear."

I say to myself, *Thank you, God,* and to Castleman, "Is Private Sloan hurt bad?"

"Leg wound, sir."

I'm relieved when I see Matt in the surgery. He took a slug in his thigh, but it's a clean wound, and the wrenched knee's giving him more pain than the bullet hole. He's dying to tell me about the fight, but most of the details have to wait while I catch up with Major Tompkins and Captain Smyser, who are leading the two columns I ordered back into Mexico after Villa.

In the next few days we overtake the bastards, kill about ninety Villistas in running skirmishes and take some prisoners. But Villa gets away again, and when I return to Columbus, there's talk of a court-martial for invading Mexico against orders.

Lucky for me the public outcry over the Columbus raid is so
great that General Funston backs me up and the War Department
upholds his decision so I receive a commendation instead of a
reprimand.

Except from Caroline. Her first words after she sees Matt hob-
bling around are harsh, but that's the mother in her talking. I get
the story of the attack on Columbus from Matt, who blames his
wound on the Benet Merciers machine gun he was firing at the
time. It's a French weapon our army was using, and ain't worth
warm piss because it jams on every third round. He was trying to
clear the belt when a Mexican rode him down and shot him. He
was lucky he wasn't killed, real lucky.

When Washington finally decides to take official action, I'm
transferred to General Pershing's command to become part of the
so-called Punitive Expedition sent down into Mexico to catch Villa.
The Carranza government don't like the idea of an American army
in their midst, but they can't catch that bandit themselves, and they
ain't strong enough to keep us out.

We go as far as Chihuahua by train, where the army breaks into
three columns. Under the protocol negotiated between Washington and Mexico, we're supposed to coordinate our operations with
the Mexican army. But Carranza's generals would rather suffer
humiliation at the hands of a dozen insurgents like Pancho Villa
than cooperate with one friendly American force.

I'm in command of five hundred men of the New Mexico National Guard and the Seventh Cavalry, making up the column on
the right, while Pershing's headquarters leads the center. He's
brought a squadron of airplanes, trucks, a gas-powered generator
and wireless sets. Modern war, they call it. Except the trucks can't
keep up with the animals, the airplanes can't fly high enough to
reach us over the continental divide and the radios only work when
you don't need them.

Matt's still limping, but he's able to ride now, and I don't have
the heart to leave him behind. According to local reports, Villa's
near a place called Babicora, fifty miles into the mountains, robbing horses and supplies from his own people to rebuild his band.
But when we get there after a long march, he ain't anywhere
around. Then when we go into camp we hear from headquarters
that Carranza's troops caught up with the Villistas at Namiquipa,
and give them a licking.

I head southwest toward Guerrero on a hunch Villa will go there
after losing the battle because it's a good supply base and friendly
to him. We pass through some of the roughest mountains in Mexico on a forced march at night. The trail is so narrow and twisted
and rocky, we're forced to dismount and lead our horses. We cross
over the continental divide the twenty-ninth of March, and it's so
goddamned cold at that altitude, the water freezes solid in our
canteens. As we approach Guerrero, I see the leg's bothering Matt,
but when I ask him about it, he just grins at me and shrugs.

The town's surrounded by high bluffs cut by steep arroyos running back from the Santa Maria River, and we thread our way down
these to get into position a little after seven in the morning. At this
point I got two hundred thirty men, the rest having stayed behind
at Babicora with Major Tompkins. Through the binoculars I see
scores of horses tethered along the dusty main street, and pass the
glasses to Matt.

"Is it Villa, Lee?"

"It is. And we caught him with his britches down."

Mexicans like to sleep late and these bastards don't know we're
here yet. I split my people into three sections. One, led by Castleman, circles around the other side of the town and sets up the
machine guns, the second, under Captain Smyser, takes the left
flank, while I lead the right with Matt at my side.

At eight on the button I order the attack and we sweep toward
that town at a gallop. It don't occur to me until years later, but we
probably made history that day with the last charge of American
cavalry into battle.

A couple of my men take spills because of the uneven ground,
and the Mexicans spot our dust when we're still several hundred
yards from the first buildings. Some of them open fire but don't
hit anybody. We kill about ten with saber and pistol in that rush,
then pull up and form again at the head of the main street.

By now they're scurrying out of buildings like roaches, running
and shooting, but caught so totally by surprise they don't know
where we're coming from. That makes me laugh because they're
supposed to be the hit-and-run experts!

For the next ten minutes we sweep up and down the streets of
that town, stirrup to stirrup, shooting and yelling and slicing at
everything in our way. Matt and me get separated in the dust we
raise, but there ain't time to look for each other. The Villistas

almost done us some serious damage with a machine gun set up in the churchyard, but just as they get it into action, two of my boys ride it down, sabering the gunner and the fellow feeding the belt.

I see another trooper leap a water trough like a steeplechase jockey and ride hard after a paunchy officer could be Villa. I take after him too, but can't get a clear shot. When the soldier's half a length behind the Mexican, he aims his pistol at his back and finds he's out of bullets. He's so mad he puts spurs to his horse, over-takes that greaser and pulls him out of the saddle. When the Mexican picks himself up and raises his hands in surrender, I see it ain't Villa. But to my great surprise, the trooper is my boy Matt.

There's about three hundred Villistas in Guerrero and they fi-nally do what I hope they'll do. Those that can, mount and make a dash right into Castleman's machine guns. If the goddamn guns had been working right, we'd of wiped the greasers out that morn-ing, but they jammed as usual, so most of the enemy escaped. But we did count thirty dead, including Elicio Hernandez, Villa's right-hand man, and another forty-odd wounded. We took sixty-two prisoners.

Questioning some of them afterward, I find out Villa wasn't even in the town that morning. He rode out with a handful of his men during the night, and was deep in the mountains by the time we attacked. They said he was moving slow because of a broken leg and a gunshot wound from the Namiquipa battle, but I couldn't chase him even if I wanted to. In seventeen hours we had covered fifty-five miles over one of the roughest trails I ever seen, and then fought until noon. The horses and men were ready to drop.

After Guerrero, Villa never made a real comeback. Most of his men dispersed, and even though we didn't catch him then or later, he disappeared from the front pages. There was rumors about him from time to time that he was in one place or another, terrorizing people or trying to raise a new army, but nothing ever happened. His wife lived on in Chihuahua until the nineteen fifties, but he was finally gunned down in Parral during the Obregon government when I was ambassador to Mexico. That was nineteen and twenty-three, and nobody mourned the son of a bitch.

I was proud of Matt in that fight, but afraid for him too, wanting him out of danger. It's one thing to be reckless and headstrong like I been all my life, but it's scary to see the same qualities in your boy. I always figured after Cuba nothing could kill me, and for eighty-nine years I been right. But I couldn't guarantee Matt's luck. All I could do was love him and worry, and remember how life already cheated me out of my little girl.

"Colonel, sir, you're getting as bad as Mother," he told me one day when I was grousing at him to keep up or keep down or stay alert or change his socks or something.

"You ought to pay her more attention."

"Then I'd have missed all the action."

"That's my point."

"Women don't understand," he says.

"I'm here because I have to be," I tell him. "But you're a harum-scarum kid looking for excitement who's going to turn his poor mother gray before her time. And me too."

"I thought you were glad to have me along."

"Sure I'm glad. As long as you got to be stirring things up somewhere, I want you where I can keep my eye on you. But I'd feel better if you went back to Yale and made something of yourself."

"Now you sound like my father."

I want to say, "Goddamn it, I am your father!" but I don't because of what I promised Caroline. What I say instead is, "Suppose I was your father? Put yourself in my place then. A father wants the best for his boy, wants him to get an education, have a family, enjoy life."

"I am enjoying life, don't you see? There's no place I'd rather be than right here with you, Lee, doing what we're doing. It's what I dreamed about since I was little."

"Then keep a deep seat and a short rein," I tell him, "because we ain't through yet."

We stayed down in Mexico until June, cleaning up little pockets of Villistas and trying to keep the peace where we was. When the National Guard was deactivated again that fall, Matt obliged me by going back to college. By that time we knew each other as well as two friends can, and had grown real close. It pained me to see that boy leave, and we both choked a little on the station platform when we said good-bye.

"Look after your mother."

"You too, Lee."

When General Pershing asked me to help him prepare the official campaign report in Washington, I agreed to stay on active duty awhile longer. We called it the Mexican "Punitive" Expedition even though the only ones we punished was ourselves. Pershing was smart, a good boss and a hard worker, the kind of general the army never gets enough of. At that time he was also trying to come to terms with his own terrible grief after his wife and children burned to death in San Francisco. His whole career was spent in dangerous places, beginning with the Indian Wars on the Great Plains, and he never got a scratch. But fate really fixed him by wiping out everyone he loved in one night, in a cruel, tragic fire.

We just about finished the report when Wilson, the great Democrat peacemaker, takes us bag and baggage into the First World War. Caroline's in Washington with me most of the time, but she still ain't quite ready to divorce Woodrow Sloan or tell Matt the truth. By then I don't even argue. After so many years it don't matter. Anyway, Pershing's working me forty hours a day, and during my spare time I'm still trying to earn my keep with Fortland Oil by herding purchase orders through the government with a little help from Albert Fall.

A lot of the deals we did came out later and were criticized during the Teapot Dome investigation, when they was trying to make Al Fall look bad. But what none of the investigators ever mentioned was how desperate the government was for oil when we went to war. It's true the oil companies made big profits, but it's also true that we was there when Washington needed us, and every man with Fortland Oil, or Texaco, or Jersey worked miracles to keep our side supplied with fuel.

The spring of nineteen and seventeen was real pretty in Washington, what I saw of it from my office window in the old War Department building. Me and Caroline was able to spend a little time together, other than in bed, mainly horseback riding early in the morning along Rock Creek. Breakfast after our rides was the only moment in the day we had to talk, with me trying to reassure her about Matt. "I'm too old," I tell her. "As soon as I finish this job for Pershing, I resign my commission. But Matt will have to serve."

"It's not fair," Caroline says.

"There's lots of safe ways to do that. I'll find one."

"Will he have to go to France?"

"Most likely."

"Oh, Lee! You must do something!"

I want to keep him out of the fighting as much as she does, but I know it ain't going to be easy. The National Guard's been called up again, and Matt's a sergeant now. I may be able to get him assigned to some hole-in-the-wall army post until the shooting stops, but there's no guaranty. And I doubt he'll sit still for it.

Then Matt surprises us by announcing that he's applied for pilot training in the Air Service. After what I seen of our flimsy airplanes in Mexico, I don't think it's such a hot idea and I tell him so.

That same day Caroline receives a telegram from Boston that contains another shock. Woodrow Sloan had a stroke and wants her and Matt at his bedside, so I take them to the train. After wishing the son of a bitch dead or blind or just out of our lives for years, I realize I'd almost got used to the idea it was never going to happen. Now all of a sudden we're facing real freedom, and I'm as shook up as Caroline.

When I get back to my office, I find a message from George Marshall that Pershing wants to see me in the war room. He's had the final draft of our Mexican report for a week or so and I figure it's about that. George and another staff officer, together with two or three colonels I don't recognize, are all sitting with Pershing at the big oak map table. Marshall hands me a folder marked *Secret* with "Lt. Col L.O. Garland" written on the cover, and Pershing motions me to sit down.

What they're talking about don't have nothing to do with Mexico. It's the Order of Battle for the American Expeditionary Force we're sending to France. I'm flattered Pershing wants my opinion on something of such strategic importance, but it never crosses my mind why. After the meeting, he tells me.

"I'd like to keep you on my staff, Lee. Do you mind?"

Of course I mind. I had enough of the goddamned army in Cuba and I never should of let Luna euchre me into coming back during the border trouble. I still got a living to make and obligations to Fortescue, and to Caroline, and to a thousand employees who are counting on me, and . . .

"Well, what do you say?" Pershing had the clearest, most honest eyes of any man I ever knew, although I don't recollect their color. But when he focused them on you and asked you a hard question like that, and you knew what he'd been through and what he was facing in France, you just couldn't say no.

At least I couldn't.

"Wonderful, Colonel," he says when I agree. "I knew I could count on you."

I had a couple of weeks to think about what I was going to say to Caroline, what excuses I'd make this time, because she was still up there in Boston, keeping a loyal vigil by Woodrow Sloan's bed. She told me that the few words he was able to get out, he spoke to his lawyers and not to her. Then he went into a coma and died without ever saying anything more, so it was nearly a month before she came back. Thus, in the space of a year, the two men I hated most in this world finally checked out of it. Charlie Bruce, who had caused all the trouble, and Woodrow Sloan, the man whose hold on Caroline I never understood.

Because of his huge fortune, his death made the front pages everywhere. The stories called him a great railroad pioneer who helped civilize Mexico, and said he was known for his philanthropies too, like a Boston orphanage and a home for unwed mothers. Little did they know.

After the funeral, Matt comes straight down to Washington, leaving Caroline to deal with whatever she had to deal with in Boston. We're having dinner in the dining room at the old Willard Hotel when I tell him I expect to be off to France in a few weeks.

"Does Mother know?"

"Not yet."

"You'll be in worse trouble with her than I am, Lee."

"She'll manage. She always has."

"Lee, how long have you been in love with Mother?" The waiter's pouring the wine when Matt asks me this. I'm in uniform and he's dignified and serious in a blue serge suit. He was almost nineteen then, but aged beyond his years by his experiences in Mexico; a tall, handsome lad with a warm smile and an easy manner. My favorite person in this world besides Caroline.

"Since I met her," I say.

"Was it love at first sight?"

"Funny you should say that."

"Why?"

"Because the day I met her, me and some friends were talking about that exact subject, how she was the most beautiful creature we'd ever seen and how we all wanted her."

"So it was."

"Was what?"

"Love at first sight."

"I guess you'd have to call it that, yes."

"Then why didn't you marry her?"

"I told you. We was just kids."

"But when you came back from Cuba?"

"She never told you anything about us?"

"No, sir."

So after all these years, with no second thoughts, and no great fanfare or consultation with Caroline, I finally blurt out our great family secret. God knows why I chose that moment, but I guess Sloan's death freed me from my obligation to follow Caroline's wishes any longer, and made me feel a bigger obligation to Matt. I didn't know when we'd see each other again with both of us going off to war so I just let it all come tumbling out.

I tell him about Tampa, and his Uncle Charlie intercepting my letters and Caroline's, about my coming out of the hospital to find her married, and then five years later meeting her with Matt for the first time in Tampico and learning the whole bitter truth.

He hears me out and he's real thoughtful before he smiles and says, "I think I always knew down deep. Since I was a little boy, I wanted someone like you for my father."

"Well, you had me, even if you didn't know it."

"You know what's so funny?"

"What?"

"Those wonderful things you used to say about my father, that he loved me and wanted this for me or that for me, even though he might not show it. Remember?"

"Yes."

"I never believed you then, Lee. But tonight you made all that come true when you told me who my real father was."

I got to look away from him for a minute when he says that, and I swallow good before I speak because I got a real tight throat. "You're a grown man now. You got a right to know."

"Remember that first time you took Mother and me to Eagle Nest. You know the way kids dream. Maybe I did suspect something, I don't know. People used to ask me about it a lot because we look so much alike. Maybe I was just waiting for one of you to tell me."

"Your mother had her reasons for not wanting to. She was always afraid Sloan would disinherit you."

"He did."

"He what!"

"He disinherited me."

"That son of a bitch!"

"He cut Mother out of his will too and left everything to some cousins and a couple of charities."

"I can't believe it!"

"Maybe he did me a favor, Lee. It relieves me of guilt because I never loved him. But he should not have done it to Mother. He owed her more than that."

"She always felt it was she owed him."

"Take it from me it wasn't. He was cold and distant except when she was around him."

"Then why? Why keep her bound to him all those years and then pull a dirty stunt like that?"

"He amended his will when I went off to Mexico, saying I was not the son he wanted, nor was Mother ever a real wife to him. And since he believed everyone is free to choose, he chose to leave us out of any bequests. It's not as bad as it sounds. Thanks to you, Mother and I are both very well off between the bank in Albuquerque and our stock in Fortland Oil."

"We'll sue the estate," I say. "Break the will."

"I won't do that, Lee. And neither will she."

"She underestimated the bastard."

"It really doesn't matter," he says, calmer than me.

"In the beginning she felt she owed him her life for accepting you and saving her from being branded a whore. Later she said she stayed because she feared he'd try to ruin me or leave you without a cent. I don't even know if she understood the real reason. Maybe she preferred me as a permanent lover instead of having me for a husband. Who knows?" I raise my wineglass. "Here's to your mother, Matt. God bless her, whatever her reasons."

"Now what happens?" Matt asks me.

"You and me go fight the Huns."

"I mean with you and Mother. Will you be married?"

"Unless she comes up with a new reason not to be."

She didn't and we was. On a sunny June morning, nineteen years from the day we met, me and Caroline became man and wife. I ask Matt to be best man and he's tickled pink. Fortescue gave the bride away, and we honeymooned at the Hotel Willard because I was needed at the War Department the next day.

On her wedding day, she's as beautiful as the first time I seen her on the hotel veranda in Florida, her figure still as slim and lithe as a girl's, her hair glistening, and her eyes teary when I slip the ring on her finger. She'd been my only real love since Tampa, my mistress for seven years, and now my wife. When we're alone after the reception Emma gave us, I ask her how it feels to be married after all this time.

"I'm not sure yet, Lee. I became so used to thinking of myself as the fallen woman, respectability won't come easily."

"It never came easy for me either," I tell her. She had a marvelous laugh that bubbled up from deep inside when she was happy, and affected everybody who heard it. You couldn't have a sour face around Caroline for long without a damn good reason, and even then, she'd usually find the cure by seeing the sunny side or the funny side, if there was one.

I miss her. Nobody ever took her place. There's more letters of hers here somewhere, but I'm having a time finding what I want. I go rooting around among my papers looking for something. God, the things old people keep. What was I looking for? Something of hers or Matt's, I think, but whatever it was I don't find it. Instead I come across a faded sepia photograph of Caroline and me with Emma Fortescue and Albert Fall, standing by a huge Packard touring car in front of the Taos pueblo. The year's marked on the back, 1915, and I remember the day that picture was taken. The photographer was Governor Luna. Albert Fall was U.S. Senator at that time. Republican from New Mexico. My friend and Emma Fortescue's lover. With the picture I find some letters of Caroline's, a couple so fragile they crumble in my hands, others like new and still with a faint scent of flowers on the notepaper. And tucked in one envelope is a snapshot somebody took of Matt and me along the Mexican border in 1916. We're both wearing them floppy old campaign hats, and trying to look military. He's on crutches, grinning at the camera, and I got my arm around his shoulder. God, how I loved that boy!

Caroline never saw the funny side of war because she had no taste for gallows humor. But like most young fellows, Matt did. When he told anyone how he got wounded in the Columbus raid, it always came out funny. He'd say, "There I was, my gun jammed, and Mexicans everywhere you looked."

People would ask, "Did you pray?"

He'd nod and answer, "Now I lay me down to sleep and pray the Lord my soul to keep. It was the wrong prayer, but it was the only one I knew and I guess it reached the right ears."

The listener would laugh and Matt would say, "It was a sticky international situation, you understand. One American with a faulty French machine gun against six hundred Mexicans."

"How terrifying!" the listener says. Matt would wink at me. "They were terrified all right. And I never understood why."

Once Wilson decided to save the world for democracy, or democracy for the world—I don't remember which—the whole United States got behind the war. Americans support a lot of foolish causes, but when we're committed to something, we usually give it our best. This war was no exception. Factories worked around the clock, and railroads moved more freight in a month than they had in a peacetime year. Like Charlie Bruce used to say, "War is good business."

Nobody knew it then, but the social changes would affect all our lives when it ended. Women don't just roll bandages, they hike up their skirts, take over men's jobs and go after the vote. The first military-draft law since the Civil War is passed to fill the army's ranks in a hurry. The stock market's booming because everything is back-ordered or hard to get, and everybody who ain't a cripple or in the army is making more money than he ever dreamed of.

In no time Washington's the mecca for every crook and crackpot, every thieving sidewinder trying to get rich off the government, and most of them seem to congregate in the halls of the War Department. They sell whatever the army's buying, which is practically everything, and one day I see a familiar face. He's wearing a dark pin-striped suit instead of his old white duster, his hair's gone all gray and his mustache is trimmed, but I'd know them pig-bristle eyebrows anywhere.

"Hello, Brewer," I say, and he jumps about a foot.

"The name's Collins," he says, quick as light.

"When did it stop being Brewer? I almost didn't recognize you without your shotgun."

He looks all around to see if anybody's listening before he hisses in my ear, "All right, Garland. Look, I've always been a good friend to you, right? You owe me some favors."

I let that go by and ask, "Why the fake name?"

"Business reasons. I'd appreciate it if you'd forget we ever met before. It could be embarrassing to both of us."

"You might be right. What happened, Brewer?"

"I drew five to ten for extortion in Kansas."

"Sorry to hear that."

"So I turned over a new leaf."

"I'll bet you did."

He hands me a business card that reads, "A. Jackson Collins, President, Eureka Hide & Leather Co., Clint, Texas." He says, "I'm just about to go into a meeting to close a deal, Garland. I need the money bad. Don't wreck it for me."

This time he's trying to still the army with some old used mule harness and pack straps, and my first impulse is to ring the bell on him. Then I think if the government can afford all these other big-time crooks, a little two-bit chiseler like Brewer ain't going to cost us the war. I'm getting soft in my old age, I tell myself, but Brewer ain't my lookout. When a nervous Supply Corps captain comes to escort him to his meeting I don't say a word, but I wonder what Brewer's paying him.

This war ain't going to be anything like the one with Spain. A whole generation of French and English and Germans was being bombed, bayoneted, gassed, shot and blown to smithereens by each other. Now we were going over to join the fun.

Our troops have yet to land in Europe, but the war is the only thing anyone talks about that spring. By June Matt still hasn't left for the air service and I'm hoping maybe they forgot about him or lost his file somewhere. Caroline begs me to talk him out of flying, but I already tried that and got nowhere. Then she starts on me to find him a job in the War Department.

"You can do it, darling. Please."

"Sure I can do it, but Matt won't buy that. Don't you know your own son yet?"

"He'd never have to know you were behind it."

I promise her I'll do what I can because I ain't any happier than she is with his airplane idea, and I don't want him marching off to the slaughter as a foot soldier either. Because our last names are different, I figure nobody will know I'm his old man when I assign him a safe headquarters job. Except Matt's already outsmarted me by going over my head. Before he can be transferred, army personnel receives a recommendation from Pershing that my son be assigned immediately to pilot training in the Army Air Service, which is the same as a direct order from God.

When I ask George Marshall about it, he says, "Why, Lee, the boy cornered the general at your wedding and claimed he got so many saddle sores riding around Mexico with you he wanted an easy war this time. The boss was amused and recommended him."

But Caroline ain't amused, and the days before Matt has to leave are the only time I ever seen her in a sulk. She can't keep it up because her natural good humor breaks through. Only the last night before he leaves, we're all three at a reception at Fort Meyer, where there's a young captain from the Air Service. Matt's pumping him with questions as Caroline listens, and this dumb cluck says seven out of twenty in his flying class crashed while in training. On the way back to the Willard Hotel she's real quiet, and once we get into bed, she lays awake a long time, staring at the dark. I hear her up before dawn and find her in the dressing room, crying.

When I put my arms around her, she says with a desperation no reassurance from me can cure, "Oh, Lee, he's all we have!"

I get mad and say, "Goddamn it, Caroline, you sound just like you did after you went to that fortune-teller in Tampa! I came back from that stupid war and Matt's going to come back from this one. He's got the Garland luck and he'll live a long happy life like me. He's just got a taste for adventure, that's all."

XXXIII

Over There

In July I'm promoted to full colonel and sail for France, and it's true I went off with some enthusiasm. Even though I'd had a gutful of war in Cuba and Mexico. Pershing convinced me that this time my presence really mattered. While he decided how and where we was going to do battle, Marshall, me, and a handful of other colonels was responsible for seeing that a million American soldiers got there in condition to do real damage to the enemy.

We made mistakes because nobody had any experience on such a grand scale. I mean the biggest problem the army command ever faced before France was moving a few thousand men around Mexico. Lucky for me Pershing worked my ass off because I had less time to worry about Matt and miss my bride.

Caroline spent those long lonely months here at Eagle Nest, fixing the place up for us to live in when we come back, writing me two or three times a week, this time without anybody intercepting our letters.

She jokes about breadless Mondays, meatless Tuesdays and porkless Thursdays that are supposed to help the war effort, but she says the worst are the loveless other days with her man away. She worries whether I'm warm enough or eating enough in France. What she don't know is that most of the time I'm quartered behind the lines in a big chateau and eating like a pig. She writes about Luna and New Mexico politics, about the changing of the seasons

435

at Eagle Nest, about Hernan's horses, and the terrible influenza epidemic that's killing people all over the country.

She also keeps me posted on the war dead from back home, which don't cheer me up any. Miguel, Hernan's kid, who rode after Fortescue years ago to return the check for the horses, is killed at Château-Thierry, as is Dave Leahy's oldest boy and a nephew of Levi Hennings. The list grows. Sons and brothers, fathers and lovers, Yale classmates of Matt's, men I eat and drink with on my tours of the front whose names turn up on the next day's casualty lists.

When I think back on that time in France, my memories are as muddy as the place. I see the tired faces of the soldiers, kids like Matt mostly, under dirty gray skies that seep rain all day and turn the battlefield to muck. The fighting had been going on in the same goddamn place for three years, and there ain't a house with a roof, or a tree standing for miles on either side of the front.

At night the heavens rumble and growl with artillery fire. Great heavy flashes outline the clouds like heat lightning. Every so often a parachute flare lights up no-man's land, catching a patrol like hares in a headlight. Startled and blinded, they freeze while machine guns cut them down. Then tracers probe the trenches until dawn.

I was thirty-nine, going on ninety then, the age of Colonel Roosevelt when he led us up San Juan Hill. An old man by some standards. I often wondered what I was doing in France, what any of us was doing there, for that matter. Schoolmarm Wilson says we're fighting the war to end wars, but nobody could ever convince me of that. We're fighting it because he blundered into it.

Mostly, my personal war was against the French command, trying to protect Pershing from a bunch of scheming, jealous foreign generals who was more interested in winning promotions than battles. They couldn't care less how many American lives had to be sacrificed to gain a yard of French mud, as long as they give the orders and got the medals. Lucky for us, my boss was a match for them.

We had our own artillery, air service, transport, supply and communications, which worked better than theirs. And our spirits were high because we haven't been living underground for the past three years. We won't take orders from the French but we stand as equals, fighting side by side. We didn't come all this way to pay for their mistakes or to make the same ones all over again.

They been hunkered down in these trenches for three years, slaughtering Germans and being slaughtered by them without a win in sight for either side. All any of them generals knew how to do was throw men at the enemy in one frontal assault after another until they run out of bodies and have to draft more. Around Verdun alone, a hundred eighty thousand dead from both sides couldn't even be identified, and they were shoved into what has to be the biggest common grave in the world.

So our allies had nothing to teach us. On the contrary. Quite a few of our troops had been on the Mexican campaign so they weren't entirely green, and many of the officers, like me and Pershing himself, had experience in Cuba or the Indian Wars.

But we weren't prepared for this. The front didn't bear any resemblance to anything except in my worst nightmares. There was a sweet stench over the place most of the time, coming from the decomposing bodies churned up every day by the shelling. Animal carcasses littered the roads too, while the vehicles they pulled lay bent and splintered among the ruins of towns. Jagged tree stumps like black broken teeth marked what once was farms or villages, and told the whole stupid story of how two great armies failed to do each other in.

In dry weather the battlefield was a parched dump, the ground cracked and scabby with shell holes, crisscrossed by barbed wire, breastworks and trenches. When it rained, the place became a soupy hell of stuck machines, soaked soldiers and panicky horses. Nothing could live there anymore except men burrowed in the ground like moles, and the infernal rats and lice that fed off them. Rain turned the trenches into a sewer. Either you waded along the bottom in liquid shit or you literally stuck your neck out on the firesteps and stood a good chance of being picked off.

As usual, we went off to war like we was playing soldiers. The amazing thing was how we kept our sense of humor. I don't know if it was just another index of our innocence, but even going into battle cold and soaked to the skin, with rain running off their helmets and no breakfast in their bellies, our soldiers could joke and horse around, prodding each other in the ass with their bayonets and yelling intimate obscenities at each other, the officers pretended not to hear.

The second week I'm in France, Pershing sends me to observe

the big British offensive around Passchendaele, which wound up costing four hundred thousand casualties without gaining a yard of ground. A good lesson in how not to fight a war. I seen terrible stupidities in Cuba, but nothing like this, and these fellows had three years to get it right.

Stepping off like they was on parade, their bayonets fixed, with only the slightest interval between them, the English formed a solid wall of flesh the worst gunner couldn't miss. Wave after wave left their trenches in the pouring rain, slipping and stumbling in the gluey clay, and being scythed down by the Huns before they could cover a hundred yards. If you didn't know these were human beings slaughtered out there, it would of been the most boring spectacle on earth. The real killers wasn't the Huns, they were the generals who kept sending men out day after day until the British army was bled white.

In August me and Captain Castleman, who'd been with me in Mexico and was now my adjutant, went to see if the French was any better at this kind of thing. We arrived at one headquarters to find a big stink because a couple of days before that particular regiment had refused to do what the British did, walk into machine gun fire and die like bugs. It wasn't the first French unit to mutiny. To make an example, several of the junior officers was shot by firing squads along with a dozen ordinary soldiers. It really convinces us they're a bunch of losers who have now gone completely hysterical.

Me and Castleman observed another regiment in action at a fort along the front. It was really just a big, hollowed-out, man-made hill with ditches on four sides and a tunnel connecting it to the main line of trenches. But it had a 75mm artillery turret that stuck out like a finger where it could do the Germans heavy damage every time they attacked across no-man's land.

The place had changed hands three times since the beginning of the war, and the French had only just got it back in a bloody underground attack through the tunnel. The Germans was trying to recover it, but each time they tried, they left scores of bodies on the slope and in the ditches. The day we came they tried again.

The barrage began at five A.M., but from inside the fort all you could hear was a harmless muffled thumping as the shells exploded against a foot of concrete and fifteen feet of earth. When the shelling stopped at sunup, the French commander let me watch the

German advance through his periscope. They didn't attack like the
Brits, but used a V-formation strung out with wide intervals like a
flight of migrating geese, so the French artillery did less damage
than they might of. But when they reached the ditches they died
just the same.

The French machine gunners don't even have to aim, just tra-
verse left to right, right to left, as scores of gray men in coal-scuttle
helmets tumble and sprawl on the slope less than fifty yards away.
Some lay on their backs like junebugs, arms and legs convulsing,
alive but unable to get up.

"They are from a Brandenburg grenadier unit," the French
commander says as we watch. "Very brave fighters." It's hard to
draw the line between bravery and stupidity, but I don't want to
offend this fellow so I say nothing. He had personally led the attack
that recaptured the fort, fighting in the dark tunnel with sawtooth
trench knives, bayonets and grenades.

I had to admire the Germans' courage as they cut and dodged,
breaking into little groups of four or five and using the shell holes
for cover. But it was like we were watching a movie. They had a
flame thrower that licked our periscope a couple of times, but
when they reached the top of the fort, they didn't do us any serious
damage even chucking potato-masher grenades through the rifle
slits.

The commanding officer decides to call his own artillery fire
down on us to clear the Germans off the turret, but our telephone
lines have been cut and he can't get through. So they release a
pigeon with the message, and after half an hour French shells rain
down on our heads. Through an observation slit I see men cut in
half, squashed, shredded and blown into bloody showers of gristle
and bone. They're my enemy, but I can't help feeling sorry for
them, remembering my own terror under the Spanish bombardment in Cuba. There's nothing worse than artillery fire when your
ass is out there in the wind.

After the last German's killed the shelling stops, and I figure
that's the end of the battle, even though it's only about nine in the
morning. But these Brandenburgers don't know when to quit. No
sooner is the first attack routed than they mount a second. And
when that fails with another harvest of bodies on the slope and in
the ditches, they do it again. And again. Somewhere during that

morning they cross the line from bravery to stupidity to madness, and if I admired their guts at dawn, by noon all I could feel was horror and pity.

The day was hot and humid, a relentless summer sun baked the battlefield, and even inside the fort the men sweated and cursed as they passed ammunition to the gun crew above. Me and Castleman each carried two canteens because I'd learned in Cuba the one thing you're always short of in a war is water. What we didn't know was just how short we was, and neither did our hosts until somebody brought the news that the cistern in the fort was dry.

The commander sends a party back through the tunnel to fetch water from the main lines, but the sergeant in charge returns ten minutes later to say there's a cave-in and he has no idea how long it will take his men to dig it out.

This means we're cut off from the French lines and there's no safe way back to headquarters until the goddamn tunnel's opened.

It takes them two days for one reason or another. Each time they get it dug out and shored up, another shower of German shells caves it in again. Three men are buried alive, and die of suffocation before they can get to them.

I seen some stomach-turning things in that place. Men so crazed they lick the damp off the walls, others wretching their guts out after drinking their own piss. By the end of the second day, they're ready to come out with their hands in the air for a cup of water, and only the threat of a firing squad keeps them from surrendering. Me and Castleman are down to our last few drops and we agree to take our chances on a run across the battlefield before we'll die from thirst.

While we're discussing our move, the Huns give us a special surprise, except this time there's no big explosions, just the whining of the shells in the air and then a faint popping sound. We hear shouting up in the gun parapet and the Frenchies begin looking nervously at each other and chattering so fast we don't understand. Then two of the gunners come sliding down the ladder, choking and vomiting, and somebody says "Gas!"

The gas didn't pass through the rubber of our American masks the way it did through the fabric of the French ones, and we was saved while Frenchmen collapsed all around us. Even so, I got a whiff of this greenish yellow vapor before I got my mask on, a pungent, putrid, dead-animal smell mixed with vinegar. I didn't know it then, but this was a new phosgene gas the Germans had developed especially to penetrate the French masks. They used it on us a few times the following year, like they did mustard gas. It's a ugly way to kill people.

Matt arrived in time for the second battle of the Marne that summer of nineteen and eighteen. He shot down three Hun aircraft and a balloon in his first month, and the French give him a medal. Then they shoot his machine down by mistake over our lines when he's flying back from a reconnaissance in August. He ain't hurt though, and they apologize, and he's back flying again the next day.

I see him every few weeks before the Meuse-Argonne offensive, and he shows off his airplane, explaining a lot of the technical things about it. I'm listening, but mainly I'm watching the way his hands roam over the fabric as he talks, the way he touches the wires and spars like a lover. He tells me he met a girl when he was learning to fly in San Antonio, and he's seriously interested in her.

"A little young to be 'seriously interested,' ain't you?"

"It was love at first sight, Lee," he says, grinning.

"That makes a difference then. But if you're aiming to follow in your old man's footsteps, you got to wait nineteen years before you marry her."

I'm watching him the whole time, lively and handsome in his uniform, and I can imagine how attractive he must be to women. He invites me to lunch with him at the squadron mess. It's a drizzly day and all the airplanes are grounded until the weather clears, so I meet his commanding officer and most of the other pilots, all kids like him. I'm real pleased when Matt introduces me as his father, but we both laugh when they call me Colonel Sloan.

After the Meuse-Argonne campaign starts in September, I don't have time to piss. For six weeks we grind the Germans down until they can't fight no more. We pound them round the clock with artillery and only let up long enough to throw waves of infantry at them. Besides the French and English troops battling on our flanks, we pour a million two hundred thousand American soldiers into that fight, and a hundred twenty thousand of them get killed. Every time I see another dead kid, I worry about Matt and say a silent prayer for his safety.

When the shooting stops at last on November eleventh, the first thing I do is drink to the fact my boy's still alive. That he can go home and finish his education and marry his girl and have kids and do all the things normal people do to be happy. I send a special dispatch over Pershing's wire to the War Department, marked for Caroline, saying, "Home soon. We love you." I sign it, "Matt and Lee."

The only Rough Rider I run into in France is Mitchell, who took leave from his film career to command a National Guard infantry battalion. He's pale and drawn from too much time in the trenches and too little sleep, but he's still the kidder he always was. We get a little drunk together, and when I ask him why he's back in the saddle at age forty-eight, he gives me the same smart-ass answer he gave in Cuba twenty years earlier.

"War's still the great adventure, Lee."

"That's what I tried to make Caroline understand, but don't you think you're a little long in the tooth for this one?"

"Sometimes I get a bellyful, old partner," he says, rubbing the sleep in his eyes. "I'm tired of writing to widows and orphans. I liked it better when Luna had that responsibility."

"Mitch, a volunteer your age needs his head looked at."

"Speak for yourself, Lee," he says. Then he declaims like he's on the stage again, " 'To this I witness call the fools of time, which die for goodness, who have lived for crime.' War is a purge for me. I crave the hardship after so much fakery. But you wouldn't understand because you're not a fake."

"I repeat—" I start to say.

"I know. I need my head examined."

Mitchell was killed in the last days of the war. Funny how that could happen to somebody like him. It was as if he'd spent his whole life rehearsing for the real thing in all them moving pictures he made. Fake shooting, fake riding, fake killing and fake dying, always looking for a better script, a nobler cause, or some high adventure. Life can bore a man like him unless he reinvents it, but it can kill him when he does.

I been going through papers and letters of Caroline's. Mixed in with the letters are old newspaper clippings, faded legal folders, land titles, records of court battles and law suits, all part of our ancient history.

God knows why I kept them or why she did. I come across a memo Dave Leahy sent me when I come out of the army, the last time listing my property holdings. Besides Eagle Nest there's parts of the Canyon de Agua, Tierra Amarilla, Espiritu Santo and all of the San Cristobal land grant.

I have to laugh. I never started out to be a big landowner, but from time to time Fall or Luna or some other friend would put me on to something, and I'd take a flyer. By 1919, besides my personal oil leases and stock shares, I own half a million acres, a lot of it desert but some prime cattle land, too. That's when Matt comes out of the army and decides to go into the cattle business.

It was Albert Fall's son Jack who got him interested. And I was happy because I thought it was a damn sight safer than flying airplanes. The boys decided to go partners on two thousand head and run them on our Canyon de Agua spread, which was the smallest, but had the best water. Jack was a few years older than Matt and already had some experience growing stock. A fine-looking young man, strong and handsome like his father, and with the same contagious personality.

Dave Leahy draws up their partnership agreement down in Albuquerque, and me and Al Fall witness it in Bungle's saloon one night. Old Ned was dead by then, and the scalps and the buffalo gun are gone from behind the bar. The new management don't offer the free lunch anymore but nobody complains. Bungle's is still an old-fashioned saloon, full of loud talk and conviviality; with dim yellow lights, the bar polished to a velvety shine by generations of thirsty cowboys, the smell of stale beer, pretzels and cigars hanging in the air like perfume.

Al Fall and me are a pair of contented fathers that night, proud of our sons and eager to interfere in their lives with more advice and counsel than they'd ever find use for. Both young men are too polite to object, but at a certain point Dave Leahy tells us to stop bullying them. Al, who was still U.S. Senator, is determined to impart nuggets of wisdom gleaned from his long political career, while yours truly is giving them the benefit of my vast experience in the livestock business, mostly with the Brown brothers.

"You're lucky you weren't shot in those days," Jack Fall says.

"Or hanged," his father adds.

To clarify the subject a little, I tell them I went straight before I was eighteen and made a hundred times more money in the legitimate cattle trade than I ever did working for Sam and Arnold Brown.

"Then you're telling us crime doesn't pay?" Matt says.

"Not unless you're a politician it don't."

"Touché," Al Fall says, smiling.

"Just keeping things in perspective," I tell him.

With Dave Leahy's help the boys are organized pretty good. Jack's already bought some prime Hereford cows from ranchers here in the Rio Grande valley, and him and Matt are going to the San Antonio cattle show to shop for bulls. I kid Matt about the trip to Texas because that's where the girl lives he met when he was learning to fly.

Jack Fall says, "Don't worry, Colonel, I'll keep him out of harm's way. He's too young to marry anyway."

"Look who's talking," Matt says. Jack himself is sweet on a pretty girl down in El Paso he's planning to visit.

After the two of them leave us, Dave Leahy orders another round and says, "Besides bulls, Matt's going to buy an airplane in San Antonio, and fly it back."

"I'll spare his mother that particular piece of news," I tell them. "She was holding her breath until he come back from France. Anyway, he got all that harum-scarum stuff out of his system."

Al Fall says, "How could that be? He's your son."

"He's Caroline's son too," I tell them. "Just wait and see."

But it don't happen that way. It don't happen in any way we could of anticipated. Not Matt, not Caroline or me or Albert Fall or anybody could of predicted the cruel turn life would take that year, robbing our boys of their future. They bought no bulls in San Antonio because by the time they arrive there, Jack Fall is sick as a dog with the influenza. Matt telegraphs that he's checked Jack into the hospital but by the time Albert Fall and his wife get to San Antonio, their fine, wonderful son is critically ill, and two days later, they lose him.

Me and Caroline are stunned, thinking, God help us, it might of been Matt. When the wings of death pass that close, you feel the chill. You huddle together, circle the wagons as they used to say, and cross your fingers and don't step on cracks, carry a rabbit's foot and wear a horsehair ring. You come up with prayers you thought you forgot. You say, "Please God, don't let that happen here to home. Send it elsewhere, anywhere, but keep it at bay."

Matt accompanies the body back to New Mexico with the Falls, and we all attend the graveside service in Santa Fe. Al's in bad shape. "Why?" he keeps saying. "Why take my Jack? I've been everywhere, done everything. Why not me, Lord?"

Privately he asks me if I think he's being punished for cheating on his wife with Emma Fortescue all these years. I tell him what he already knows but wants to hear again. Life and death don't work like that. There may be a couple of physical laws that follow some kind of logic, but nothing else does. God ain't mean or nasty or vindictive. He ain't out to get us for our piddling little sins, in spite of what the preachers would have us believe. He's blind, indifferent and arbitrary, and that's more terrifying than if he took an interest. It's like having a drunk for a father.

So we try to ignore reality and keep playing our little games, inventing values that make things seem more comprehensible and us more important. Meanwhile the real world goes on, a speck in God's eye if you lean toward a religious explanation, or just another dust mote in space, with no more purpose, hope or future than a fly flushed down a drain.

Caroline thought otherwise, but her faith took its hardest lick that year. When we get back to Eagle Nest after Jack Fall's funeral, Matt starts hacking and shaking and shooting a fever, and the doctor says he's got the flu too. That bug killed millions all over the world between 1918 and 1920. There wasn't no antibiotic or anything against it, and Caroline and me panic.

Matt's throwing up and in severe pain with terrible cramps and headaches. I'm scared for his life, but I reason that it can't be that bad. Jack Fall's succumbing to it was just freakish bad luck. Matt's strong and healthy, and always sailed through all the kid diseases without alarming nobody. He also had my Garland blood, and if I could beat typhus and malaria, Matt would whip this goddamn thing.

Then Caroline comes down with it too after nursing him for three days almost without sleep. She's pale and delicate as a hot-house flower, transparent from the fever, and now I'm praying to God nothing will happen to either one of them. Somehow I'm sure Matt will make it, but I'm worried sick over Caroline.

On the fourth night, Matt calls out for her around three in the morning. He's burning up and not making a lot of sense, and of course she can't come so I bathe his brow and hold his hand for a while. Then along toward dawn he cools down and seems to be sleeping okay. But when I go in about seven to check on him after sitting up the rest of the night with Caroline, our boy is gone.

I couldn't deal with it, just plain couldn't. Couldn't believe it, couldn't accept it and couldn't understand it. Sick as Caroline was, she had to take care of me after that. There was no way I could allow my son to be snatched from this life so quick and stupid, and still keep my sanity. After little Emma died, things was as bad as they could be. But with Matt . . . Jesus! Like he forgot his manners and just left us. Like he didn't know how much we loved him and how much our own happiness depended on his staying around.

After Mexico and France and everything, he just had to be a survivor like me. But he wasn't, and after we lost him, for a while I wasn't much of a survivor either. I spent days locked in the library with my Colt in my lap, drunk a lot and feeling sorry for myself, cocking and uncocking that old revolver as I tapped the barrel against my teeth. Until one day I looked up and saw how Caroline was suffering, and realized I was the only one could help her.

XXXIV

Bad Times, Good Times

Albert Fall resigned from the Senate shortly after that to be appointed Secretary of the Interior. He never got over his boy's death any more than I got over Matt's. Only the passage of time eased the hurt. It helped too when Harding made me ambassador to Mexico in 1921 because it gave us an excuse to get away for the next three years.

I was older and less tolerant, but I found the place poorer, dirtier and more savage than ever. The so-called Mexican revolution hadn't solved anything, just added more problems to the ones the country had always faced. The struggle was in its twelfth year when we returned this time, and was more confused than ever. Every bandit who could hold a hundred men together and terrorize a province, called himself a general. Instead of one Pancho Villa, there was a dozen, and none of them with any hope of winning. Mexico was the kind of place where any sensible man had to be more afraid of living than of dying.

The money made there over the centuries from mining and cattle stayed in the same pockets, and the prosperity we brought to places like Tampico didn't last because one bandit government after another stole the oil revenues outright or squandered them on war and revolution.

The great "visionaries" who claimed to be saving Mexico from Yankee exploiters were the worst. They ruled in the name of the

447

people yet they made the old Diaz crowd look like angels. Under Diaz there was always some table scraps for the poor peon. Now his belly stayed empty.

The country was crawling with arms brokers peddling leftover toys from the Great War. While I was ambassador enough guns and ammunition was landed in Mexico to win a hundred revolutions, most of them made in the U.S.A. For a while I thought it was just more of the same chaos I'd lived through ten years earlier in Tampico. But it wasn't.

One difference was the new Communists and Socialists. Every two-bit revolutionary general had a political adviser by that time, and a lot of them were fresh from the Russian revolution. At first they was so busy slaughtering priests and burning churches that they didn't get too involved trying to govern. That came after they really got their paws on the tax-collecting system and expropriated most of the private property in the country, including practically everything owned by the American cattle and oil interests.

Most people don't know or remember that we came about as close to going to war with Mexico in the twenties as we ever would. Many of my own friends were all for it. Doheny, for example, always believed everything we owned would go down the drain if we didn't take over the country. He wasn't far wrong, but I always held the view that the worst goddamned shaky peace is better than the best war, no matter what countries we're talking about. Lucky for everybody, both Harding and Coolidge thought the same.

I can't claim to have kept us out of a war with Mexico, but when I was ambassador I did manage to eliminate our main reason for invading the country, even though I come under a lot of criticism from the pantywaists back home for the way I did it.

When the strongest of the generals, Obregon, finally took over as president I got Washington to recognize his government. It wasn't that I liked him especially, but in exchange for American recognition he was willing to guarantee cash indemnities for all foreign property seized, damaged or destroyed since the revolution started in 1910.

Some say I got the concessions by force, like a lot of things in my life, and I know what give rise to the rumor. "Gunboat diplomacy," the New York *Times* called it, which wasn't strictly true because no gunboat was involved. It was the battleship *Nevada*.

When I heard the U.S. Navy was planning maneuvers off Key

West, I suggested to some Washington friends that we move the fleet a little closer to the Mexican coast. I reckon our good neighbors would get a real kick out of seeing these big ships in action, because a friendly power like us can only be a comfort to them since they don't have a navy of their own.

I invite General Obregon to a little party over in Veracruz, where him and his hangers-on can watch our battleship pot targets with her fourteen-inch guns just outside the harbor mouth while we sip cocktails on the yacht-club terrace. They was very impressed with our ability to defend them and signed the agreement to pay up the following week.

The revolution finally petered out. They shot most of the Communists in the thirties. Then over the years they lost a few million wetbacks who come here to pick lettuce and stayed. The priests recovered some influence, but not the bandits, which may explain the Mexican population explosion.

When rich and poor are shoved so close against each other, like we are with Mexico, either the rich better look after the poor, or the poor will take what they want. Mexico and all them other little so-called banana countries are a time bomb. We can't feed them and we don't want them coming here, but we can't make them disappear either, without killing a few million people.

Prohibition turned Mexico into a giant liquor lake with booze sloshing over the border all through the twenties. And immigration. Until the first war, we only kept out Orientals, paupers, prostitutes and imbeciles. Afterward, the Johnson Act tried to keep out practically everybody.

That's how Mountain got into trouble with the law again. After several years of keeping the peace with Tom Isbell around Tampico, he's homesick for New Mexico, so we make him superintendent at our Hobbs field. He brings his Mexican housekeeper and her six or seven kids, most of whom are his. Knowing he can't find whiskey anymore back home, he also brings about a year's supply.

Somehow he gets over the border with all this baggage, but federal alcohol agents and immigration inspectors smell something fishy so they raid him and his family in their El Paso hotel. As soon as Levi hears about it, he calls Fortescue, and Fortescue wires me and I wire Albert Fall to lean on some Republican friends before I take the train up to Juárez and cross the Rio Grande into El Paso.

There I am, the United States Ambassador to Mexico, visiting the same big old brick jail me, Mountain and Cody was confined in all those years ago. Before I ask to see Mountain I talk to the federal officers in charge. The immigration inspector is an ass-kisser who assures me he's willing to let Mountain's family continue on to Hobbs if Mountain will just sign a declaration recognizing the woman as his wife.

"Is she?"

"He admits she's the mother of his children, but he insists she is only an employee. As such we can't let her into the country."

"What does she say?"

"She doesn't speak English."

"And I suppose you don't speak Spanish."

He smirks and shakes his head.

The alcohol agent is a different story. His arm's in a sling, he's got sticking plaster covering his nose, and both his eyes are black. In the corridor behind the holding cells I see fifteen cases of scotch whiskey, the evidence against Mountain Moore, who at the very least seems to be looking down the wrong end of a seven-year jail sentence for bootlegging. And on top of that, this beat-up bastard found out M. Moore is still wanted in the state of Colorado.

I take the agent aside and tell him real quiet that if he can find a way to release my friend and forget the whole thing, not only will he be able to get rid of the whiskey as he sees fit, but a very substantial cash honorarium will be placed at his immediate disposal.

"You can't bribe me," he brags, like he's really caught me out in something terrible.

"I was thinking more in terms of a scholarship."

"I know what you're thinking and it won't work!" His eyes are mean and squinty, and his big round face is flushed with righteousness. "Criminals like Moore think they own this country! Well, not anymore! I'm going to put that scoundrel and his greaser girl friend behind bars where they belong, you wait and see!"

"I'm sorry you feel that way," I tell him.

But there's no reasoning with this fellow. I mean, the country's divided then between wets and drys, and maybe some of the drys got a case, but this monkey's a fanatic. "I know who you are," he says, leaning in close and spraying me with spit. "People like you think you can buy anything. Well, you can't buy Malcolm B. Swinnerton!"

"Is that your name?" I say.

"You bet it is, mister. Try throwing your weight around and you'll learn there is such a thing as an incorruptible alcohol agent!" I swear to God that's what he said.

When I go to visit Mountain, what I see almost makes me laugh except the pickle he's in is serious. His two little girls are asleep in one jail cell, two huge adolescent boys in the next and Mountain with his three middle sons sharing the last two cells like a suite. Laundry's strung from the bars of one cell to the next and the pungent smell of Mexican food's coming from the jailhouse kitchen, where his woman's frying tortillas. Half the cell doors are ajar, and they could all walk out if they want. Except Mountain's got irons on his wrists.

"Why, Lee, what brings you way up here?" he says, happy as a bird to see me. Then his face clouds over. "They arrest you too?"

"If Ransom and Cody was alive," I tell him, "the reunion would be complete. What happened to that alcohol agent that pissed him off so?"

"He busted into our hotel room when we was, well, you know, busy." He nods in the direction of his smiling Mexican lady, who's half his height but just as big around, with arms like sugar-cured hams.

"Looks like you been busy for the last several years," I say, indicating all the little Mountains in the adjoining cells.

"Can you get us out of here?"

"I'm working on it." I tell him his immigration problems is solved if he just says the woman's his wife.

"But she ain't."

"You want her sent back to Mexico?"

"Hell, no. She's a wonderful person."

"Then tell them you're married."

"Would she have to know if I tell them?"

"I don't suppose so. Why?"

"The way things are, she still thinks I can fire her."

"Don't tell me you're afraid of the woman!"

"Go ahead and laugh. You seen what she done to that agent."

That night some of Ransom's old friends on the El Paso police force help me make the whiskey disappear so there's no evidence. We also reply by telegraph to the Colorado authorities that the person in their custody can't be the same M. Moore wanted for that old murder because one in custody is an Oriental female five feet tall.

Another telegram guarantees the immediate transfer of Malcolm B. Swinnerton to Nome, Alaska, where the incorruptible agent should pose no serious problem for the Eskimos.

Mountain ain't the only one who found himself a compatible Mexican lady. While I was still in the army in France, Fortescue announces he's marrying one of the most beautiful girls in Mexico. Me and Caroline give up on him a long time ago. I mean he's forty-five years old when he finally takes the big step to the altar with Luz Candelaria Maria-Carmen Ortiz, age eighteen, daughter of Paco Ortiz, who owns the main newspaper in Mexico City.

I've known some good-looking women in my time, including my own beautiful Caroline, but this Lucy Ortiz took your breath away. She wore her hair up in black braided coils, sometimes with little sprigs of flowers. She had dark, flashing eyes like a gypsy dancer's, a tall, curvy figure, velvety skin and a smile that captured everybody's heart. She was smart and stylish, and Fortescue spoiled her rotten. When his friends told him she was worth the wait, he was real pleased.

Lucy gave birth six months later in New York to twin girls they name Consuelo and Mercedes, two cherubs with dark raisin eyes like their mother, and light-colored hair like Emma Fortescue's. That's when Fortescue starts devoting less time to Fortland Oil and leaving the management to Levi. I been doing it for years and the company's coined money, so we figure if he plays hooky too, we should double earnings.

Fortland's success results mainly from the single greatest phenomenon of the twentieth century, the rise of the American automobile. Fortescue saw it coming all those years ago in Bungle's saloon. Others may have seen it too, I suppose, but not too many. Until the twenties, the country was geared to the horse. Motoring was more of an adventure than a habit, and people still traveled long distances by train. Then, almost overnight, when Americans took to the road in a serious way after the war, Fortland Oil was waiting for them.

Our filling stations were soon known nationwide, with the familiar white bronco kicking up his heels inside the red diamond. Levi's advertising people spent a pot of money on billboards and the new radio commercials, until Fortland No-knock gasoline and Fortland Superlube were household words. When I tell Levi he'll be known to posterity as one of the great pioneers of the gasoline age, he just blushes. Fortescue says, "Every woman is in your debt, Levi! What Edison did for electric light and Bell for the telephone, you've done for clean restrooms coast to coast!"

The richer Levi got the more eccentric he became. After Heinz died and we made Levi president of the company, he married a Texas millionairess who was a head taller and fifty pounds heavier than him, and looked like Jack Dempsey in a skirt. Nobody knew what they ever saw in each other because they fought from the day they met. But the marriage lasted thirty years until he died.

Levi really hated her, and relished every chance to get her goat. He would deliberately turn up late when she was waiting for him, or take his limousine and driver home from a party and leave her to beg a ride or call a taxi. She had most of her money in the stock market by then, just like him, and the only thing she respected him for was his financial expertise. She never bought or sold a single share without consulting him.

It took him a few years to wake up to this, but when he did, only God could help her. He'd call her at home sometimes two or three times a day to give her advice on the market. Whatever he was buying, he'd warn her to sell, and vice versa. When she'd cry later about how many thousands she lost, he'd hang up the phone, slap his knee and roar with laughter. "Serves her right, stupid old bag!"

Why she never caught on, I don't know, but in the end it was lucky she didn't. Just before the big 1929 crash when he was buying everything in sight, he told her to sell out and not buy back. She did, and she survived with her millions intact while Levi lost everything except his Fortland Oil salary.

I should of done the same as Fortescue and stayed away from the office after we come back from Mexico, but instead I get caught up in the oil business again, a mistake I was soon to regret. A printed title on one of my dusty old legal files tells the whole squalid story. It's dated May 27, 1925, and reads: "Indictment Violation Section 37, United States Penal Code: Conspiracy to Defraud the United States."

At the bottom is a note in my handwriting: "Supreme Court Hearing," and another printed title that reads: "Case concerning Naval Petroleum Reserves. Criminal #433325. *The United States of America, plaintiff,* versus *Edward Laurence Doheny, Harry Sinclair, Lee Oliver Garland and Albert Bacon Fall, defendants.*"

What a mess that was! The case against me and Doheny and Fall and Harry Sinclair was blown out of proportion in the press and became known as the Teapot Dome scandal. The whole thing was a sham and a political vendetta, but they nailed Al Fall in spite of that, and he went to prison. He was Secretary of the Interior when it started, and they said we bribed him to let us take oil that belonged to the navy out of the Teapot Dome over in Wyoming. The truth is we didn't bribe nobody. It was just an exchange of favors between businessmen and politicians, the kind of back-scratching exercise that's been going on for centuries, and won't stop until the last politician and the last businessman bite the dust.

Lucky for me, all during the investigation and trial Fortland Oil continues to make more money than I'll ever need, and Fortescue helps out by politicking around the Republican party and down in Washington. He was one of the best friends and certainly the finest associate I've known in my long life. I treasured that man.

I told him, "If you want to disengage yourself from this Teapot Dome stupidity, now's the time. It's my fault and Doheny's. You wasn't involved so there's no reason to share the scandal."

"You once said you wouldn't kill me to save my pride."

"So?"

"We're friends. Nothing as insignificant as a little scandal could scare me off. Why, this promises to be more fun than being beaten up or getting shot in the foot or scorched by a Tampico tank fire. After all the wonderful times we've shared, why would I want out now?"

He makes me laugh.

"Exactly," Fortescue says.

"Okay. I get the message."

"You may be a trial to those who know you, Lee. Sometimes you're even an embarrassment. But as my dear mother always said, knowing you makes it all worthwhile."

"I appreciate your vote of confidence."

"You have a talent for making things happen."

"That ain't a talent, it's a curse. All I ever wanted was peace and quiet, and some time alone with Caroline."

Fortescue looks at me for a long time with those clear, candid eyes of his, smiling, before he says, "I know better. You want justice and fairness more than anything, even Caroline, and when you don't find it, why, you shake the very tree of life."

"And *you* can still talk the ears off a army mule."

"If I'm wrong, explain why you went to fight again in France."

"I just got caught up in it."

"You never got caught up in anything you didn't want to be caught up in. At the risk of hurting your feelings, let me say you can find more ways to show off than a highwire artist because you're never happy unless you're risking life, limb and precious reputation."

Fortescue wasn't entirely right, but he had a point. I was determined to fight this Teapot Dome thing through because the real scandal was the way them senators went after poor Albert Fall. Every politician makes a few enemies in his career, but Al's cockiness probably earned him more than his share. And when some of them saw a way to knock him off his perch, they had a picnic. He never was smart about money and not lucky with it either. When he ran the Interior Department, he looked after his friends. Me and Doheny and Sinclair and some others. And we loaned him money. The Democrats didn't see it like that. They said the money was a bribe so he'd give us the right to pump out oil.

They persecuted that man until they finally put him behind bars. Which was unjust because they never could prove anybody bribed him. Nothing happened to me or Doheny although they locked Harry Sinclair up awhile for contempt because he told them where to shove their investigation. I've talked to lawyers and judges about that case over the years and most of them agree the court was wrong. I mean, it takes two to tango. How can you convict a man of *taking* a bribe when you can't prove somebody gave it to him? But political justice works like that. It's different from any other kind.

So Al Fall's public career ended in jail, where I visited him every week, to the distress of some of my proper friends. He was allowed to serve his time as a federal prisoner in the state penitentiary here in Santa Fe, which was both a mercy and a humiliation. Among the hardened old-time criminals in that jail was more than a few he'd put away when he was judge, but they didn't hold it against him.

On my visits I learned a lot about his early life in the Territory, like the fact that him and Ed Doheny knew each other way back in the eighties. Doheny worked a gold claim in Kingston, which is now a ghost town. Al Fall was already a lawyer at that time but trying to dig his fortune out of a mountain too. He told me about it in a way that showed he hadn't entirely lost his sense of humor.

"I suppose Thurston Byrd is responsible for all this."

"Who the hell is Thurston Byrd?" I ask him. That's a name I never heard anybody mention at his trial.

"Was, not is," he says.

"Well, who was he?"

"A villain who once tried to kill Ed Doheny. That's how we met. You might say Thurston Byrd also rekindled my interest in the law."

Al says this Thurston Byrd raided Doheny's camp at gunpoint one day back in the eighties and robbed him of gold dust worth several thousand dollars. Doheny tried to stop him and nearly got killed. His partner tried too, and *did* get killed.

The other miners form a posse and catch up with Byrd on the lava beds east of Grants. They bring him back to Kingston, try him for murder and hang him. After about ten minutes they cut him down and put him in his coffin. They're taking the body to the cemetery in a wheelbarrow when Byrd kicks off the lid and climbs out.

Doheny points a gun at him and they march him back to town. Byrd's got a touch of laryngitis from choking on the rope but he finally makes them understand there's a point of law at stake here called double jeopardy, which says a man can't be hanged twice. The judge never heard of this, but he wants to be fair, so he says to go get Al Fall because he's the only bonafide lawyer around who owns a set of law books.

Al looks up double jeopardy and confirms that a man can't be *tried* twice for the same crime, but the law don't say nothing about how many times he can be hanged for it. So they string Byrd up again and this time they leave him an hour so there's no doubt.

Emma Fortescue didn't live to see Al Fall brought low. She died of a cancer in her womb some months before the scandal broke, with Albert Fall at her bedside. Losing Emma at that critical moment was a great sorrow for him and all of us, although he always said he was glad she wasn't there to see the wolves eat his liver.

The newspapers decided he was the most exalted example of moral and ethical corruption since Benedict Arnold. He wasn't guilty of any crime that I could see, except friendship.

After he come out of jail he wouldn't let nobody help him because all he had left, he told me, was "a little pride and dignity." So that's what he kept to the end. (He would die during the Second World War down in El Paso, alone in a furnished room where he'd lived the last years of his life. A man who could of been president.)

Luna's comment on what happened, as usual, was closest to the grain. He said, "It's not so much the act that counts in politics, Lee, but the outward appearance of it, and what Al Fall did had all the outward appearance of taking a bribe."

"You know he's innocent."

"I don't believe either of you is innocent because I know you both. But neither do I think you were consciously committing a crime. You're the kind of man who'd loan a friend money and not give two hoots if you ever got it back. And he was the sort who would borrow it and not be overly troubled in what coin he paid you."

"Well, there you are. That's exactly what I told them federal attorneys. If that ain't innocence, what is?"

"Lee, in politics you're guilty unless you can prove otherwise, and Albert Fall couldn't do that."

"Neither could I, but nothing happened to me."

"You held no public trust."

When I think back on it, Luna was right. Albert Fall paid a heavy price for being a friend to all of us, for being careless and for misunderstanding the rules of the political game he played all his life. He couldn't believe it when they turned down his appeal. For a politician, Al was pretty naive. He never lost his faith in the tooth fairy. He came a long way from frontier lawyer to Washington, and he had more friends than any man I ever knew, with the exception of Ben Butler. Yet all but a handful of them deserted him when he got into trouble because nobody wanted to be tarred by the brush of scandal. That's a laugh. Most of them same Washington people would sell their mother for small change if they hadn't already sold her to get where they was.

I spent as little time in Washington as possible after coming back from Mexico. Mostly Caroline and me lived quietly here at Eagle

Nest, only leaving to visit the oil fields from time to time.

I seen a lot of Luna then. He'd served three terms as governor
and the party wanted him to go to the Senate, but he said no, he
had enough of politics after thirty years. He also turned down a
couple of cabinet offers from Hoover, and for the rest of his life
dedicated himself mainly to raising cattle for his family and money
for charity.

He was in demand as a fund-raiser because he knew how to
intimidate an audience. He'd menace them, embarrass them, flat-
ter them and trick them, all the things he used to do to us in the
army to get his way. He knew everybody in the state and what they
was worth, which helped. I remember once during the Depression
he was talking to a banquet hall full of people at the Alvarado Hotel
in Albuquerque when old Walt Wideman got up to leave. By this
time Wideman was one of the richest men in the southwest and
proud of his image, but not easy to put the touch on.

Luna called out, "Hold on, Walt. I don't have your check yet."
The money was to feed homeless migrant families or something.

"You can have it right now," Wideman says, smiling at the
crowd.

"For the usual amount?"

"That's right," Wideman says, taking out his checkbook.

"I want a big hand of applause," Luna calls out. "Let's hear it
for Walt Wideman's generous gift of one thousand dollars!"

Wideman was usually good for only a hundred, but with the
crowd applauding, and a clerk waiting at his elbow for the check,
he had to add the extra zero to save face. When he complained
about this to Luna the next day, Luna said he was sorry but he must
of got him mixed up with some other benefactor who always gave
a thousand.

Luna used to visit Albert Fall in jail too, and the hell with public
opinion. It was a funny friendship. They mainly played cards because Luna was not a great talker, and he said he'd heard everything Al Fall had to say when Al was on the bench. But good
friends they was, and nobody could criticize Albert Bacon Fall to
Max Luna without running a certain risk.

Ed Doheny made that mistake once and Luna ordered him out
of his house. All Doheny said was Al was a damn fool for getting
caught.

"Caught at what?" Luna demanded.

"Well, you know," Ed said.

"No, I don't."

"We did give him money."

"Lee said it was a loan."

"And Al did us some favors."

"Lee told me that."

"Well?"

"Well, what?"

"We didn't expect the money back."

"So you're telling me you bribed him."

"Not exactly."

"Then let me get it right. You're telling me he took a bribe, even if you didn't bribe him."

"That's more like it," Ed says.

"Get out!" Luna says.

"What the hell's the matter with you?"

"Out!"

Doheny's still angry a few days later. He's a big contributor to the Republican party, and Luna's made him feel like a crook and look like a horse's ass.

"I don't understand that bastard," Doheny says.

"Al Fall's his friend," I tell him.

"He's my friend too," Doheny says, "but he never should have got caught."

"That's the point," I say. "You think he's guilty, and you couldn't care one way or the other. What you don't understand is Luna couldn't be friends with Al if he thought that."

Doheney says, "It's just his convoluted greaser mentality."

"Don't ever let him hear you say that."

Doheny laughs. "Why? You think he'd shoot me?"

"He's shot men for less."

"Look, I like Luna. He was a good governor and he's got a lot of class. But he's still a Mexican."

"You really are lucky," I tell him sincerely.

X X X V

My Boy Ben

Caroline rarely read the financial news, hardly ever looked at a newspaper. Yet six months before the stock market crash in 1929, she took the Southwest Century Bank out of Wall Street. She did it because a *brujo* she trusted told her New York was going to collapse, and he gave her the date as September. He seen a vision of people jumping out of windows, screaming, filling the streets in panic. More damage, he told Caroline, than the San Francisco earthquake.

"New York don't have earthquakes," I told her.

"He didn't exactly say that's what it would be."

"Well, you ought to get it straight before you go redefining the whole investment strategy of your bank."

"You said yourself Wall Street is riding for a fall."

"That's only a way of talking, Caroline."

"I don't see you rushing to buy stocks."

"You never will. We own a nice piece of Fortland Oil and a lot of land. What do I want stocks for?"

"Suppose you were running the bank?"

"Listen to the bankers. You got some good ones on your board."

"Perry says they're wrong." Everybody's got a right to believe in his or her own foolishness, and Caroline always had this weakness for fortune-tellers, witches and mediums.

Perry Sandoval was a neighbor of ours here at Eagle Nest who owned a little one-horse spread high up on the mountain, with pastures so steep we used to joke about his sheep having one set of legs shorter than the other. He was married to one of Hernan Montoya's granddaughters, so you could say we was kind of related. I always thought he was harmless enough until he started giving out financial advice.

I said, "Perry's a good fellow, Caroline, and maybe he's a spectacular *brujo,* but he's got a plate in his head and he ain't always home upstairs." I wasn't kidding about the plate. He'd been shot up bad at Chateau-Thierry and was more than a little shell-shocked. I think that's where his visions come from, but I could never convince her, especially after the crash came in October and the Southwest Century remained one of the few solvent financial institutions in the state.

She reminded me how I doubted Perry's prediction, and I said, "Wait till he comes to collect," but he never did. I felt that he earned himself a hell of a fee for his Wall Street advice but he didn't see it that way.

Caroline kept him from starving by giving him odd jobs here at Eagle Nest, but he was never well enough to work a whole week and he refused to take more than an hourly wage. His eldest boy was fourteen and worked for her after school in the garden. On what they made, plus a pitiful little army pension, Perry fed four more kids and a wife. The Sandoval family survived, but barely.

What Caroline didn't know was that Perry Sandoval was also *Hermano mayor* of the local *Penitente* sect, a supersecret religious brotherhood whose members were pledged to look after one another. The only trouble was most of them was as poor as Perry. The sect was illegal in New Mexico, and the Catholic church would excommunicate any man they found out belonged. But it went back four hundred years, and nobody ever has been able to stamp it out.

Perry Sandoval wouldn't take money for himself, but he accepted my donations to the brotherhood and they made me an honorary member. Luna got a kick out of that. His father had belonged to the *Penitentes,* and his grandfather before him, and so on. But like every other recent governor, he condemned their practices because he believed they had no place in the modern world. "Now I know they're doomed if they took you in," he tells me. "I can just see you stumbling up a mountain with a cross on your back."

That's one of the things they do every Holy Week. Before Luna got wound up on one of his sermons, I reminded him that my membership was only honorary. "They just wanted to say thanks for the money. I got no intention of joining in their ceremonies."

"I'm relieved to hear that, Lee. Because if you got serious about religion, I'd have to reexamine my whole set of values."

"Hell, Max, I'm as serious about it as the next man."

"If that were true, I believe I'd take the veil."

Beginning on Palm Sunday the *Penitentes* hold nightly processions from their lodge to a mountaintop shrine. They march barefoot, stripped to the waist, some with candles chanting Ave Marias, while the rest flog themselves with straps and barbed-wire whips. The trail would be wet with their blood after a few minutes.

The brothers who don't take part in the march stand guard to keep sightseers away. Then on Good Friday they elect one man to carry a heavy cross over the same route. When they get to the top of the hill, they set up the cross and tie him on it and leave him there until Sunday, just giving him a little water. After ten or fifteen hours, he's usually unconscious, and sometimes he dies.

The State Police raided these ceremonies more than once and locked up some of the brothers. But it was always too popular an organization to stamp out. People still lead hard lives in these poor, remote mountain villages. There's no priest and no church, so they invented their own way to keep the faith.

None of our New York friends had the benefit of Perry Sandoval's witchery and the market crash wiped out quite a few of them. Some, like Fortescue, actually made money because he got out early. Others like Knoblauch lost heavy fortunes, even though what was left was more than they or their descendants could ever spend.

The Fortland Oil Company stock price shrank by almost a third, but that still left us well off. The petroleum industry in general was the least affected by the crash at the beginning. And by the time we began to feel the pinch, we had pulled in our horns and reorganized ourselves.

The first year, 1930, passed with a lot of optimism and up-beat talk. It was clear that regulation of the stock market was long overdue, but everybody had a different idea how to go about it.

Nobody really understood what had happened, and while the politicians argued about what to do, the country was like a raft headed over a waterfall.

The big drop and deep trouble lay ahead. By 1932 thousands of businesses had closed, banks collapsed and factories shut their gates. The ordinary institutions couldn't cope with a disaster on such a scale. For the first time in our history, whole families were going hungry and whole states were begging Washington for help.

Any half-baked crackpot with a soapbox and a crazy idea could find an audience willing to listen. Communists, Fascists, Socialists and Anarchists all claimed it was the collapse of the capitalist system, and some of us dyed-in-the-wool capitalists wasn't too sure they were wrong.

Me and Caroline go to the Republican convention in Chicago that year where I'm a delegate. A week of boozing at the Blackstone Hotel and dying of the heat to renominate Hoover and Charlie Curtis on the presidential ticket. Then we take the train to New York with Pat Hurley and his wife. I'd known Pat since he was a young National Guard officer and now he's Secretary of War. A tall, handsome man, some years younger than me, with an ambitious streak not unlike Albert Fall's. Like me, he had made a sizable killing in the oil business and dabbled in politics. We saw eye to eye on most things except he was more optimistic about Hoover's chances than me.

"He'll win, Lee, you'll see."

"I don't know. There's too many men looking for work out there." I point to a closed-down steel mill beyond the train window. "And too many Democrats blaming it on us."

Like most Westerners, Hurley felt that the greed of the Eastern brokers was responsible for the craziness in the stock market and the crash that followed. But he had blinders on, too, and failed to see that the people had to blame somebody for the Depression, and Hoover was the favorite scapegoat.

After soaking in the springs at Saratoga for a few days, Caroline and me spend part of July with the Fortescues at a place he had built out near East Hampton. The twins are beautiful, but awkward and leggy, twelve years old and madly in love with their daddy and their horses, sneering if you mention boys. Consuelo, the older one by five minutes, talks a streak and is always first at anything she does, while Mercedes is shy like her mother.

Fortescue had his own stables and polo grounds on the estate, and weekends friends came to play. Some of the younger players are sons of men who'd served with us in Cuba. And one that I invite especially is my own son Ben, now twenty-four and a Harvard graduate. He's a little embarrassed having a father with such rough ways, but he makes a real effort to get along. When Fortescue organizes a father-son game, me and Ben play with C.E. Knoblauch and his son against some of the best players around. We lose, but the game at least is the beginning of something between me and my boy at last.

"You're good, Dad," Ben tells me when we finish.

"Nice of you to say that, Ben." But I'm fifty-two by then and got no business crashing around the Fortescue estate on a polo pony. Except it was good exercise and a way to know my boy.

He was no Matt, far from it, and most of the time I suppose I found that hard to forgive. But he was a good fellow at heart, just so damned stuffy and correct and conservative that I always felt like some kind of wild animal around him. He was a fine horseman but he rode like he did everything else, cautious and defensive, with no real flare or style. He was as different from me as a boy could be.

The thing I notice most about that polo crowd at Fortescue's is how far removed they are from the Depression that grips the country. I mean it ain't a popular subject of conversation, except among the few who see a Communist under every bed and a revolution in every hunger march.

One day me and Fortescue drive over to Montauk and find the place where we'd landed when we come back from Cuba more than thirty years before. Some fishing boats are putting to sea, and gulls screech over the harbor. We walk around the piers and watch the fleet of big, squat potato boats loading, then past the railroad station and through the little town and toward the lighthouse on the point. There's nothing now where our army quarantine camp had been. Nothing where we'd mustered for the last time and said farewell to the colonel. Not a marker or a flag or a plaque or anything. Just sand dunes in the wind.

When I ask Fortescue what he's thinking, he says, "The same as you, I guess. Remembering old friends." He shrugs and picks up the dried-out shell of a horseshoe crab. After all these years he still don't talk much about the war, except the funny parts. He hands me the shell. "You think the twins will like this?" When I nod, he says, "Well, we better find another then, because I can't bring them one of anything."

While Caroline stays on with Lucy and the girls, me and Fortescue travel to Washington for meetings with the bosses running Hoover's reelection campaign. We're on one of them advisory committees politicians like to put together because it gives them a way to spread the blame when they guess wrong.

In Hoover's case, the committee itself is a wrong guess. I mean it's made up of bankers and brokers and business men like us, which means he's listening to some of the same people who caused the country's problem in the first place. But whatever advice he gets, there's no way the voters are going to send him back to the White House. And the advice was mostly bad. The country was suffering, and nothing short of some fast, heroic action was going to pull us out.

When we get out of Fortescue's limousine at Pennsylvania Station, the people crowding the sidewalks break your heart. Apple sellers and beggars of all shapes and ages. Lean, hungry-looking men holding crude pathetic signs saying things like, "I'll do Anything!" "Skilled Plumber! Hire Me!" and "Work, please! Before My Family Starves!"

On the train Fortescue puts down the newspaper he's reading and says, "The great American dream, Christ! What went wrong? You saw those faces. They're not beggars, they're ordinary people forced to beg." He slaps the paper on his knees. "On top of everything it hasn't rained on the great plains in four months, there's a grasshopper plague in Kansas and the West is turning into a dust bowl. Billy Sunday claims it's God's vengeance."

"Who?"

"The evangelist preacher."

"Since when do you pay attention to that kind of air?"

"Do you feel any guilt?"

"Should I?"

"According to Franklin Roosevelt, you should. On the radio he said the 'forgotten man' is the fellow in the street, and fat cats like you and me are the ones who forgot him."

"You think people believe that?"

"He's got a great gift of gab, and his New Deal pitch is very clever politics."

"Maybe Hoover should get on the radio too."

"To keep saying what he's been saying? 'Vote for me because better days lie ahead.'? How do you convince a man who's lost his job, his savings and his self-respect, and can't feed his family?"

At first glance, Washington ain't as depressing as New York, but that's a false impression. Eleven thousand war veterans from all over the country are camped in tents and tar-paper shacks on the flats in Foggy Bottom, sending daily delegations to Congress and the president to collect a bonus they been voted.

Pat Hurley is convinced the ringleaders are all Reds and he tells Hoover this. Rumors are around town that they're plotting to kill the president and overthrow the government. One day after a meeting I go over to where the main camps are, to have a look for myself. If there was any revolution brewing, I missed it. Mostly they are poor devils desperate for food or work or money, many of them with gaunt-eyed wives and sickly looking children.

When I ask around if there's any New Mexico boys there, a polite young fellow points me to one tent that's got a Hopi sun figure painted on the flap and an American Legion flag stuck in the mud out front. I stick my head in and who do I spot but Perry Sandoval.

He's happy to see a familiar face from home, but embarrassed too. "Colonel, what brings you here?"

"Perry, I could ask you the same."

"Just the bonus they voted, the money we're entitled to."

"Maybe this ain't the way to collect," I say.

"We tried everything else," Perry tells me.

"I'll see what I can do for you," I say.

I talk to Pat Hurley but I can't convince him. "If they abandon the protest and go home," he says, "they'll get their money."

"Most of them need it to get home."

"Well, this administration won't be coerced by Communists."

In the end, what happens is a disaster. Hurley and MacArthur, who was then the army's chief of staff, blitzkrieg them poor bastards with tear gas and armored cars. Three thousand regular troops from Fort Meyer, with bayonets fixed, go stomping in there that summer under Ike Eisenhower's orders led by Georgie Patton. It's one of the more shameful chapters in our history, and I believe the public reaction to it gave Roosevelt the election on a plate.

For a while after Caroline and me get back here to Eagle Nest, we try to ignore what's happening to the country too. That's the beauty of this place. The rhythm's different. Wars and panics come and go, but the birds and animals and most of the people still mark the time and seasons by the sun on the mountain and the changing color of the leaves.

When I tell Caroline about running into her witch friend Perry Sandoval in Washington, she ain't surprised, but she's as shocked as I am by the unnecessary way the government run them fellows off. There was quite a few gassed and hospitalized, and I heard a child was killed too. It sounded like the kind of thing old Simon Glasinsky told me used to happen in Russia, riding people down with mounted troops and bayonets and burning their dwellings.

But there's always violence when people are hungry, and if a whole country don't know where its next meal's coming from, it can take on a real ugly character. The early thirties was a time of failure and misery for too many folks. New Mexico was luckier than most states because our population was small and there was no industry. But that didn't mean one man's misfortune was any the less because he lived in Albuquerque instead of Chicago. Disaster is personal wherever it strikes.

Take the Sandoval family. After Perry come back from the bonus march, he's so depressed, according to Caroline, he even stops having visions and just goes around mumbling to himself. Old war wounds pained him so much he couldn't work, so they mainly lived off what the boy earned, and what the *Penitente* brotherhood gave to the wife. I mean they was no strangers to poverty. That's when they get a notice the bank that holds their mortgage is foreclosing.

By the time I hear about it, the court has ordered the sale and it can't be stopped. There's dozens, maybe hundreds of these auctions every week, and small farmers and ranchers are going belly up all over the West.

The day before the sale Perry Sandoval takes down his hunting rifle and blows his brains out, leaving the wife and five kids to deal with their leftover lives. As far as I'm concerned, it's the United States government pulled the trigger on that man. He never was too stable or too bright, with his crazy visions and his magic spells and charms, but that ain't enough to condemn a man to death. Old Perry worked hard for his family and suffered for his country, and if that country hadn't let him down, he'd of paid off his goddamn mortgage, kept his pride and squeezed a living somehow out of that fifty-acre rock pile he called home.

The day of the auction is also the day of Perry Sandoval's funeral, and I decide to attend both. My son Ben arrives early that same morning from Santa Fe. The visit is Caroline's idea because she likes Ben and wants me to be more of a father to him. It's a little late, but I'm willing to make the effort, except that particular morning I'm mad as a snake about poor Perry Sandoval.

I put on an old black suit and a dark Stetson I keep brushed for such somber occasions, and we all three drive to the cemetery. By the time prayers are said and the *Penitentes* brothers put Perry in the ground, I've had time to reflect on the unfairness of what happened. It ain't enough the man was wounded and gassed in Wilson's war, but he couldn't hold a steady job after that. He couldn't live on his miserable pension either, or pay his mortgage after the Congress held up his bonus.

I don't believe in layabouts and bums getting free handouts. I don't believe in drunks and drug addicts living off the rest of us either. Just keep them locked up where they can't hurt anybody. But if we're being true to ourselves, we got to look out for people like Perry Sandoval. They're poor devils who don't deserve to fall through the cracks in an imperfect society.

I say some of this to Ben and Caroline on the drive home. I say it ain't just the charities and the government got an obligation, but anybody cares about his country. She agrees in a gentler tone because she's more tolerant and forgiving than I ever was.

Ben says, "I don't see why you feel sorry for him, Dad. The man took his own life and left his family to fend for themselves. It's them I'd be sorry for, if you're going to feel sorry for anyone."

"Who's talking about feeling sorry? I'm talking about America! About a poor shell-shocked bastard who lost his health on a battlefield. I'm talking about living up to promises."

I drive Caroline and Ben home, and before going out again, I do something I ain't done in years. I strap on my Colt. When Ben sees the gunbelt, his eyes grow.

Caroline says, "Lee . . . what on earth?"

"Don't ask."

"Please. I know you're angry but . . ."

There's about fifty people at Perry's place when I get there, but the auction ain't started yet. I know most of them, and except for two or three who might try to buy the farm for peanuts, the rest don't have two cents to rub together. I already decided to buy it if I have to, to keep Perry's family from being thrown out, but I really don't want the property to change hands. My Colt causes some sidelong glances and whispering behind cupped hands, but nobody mentions it to me.

The auctioneer is a dapper young fellow, one of them hearty, booster types always smiling and slapping strangers on the back. He tells everybody to quiet down when there ain't hardly any talking, and hikes himself up on the tailgate of his truck to start the auction.

I wander over to the pathetic pile of possessions Perry Sandoval accumulated from a lifetime of hard work and sacrifice. A couple of worn-out saddles, some sheep shears and branding irons, a broken victrola, a wooden icebox and an old sofa with half the stuffing hanging out. Junk mostly, not worth ten dollars. Laying on the sofa is a rope I pick up before I sit down.

This auctioneer sees me and says, "Mister, you had all morning to inspect the items!"

"That so?"

"Move back so we can start!"

I shake out a loop and give it a turn or two till I got their attention. Then I throw it over his head so it lays on his shoulders. Men start laughing, but this auction fellow don't see the humor.

"Ha, ha, very funny," he says reaching up to shake it off. But I jerk the loop so tight his eyes pop. He grabs for the tailgate with one hand to keep his balance, and tugs at the noose with the other to loosen it. "What the hell do you think you're doing?"

"What do you think *you're* doing?" I say.

"Conducting an auction," he gasps, his wind almost cut because every time he tugs, I tug.

"Well, I'm conducting a hanging," I say, and by now everybody's laughing.

Some of the men shout, "That a boy, Colonel! Teach the bastard a lesson! String one up for old Perry!"

"I'll make you a deal," I tell him, keeping the rope taut. "You suspend your auction and I'll suspend my hanging."

"You can't hang me!"

"Want to bet?"

About then a bank employee who's been helping him steps up and says, "Come on, damn it, do as he says!"

"What about my commission?" the auctioneer whines.

"Hang your commission and let's get out of here!" The bank fellow hustles him to his car and the rope catches in the door when they slam it. This poor auctioneer's still struggling to get free of the noose as they drive off in a hurry.

When I get home and put up my gun, Ben don't say nothing, just makes himself scarce. He's embarrassed because some neighbors have already called Caroline to tell her I tried to hang the auctioneer. It just shows how even your friends can distort the truth.

They was hard years for most people, but I have to give Roosevelt credit. He gained the confidence of the voters in a way Hoover never could of. I personally disliked them alphabet agencies and giveaway programs of his, but he did put men back to work, building highways and post offices and a lot of other things the country needed.

In 1934 me and Fortescue inaugurated the Fortland Tower in New York, a sixty-story headquarters in the art-deco style that changed the skyline along Central Park South. There was a lot of soul-searching before we went ahead with the project, but we decided either we believed in what we was doing or we didn't. And if we did, then the time had come to put up the Fortland Tower. Seven hundred construction workers labored a year to finish it at a cost of half a million dollars a floor.

A three-story waterfall cascades into a pond on the lower level of the half-block site. Swans swim there in the summer, and in winter people can iceskate. A garden Caroline designed attracts secretaries and clerks from all over midtown who come with their lunches.

The official opening brings out the governors of New York and New Mexico, ex-President Hoover, some senators and ambassadors, Fiorello LaGuardia, and the movie stars Doug Fairbanks and Faye Wray. I invite Albert Fall, but he declines because he thinks it will embarrass us. I insist, but he won't change his mind. Doheny shows up and gives a funny speech about the early days. He has everybody in stitches with his tales of us hosing down Mexican bandits on the *Molly Pratt* and spudding in our first producing well near Tampico.

But the high point for me is when Fortescue asks my boy Ben to say a few words. Ben has just joined the company from business school and is one of our youngest managers. To my surprise he's a good speaker, measured and controlled, with a nice manner and poised gestures. He says the Fortland Tower is a monument to tenacity and patience, to the vision and risk-taking expertise of me and Fortescue. He also calls the building a testament of our faith in the country's future.

"I've listened to a lot of speeches in my time, most of them terrible. But Ben's talk that day stands out even now as one of the best, maybe because he articulated a few thoughts on free private enterprise I felt strongly about all my life.

He called Fortland Oil a machine, not just a oil company, a gigantic machine designed to convert, invent or produce practically anything. He said a whole new world would soon be opened for us by petrochemicals. Wonderful new textiles, paints, wrappings, fertilizers and even medicine would come from the laboratories of our oil chemists. This great machine would make them cheap, while the men and women who operate it would continue to enjoy the highest living standard in the world.

That is what an honest capitalist system gives everybody, he tells the crowd. Not socialism or communism. And not the kind of irresponsible, reckless speculation we've seen lately by unscrupulous brokers and bankers. Not political promises of pie in the sky either, but *open* competition, *efficient* production, *responsible* management, and above all, the fired-up enthusiasm and imagination of all of us who work here.

When he finishes, the applause goes on for five minutes. I kid him he'll have to do an encore like the prima donnas at the Metropolitan Opera, but Ben don't think I'm funny.

"You were good," I say again at the luncheon afterwards.

"Like you at polo," he says, smiling. "Thanks, Dad."

Fortescue seems to understand him better than I do, and when I ask him why in hell Ben and me have so much trouble communicating, he says it's because I intimidate him.

"I never intimidated nobody!"

"Lee, he told me the last time you were in New Mexico together, you went after some guy with a pistol."

"I was only trying to make a point."

"Anyone would be intimidated by that."

"Hell, he just crawled into a corner."

"There you are."

"Ben don't need me to intimidate him. He intimidates himself."

"That's where you're wrong. You saw him handle that crowd today. Not nervous or awkward. It's only around you he loses confidence."

"What am I supposed to do about that?"

"Ease up on the boy."

"I never been tough on him. How could I be? He wilts before I even open my mouth."

"Stop treating him as some kind of weak-minded copy of yourself. He's not. He has his own style and it's effective. It's different from yours, but I'll tell you one thing you've got in common."

"What's that?"

"A way with women."

"Ben with women? He's scared to death of women."

"Not all of them."

"He gets on with Nora, but she's his mother. And with Caroline."

"I'm talking about young women."

"For instance?"

"My daughter."

"I can understand that. Mercedes is quiet, shy, brainy. Sure, I can see that. But he's way too old for her."

"I mean Consuelo."

That really makes me laugh. Fortescue's twins are about fourteen or fifteen by that time, as pretty as their mother, but Consuelo is a rough-and-tumble tomboy and a fine little horsewoman. The idea of this lively, vital girl being interested in stuffy old Ben is really funny. I can only blame it on the difference in their ages.

Fortescue always said Connie should have been a boy. I mean, when they was little and Mercedes was playing with dolls, Connie'd take off alone on her pony or be up climbing a tree. Fortescue let her play polo with us a few times and she was as good as any boy her age. Of the two girls, she was the one loved to hear about bear hunts and soldiering and our early days in the oil business. While her sister Mercedes was reading novels, rouging her lips and putting on her first silk stockings, Connie was planning how she could disguise herself to join the navy, or ride as a jockey in the Belmont Stakes.

She was a trial to her parents, and for a long time, the only thing made her happy was horses. She filled her room with cups and trophies and spent all her spare time around her father's stables.

Until she got this fix on Ben about the time we opened the Fortland Tower building. He was rich enough to do anything he wanted or nothing at all. I give him credit for choosing a business career when he could of been just one more New York playboy with a big bank account.

On the other hand, Ben wasn't cut out for the late hours and dissolute ways of a playboy. He was a born puritan, a worker and a worrier. Although he never had less than a million dollars to his name in his life, he was always looking over his shoulder, expecting the worst. The stock market crash only confirmed his deepest suspicions. At twenty-one he was telling anybody who'd listen, "I told you so!"

For a couple of years he don't give Consuelo a tumble. After all, he's a sophisticated young business executive and she's like a kid sister. Also Ben's the kind of man gives everybody the impression he don't have time for girls.

He never had a steady flame that I remember, which made him popular in New York society. For every eligible, uncommitted young dude like Ben, there was ten mothers after husbands for their daughters. He never come close to being caught, which shows how serious he was.

But when he's playing polo—which is about the only fun he allows himself—Connie's always there. She also comes to her father's office a lot, stopping by to see Ben on the same floor. Lucy notices it first and tells Fortescue. He laughs and tells me that if Connie's set her cap for Ben, he's as good as caught.

"But he don't even know she's alive. As a woman, I mean."

"That won't stop her. She always gets what she wants."

"I can't imagine why she'd want Ben, but I ain't a woman."

At the beginning of the 1937 social season Connie and Mercedes come out as debutantes and Life magazine puts them on the cover, with a story inside on the good life lived by society's most beautiful twins. Fortescue ain't too happy about it. He never liked personal publicity of any kind. But the girls are thrilled by the limelight, and Connie asks Ben to escort her to the big debutante cotillion.

He says he'll let her know, and then typical businessman Ben, he don't get back to her in time. So she asks some North Carolina tobacco prince who plays polo too, and who's as handsome as sin. That's when Ben wakes up. Consuelo and Mercedes are the reigning queens that night, as pretty as twin angels in their white gowns

and diamonds. Ben ends up going to the ball by himself to find all
Connie's dances are taken. Cutting in ain't allowed so he spends
the evening standing around or dancing with the mothers, including Lucy Fortescue, while Connie goes gliding by, gazing at Prince
Tobacco with stars in her eyes.

According to Lucy, the telephone calls from him start the next
day. Amazing what a little attack of jealousy will do for a Garland,
even one as stuffy as Ben. The girl keeps him guessing for a few
weeks, makes him sweat out each date and stands him up a couple
of times until nobody recognizes the old Ben. He's desperate,
distracted, hollow-eyed. Consuelo and her sister are not only the
top social attraction in town that season, they're wanted by every
photographer and magazine editor in the country. Next to King
Edward and Wally Simpson they are the big news in society, and
anything they do gets reported.

One day a few months after the coming-out dance when I'm in
a New York meeting arguing with our lawyers and geologists about
some new Fortland concessions in Venezuela, Ben calls me.

"Dad, can I see you?"

"Right now?"

"Soon as possible."

"What's it about?"

"I'll tell you when I see you."

"Meet me for lunch."

He's waiting for me in the Plaza grill when I walk in a half hour
late because of the meeting. With his usual great tact, before I even
sit down, he blurts out, "I'm getting married."

I lean across the table and take his scotch, raising it in a toast.
"Congratulations! To whom?"

"Consuelo, of course. Who else?"

"Does she know?"

"Dad, please. This is serious." Only then do I realize my stiff-
necked son is half smashed, and even in his present condition, it's
costing him blood to confide in me.

"Does Nora know?"

"I haven't told Mother yet. I wanted to speak to you first."

The truth is, I'm flattered by this declaration, and after thirty
years I'm almost beginning to warm up to this pompous young
prig of a son. "Why me first?" I ask him.

"The circumstances."

"What circumstances?"

"We'd like to marry quietly, away from New York."

"No parties? No big church wedding? You'll disappoint about a thousand people, not to mention the loot you'll lose by not putting on a good show."

"You mean you approve?"

"She's a wonderful girl. Practically family. I think she's a little young for you, but why wouldn't I approve?"

"My great concern is about her parents," he says stiffly.

"They'll come around. Lucy wants her daughters married, and Fortescue thinks you're the cat's pajamas. If you're so hellbent on doing this out of New York, you can do it quiet in Eagle Nest."

"Dad, Connie's pregnant."

"By you?"

"That's insulting."

I start to laugh. "Don't get up on your high horse. I'd be more insulted if I couldn't get a girl pregnant."

"I meant it's insulting to Consuelo."

"Well, I don't know her as well as you do."

"What a terrible thing to say!"

"I don't mean she's going to bed with other fellows besides you. How would I know who she sleeps with? I always considered that a woman's private business same as a man's."

"I can't believe I'm hearing such things from my own father!" He stands up, swaying back and forth, while I'm chuckling at all this.

"Look, don't make it worse by being ridiculous. Sit down! You don't even know why I'm laughing."

"Consuelo is the woman I love," he declares, "and she's a virgin. I don't know why I ever thought I could talk to you about it."

"A pregnant virgin!" On that one I got to take my handkerchief out. "Christ on a crutch, Ben," I tell him. "You done it this time! This could be bigger than the oil business!"

But he ain't listening as he weaves his way toward the hotel lobby. It takes me a few minutes to stop laughing and realize he ain't coming back for his lunch. If there's one thing that boy was born without, it's a sense of humor. I mean it's as serious a defect as a missing leg even if it ain't as obvious.

He and Connie are married over in Maryland a few days later, and I hear about it through Fortescue, who ain't exactly delighted with his kid or mine either. The only problem he's got is calming Lucy down. It ain't the pregnancy or anything that silly. As far as I can figure I'm the only one knows about that. But a girl's mother puts a lot of stock in big church weddings, fancy receptions and all that, and Lucy Fortescue feels cheated.

When I keep calling Ben after the wedding, he don't return my calls. Then a week or two later he asks for a transfer to Venezuela, and Fortescue gives it to him without consulting me. Caroline says, "What on earth did you say to the boy, Lee?"

"Nothing. You know how careful I am around him."

"You must have said or done something."

When I tell her finally, all she says is "Oh, Lee!" and we don't see Ben again until my grandson Pete's about a year old and they all come back to the States. I still don't know what all the fuss was about. One of the few natural, lovable things that boy ever done in his life turns out to be the cause of a powerful misunderstanding between us. I mean pregnancy before marriage was practically a Garland tradition by then. But pregnant virgins was news!

Sitting One Out

Hindsight ain't any more use to us than it is to a fish in a frying pan, but we never get tired of acting like it is. Somebody says, if I'd done this or that different, wouldn't I be hot stuff? Maybe, but then they wouldn't be the same person. Pete says at any given second, a man is always what he was and what he will be. Maybe he was just a poor nobody, but what he will be some day is president or a rich movie star. Then again, maybe he was president or a movie star, and what he will be is fish bait or worm food.

By 1939 I figure I'm in my twilight years. Hell, I'm sixty, and like Churchill, I'm a has-been. If anybody'd told me I'd witness three more wars and another president killed, I'd of called him a liar. Even crazy Perry Sandoval couldn't of seen that much grief in our future.

That's the spring Caroline finally sells me on the idea of going to Europe. Whenever I had time to do nothing, I liked doing it in Eagle Nest, but I know she's got her heart set on this trip. When she was married to Woodrow Sloan, she went to all the fashionable places. Matt was born in London and she's got fond memories of that moment and friends there. My memories of France ain't so happy except for the visits with Matt, but all that's twenty years ago so I say, okay, why not? We also got a slew of invitations from people I do business with, and from diplomat friends we made when we was in Mexico.

477

I'm having lunch at the New York World's Fair one day in May
with Ben, Fortescue and Ben's friend Juan Trippe, who says, why
not fly to Europe. Well, Trippe owns an airline so I guess he knows
what he's talking about, but I ain't thought about anybody flying
the Atlantic since Lindbergh did it back in 1927.

I tell him I didn't know they was taking passengers yet.

"We start scheduled flights in two weeks," he says. "New York
to Lisbon. I can still get you on."

"I'll see if my wife goes for it," I say.

Fortescue thinks I'm crazy, but the idea tickles me. It's an overnight trip instead of a week on a boat, and on top of that we'll be
among the first paying passengers to fly the Atlantic Ocean.

"You may be the last, too," Fortescue says after Trippe leaves.

I got to work on Caroline a little because she's never been up
in an airplane before. She ain't afraid, she says, but the fifteen-
pound baggage limit worries her. For a clotheshorse like Caroline
that's hardly more than some jewelry, an extra pair of shoes and
a toothbrush. When I tell her we can ship the steamer trunks ahead
by ship and pick them up when we get there, she says, imitating
my voice, "Okay, why not?"

Ben and Connie come to see us off. I don't know whether Ben
figures it's the last time he'll see me alive or if we're really becoming friends, but I like it. The fare is three hundred seventy-five
dollars apiece, and we take off from the harbor at Port Washington,
Long Island, in a Boeing flying boat called the *Yankee Clipper.* It's
a big son of a bitch. I mean the propellers measure about fifteen
feet and there's four of them, plus two carpeted decks and five
passenger compartments. The men's toilet even has two pissers on
the wall, besides hot and cold water, and they give us sleeping
berths bigger than a Pullman's. Caroline's thrilled and when I
laugh, she asks me what's the matter.

"I was thinking of all the miles I covered on foot and horseback,
and now look at me. Flying the Atlantic at a hundred fifty miles an
hour!"

There's no liquor sold on board, but some of us bring along
enough to take the edge off the evening. We mix cocktails and
mingle in the aisles, watching the stars come out, forgetting all that
ocean eight thousand feet below. I think about Matt. This is what
he'd be doing if he'd been luckier. Yes, indeed, our Matt would
love this ride!

Dinner's served on a fancy white tablecloth in a paneled dining room. Trippe's wife is aboard and that relaxes Caroline because unless her husband's trying to get rid of her, he must consider his airplane pretty safe. Another passenger is Sonny Whitney, who flew with Matt during the war, and now is chairman of the airline. Sonny's a well-known playboy and polo player who was always getting married and divorced. All he talks about on the trip is how him and his brother Jock just put up four million to finance the movie *Gone With the Wind*. Caroline read the book, and her favorite star Clark Gable's going to play the lead.

"Do you know Mr. Gable?" she says to Whitney.

"Yes, I do."

"I'd love to meet him," Caroline gushes.

"Well, he doesn't get to New York too often," Whitney says.

"Oh, I'd go to California any time to meet Clark Gable," she says, like some teenage kid with a crush. Women are funny that way, and Caroline was no exception.

After Caroline turns in, me and Whitney and two other passengers play poker while the plane drones on through the night. Sonny may be a whizbang polo player, but he's got no head for cards. And like most men with money and no card sense, he likes high stakes. I'm always happy to oblige, and that night I pay our trip to Europe, and then some.

At dawn we land in the Azores to load gasoline, and some of the passengers get a little seasick while the flying boat's bouncing around on the mooring. It's the only time we're uncomfortable on the whole ride. Late that afternoon we glide down over the Tagus River at Lisbon for a real smooth landing, less than twenty-four hours out of New York.

Caroline and me take the train to Madrid and then on to Paris, and she's like a girl on her first outing. All the time she was planning this trip she was studying her Baedekers and maps and histories, so we hardly need a guide. She knows more about Paris and about France than I ever would of guessed, but that was one of the things made her such a remarkable woman. Everything she read she remembered, and she read nearly everything except newspapers.

I like France even though I can't wrap my tongue around the lingo too good. In the army I always had an interpreter, so it's lucky for me Caroline is pretty fluent or I'd of starved. We spend a couple weeks in Paris, where she drags me around to museums and parties and fashion shows, and I take her to some cabarets that shock her a little, and to the races at Longchamps.

Like most women she loves to gamble, but her handicap system at the track would baffle experts. I dope every race and drop a few hundred dollars on some of the most beautiful horse flesh I ever seen, except they can't run worth a damn. Meanwhile she's betting heavy, a hundred dollars a race, and paying no attention to past wins or pedigrees.

In the second race she lays her hundred on a sixteen-to-one shot called *Chanel* because it's number five and that's the perfume she uses. She also bets this horse for the triple and wins. Then she bets on a nag called *Aiglon,* at nine-to-one odds because it's French for eagle, like in Eagle Nest, and she wins again, taking two out of three for the triple. Then in the ninth race, which ends the triple, she backs a filly called *Femme Fatal* who's the favorite.

After two longshots this makes no sense to me, so I ask her, "Why'd you bet this *Femme Fatal,* Caroline?"

"Because it's the favorite," she says as if this fits perfect into the logic of her system. Well, *Femme Fatal* comes home second, so I say I'm real sorry, but then the first horse gets disqualified so Caroline wins anyway. She's jumping around like a scalded cat, grabbing me and crying. I mean we ain't that young anymore, even though you'd never know it to look at her. She's the most beautiful fifty-seven-year-old girl in France at that moment, and winning that triple made her feel like sixteen again.

"Lee, how much did I win? How much?"

I do the calculations on the back of the racing form because she's too hysterical to count, and I don't believe my own numbers. I come up with 90,000 francs, which works out to about $20,000 on her original hundred dollar bet. Caroline's got dozens of trinkets and little pieces of jewelry each worth more than that, but no pair of earrings ever excited her as much as winning that triple.

We had a few bad minutes right after I gave her the numbers because she couldn't find her betting stubs among all the junk in her purse. She finally come up with them from the pocket of her skirt. I tell her that between her system at the track and my poker luck we could live off our wits like this forever.

"Oh, Lee, wouldn't that be wicked fun? You be the gambler and I'll be your moll. But we're a little old to start, aren't we?"

"You and me are never too old to start anything," I tell her, and to prove it we have some wicked fun on the bed before dinner, scattering our clothes on the carpet while I get it up twice.

Then we motor down along the Loire to see all the châteaus and castles, and it would have been like a second honeymoon. Except she points out we never really had a first honeymoon, so I owe her. We kiss in the back of the car like two kids, and when I start to grope her again, she says, "Lee, what will the chauffeur think?"

"We're married, Caroline."

"But he's French," she says. "God knows what he's imagining."

After a week of poking around the Loire we drive east to the Meuse River and the Argonne forest, where I was in 1918. We visit the American cemetery and I take her to some of the places she heard me mention. None of it looks like what I remember. The weather's beautiful, not rainy and gray, and traces of the war are few. After searching half a day I finally find the remains of that fort where me and Castleman was stuck and thought we'd die of thirst.

I tell Caroline about it while we're walking across the battlefield, which is all green pasture now. I can see that her imagination is working overtime trying to visualize what I'm describing. I mean the trenches was filled in ages ago, the only barbed wire around is for fencing milk cows and the old fort is just an innocent-looking hill where a farmer walks behind a plow. It's like I dreamed it all and the war never happened. We walk to the top of the fort and stand where I seen them waves of Germans blown to pieces

She says, "It's hard to believe this was a battlefield."

And I say, "I don't believe it no more myself. I'm hungry. Let's go get some lunch."

She takes my arm and says, "I thank God every day I didn't lose you here. After Matt, I never . . ."

"There was no chance of that," I tell her. "Them things are fate, Caroline. I was born to die in bed making love to you."

She smiles but she don't think it's funny. I can see she's thinking about other things when she asks me, "How do you explain why Matt was taken? Was that just fate?"

"I don't know, darling. I got no answer to that. I'd of died a thousand times if our boy could of lived out his life normal."

She squeezes my hand and there's tears in her eyes, thinking about her baby. To get her mind moving in another direction I say, "Talk about fate, I knew a fellow once who walked away from a

dozen car smash-ups, an airplane crash and two train wrecks
before he died of a tetanus shot."

"Why, I don't believe that at all. You're making it up."

"Well, he did die of the tetanus shot. That part's true."

From our battlefield tour we head down to Switzerland, where
the Knoblauchs have a summer place on the lake near Lausanne.
Old C.E. is still holding up pretty good for sixty. He's already got
about five grandchildren and most of them are running around this
lake house that summer. What I remember mainly is how peaceful
it all was, them cool evenings with Caroline, sitting on Knoblauch's
veranda, looking out over the dark lake at the mountains. C.E.'s
wife plays the piano beautiful, and I remember that too, listening
to her magical, tinkling music in the twilight.

There was a lot of stuff in the news about what the Germans
would do next, but nobody really believed they'd go to war. I mean
they already got the Ruhr back, and Czechoslovakia and Austria
without firing a shot, so there's no need. And mostly we think
Hitler's a joke. One evening Knoblauch's grandchildren put on a
show for us with Victrola music, cute as hell. The girls do a cancan
number dressed in stockings and garters borrowed from Caroline,
while one of the boys does what I think is a great imitation of
Charlie Chaplin. Only he's imitating Hitler. But that's the way we
saw him then, with his Chaplin mustache and hair falling over his
eyes. He was a joke to any American.

One of Knoblauch's banker friends, a German aristocrat from
Frankfurt, visits with us a few days. Graf von Bruckner is no great
admirer of Chancellor Hitler because the graf's a snob. But he's
also a shrewd financial brain who respects ability in anybody, even
if the person come up from the gutter like Hitler. The *graf,* which
means count to us, says Hitler could have been the greatest figure
of this century.

"Why do you say 'could' have been?" Caroline asks him.

"Because he's doomed to failure. In spite of his intuitive genius
for politics and his vigor, he has failed to learn from history and
has already made his first fatal mistake."

"What mistake is that?" Knoblauch says.

"His grotesque partnership with the Russians. It cannot last, and
the Communists will be his undoing."

"What about the way he's come down on the Jews?" I ask him.

The graf says, "It's deplorable because they represent an old and valued part of European culture. But the baiting of Jews has always been a popular pastime in Germany, almost a cherished tradition."

"Only now he's kicking them out," I say. "Taking their property and telling them to find another country."

"I daresay they may be the lucky ones," says the graf.

"Do you know Mr. Hitler?" Caroline asks him.

"We've met," he says, making a face.

In August, at the graf's invitation, we spend a few days with him at his family castle overlooking the Rhine River. Like me, he was in the First War. He says he survived it only because he was taken prisoner by the Brits at the beginning. Most of the other house-guests are bankers or nobility, and I get the impression for the first time that they are seriously worried there could be a war, because they keep asking me what I think America will do.

"Stay out," I say.

"How can you be sure? If England goes to war against Germany, wouldn't you Americans join her?"

"I don't see it," I say. "Roosevelt's a Democrat but he ain't a damn fool. He knows we can't afford a war right now. Nobody can."

"Germany can," one man says.

"Against whom?"

"If Poland attacks, we must defend ourselves," he says.

"But why would Poland attack you?" Caroline asks him.

"There have been many provocations," this fellow says, avoiding the question, "and our patience is running out."

Fred Kaltenbach, an American friend of the graf's from Berlin, stops by for the weekend on his way to Nuremburg. He works for the Hearst newspaper chain and raves about how fantastic the German chancellor is, man of the hour and all that. With him is a German named Putzi Hanfstaengl who claims to be Hitler's best friend. Hanfstaengl plays the piano and tells jokes in perfect English. He went to Harvard so he's very pro-American. He says if the Germans do go to war, this time the Americans will fight with them.

"Are you serious?" I ask him, amazed anybody can believe that.

He's a great success with the ladies because of his line of gab, his jokes and his tunes on the piano, and right away he has Caroline eating out of his hand.

Sunday morning there's a lot of commotion because it seems Hitler's on his way to Nuremburg too, and some of the guests are joining him for tea at a place he's stopping along the river. I'm curious but I decline because I'd rather go boar hunting with the graf, but Caroline tags along with Fred Kaltenbach and Hanfsta-engl to meet Hitler.

She wrote down her impression afterward in a letter to me, which I got here somewhere. It don't have no historical value I suppose, but when you think about what this Hitler turned out to be, the impression he made on my gentle wife is interesting. She comments on the warmth of his smile and his soft hands. Shy but gracious, she calls him.

"And, Lee, darling, I know you won't be jealous if I say he has the most penetrating liquid blue eyes I've ever seen. Kindly one moment, intense and animated the next. One peculiar thing. Facing you he gives the impression of great gentleness and perhaps intelligence, but when you see him from the side, the illusion is destroyed by the disproportionate size of his face, the pronounced, almost Neanderthal ridge of his brow, and nothing at the back of his head. You'll laugh, but several times over tea he broke wind in a most audible way and no one even looked up. He talked nonstop and people hung on ever word.

"I was the only woman present and he deferred to me constantly. Putzi translated his words and the gist of what the chancellor said is that he doesn't understand the Poles. They continue to antagonize the German people by threatening and menacing their eastern borders. I get the impression this is a speech he's given many times, but still those around him are mesmerized. He says that what others expect of Germany is a matter of supreme indifference to him. Only he understands the soul of the German people, and only he can chart their destiny because he is that soul's embodiment. The odd thing is this doesn't make him sound arrogant or egotistical. Although he expresses sentiments that would make another man blush, he does it so naturally and with such assurance that one is persuaded by his conviction and his eloquence, even though I don't understand the language. It is only now, hours after meeting him, that I realize how preposterous were many of the things he said. The man is a great spellbinder!"

I'll say. Two weeks later he attacks Poland, and World War Two gets off to a running start when France and England jump in. We sail home on the Normandy, which is a little like being cooped up in the Waldorf-Astoria for five days. Except the food's better. Roosevelt declares us officially neutral, but I sweat out the crossing anyway because I don't know if them U-boat captains heard his speech.

Back at Eagle Nest we follow what's happening by listening to the radio. Besides the Nazis going after the Poles, the Russians attack Finland and all of a sudden it seems like the whole world's gone loco. I mean for months even the war itself don't make any sense. The Finns kick the stuffing out of the Russians, which surprises everybody, and the French and the Nazis don't fire a shot at each other. Roosevelt keeps talking neutrality but wants our factories geared to make fifty thousand airplanes a year. For who?

When the shooting war in Europe heats up again the following spring and the Nazis march into Paris we are already committed and everybody knows Roosevelt's neutrality talk is a joke. It's no longer a question of "if," just a question of "when." Sixteen million boys sign up for the draft, and people start calling our factories "defense plants."

Fortland Oil's business has never been better, but in the fall when one of our tankers is torpedoed in the south Atlantic, the war gets personal. Fortescue is asked to head up the National Defense Advisory Commission in Washington while I run the store in New York, so me and Caroline take an apartment in the Ritz Towers for the duration.

For nearly two years America waits for the spark that will light our fuse. By that time we got an industrial war machine that's growing like Gargantua. Billions of dollars worth of everything is going to the Brits and the Russians, while we're stockpiling the excess.

General Marshall's the new army chief of staff now and the main architect of our war preparedness effort. When I call on him in Washington, before he can open his mouth, I say, "This is strictly social, George, so don't offer me a job. This time you'll have to excuse me. I'm too old for the draft and I got an oil company to run."

He smiles and says he already crossed me off his list, but as long as I'm there, he'd like to check a reference on a young reserve officer who's volunteered for active duty at the War Department. "He works for you."

"What's his name?"

"Benjamin Butler Garland."

"I guess you'd have to say I can't recommend him too highly," I tell Marshall.

Ben's been running our U.S. refining operations and doing a hell of a job. Although him and me still don't find a lot to say to each other, we're doing better and I'll hate to see him go. This war's going to get a lot uglier before it's over, and when I think of Connie and little Pete, I'm real pleased Ben will do his time on Marshall's staff and not in some goddamn muddy trench in France.

I couldn't of been more wrong. Ben is thirty-three years old by this time, and he goes on active duty as a major. Within a year, Marshall jumps him to lieutenant colonel, then to colonel, and makes him his eyes and ears, assigned to bring back firsthand reports on what we're doing wherever we're engaged with the enemy. What this means is that although Ben never gets a combat command, he sees more combat in that war than practically anybody. When he ain't flying to one battlefront or another, he's hunkered down in foxholes or shelter-halfs from Guadalcanal to Remagen.

He observes the Oran landings in North Africa, watches tanks battle in Tunisia, goes ashore at Sicily, Salerno and Omaha Beach and flies out to Australia and New Guinea to be snubbed by Doug MacArthur. Aside from being dangerous, Ben's job was tough because of the jealousy at the top of the army. Everybody knew he was hired to carry tales back to Marshall, and except for MacArthur they all tried to put the best face on whatever they was supposed to be doing. This gave him a lot of power for somebody so young, and it's to his credit he never abused it.

The outstanding thing about my boy, which men like Fortescue and Marshall seen right away, but what took me forty years or so to recognize, was his discretion, as well as his honesty. Ben just called every shot like he seen it, and because he had a clear, balanced, unprejudiced way of looking at everything and everybody except me, his conclusions were pretty sound as well as carefully presented.

These are as rare qualities in a staff officer as they are in a businessman, and cause people to value your opinions. As a result, by the time Ben comes out of the army, he's got a reputation for scrupulous dealing and a wisdom far beyond his years. He's no politician, and he can rub people the wrong way without meaning to, especially me. He couldn't put icing on anything if his life depended on it. But I'm beginning to recognize his talent even if he never had no flare or style. Thank God his wife Connie's got enough for both of them. But Ben is good solid value, if that's what you're looking for. It's just that where I see a glass half empty, he always sees it half full.

Toward the end of the war, Caroline and me have more chance to get home, and we usually take Connie and little Pete back to Eagle Nest with us. I could never get over the resemblance between Pete at that time and Matt when he was little. I mean both of them looked like me, which Ben never really did. Caroline saw the likeness too and one day when we was in the garden watching Pete play, she says, "It's almost as if the Lord decided to give Matt back to us, isn't it, Lee?"

"Maybe. But every child's unique. I'm satisfied with him being just plain little Pete, and not a reincarnation."

"You're right, of course," she says. "And I'm being foolish."

"No, you ain't. But don't put a burden on the little boy of being like someone else, even if he is. He's got to be himself."

As our armies close the final trap on Hitler and the German people in the spring of 1945, Ben's letters, which Connie reads to us, gives us a pretty clear idea of what's going on right up to the German surrender. Ben didn't get home for seven or eight months because Marshall has him running back and forth across Europe while they're mopping up. Then on the Fourth of July, with everybody in the house still asleep, I go for my usual morning ride and hear a plane circling. It's one of them little army spotter airplanes and when it lands on our airstrip, out steps my boy Ben, dressed in dusty flight coveralls with no rank or insignia or anything.

I'd be a terrible liar if I said I wasn't happy to see him, but he ain't on the ground five minutes before we're arguing about where to park the plane and who's going to carry his Valpack. He has fifteen days leave, his first real holiday in three or four years, so Caroline and me keep little Pete amused as much as we can the first few days while Ben spends time with Connie alone.

In the middle of his leave there's a call from the Pentagon for

General Garland. I correct the operator that it's Colonel Garland and that's when I find out Ben's been promoted to brigadier, and just forgot to tell us. He has to go down to White Sands for a meeting with army brass, which will cut into his leave a day or two.

When I see how this upsets Connie, I volunteer to call Marshall personally and get Ben off the hook. I mean he ain't had more than an occasional weekend or two with his little family since he went in the army, and that's four years ago.

Ben says, "Dad, please stay out of it. I don't want you interfering. If the general wants me in White Sands, I'll be there."

"Just because you're too shy to speak up, don't mean I can't put in the word. Me and George Marshall go back a long time."

"I'm aware of that. I'm asking you to butt out, as a favor."

We argue about it some more, but he's so stubborn and intractable, Connie finally asks me please, to let him do as he wants. I agree for the sake of peace in the family. Hell, I don't want to fight with my only son during the few days he's home, but it burns my ass. What can be so damn important at White Sands that my Ben's got to be there? I mean, George Marshall must have twenty other generals he can send in Ben's place.

I back off and then another idea occurs to me. After making the arrangements, I tell little Pete and Connie and Caroline I'll take them all to Elephant Butte Lake, which ain't far from where Ben's got to be, and we can wait for him there.

Some friends of ours got a fish camp on the lake, with a boat and all, so me and my five-year-old grandson can do some serious fishing while we wait for Daddy. The weather's as hot and dry as any desert summer in New Mexico, with the sun like a big fried egg hanging against the sky. But like me, the kid thrives on it. We don't catch much, just a few sunfish and crappies, but they might as well of been whales for the thrill that little boy gets out of it. Connie has to cook them and I have to eat one, and three days go by without Ben turning up.

Me and Pete are out on the lake on the fourth day but our luck's poor and the child's bored after two hours and only one fish. I dig a coke out of our ice bucket for him and tell some yarns, but it's hard to hold his attention. I'm about to crank up the little outboard and head home when there's a funny bright flash in the sky to the southeast of us, like a second sun coming up behind the first. It's so brilliant for a few seconds I have to shield my eyes. Pete is frightened by it, and to tell the truth so am I because I don't understand it. Then it kind of wavers and dies out. While I keep watching in that direction, I don't see nothing else except the distant outline of a cloud in a sky that's cloudless that time of year.

I make a note to ask Ben about it when he comes back. White Sands is over in that direction, and whatever the flash was, he must of got a better look at it than we did. Caroline and Connie seen it too from the camp, and Caroline says with a shudder that for a minute or so she thought the world was coming to an end. When Ben finally shows up, he's pretty closemouthed about what happened, but he does admit it's a new kind of bomb they're testing and it works.

XXXVII

The Last Man

They say if you live long enough, there comes a time when the best page of the newspaper is the obituaries because as long as you can read it, you ain't on it. There's also a perverted pleasure in watching friends die off while you go marching on. I mean it just confirms what you always believed about yourself, that you're immortal after all. By the time we held the 1952 national reunion of the Rough Riders at Las Vegas, New Mexico, there was still more than fifty of us left, according to the pension people in Washington. But only about two dozen was in good enough shape to make it to the meeting.

Me and Caroline attended, driving up with Luna from Santa Fe. His wife had died the year before, and he'd already had one heart attack, so a lot of the starch had gone out of him. He was pretty old by that time, almost as old as I am now, a fragile little man in a natty blue suit and palm beach fedora. His hands shook but his voice was still firm, and the eyes that looked out from under them thick white eyebrows could still pin a liar or equivocator to the wall.

After so many years, I guess we look more like a nursing home outing than a soldiers' reunion, and except for the men I still see regular like Luna and Mountain and Tom Isbell, I don't recognize too many of the others right off. It's a collection of bald, potbellied, shrunken old geezers for the most part, and where we once carried

490

Krag carbines, now half of us are leaning on canes.

Tom Isbell's eighty-five years old then but don't look sixty. Same weight and stocky Indian build he always had, with all his teeth as white as ever, and a thick shock of hair that's slicked down and parted toward the cowlick on one side of his forehead. He's retired from Fortland Oil like Mountain, and got some money put away. The two of them still got a drinking capacity beats all the rest of us put together and both are widowed so there's no woman around to cut into their bar time.

Dave Leahy shows up with his third wife, who's thirty years younger than him. He's retired from the federal bench and still lives down in Albuquerque. There's a meeting the first morning, with a few minutes of silence in memory of dead comrades. Luna's the senior man so he reads off the list, beginning with Ben Butler. Then he reads letters and telegrams from others like Knoblauch who can't make it because of ill health. Then the list of them we know about who died since the last get-together, which includes Levi Hennings.

Levi retired to Florida after forty years with Fortland Oil, the last fifteen as president. He built himself a small palace on the water at a place called Longboat Key and spent his final years deep-sea fishing, when he wasn't tormenting his wife. He was doing a little of both the day he cashed in.

His captain tells me the trip started out like any other, with Mr. and Mrs. Hennings fighting on the dock because he wants to go fishing alone and she wants to invite friends. He wins and it's a hot, hazy day on the Gulf. Before long both the Hennings have cruised through a fair amount of beer while they're arguing about who gets which fishing chair. She's screaming at Levi and he's calling her names. Just an ordinary morning at sea with the Hennings family, the captain says.

Then Levi sings out, "Tarpon! I got him!" and Mrs. Hennings says, "If that's a tarpon you got there Levi, I'm a monkey's uncle!"

And he says, "Right on both counts, you talky old bag!"

"It better not be a tarpon, you little runt," she screams at him. "It by God better not be!"

The captain says by now Levi's laughing like a idiot because what he's hooked into is really big and leaping ten, twenty feet in the air far astern of the boat, while his wife ain't had a bite.

He's feeding it line and shouting at her, "See him and weep, you dowdy old bat!"

"Look who's calling me a dowdy old bat, you limp dick!"

The captain says that about this time, before the big fish is close to being tired, Levi seems to lose interest and the line pays out like crazy, practically smoking the reel.

"What are you doing, you numbnuts!" she screams at him. "That fish will get away if you don't wake up and land him!"

The mate goes to see what the trouble is, and finds Levi dead in the harness, a half-smile on his face. When he tells this to Mrs. Hennings, she helps lift old Levi out of the fishing chair and takes over his rod, saying to him, "Don't you worry, little sweetheart! I'll land him for you, baby! You'll see, my little honey! I'll bring him in for you, darling!" And she lands the big fish single-handed.

According to the captain, the tarpon is mounted over her fireplace now, and she tells everyone, "That's the one didn't get away, the one me and my sweet baby caught the day he died." When the captain called on her to say he's sorry about Levi's death, she says, "Wasn't that just like him? He always had to be first at everything."

But she cried a lot too, the captain said, and put a huge stone on the grave where she goes every week with flowers. They was a funny pair, Levi and her; they fought a lot, but stayed together thirty years.

That first night of the reunion Mountain entertains everybody in the hotel bar with tales of our escapades in San Antonio. Most of the wives have heard the stories a hundred times before, but Mountain knows how to yarn with the best. When he gets to the choir riot, it's satisfying to see Luna grin. I'm a little nervous when Fortescue recalls Rose-of-Sharon Moriarty and her friend, but the refined way Fortescue tells a story, it's never off-color. And we're all so old by that time, a wife can laugh at something she wouldn't of found funny fifty years before.

But the best yarns are about Levi and his dog Heinz, and Levi coming aboard the *Yucatan* in irons just before we leave for Cuba. Old Heinz lived twenty years after the war, and died in his sleep. But he had sons and grandsons and great-grandsons, a whole dynasty of dogs that looked like him, sawed off and spotted, with bat ears and terrier brains. I got one of them still, and he's old and blind now. Heinz the Tenth, I call him, but Pete's kids shortened it to Tenth.

Anyway that 1952 reunion was memorable for a couple of reasons besides it being the first one Levi missed. It was the last time we formed up mounted and posted by the grandstand where the governor and some army brass reviewed us. Not everybody could sit a horse by then, but ten of us made it. Me and Fortescue, Isbell and Mountain, McGinty, Tuttle, Shanafelt and Jesse Langdon was among them as I recall, four or five of the men in uniform, me in a black suit and Stetson.

Caroline stood between Governor Ed Mecham and Luna, and she said it made her cry when the band struck up the "Garry Owen" and the "Stars and Stripes Forever" and we trotted by with the colors, ten proud old men sitting tall in the saddle.

Me, I was grinning, because I can't ever hear the "Stars and Stripes Forever" without remembering the other lyrics. "Oh, the monkey wrapped his tail around the flagpole! To see his asshole!" etcetera.

We held two lines abreast pretty good, which put me in mind of something about Levi Hennings when we was in the army at San Antonio. Before our horses come, Levi was as hopeless as a man could be for keeping step, worse than any cowboy. When I bawled him out about it, this ex-jockey puts his hands on his hips and says, "Goddamn it, Lee, if I was mounted, I'd keep step!" And he was right. After we got our horses, his precision was something to behold, and we all guided on him.

Although Caroline admits she was moved by the sight of us, at the same time she knew if she lived forever she would never understand men or their love for the trappings of war. When I try to explain, she just holds up her hands. "No, I see you all together, listen to your boasting and hear the funny stories. Yet I know so many died. To tell the truth, while I loath the senseless brutality, I envy the bond it forges. Women share nothing like it."

Some reporters from Albuquerque and Santa Fe come to do stories on our get-together, and one of them writes up an interview with one of the late arrivals, who complains about the piddling size of the veteran's pension we all get, that him and his wife can't live on it. Luna passes me the newspaper over the breakfast table, saying, "Wonders never cease," and when I read the article I don't believe my eyes.

"He's here?" I ask Luna.

"Looks that way."

When we go into the card salon for our morning meeting, which ain't a meeting at all but just an excuse to sit around and renew old friendships, the man who gave the interview is grinning and shaking hands with some of the other Rough Riders. When he sees Luna he sticks out his hand and says, "Good morning, Captain."

Luna says, "Hello, Holman. What are you doing here?" But he don't shake hands, just stares at him. The other men are shifty and nervous with Luna there, like kids caught doing something wrong.

"I read about the reunion and thought I'd come," Red Holman says. "I thought after all these years I'd look up old friends."

"You have no friends here," Luna says.

"I got a right to be here," Red protests. "I'm an honorably discharged veteran of the First Volunteer Cavalry just like you."

"Not just like me, Holman. You were awarded an honorable discharge over the objections of every officer in the regiment because Fifth Corps headquarters didn't want to brand any soldier a deserter."

Mountain says, "If he stays, I go."

Tom Isbell says, "You got a nerve showing up here, scrimshanker! When you ran at Guásimas, you should of kept running!"

Fortescue takes old Red by the elbow and gently leads him aside. Red looks the worse for wear, real old and wizened, his mouth caved in from lack of teeth, pale as paint and with the collar of his shirt three sizes too big. "See here, Holman," I hear Fortescue say, "you must understand how embarrassing your presence is for everyone." Then we notice a little old lady in a faded housedress, tagging along behind Red. She's peering out from behind thick eyeglasses and clutching an imitation-leather purse. "Mrs. Holman?" Fortescue says.

"Red just came to say he's sorry," she tells him. "He knows he done wrong back then and he's sorry, ain't you, Red?"

"That's right," Red mutters.

When the men vote to decide if Red Holman can stay, the vote goes against him. Even after fifty years nobody wants him around.

"I'm sorry, Mrs. Holman," Fortescue says.

"I understand," she replies. "I told Red this would happen."

After the Holmans leave, Luna says, "Can you beat that?" and Dave Leahy says, "Why do you suppose he came? He sure as hell knew he wasn't welcome."

The answer seems to be in another newspaper story a day or so later written by the same reporter who interviewed Red Holman at the reunion. Red and his wife are found dead in the furnished room they occupy in Raton, with the windows taped shut and the gas turned on. A note says they couldn't hang on no longer. She's got cancer and they can't pay the doctor. They've been living on fifteen-cents-a-can dog food because his meager veteran's pension is all they got.

Some of the men feel bad because we could of taken up a collection or something. Fortescue says he guesses one way or another Red Holman finally paid his dues. We pass a resolution before we break up, adding his name to the list of our honorable dead, and vowing to hold a meeting each year down to the last man.

Fortescue went soon after the 1952 reunion. It was toward the end of the Korean War and he was working on another one of them Washington advisory committees. He'd been slowing down a little but I figured it was just the years catching up. I mean we was both in our seventies by then. But it was more than that. He was giving an interview to some reporters right after a meeting with Ike at the White House when he complained of a bad headache and had to excuse himself.

Later when he's taking a shower in the hotel, a stroke fells him like an ax and he never gets up again. He hung on for nearly three months with Lucy at his bedside, and the twins.

We shared a lot of things in life besides business, and I miss him something terrible. For all his fancy manners, he was a sensible and fair-minded man to the core, a loyal friend and a great gentleman. His dying left Lucy and the girls among the richest women in the country, and Pete, who was then in medical school, with enough to buy his own hospital if he wanted, and still have a hundred million left over. Fortescue and me used to joke a lot about Pete being the best thing we ever produced together, him being grandson to both of us.

We lost Mountain a few years after that too, only not to a bad liver or any of the other things might of killed him. From the time he first come with us at Fortland Oil until he retired, Mountain's only real extravagance besides his kids was buying a new car every few months. He was a terrible driver and he used to go through Cadillacs and Lincolns the way other people go through beer cans, leaving them crumpled up by the side of the road. I lost track thirty or forty years ago of the accidents he had.

Lucky for all concerned, he never killed nobody, just wrecked one automobile after another, usually when he'd been drinking. We had to get him special liability insurance because no regular company'd go near him. And every highway cop in the West knew if they picked him up and looked after him, they was good for a thousand bucks from yours truly just for the favor. He never bothered to get a license, not that any state would of give him one. I mean, he never did learn to read or write.

In his later years, besides boozing and spoiling his kids and his grandchildren, and wrecking cars, he liked the moving pictures and television, always saying they was invented for people like him who couldn't read. He never got real fat, just stood tall all his life, big all over, in his heart as well as his great bulk, healthy as an ox. Then he got cataracts, and even though he had them operated, his sight wasn't quite the same so he saw things blurry on the TV.

He never should of been allowed behind the wheel of a car, but who could stop him? He was in his eighties by then, but in so many ways he was still just a big, good-natured kid. Lucky he made enough money to go around, because his numerous family all took advantage of his sweet nature and only a couple of them ever amounted to a damn.

I got the call from one of his granddaughters. "Colonel Garland, Grandpa's in the hospital." He was in the Presbyterian down in Albuquerque and was asking for me.

"What's wrong?"

"He had an accident."

"That don't surprise me. How is he?"

"Bad."

I get one of the hands here at Eagle Nest to drive me down, and we arrive at six in the morning. I go straight to the floor where they got him and meet the granddaughter in the corridor. She's been crying and for a minute I think maybe I'm too late. Mountain just took delivery on a new Mercedes and it looks like the goddamn fool wrapped himself around one lamp post too many this time.

"What happened?"

She just shakes her head and daubs at her tears. "Someone ran into him on Bataan Boulevard."

"Anybody else in the car?"

"Oh, Grandpa wasn't driving. He went out for a walk. Whoever hit him didn't even stop. I guess he didn't see the car coming."

So Mountain Moore finally meets his match in a hit-run driver. When I find out he's on the critical list but still conscious, I have the usual argument with the nurse because he ain't allowed any visitors. But she's half my size so I barge in anyway.

My friend is in a bed built for a normal person, which means his big feet stick out a mile from under the covers. His head is bandaged and so is his chest and both shoulders, and he's got tubes running in and out of his arms and his nose, so he can't talk too good. But he opens his eyes when he hears me.

"Knew you'd come," he gasps.

"Yeah, well, I happened to be in the neighborhood."

"Never thought I'd die in bed," he says, and I barely hear him.

"You ain't going to die. Not yet."

"Everything's broke inside, Lee. Can't even swallow."

"You been in worse shape."

"I don't think so. . . . Lee?"

"Yes."

"Remember . . . remember the bed in Mexico? The one was witched?"

I'm thinking, of all the foolish things to pop into a old man's head when he's dying. Sparks in a bed! How many years ago was that? Sixty, easy. "Sure, Mountain, I remember."

"I was thinking of that when you come in."

"Well, you keep thinking about it and get your mind off dying."

"You know . . . ?"

"What?"

"I . . . never . . . understood it."

"Never understood what?"

". . . That bed."

"Static electricity, like when you scuff a carpet."

"Thanks, Lee."

"For what?"

"For taking the time."

And with that, he just slips away, never says another word, goes out of my life forever, the man who saved it so often in so many places. It's the only time Mountain ever give up without a fight and it takes me a while to get used to the idea that he's dead. Somehow it don't seem right that such a big fellow should go so quiet.

Pete tells me later he might of survived the fractures, but it was the internal injuries done him in. I hire special investigators to

track down the son of a bitch who ran over him, and they work on
it a few weeks, but they never come up with anything. I figure it
couldn't of been just an ordinary car. It had to be at least one of
them big tractor rigs to take somebody as big as Mountain out of
circulation.

I said at one point that what I'm telling is for my grandson Pete
and anyone else who's interested. That's only half a truth. I'm
telling it for myself, too, to get it straight before I die. Not that I
forget. Hell, my memory's too good, if anything. But when you're
old, you run the risk of losing your perspective, something I been
accused of lately. After the hair thins and the waist thickens and
the teeth start to drop out like flower petals, the mind starts playing tricks. Dreams get mixed with memories and all the edges blur
a little.

Pete told me once it don't matter if a man talks to himself. What
matters is what he says. Lies wear out in a hurry, but the truth lives
forever. There's nothing sadder in this world than an old liar,
especially if he believes what he tells himself. I'm making a special
effort to tell the truth, but it ain't easy. When I talk about Caroline
I think of her beauty, her sense of humor, her charm and her
brains. I overlook the vanity and snobbishness she sometimes
showed, or the little streak of cruelty that also marked her character.

Sometimes I pretend Caroline's just gone out or she's in the
garden or away for a few days visiting friends. I tell myself it's a
harmless kind of game, but maybe it ain't. Maybe it means I'm
entering senility at last.

The truth is Caroline and Matt are dead. I know because I buried
them both. Yet they live as long as I live. I wouldn't try to explain
that to nobody except Pete, but goddamn it, when you get to be
as old as me, almost all the people who count live inside you.
Otherwise they're just names on a tombstone or brown faded
pictures in an album.

When you reach your eighties, survival is the name of the game.
Especially when you see youngsters in their sixties falling like
snowflakes in winter. But I'm lucky. Pete's kids put things in perspective without being a constant reminder of how little time I got
left, and Pete himself keeps my suspicions alive that there might

be some point in living this long after all. Otherwise, what happens
in a old man's life would just be a jumble of people and events that
have lost the power to astonish.

Indians know this better than we do. Navaho seek a little meaning in their sand paintings. Comanche find hints of a grand design
in the stars. Apache dream peyote dreams.

I tried peyote once with Pete, got sick and seen colors that don't
exist. Poisonous lilacs and vomity fuschias. Then, like a lunatic in
electroshock, I feel eighty years of memories explode in my brain,
leaving me not one perspective but a thousand.

I see mountains and armies and birds, and a ballroom where
jewels glitter at a woman's throat. I see tall buildings and the
people in them; at the same time, I see a fox's footprints in the
snow. I watch a great green snake stir the waters of a swamp as a
ocean liner cuts a foamy wake on the face of the sea.

I understand the pattern in a leaf and why the sun shines. I see
the rotted dust and pale bones of my beloved little Emma, and
understand even *that* as I catch my own terror reflected for a
lifetime in a Spanish soldier's eye.

I dream a marble bath where a woman soaps her tits, skaters on
a pond, a baseball game and eggs in a skillet. I see corpses on a
battlefield and children playing in a park. Everything's visible as I
travel at the speed of light without moving, comprehending the
how and the why and the what-for.

I'm being let in on the vast slippery secret of the universe and
I got to bring it back from the dream. But after my head clears, I
can't pin down what it was I understood. When I tell Pete that I
was one of the kids in the park at the same time I was the old man
dreaming it, he says, "Hey, Lee, maybe that's the secret!"

I dabble in the cattle business on and off over the years, but
ranching's always more of a pleasure than a way to make money.
One of the places I own, the Tierra Amarilla, is in dry and desolate
country, with poor water and sparse grass. Ben took an interest in
it after the second war when he found coal in commercial quanti-
ties and wanted to mine it. But I said, "Leave it be! There's enough
dug-up places around this country without making another hole."
Then, a few years later, a geological survey shows great deposits
there of some of the purest uranium ore in the United States.

It's what you'd call an embarrassment of riches. I can't spend a tenth of what I make, and all of a sudden six companies and the U.S. government are beating a path to my door here at Eagle Nest, offering me millions for the right to mine the uranium.

I say no thanks. Even though the Tierra Amarilla ain't much good for growing anything besides mesquite and Gila monsters, I don't like the idea of them digging it all up now anymore than I did for the coal. But these bastards can't take no for an answer and they start pressuring. First they say it's my patriotic duty because the country needs the uranium for bombs. When I still say no, they get tough. They're going to force me because uranium is a strategic mineral, and the government can take the Tierra Amarilla away from me if it wants, in the interest of national defense.

Well, that gets my dander up so I just dig in. I get me some fancy Eastern lawyers, plus Sy Glass here in New Mexico, and we fight. That's when Pete asks me, "Lee, do you really think you'll win?"

"I don't know. Why?"

He says. "Sy Glass says you'll lose eventually. I know you don't care about the Tierra Amarilla, so why not take their offer now?"

"Just ornery."

"I've got another idea."

"Let's hear it."

What he says makes so much sense I start to listen. Pete figures I'm just dragging out a long and costly legal battle that don't help nobody but the lawyers. So he says get the best possible contract for the Tierra Amarilla and use the money to set up a foundation.

"What kind of foundation?"

"I don't mean just the usual tax dodge, but something important enough to do some real good in the world."

"Such as?"

"Scholarships, medical research, whatever you want. You're always talking about what needs doing. Here's your chance."

"You mean put my money where my mouth is."

"In effect."

And that's what I done. The mining outfit paid me thirteen million for the rights to dig the ore, and seven dollars for every ton they took out. The income to the Fortland Foundation exceeded a million dollars a month for the next few years and we had a good time giving it away. I was sorry Fortescue wasn't around to play Santa Claus too, because he'd of liked nothing better in his old age.

I put Lucy on the board, as well as Caroline and Pete, which made for some diversity of opinion. The women had their pet projects like Caroline's Indian art center and Lucy's college scholarship program. Pete used a chunk of foundation money to build and endow the Fortescue Rehabilitation Clinic where stroke and accident victims could learn how to walk and talk again.

I spent a few million and several years setting up the Fortland School of Inter-American Commerce at the University in Albuquerque, and down in Lima, Peru. The original idea was to exchange young business and professional people between here and South America for a year or two of special study, all expenses paid, in the interests of international relations. It's one of the better notions I had in my life, and I figured it would occupy the rest of my days. But that was not to be.

Right after Johnson decides we can win a war in Vietnam, the U.S. government informs me that my ranch here at Eagle Nest is needed because they're expanding some secret testing facilities. At first I don't take it serious, figuring if I don't want to sell, they have to look someplace else. Then I get a second letter asking why I didn't answer the first letter, telling them how much I want for Eagle Nest. I call Sy Glass to find out what that's all about, and he says, "It means they're buying your ranch, Lee, and you have to get out."

"Eagle Nest ain't for sale."

"Eventually you'll have to do a deal with them."

"They can't throw me off my land."

"They'll claim right of eminent domain. Remember the negotiations for Tierra Amarilla almost reached that point."

"That was different. I live here."

"It's all the same to them."

"We'll see."

"It's not worth litigating."

" What are you talking about?"

"This is the Department of Defense, the Military Industrial Complex. What they want, they *get*, and one man can't stop them."

"I'll spend whatever it takes."

"That is not the point. You simply can't go up against them. They're too powerful and even the law is on their side."

"The hell with the law."

"Then why call me? You won't take my advice. Lee, it's not

worth the hassle or the grief or the money it will cost you."

"That's where you're wrong. Eagle Nest is worth whatever I have to do to hold onto it."

"Lee, let me negotiate a fair price and then forget it. You can't fight city hall, and this is all of Washington."

"No, sir."

XXXVIII

The Siege of Eagle Nest

They'll be back. The question is how many more will they bring, and when? Just because I ordered them off the property don't mean they'll stay away. The fat fellow says when they come again they'll arrest me and charge me with criminal assault. Ain't that a pistol! Well, it won't be the first time I been charged with something. But this country's in a hell of a shape when the government can kick a man off his own land and then arrest him into the bargain. I was willing to make a deal. I said from the beginning I'd even donate four thousand acres for their atom research or rocket range or whatever the hell it is they want it for. Just leave me the ranch house at Eagle Nest and the south pasture on the river. The rest they're welcome to.

But no, they got to have it all and they got to have it right away. Three years in the goddamned courts for what? I'm eighty-nine years old, so time's more important to me than it is to them. Well, I ain't leaving now, and no goddamn federal marshal's going to make me.

The younger one, a black fellow who looks to be decent enough, at least apologizes. "This is a sad day for me, Colonel Garland," he says, "but I don't make the law. We have our orders. Please try to understand that you have to leave."

"Understand what? That a bunch of pantywaists in Washington who never set foot in New Mexico can throw me off my land?"

503

The fat officer, who's white, says, "As of twenty-four hours ago, it's not your land and you're a trespasser."

"Colonel Garland, sir," the young one pleads, "don't make it harder for us than it is already. We don't want to arrest you."

"Then just get on back to Santa Fe and leave me be."

"We can't do that, sir," the young one says.

"And we can't hang around here all day waiting for you to make up your mind," the fat one tells me.

"My mind's made up and no one asked you to hang around."

They're both down at the bottom of the steps when we're having this conversation, while I'm on the veranda, looking beyond them at the most beautiful scenery in the world. The mountains are bathed by the early morning sun, while the river valley still lies in shadow. The peak that gives the place its name rears up behind me where the house is set against the cliffs. I literally got my back against a wall. It's golden this time of day, and even though it's spring, patches of snow still glint and sparkle like jewels along the crest. What these two don't know, and all them Washington lawyers would never understand, is that the only way they'll ever get this place is over my dead body.

The eagles that was here when I was young are gone like a lot of the wildlife, hunted down or chased away. But nobody's chasing me away, even if the Supreme Court did refuse to hear my case. Right of eminent domain, my ass! The Constitution says it clear enough. No unreasonable seizure! Well, nothing could be more unreasonable than trying to take Eagle Nest away from me!

They talk in low voices between themselves, trying to decide what to do in view of me being so obstinate. They already got rid of the hands who worked for me here, including my housekeeper, by threatening to arrest everybody if they didn't leave. So I'm alone now, except for my dog Tenth. He's old and half blind from cataracts and smells raunchy, but his hearing's sharp. I should of put him down ages ago but never had the heart because he don't want to leave Eagle Nest any more than I do.

There ain't nothing left of the original house that was here when I was a kid. I put up the main house before the First War and added on over the years until it's the size of a small hotel. The part I live in now is the west wing with thick adobe walls and rooms on two levels. Real pretty with fireplaces and stone floors and Navajo rugs scattered around like my memories. It's cool in the summer and cozy in the winter.

The fat marshall watches me like he expects me to grow horns. He's in his forties, big gut like an old mare's belly, red-faced and impatient, puffing one cigarette after another. He looks like the kind of fellow blames the cards when he can't learn the game, an unappetizing gink whose gaspy breathing even alarms his partner when they walk the hundred yards from their car up to the steps. The young negro now, he's fit, and appears like he can handle himself in a set-to if there is one.

He touches his hat brim in a polite salute and says, "Colonel Garland, you're a prominent man. We don't want trouble and neither do you. I'll give you another hour, but I have to tell you, sir, that if you don't leave here voluntarily, we will have to evict you."

They walk back down the rise and sit in their car with the doors open, the fat one smoking and the younger man just watching the house and hoping I'll show some good sense and get out.

What they don't know is I can't do it and won't. And it ain't easy to explain the reasons why because I don't understand them all myself. A man does what he is, I guess, and that's the only explanation he needs. Anyway, that's what I tell myself.

I go back inside and fix a cup of coffee. Can't let my mind wander right now. Got to be sharp for these fellows when they come back. I keep one eye on the clock while I wait for them to get tired of sitting in their car and come after me.

The main story on the television news is about President Johnson, who says, "I shall not seek nor will I accept the nomination of my party as president." If ever there was a unnecessary speech, it's that one. This Texas sidewinder takes the cake, claiming he's the great defender of poor black people when it's mostly kids from that kind of family he sends to Vietnam, a place nobody even heard of ten years ago. He don't dare run again because he couldn't get elected dogcatcher by black or white.

The Republican candidate's just as big a liar. If I'm still around at election time, I won't vote for him either. There's church music on the television so it's probably Sunday. I'm losing track of the days lately. They're singing "Rock of Ages," which I always associate with funerals because that's the only time I ever go near a church.

The young marshall's right about me not wanting trouble, but I don't see no way to avoid it, short of giving in, which I can't do. So I buckle on my Colt and sip my coffee, thinking I been in tighter places than this, but not lately. Not in the last forty or fifty years anyway. When the hour's up and they get out of the car again, I take down my Winchester and pump a round in the chamber. Then I walk back out on the veranda.

The fat one's gasping as he waddles up to the first step, and he don't look like he's long for this world. It's the young black fellow sees my Colt and the Winchester first, but he politely ignores them. "Are you ready to leave, Colonel?"

"No, I'm not."

"We don't want to use force." They're both carrying holstered revolvers and handcuffs on their gunbelts.

"I'm not leaving."

"Then I'm sorry but we'll have to take you in."

"Don't try it, son."

I got the Winchester cocked now and it's pointed at them.

"You're crazy, old man!" the fat one says. "Put down that rifle before somebody gets hurt!"

The young one says, "Colonel Garland, I'm asking you. Please don't make us do this."

"He's bluffing," the fat one tells his partner. "He wouldn't shoot a U.S. marshall."

"Not unless I have to," I tell them.

"I've had enough of this," the fat one blusters, and starts up the steps toward me, reaching for his handcuffs. I aim between his legs, and the shot echoes off the mountain.

You can hear a fly fart in the silence after that, with both of them freezing where they are and the fat fellow's color gone from red to white because I don't think he ever heard a shot fired in anger before. I pump another round into the chamber and keep the rifle leveled at them.

After they get their wits together and the shock of what I done passes, the fat officer tells me what's going to happen to me now for shooting at them.

"If I'd been shooting at you, you'd be down," I say.

He starts to argue, but the black marshall raises his hand and stops him. "This is out of our hands now, Colonel Garland. I'm sorry. I really am, I hoped we could settle this friendly." And they go away.

Now I done it! If I had half a brain I wouldn't be so ready to take on the whole U.S. government by myself. All I want is to hold on

so Pete and his kids got this place to come to. I like having the kids.
It gives me a chance to teach them something. And them me.

My lawyer, Sy Glass, and me still argue a lot. He said it was
throwing money at an indefensible case. "You did all right when
we negotiated Tierra Amarilla," he tells me.

"That was different. I was raised here and I aim to die here."

"Well, you just might," he says, "being so stubborn."

Caroline liked to say God works in mysterious ways. I never saw
no mystery about it. I don't believe He works much at all. If He'd
been paying attention, I'd of been sent to the big clearing house
in the sky years ago. She believed in the hereafter. I let her think
I did too, but I don't. The here-and-now is good enough for me
as long as I can hold onto Eagle Nest.

Just before sundown a power company truck comes to the bottom of the mountain, and a few minutes later my electricity's cut.
That's their game now. Cut my water off and see what I'll do. But
I got my own generators so I push a button and everything's
working again. I got food to last for months and my water comes
from a artesian well on the patio.

The next morning a National Guard helicopter flies over with
two fellows watching me through binoculars. When I wave, they fly
off, but the racket starts Tenth to barking. I wish Pete was around
to talk to, but maybe it's just as well he ain't. Yet he'd understand
there's some situations don't give a man an easy out.

Sy Glass is as fine a fellow as his granddaddy Simon Glasinsky
who I knew sixty years ago, but like most lawyers Sy's led a pampered life and don't always see that sometimes there's principles
at stake more important than the law. He did what he could about
Eagle Nest, but as he said, some causes are lost before they start.
I'm afraid he washed his hands of me yesterday when I told him
I wasn't leaving.

"You're not planning to resist, I hope?"

"Not unless they push."

"Of course they'll push. They have guns."

"So do I."

"God help us!"

"I'm committed, Sy, don't you understand?"

"Not yet you aren't, but you sure as hell should be! Committed
to the State Hospital for the certifiably crazy!"

"Sy, the law ain't always right."

"Don't lecture me on the law! This is 1968, not the Wild West. You're rich and you can live any place in the world but here. The government paid you twice what that old ranch is worth, so leave it."

"I sent back the check."

"Lee, they'll drag you out of there like a squatter."

"No, they won't."

"Don't call me when they do. I don't want to know."

"They won't drag me anywhere."

Over the next couple of days the helicopters keep a constant vigil, blatting over the house at all hours, with soldiers and police watching me through binoculars. I'm amazed at what I started.

On the third day around noon a private machine lands in the south pasture, and three men jump out. I'm on the veranda with the Winchester, and one says he wants to interview me for the television while his partners set up their cameras. He asks a bunch of questions while they film what I got to say.

It ain't much really. Just what I told the courts a dozen times and what I told Sy Glass. "Do you know they're coming back in force, Colonel?" the television fellow says. "Federal marshalls are being brought in from all over the country. State police, FBI, National Guard. You're a big story."

"Don't they have nothing better to do?"

After these television fellows leave, some vans pull up at the bottom of the rise. My eyes at a distance are as good as ever and so's my shooting. I count about thirty men, all of them with guns. If this keeps up, I can sell tickets. I don't know what else I expected, but it does seem like a overreaction to me, and I can't help wondering what all this foolishness is costing the taxpayers.

At sundown I see three of them trying to sneak around the corner of the corral. They got helmets and a tear-gas gun, but a rifle shot over their heads sends them scurrying back down the rise to the vans. Later Sy Glass telephones again to ask if I've gone totally bananas. He's been trying to get me a thirty-day extension from the court, to call off the dogs, but my television appearance killed any chance he had with the judge.

"Don't worry about it," I tell him.

"You're going to get yourself or somebody else killed if you keep on. For God's sake put those guns away and give up!"

"I can't, Sy."

"You must."

I know I sound like a damn fool, but I'm still convinced I'm right and they're wrong no matter how many legal words the courts wrap around it. It ain't easy for a man to know where he stands anymore, ain't easy at all. Today everything's more complicated, watered down, lacks salt. Or is it just that I'm so goddamn old? Maybe I'm deluding myself. Maybe I am senile like some people think.

They don't cut the phone, but I unplug it for a couple of hours to give myself a rest. I'm tired of Sy Glass's fulminations, and the other calls are from reporters. I already said everything I got to say so there's no point in repeating myself.

The governor came to talk this afternoon. He's a good fellow for a Democrat. He ordered the state troopers to stay out of it, but he's got no control over these federal people. "Colonel, you'll have to give into them. I personally agree with your position and believe what they're doing to you is criminal. But my hands are tied."

"So are mine," I say.

"I don't want anyone hurt," the governor says. "Can't we find a solution between us, as friends?"

"Sure. Call Lyndon."

"The president won't intercede," he says.

"I ain't leaving."

"If I persuade the marshalls to withdraw, get rid of all the vehicles and choppers and people? So that you can just drive out without being bothered? Would you go then?"

"No."

"I don't know what else to say."

"You want some coffee? It's hot."

"Please reconsider."

"I'll think about it."

"Thank you, Colonel. I guarantee nothing will happen if you do."

We shake hands and he walks back down the hill.

That afternoon on the television news, he says he's talked to me and that I accepted a proposal he made, which will bring this bizarre disturbance to a peaceful and satisfactory halt. I believe there's been a serious misunderstanding.

Nobody bothers me that night and I wake up to a beautiful warm day, with a trace of pink showing in the south pasture, which means the verbena's coming to flower. A robin builds a nest at one end of the veranda and I watch her work. More lawmen arrived while I slept and are camping by the cattle gate now in tents and trailers, like a circus. But even with all that hardware, they don't know whether to squat or piss up a rope.

The television news says I'm a living legend, a relic of the Old West like the Colt Forty-four or the last longhorn. On a talk show Bill Buckley calls me an authentic symbol of personal freedom in an age of government abuse, but the fellow he's arguing with says I'm the last of the robber barons, a dangerous, posturing old rogue. Hell, they're both right. Sy Glass calls to tell me my picture's on the cover of Time magazine this week, which he says will only make the government men angrier.

According to Sy the attorney general himself give the order to throw me off Eagle Nest but not to hurt a hair on my head because I'm the retired chairman of the Fortland Oil Company, an ex-ambassador and a war hero, even if I am a little nuts. It's amazing how people get taken in by titles and appearances, but if they work in my favor, so be it. The TV's talking about me again today like they dug up a dinosaur.

That's when it happens. After I turn down the television set, when I'm savoring my notoriety and getting used to the helicopter traffic, they think they'll catch me napping. Except good old Tenth hears them before they charge the house.

I shoot over their heads but they just hunker down and keep coming. The two marshalls who tried to evict me are in the lead, with more fanned out on either side. The colored one fires a tear-gas grenade in a window but I toss it back at them. When they're no more than fifteen yards away, I aim close and kick dust around their knees. The fat fellow drops, which surprises me, because I wasn't aiming at him. The others fall back then, and I hold my fire while the black marshall helps carry the fat one down the slope.

Over the bullhorn they yell that he's hurt bad, and I better surrender or I'll be charged with attempted murder. I ain't worried because if he's hurt, either he shot himself in the foot or it's from the fall. I sure as hell didn't do it.

It won't be the first time I been blamed for something I didn't do. That's practically the story of my life. I settle down near the window again with the rifle in my lap. I don't need much sleep, and the dog's there, so it'll be hard for them to sneak up on me again.

I sit trying to concentrate on what I'm doing and not let them marshalls catch me napping. Then something sets me remembering, like a shaft of sunlight through the aspens or a whiff of some familiar fragrance, and I lose track if I'm here and now, or back then. I doze a little and think about Caroline, a habit I been falling into a lot lately. She comes into my dreams and sometimes it's hard to tell where the dream leaves off and the recollection begins. If I concentrate I can even summon up the sound of her voice and the feel of her small breasts under my fingers. In the memory or the dream we're what we was at the beginning. Young again and in love, and when this dream happens, I wake from it always with a sweetness that stays with me for hours. She's never far from my mind these days, and I miss her as much as ever.

I don't know how long I been dozing. I got to watch that. I got to eat something too, and feed Tenth. I don't remember when I ate last. They won't go away, they'll try it again. On the tube they're calling this "The Siege of Eagle Nest" now.

"Colonel Garland! Do you hear me?"

"What?"

There must be a hundred men on the place now. Creeping around by the cattle gate, hunkered down along the drive and in among the aspens, scooting back and forth trying not to show themselves.

"GARLAND!" The bullhorn echos around the cliffs, and now the phone's ringing too.

"Shut up, Tenth!" I scratch his ears but he won't quiet down. Blind as he is, he's quivering and sniffing like he's got a scent but can't find the direction, can't pin it down. But I can. All of a sudden I know where they're coming from.

"Colonel Garland! This is the attorney general speaking! Please answer your telephone! We have an open line and I would like to talk with you!"

They think they're cute, all right. Somebody's rappeled down the cliff behind the house and now he's on my roof. What's he going to do, drop down the chimney like Santa Claus? No, he's going to try one of the rear windows while they think my attention's on the telephone. Only my attention's going to be on the windows. I pick up the phone and say, "Garland, here."

"Thank you, Colonel . . ."

"Hold on," I say.

"Colonel Garland . . .?"

I put the phone down and kneel beside the window Tenth is pointing at. Bang! Crash! Just like on television the man comes through feet first in a hail of broken glass. His helmet flies off as he lands in a crouch, which is lucky for me, and unlucky for him.

Before he can turn I whack him on the side of the head with the barrel of the Winchester. He goes down on all fours but he's only stunned. Tough cookie. I clout him again and this time he sags forward, spread-eagled, out cold, with Tenth circling and growling around him.

The second one's outside the window with a shotgun pointed at me. "Drop it, old man!"

But I don't drop it. I shoot first and he tumbles backward as his shotgun goes off, and the son of a bitch splinters half the dining table and part of my leg. I figure I killed him because I shot for the chest, but he gets to his knees, raising his hands as I aim again.

"Don't shoot! Please!"

"Get! Go on, get! Or you're dead!"

I don't know why that fellow's still alive until I go over to the unconscious one and see his armored vest. He's the black marshall been persecuting me from the beginning, the same one who charged the house with his fat friend. I see he's bleeding from the knock on the head so I press a towel against it before I handcuff him with his own handcuffs.

I tie another towel around my knee, which is bleeding heavy and hurts like thunder, but I can still get around. I must of took a dozen pellets and they're big ones. If I had a nickel for every time I been chewed, nicked or winged by something, I'd have another fortune.

But I'm giddy just the same, and have to sit down. Too goddamn old for this kind of thing. So why not move to Taos like Sy Glass says, and let the bastards have the place? Right now, I'd do it, but if I back down, I'm just what they said I was, a senile old goat who ought to be shut away some place. Got to keep my dignity, stick it out until they give up, which they will. At some point they have to feel more ridiculous than I do.

"You always talk to yourself like that?"

"What?"

"I said . . . oh, never mind." The marshall jackknifes himself around so he can look at me. "They say you're crazy."

"Don't believe everything you hear."

"I'm willing to believe that part, Colonel. What do I have to do to impress you, die?"

"Feeling better, are you?"

"That's not likely. My head's split."

"I'm sorry about that."

"Colonel, give it up!"

"I'm eighty-nine years old, son, and this place has been my home since I was five. Don't tell me to give it up."

I put the kettle on and make us both some pipsissewa tea, which he spits back in the cup because it's so bitter. "Jesus, you *are* trying to kill me! What the hell was that, hemlock?"

"Drink it down, you'll feel better. That's a bad cut, son."

"I need a doctor."

"My grandson Pete's a doctor."

"Then let's call him. You won't go far on that leg, either. You've lost a lot of blood." He's right because there's a big red puddle on the floor around my foot. No wonder I'm dizzy.

Why don't I let this fellow go? One crazy old man like me against the U.S. government. It's funny when you get down to it, but every oath I ever took in my life was to uphold the Constitution. Believe it or not, that's what I'm still doing, upholding the Constitution. Unreasonable seizure is what it's called, and I'm resisting it. Look it up. It's in the Bill of Rights.

"While you're resisting," this black officer says, "how about giving me a break. There's no feeling in my hands."

It costs me to move, but I hobble over to where he is and loosen his handcuffs a notch. He sits up, working his fingers to get the blood running again. "Thank you, sir," he says. "I'm very much obliged." He looks at me for a long time, studying me like I'm some kind of specimen, and then he shakes his head. After that we sit in silence.

The leg's throbbing like the devil now but Tenth is sound asleep so I guess they ain't up to anything more for the time being. The colored fellow's looking at me with some curiosity, but he still don't say anything. I notice what a handsome man he is, and big. Six-three or -four and built solid. Good thing I conked him when I did or he'd of taken me out easy. Muscles on him like knots on a oak tree.

The sun's going down outside now and the aspens throw long

shadows across the road. The robin must of give up on her nest and went some place else to sleep because I don't see her. But the men are still milling around the cattle gate at the bottom of the drive, armed to the teeth and buckled into their armor vests and helmets.

Seems like there's more of them than when I last looked. Will they try to take me again tonight?

"You can bet on it," my guest tells me.

"How you feeling?" I ask him.

"Foolish," he answers.

There's a hell of a noise down on the drive now, a grinding, clanking racket, and when I look out to see what it is, I don't believe my eyes. "Tanks!"

The marshall raises himself up. "You're joking."

"See for yourself." He takes himself over to the window to look. "There! Down among the aspens."

"They're APCs, colonel. Armored personnel carriers."

Whatever he calls them, they look like tanks to me. The United States government sending tanks to throw Lee Garland off his ranch! How do you like that? Helicopters, guns, grenade launchers, soldiers and now this. All for one man? And they call me crazy!

"It does seem like overkill," the marshall admits. "Give it up, Colonel. Obey the law."

"Gravity's the only law I obey because old bones are brittle."

"Think of your family."

"Caroline's dead. And Matt's gone too."

"Was she your wife?"

"Wife and son."

"I'm sorry about that."

"So am I. He was the boy every father wants."

The tanks or whatever the marshall calls them are growling around the cattle gate, and the powerful lights of the television people got the whole aspen grove illuminated. I can't hardly stand on the leg at all now without growing faint, but I can't pass out or they'll get me. Got to concentrate. Got to keep busy. Got to feed the dog.

"The dog's dead, Colonel."

"Tenth? He's a heavy sleeper, that's all. He's as old as me in dog years and needs his rest."

"See for yourself."

Tenth ain't moved in hours, come to think of it, after the excitement this morning. When I call him he don't wake up. I drag myself over to where he's lying and touch him with the rifle. "Tenth? Hungry boy?" But his carcass is limp.

I bend down to scratch his ears anyway. He was a good old dog, the last of the line. His heart must of give out and he's gone.

"Get some sense and quit before the same thing happens to you."

"How often do I have to tell you? This is my home."

"You're never going to live in it."

"I'm living in it right now, son."

"For a few hours maybe, until you bleed to death or get shot."

"Right. Well, I'll tell you something might interest you. They ain't going to shoot me."

"There's some trigger-happy dudes out there with live ammo in their magazines. No rubber bullets."

"I believe you, but it won't happen."

A helicopter clatters overhead and for a minute I can't hear a thing above the racket. After it passes, he says, "Are you looking for a way to commit suicide? Is that it?"

"No, I just got myself into something I can't back down from. It ain't the first time. Is that so hard to understand?"

"Put that rifle up and walk away while you still can."

"It don't matter."

"If it doesn't matter, then quit."

"I can't."

"Just say, 'That's all, folks!' and everybody goes home."

"I am home."

He shakes his head and heaves a great sigh, like he don't know what to do with me. Hell, at this point, I don't know what to do with myself. I never meant for things to go this far, but goddamn it, I didn't start the trouble, they did. Eagle Nest will still be here when I'm gone and when they're gone, so what point am I trying to make? I'm so whoozy now I forget. He's inching his way closer to me, like maybe he might make a grab for the rifle even if he is handcuffed.

I say, "Don't try it, son. You'll lose."

He gives me a guilty smile. "You're pretty handy with a gun."

"I knew the best shooters there was. Max Luna. Ben Butler."

"Gunfighters?"

"Peace officers like you. Ben saved me from Luna and Luna saved me from myself. Nobody around to do that anymore."

"Let me be the one to do it, sir."

"You believe in the Constitution, Marshall?"

"Yes, sir, I do. Absolutely."

"The fourth amendment says people got a right to be secure in their persons, houses and effects, against unreasonable seizure."

"It also says no warrant shall issue, but upon probable cause, and the court found such cause. The warrant's in my pocket."

"I offered them the land if they let me keep the house and the view. But that ain't enough for them."

"They'll kill you."

"That's a bad cut, son. How'd you get it?"

"Don't you remember? You clubbed me with that rifle."

He's right, and I won't make it if I can't keep simple things like that straight. But an old man's grip is weak, and Eagle Nest ain't easy to hold onto.

Pete understands that. My son Ben, now, he don't want to know. How could a dry old stick like Ben ever have such a fine, sensitive boy as Pete? They say some things skip a generation, but Pete understands the same way Matt always did. Where is he? Why don't he come?

"Who?"

"My son Pete. I mean my son Matt. Gone. Everybody's gone."

"Gone where? Where did your son go, Colonel?"

"What?"

"Let me get you a doctor."

"I'll be all right. Just a little dizzy for a minute. My little Emma was six years old when she drowned. If it wasn't for Caroline, I'd of gone crazy. You got kids?"

"Two."

"Then you know what I'm talking about. You can't replace one and you can't cauterize the hole they leave in your life. I lost all mine, one way or another. Even Ben."

"Call your grandson, Colonel. You say he's a doctor."

"Pete's off climbing mountains some place in South America. You're a climber too, that's how you got in here."

"That's correct, sir."

"Caroline planted them rose bushes you trampled. Her heart

give out one morning in the garden. I found her with the pruning shears still in her hand, looking like she'd just dozed off. She was an old lady by then, but still beautiful. I carried her into the house, laid her on the bed and combed her pretty hair. As many years as we was together, we never got everything said we had to say to each other. One lifetime just wasn't enough. It was after midnight before I called Pete."

"Is that her picture?"

"Taken when we was married. She always said pictures was no substitute for the real person, but it helps me remember now I'm so goddamn old and forgetful. She showed me when you love somebody enough, you never really lose them."

"GARLAND! Colonel Garland! Do you hear me?"

The marshall backs away from me when I raise the rifle and concentrate on whoever's shouting outside the window.

"They want you on the telephone."

"I got nothing to say."

"Then listen."

I don't know if I got the strength to make it to the telephone. I'm so dizzy, it takes a while to find the damned thing, but I pick it up and collapse into a chair. "Garland here."

"Lee! It's me! Don't shoot. I'm coming up."

I don't believe the voice I hear.

"I'm at the gate."

"Gate? What gate?"

"I'm here, Lee. Hold on. For God's sake don't shoot me!"

I'm so weak all of a sudden I drop the receiver on the floor. I can't focus on nothing, can't hold a thought in my head. Is it really my boy come back? Is it really Matt? He don't have to worry none.

The next thing I know the place is full of people and one of them takes the gun. I don't see Matt, though, but I can't make out all the faces too clear. Then I feel cool hands on my forehead.

"Get an ambulance up here quick!"

"Matt?"

"It's me, Lee. Don't talk. You'll be all right."

"I know." I feel the prick of a needle in my arm. Somebody's cutting away the leg of my pants.

"Colonel?" It's the handcuffed marshall talking.

"Matt, this here is Marshall . . ."

"Colonel Garland, you're under arrest."

I hear my boy say, "First I've got to get him to the hospital. You can arrest him later."

"Doctor, he's a federal prisoner. One of us will have to ride in the ambulance with him."

"Suit yourself," Matt tells him, only I'm mistaken because it's not Matt. It's my grandson Pete talking as he ties something around my thigh. I was confused there for a minute. I'm real dizzy again, and my eyesight's fading, but at least the leg's stopped hurting.

A voice says, "Colonel, I have to read you your rights."

I laugh at that, only it comes out a croak.

Pete tells the marshall I ain't in no shape to listen.

"I know my rights," I say.

"Sorry, sir. You'll have to speak louder."

"Goddamn it!" Pete says. "Leave the man be! Can't you see he's too weak to answer questions?"

"Pete?"

"Easy, Lee."

"I thought you was Matt for a minute. Could of sworn it."

"It's okay, Lee."

"Things got out of hand. I'm sorry."

"Sure, Lee."

"I couldn't do it different, Pete. None of it."

"Just lay back. We'll have you patched up in no time. Relax and let the paramedics do the work, okay? Lee, do you hear me? We're taking you to the hospital now. Lee? Lee?"